Collins

NEW GCSE SCIENCE

Additional Science

For Specification Modules B3, B4, C3, C4, P3 and P4

OCR

Gateway Science

Series editor: Chris Sherry

Author team: Louise Smiles, Ian Honeysett, Pam Large, Sandra Mitchell and Maureen Elliott

Teacher Pack

William Collins' dream of knowledge for all began with the publication of his first book in 1819. A self-educated mill worker, he not only enriched millions of lives, but also founded a flourishing publishing house. Today, staying true to this spirit, Collins books are packed with inspiration, innovation and practical expertise. They place you at the centre of a world of possibility and give you exactly what you need to explore it.

Collins. Freedom to teach

Published by Collins
An imprint of HarperCollins*Publishers*
77 – 85 Fulham Palace Road
Hammersmith
London
W6 8JB

Browse the complete Collins catalogue at:
www.collinseducation.com

10 9 8 7 6 5 4 3 2 1

ISBN-13 978 0 00 741532 8

British Library Cataloguing in Publication Data
A Catalogue record for this publication is available from the British Library

Commissioned by Letitia Luff
Project managed by Tammy Poggo
Editorial, layout and production by Hart McLeod, Cambridge
Proofread by Lumière Chieh
New illustrations by Tim Oliver and Sarah Channing-Wright
Word template design by Jerry Fowler
Cover design by Julie Martin
Production by Kerry Howie

Printed and bound by Hobbs the Printers Ltd, Totton, Hampshire

Health and Safety: All practicals in this book have been safety checked (but not trialled) by CLEAPSS (www.cleapss.org.uk) and the publisher and authors have made every reasonable effort to ensure that the experiments and activities in this book are safe when conducted as instructed. However, the publishers assume no responsibility for any damage or injury caused or sustained while performing the experiments or activities in this book to the full extent permitted by law.

CLEAPSS

Parents, guardians, and/or teachers should supervise students who undertake the experiments and activities in this book, and carry out full risk assessments before carrying out any practical work.

CLEAPSS is an advisory service providing support in science and technology for a consortium of local authorities and their schools including establishments for pupils with special needs.

Acknowledgements
Every effort has been made to trace copyright holders and to obtain their permission for the use of copyright materials. The publishers will gladly receive any information enabling them to rectify any error or omission at the first opportunity. A list of photo acknowledgements can be found in a separate file on the Teacher Pack CD

Contents

On the Teacher Pack CD-Rom accompanying this book, you will find all the lessons in this book, available as editable MS Word files. In addition, you will find editable

- Worksheets
- Practical Sheets
- Technician Sheets
- Answer sheets per subject: Biology, Chemistry, Physics

Lessons are organised in folders, with all the materials you need for a particular lesson in one folder.

How to use this book

Welcome to the Collins New GCSE Science Teacher Pack for OCR Additional Science B Gateway, which has been written by experienced authors and teachers to help you deliver an effective and successful GCSE Additional Science course.

Overview of Additional Science B Gateway

Unit B721	Modules B3, C3, P3	Tiered written paper	35% of the qualification	Structured questions
Unit B722	Modules B4, C4, P4	Tiered written paper	40% of the qualification	Structured questions and analysis of data
Unit B723	Controlled assessment		25% of the qualification	

Lessons

The Teacher Pack has been matched lesson-by-lesson to the Student Book and clear specification references on every page allow easy navigation throughout the books.

Lesson outlines cover the following:

- Resources
- Learning objectives and learning outcomes
- Key vocabulary
- Obstacles to learning
- Stimuli and starter suggestions
- Learning activities (differentiated into low, standard and high demand)
- Plenary suggestions
- Assessment opportunities

Lesson outlines are supported by **Worksheets**, **Practicals**, **Technician sheets** and all answers.

- **Worksheets**: Each lesson includes a differentiated worksheet, with varied, level-appropriate tasks at low demand, standard demand, and high demand.
- **Practicals:** Practicals sheets provide step-by-step guidance for students to ensure that they carry out their investigations safely and successfully. The section at the back of the book, **Carrying out practical investigations in GCSE Additional Science**, can also be used as a reference section for all practical work.
- **Technician sheets:** Detailed technician sheets are provided for every lesson with resources lists and overviews of practical methods.
- **Answers:** Every lesson plan in this book includes the answers to the questions in the Student Book and the Worksheets. In addition, on the Teacher Pack CD, you will find a document with all the answers arranged per subject so that you can make these available to students and that they can mark their own, or a peer's work.

Optional resources: Our integrated scheme includes the Interactive Book, Homework Pack, Assessment and Revision Guides. All components work well together and on their own, and you have the flexibility to include the resources in your lessons as and when appropriate.

Introduction and checklist

Every module in the student book starts with an introduction linking what students should already know to the content of that module.

At the end of every module, a detailed **Checklist** provides a summary of the content that students need to revise. Students are reminded that they will need to be able to use these ideas in a variety of ways, such as interpreting, applying, explaining, suggesting, and drawing conclusions.

Editable checklists that students can tick off as they progress are provided on the Teacher Pack CD.

Preparing for assessment activities

Each section contains two **Preparing for assessment** activities. The tasks will help students build the skills they need to successfully complete their controlled assessment, and develop confidence in answering questions within a new context.

Each type of Preparing for assessment activity builds different skills.

- **Applying your knowledge** tasks require students to look at a familiar scientific concept in a new context.
- **Skills based** tasks require students to think about preparing for their controlled assessment. There are three types of task:
  - Research and collecting secondary data
  - Planning and collecting primary data
  - Analysis and evaluation.

Exam-style questions and worked examples

Every section has two sets of **Exam-style questions**, for Foundation Tier and Higher Tier. Questions are labelled with the Assessment Objectives that they address.

The Worked examples take the students through a sample candidate answer with examiner tips showing them how to improve their grades and remind them about good exam technique.

Assessment skills

The assessment skills embedded throughout the book are covered in detail in the two-part assessment skills section at the back of the Student Book.

- **Carrying out controlled assessments in GCSE Additional Science** covers the different skills that students need to master in order to successfully complete their Controlled Assessment.
- **How to be successful in your GCSE Additional Science written examination** covers the written assessment skills that students need to master in their Written papers.

Assessment tips give further guidance and *Definition* boxes highlight essential terminology.

Bad Science for Schools

Based on the work of Ben Goldacre, the **Bad Science for Schools** lessons have been created to encourage your students to critically evaluate scientific claims made everyday in the media. These lesson plans are also available on the Collins Education website.

Scheme of Work

The detailed Scheme of Work at the back of this book provides a comprehensive overview of the Additional Science course, matching the Learning Objectives and Outcomes for each lesson to the OCR Additional Science B Gateway specification so that you can plan and teach the 2011 specification with confidence.

Teacher pack CD

On the CD accompanying this book, you will find all the material in this book, available as editable MS Word files so that you can adapt the lessons to suit your class if required.

In addition, you will find editable **Worksheets**, **Practical Sheets**, **Technician Sheets** and all the answers.

The content has been arranged in folders per lesson, with all the materials you need for that lesson in one folder so that you can quickly and easily prepare for your lessons.

B3: Introduction

Pages 8–9 in the Student Book provide an introduction to module B3.

When and how to use these pages

These pages summarise what students should already know from KS3 or previous GCSE units and provide an overview of the content that they will learn in this module.

- Use these pages as a revision lesson before you start the first new topic.
- Brainstorm everything that students remember about the different topics using the headings as a starting point. Compare your list with the points in the Student Book.
- Use the questions on the left-hand page as a starting point for class discussions.
- Ask students if they can tell you anything about the topics on the right-hand page.
- Make a note of any unfamiliar / difficult terms and return to these in the relevant lessons.

You can revisit these pages at the following points:

- before the lessons on Respiration pages 18–21
- before the lessons on Cell division pages 22–25
- before the lessons on The circulatory system pages 28–31.

Overview of module

In this section students will learn about DNA and how it codes for proteins. They will develop ideas about enzymes as proteins and how changes to the DNA can prevent the proteins from working.

Students will then look at how blood is circulated around the body and respiration. Different ways of measuring respiration will be investigated.

The different types of cell division will be studied along with how organisms can be selectively bred or cloned.

Barriers to learning

Students may need extra guidance with the following terms and concepts:

Terminology

It is vital to use terminology with precision. Avoid confusion over chromosomes, genes and DNA.

Protein synthesis

Making the link between DNA base sequence, protein structure and characteristics is a complex idea.

Genes

Understanding that the cells of the body contain all the genes but only a few work in each cell is often a confusing concept.

Describing patterns

Some students find it difficult to describe the pattern in a graph; they need to be encouraged to refer to the dependent and independent variables.

Terminology

Some students will find it difficult to understand the difference between breathing and respiration.

Terminology

Students may confuse the equations for anaerobic reaction with aerobic respiration.

DNA replication

It is important that higher tier students understand that DNA replication takes place before the cells divide. Some students will think that 'unzipping' occurs when the chromosomes separate.

Terminology

Many students will confuse mitosis and meiosis

Terminology

Students may be asked about how the structure of red blood cells are adapted to their function. Some students struggle with the terms, structure and function.

Heart structure

Students find it difficult to transfer the labels of the heart from one diagram to another.

Terminology

Some students will find the concept of cell differentiation difficult.

Growth curves

It is important that students can interpret growth curves.

Selective breeding

Students need to be able to describe the process of selective breeding even at low demand. They often get the process confused with genetic engineering.

Terminology

It is important that students understand the difference between selective breeding and genetic engineering.

Clones

It is vital that students understand that clones are genetically identical and not just identical.

Asexual reproduction in plants

It is vital that foundation students are able to describe how different plants reproduce asexually. They often mix up the different ideas.

Practicals in this unit

In this unit students will do the following practical work:

- Making a model of DNA using pasta
- Enzymes practical using lipase, however alternatives can be used
- Students measure rate of oxygen uptake in woodlice or germinating beans
- Measuring recovery rate after exercise
- Looking at mitosis in root cells
- Heart dissection
- Looking at cells under the microscope
- Taking cuttings or tissue culture

Key vocabulary covered in this unit

chromosomes • DNA • genes • mitochondria • ribosomes
base code • complimentary • double helix • protein synthesis • mRNA
collagen • enzyme • haemoglobin • hormone • mutation
active site • denature • lock and key • pH • specific • temperature
aerobic • ATP • metabolic rate • mitochondria • respiration • respiratory quotient
anaerobic respiration • lactic acid • muscle fatigue • oxygen debt • recovery rate
base pairs • cell division • DNA replication • mitosis • multicellular • unicellular
acrosome • fertilisation • gamete • genetic variation • haploid • meiosis • mitochondria • sexual reproduction • zygote

artery • capillary • haemoglobin • oxyhaemoglobin • plasma • platelet
red blood cell • vein • white blood cell
atrium • bicuspid valve • double circulatory system • tricuspid valve • ventricle
bacteria • cell differentiation • cellulose • chloroplast • mitochondria • stem cells • 'true' nucleus • vacuole
cell enlargement • dry mass • finite size • growth curve • meristems • wet mass
characteristic • cross-breed • gene pool • inbred • selective breeding • variation • yield
genetic engineering • genetically modified • gene therapy • insertion • isolation
asexual reproduction • clones • Dolly • nuclear transfer • stem cells • surrogate
genetically identical • plantlet • tissue culture • variation

B3a: Molecules of life

Resources

Student Book pages 10–11 • ICT equipment
Interactive Book Quick starter: Differences in specialised cells • Drag and drop: Cells and cell structure
Files on Teacher Pack CD: b3_a_01_worksheet; b3_a_01_technician

Learning objectives

- Explain that DNA is found in the nucleus of the cell.
- Describe how Watson and Crick built a model of DNA.
- Explain the function of mitochondria and ribosomes.

Learning outcomes

- Recall that mitochondria are needed for respiration.
- Recall that Watson and Crick used data from other scientists to develop their ideas about the structure of DNA.
- Explain why new discoveries are not always accepted and that ribosomes are the site of protein synthesis.

Prior knowledge

Students should know that DNA is found in the nucleus of a cell.

Some students know that everyone has their own unique DNA.

Key vocabulary

chromosomes • DNA • genes • mitochondria • ribosomes

Barriers to learning

It is vital to use terminology with precision. Avoid confusion over chromosomes, genes and DNA.

Using key cards that can be matched to definitions may help.

Curiosity and starter suggestions

- Show a short video clip of the discovery of DNA on YouTube (The Secret of Life – Discovery of DNA Structure) (http://www.youtube.com/watch?v=sf0YXnAFBs8)

OR

- Ask students to work in small groups (perhaps using mini-whiteboards) to:
  - say what they know about chromosomes, genes and DNA
  - write down what they know about DNA

Learning activities

Worksheet b3_a_01

Low demand

Use the starter activity to lead into a discussion about DNA. Then discuss the role of mitochondria in the cell.

Ask students to complete worksheet question 1a and 1b *Cells and DNA*.

Teaching and learning notes: *Question 1b is standard demand, therefore, higher tier students will need to cover this. Question 1 could be used as a starter activity for higher tier students. Page 10 of the Student Book has a similar diagram that students can use to help.*

Standard demand

Students should complete the low demand activity as background for both standard and high demand.

Ask students to research the work of Watson and Crick. They should follow the instructions in worksheet question 2 *The discovery of DNA* to produce a leaflet about the discovery of DNA.

***Teaching and learning notes:** How this is tackled depends on time available. Most of the information can be obtained from the Student Book.*

High demand

Students develop their ideas to complete worksheet question 3 *The discovery of DNA extension*.

Plenary suggestions

Read out some definitions of the key words and ask the students to write down the word.

OR

Have a quick class debate to answer the question – 'Should Watson and Crick be the only scientists to get recognition for the discovery of DNA?'

Assessment opportunities

The leaflet students produce should reflect their understanding.

The first plenary might provide good checkpoints for students' progress.

Answers

Student Book

Q1 Nucleus • **Q2** Gene • **Q3** Watson and Crick • **Q4** Muscle cells need a lot of energy and mitochondria release energy during respiration **Q5** Bases • **Q6** X-ray crystallography • **Q7** Erwin Chargaff • **Q8** Too small • **Q9** Confirmed DNA was a double helix not a triple helix • **Q10** To make the results more valid

Fig 2 nucleus • **Fig 3** DNA • **Fig 4** for respiration to release energy • **Fig 5** four • **Fig 6** proteins are made on the ribosomes and proteins are needed to repair damaged tissue

Worksheet

Q1a Top to bottom: membrane, nucleus, cytoplasm, chromosome, DNA, gene • **Q1bii** Because liver cells need more energy from respiration

B3a: Molecules of life

Resources

Student Book pages 12–13 • Equipment for practical
Interactive Book Quick starter: The genetic code
Files on Teacher Pack CD: b3_a_02_worksheet; b3_a_02_practical; b3_a_02_ technician

Learning objectives

- Describe the structure of DNA.
- Explain how DNA is used to make proteins.

Learning outcomes

- Recall that genes are made from DNA and that DNA controls the production of proteins.
- Recall that DNA is a double helix and that each gene contains a different sequence of bases.
- Explain the base sequence is used to determine the order of amino acids in a protein.

Prior knowledge

Students should know that genes are made of DNA.

Some students know that DNA controls individual characteristics.

Key vocabulary

base code • complimentary • double helix • DNA • protein synthesis • mRNA • ribosomes

Barriers to learning

Making the link between DNA base sequence, protein structure and characteristics is a complex idea.

Building models to show protein synthesis can help visualise the process.

Curiosity and starter suggestions

- Ask the students to crack the code on worksheet b3_a_02 question 1 *DNA code*. Link this to the idea that DNA is a code.

OR

- Ask students to suggest how the DNA in their cells is linked to the enzyme amylase in their mouth: they may need to be reminded that enzymes are proteins.

Learning activities — Worksheet b3_a_02 + Practical b3_a_02

Low demand

Use the first starter activity to lead into a discussion about DNA as a code for making proteins.

Ask students to complete questions 11 to 13 on page 12 of the Student Book.

Teaching and learning notes: *The standard demand activity will take up most of the lesson and will build on low demand ideas. Therefore, there is no need to spend much time on the low demand activity.*

Standard demand

Introduce the model-building activity described in the practical. Divide the class into small groups and ask them to carry out the activity. It is easiest to do this in groups of about four. Two students concentrate on a strand between them. Each pair of students takes a length of wire – it can be 50 cm, 1 m or longer depending on how much space, time and patience you have. You may wish to give less-able students a base sequence consisting of 20 base pairs.

Discuss with the class how DNA is involved in protein synthesis. Students then complete question 2b *Evaluating your DNA model.*

Teaching and learning notes: *High demand students will need to spend more of the lesson on protein synthesis, the model-building activity could be set as homework.*

High demand

Students develop their ideas on DNA structure and protein synthesis by watching a short video clip. (http://www.youtube.com/watch?v=NJxobgkPEAo) Students complete worksheet question 3 *Protein synthesis*.

Teaching and learning notes: *The website mentioned is just one example of many. Most are pitched at A Level so it might be more appropriate to play the clip without sound and then add your own commentary at the required level for your group.*

Plenary suggestions

Role play protein synthesis using students as the bases in DNA and mRNA.

OR

Judge which group has made the best DNA model.

Assessment opportunities

Worksheet b3_a_02 provides staged opportunities to assess students' learning.

The first plenary might provide good checkpoints for students' progress.

Answers

Student Book

Q11 DNA or chromosomes • **Q12** For growth or repair of damaged tissue or cell division • **Q13** DNA • **Q14** Sequence • **Q15** They may not have the correct code in their DNA to make insulin • **Q16** G • **Q17** 10 • **Q18** TTTATAGAGGGGAGTTGGCCCGCCATTTAC • **Q19** It is a copy of the DNA that can leave the nucleus to go to the ribosomes where it is used to put the amino acids together in the correct order

Fig 7 gene • **Fig 8** nucleus of your cells • **Fig 9** the DNA code for insulin will have a different order of bases to the code for collagen • **Fig 10** mRNA has a the letter U but no T • **Fig 11** yes – second line down (AA)

Worksheet

Q1 Genes are made of DNA. Your DNA contains a genetic code. The code is used to put amino acids together to make proteins • **Q2** Depends on their model • **Q3a** A–T and C–G • **Q3b** So that the mRNA can leave the nucleus because DNA is too large to leave the nucleus • **Q3c** 3 • **Q3d** similar to Fig 10 on page 13 of Student Book

B3b: Proteins and mutations

Resources

Student Book pages 14–15 • ICT equipment
Files on Teacher Pack CD: b3_b_01_worksheet, b3_b_01_technician

Learning objectives

- Describe the function of some proteins.
- Explain how DNA mutations can affect the function of the protein.

Learning outcomes

- Recall example of proteins and describe a mutation as changes to genes.
- Describe the function of different proteins and understand that mutations can be harmful or beneficial.
- Explain that genes can be switched on or off and that mutations can alter the sequence of amino acids in a protein.

Prior knowledge

Students should know that genes are made of DNA.

Some students know that DNA controls individual characteristics.

Key vocabulary

collagen • enzyme • haemoglobin • hormone • mutation

Barriers to learning

Understanding that the cells of the body contain all the genes but only a few work in each cell is often a confusing concept.

Use the analogy of a cookbook full of recipes, it is unlikely that you are ever going to use every recipe in the book, but they are there if you need them.

Curiosity and starter suggestions

- Put a list of proteins on the board – e.g. collagen, insulin, haemoglobin and amylase. Ask the students to discuss what they might all have in common.

OR

- Show the students some images of mutations – there are plenty on the internet but choose carefully (safe examples could be sickle cells, albino animals or dark peppered moths). Ask the students to discuss what might have caused the mutation.

Learning activities

Worksheet b3_b_01

Low demand

Use the first starter activity to lead into a discussion about the link between genes, proteins and mutations. Ask students to write down a definition of mutation in their books.

Teaching and learning notes: *The low demand concepts are also covered in standard demand due to the way they are linked. So it is possible to just jump to the standard demand activity.*

Standard demand

Extend the discussion on proteins to describe the functions of different proteins.

Ask the students to complete worksheet question 1a *Protein function*.

Remind the students how genes code for proteins and if the gene is wrong the protein may be different. Use sickle cell as an example to show how a different gene can change the shape of a protein molecule.

Divide the class into small groups. Give them the list of mutations (question 2b *Mutations*) and ask them to consider if they are beneficial or harmful. The students complete worksheet questions 2a and 2b *Mutations*.

Teaching and learning notes: *The ideas about beneficial mutations could be extended by asking the students to research the link between sickle cell and malaria, either in the lesson or as homework.*

High demand

Provide the class with some different words and ask them to change one letter in the word to form another word. Link this to the idea of mutations being changes in the DNA code, which result in different proteins being produced.

Discuss with the students why some genes only function in certain cells. The students complete worksheet questions 3a and 3b *Switched on.*

Teaching and learning notes: *If students are studying this topic as part of Biology Unit 1 then this lesson could be linked back to natural selection by discussing gene mutations in bacteria and why they are beneficial.*

Plenary suggestions

Students report back on their discussions about harmful or beneficial mutations.

OR

Ask students to write a summary of why a gene mutation results in a protein that may not function. They should link protein synthesis from last lesson to mutations and protein function.

Assessment opportunities

Worksheet b3_b_01 provides staged opportunities to assess students' learning.

The second plenary might provide good checkpoints for students' understanding at high demand.

Answers

Student Book

Q1 Haemoglobin • **Q2** Makes the walls stronger • **Q3** Mutation • **Q4** Collagen • **Q5** E.g. digestion **Q6** Radiation and chemicals in cigarettes • **Q7** Codes for the order of bases in the protein • **Q8** Gene is switched off • **Q9** Mutation which changed the sequences of bases in the DNA

Fig 1 yes, there is one on left-hand edge • **Fig 2** insulin • **Fig 3** mutation

Worksheet

Q1a Collagen provides structure; insulin is a hormone that lowers blood sugar levels; haemoglobin carries oxygen around the body; amylase breaks down starch • **Q2a** Radiation and chemicals such as tar in cigarette smoke • **Q2bi** Harm, harm, benefit, benefit, benefit • **Q3ai** Nucleus • **Q3aii** Gene is switched off in the white blood cell • **Q3bi** One less amino acid • **Q3bii** May have a different shape

B3b: Proteins and mutations

Resources

Student Book pages 16–17 • Equipment for practical
Interactive Book Matching pairs: Enzymes
Files on Teacher Pack CD: b3_b_02_worksheet; b3_b_02_practical; b3_b_02_technician

Learning objectives

- Describe the role of enzymes in the body.
- Explain why enzymes are specific.
- Explain how enzyme activity is affected by temperature and pH.

Learning outcomes

- Recall that enzymes are proteins that speed up chemical reactions.
- Describe the effect of temperature and pH on enzyme activity and use the lock and key mechanism to explain why enzymes are specific.
- Explain the effect of temperature and pH on enzyme activity and calculate Q_{10} values.

Prior knowledge

Students should know that enzymes are found in the body.

Some students know examples of different enzymes especially those involved in digestion.

Key vocabulary

active site • denature • enzyme • lock and key • pH • specific • temperature

Barriers to learning

Some students find it difficult to describe the pattern in a graph; they need to be encouraged to refer to the dependent and independent variables.

Showing them images of graphs and ask them to describe the pattern using the **'er**, **er'** idea, e.g. the high**er** the temperature the fast**er** the reaction.

Curiosity and starter suggestions

- Put a lump of cheese on the desk and ask students to describe what happens to the cheese in their bodies – link this to the importance of enzymes.

OR

- In 1 minute, ask the students to write down everything they know about enzymes. Report back what they have written to the rest of the class.

Learning activities — Worksheet b3_b_02 + Practical b3_b_02

Low demand

Class demonstration – add a small piece of liver or yeast to a boiling tube containing 20 cm^3 of hydrogen peroxide. Discuss with the class how enzymes can be used to speed up a chemical reaction in living cells. The students complete worksheet questions 1a and 1b *Enzymes and chemical reactions.*

Teaching and learning notes: *This activity should be kept short to give plenty of time for the practical.*

Standard demand

Divide the class into small groups and ask them to follow the instructions in the practical. Each group can carry out the experiment at a different temperature and the results are then collated. The data can be recorded by hand or using a data-logger.

The class should discuss the collated results and complete worksheet question 2 *Enzymes experiment.*

Teaching and learning notes: *There are many alternative experiments that can be done. If time permits investigating the affect of pH on pepsin would develop ideas about pH and enzymes.*

High demand

The students complete worksheet question 3 *Explaining your results.*

Plenary suggestions

Sketch some different-shaped graphs on the board. Ask the class to describe the pattern they see in each graph (you could use the graphs in the Student Book on page 17).

OR

Ask students to evaluate their investigation and suggest improvements.

Assessment opportunities

Worksheet b3_b_02 provides staged opportunities to assess students' learning.

Ask the students to verbally explain their results to another student who then assesses their explanation.

Answers

Student Book

Q10 E.g. rennin, amylase, pepsin • **Q11** Speeds up the reaction • **Q12** Biological catalysts • **Q13** Increasing the temperature increases the rate up to about 40°C after that the rate falls • **Q14** Diagram drawn to show that a starch molecule is the wrong shape to fit into a pepsin's active site • **Q15** The enzyme denatures • **Q16** 12/5 = 2.4

Fig 4 rennin or enzyme • **Fig 5** pH 7 • **Fig 6** enzyme is destroyed / denatured • **Fig 7** idea that each enzyme has a different shaped active site that only fits one type of substrate

Worksheet

Q1a Enzyme, oxygen, protein • **Q1b** Enzyme, active • **Q2a,b** Answers will depend on the outcome of the experiment • **Q2c** Starch is the wrong shape to fit into the active site of lipase • **Q3a** As temperature increases the molecules have more kinetic energy so there are more collisions; when temperature gets too high the enzyme denatures, the fats cannot fit into the active site so the reaction stops • **Q3b** Enzyme denatures, the fats cannot fit into the active site so the reaction stops • **Q3ci, cii** Answers will depend on the outcome of the experiment

B3c: Respiration

Resources

Student Book pages 18–19 • Equipment for practical
Interactive Book Naked Scientist animation: How do cells get their energy? • Practical investigations: Plant growth
Files on Teacher Pack CD: b3_c_01_worksheet; b3_c_01_practical; b3_c_01 technician

Learning objectives

- Describe the process of aerobic respiration.
- Describe how to measure the rate of respiration.
- Explain why respiration rate is affected by temperature and pH.

Learning outcomes

- Recall the word equation for aerobic respiration and be able to name some processes that require energy from respiration.
- Recall the balanced symbol equation for aerobic respiration, use data to compare respiration rates and be able to calculate RQ values.
- Explain that respiration is controlled by enzymes which are affected by pH and temperature; they should also recall that ATP molecules are produced during the process of respiration.

Prior knowledge

Students should know that respiration releases energy from food.

Some students know the word and symbol equation for respiration.

Key vocabulary

aerobic • ATP • metabolic rate • mitochondria • respiration • respiratory quotient

Barriers to learning

Some students will find it difficult to understand the difference between breathing and respiration.

Using key cards that can be matched to definitions may help.

Curiosity and starter suggestions

- Burn some food in front of the students and discuss the idea of chemical energy being converted to heat energy – link this to respiration.

OR

- Write the words respiration and breathing on the board.
  Ask students to compare the two processes.

Learning activities

Worksheet b3_c_01 + Practical b3_c_01

Low demand

Use the starter activity to lead into a discussion about respiration being a chemical reaction.

Ask students to complete worksheet question 1 *Respiration*.

Teaching and learning notes: *This should be a quick introduction to the lesson as the practical will take up most of the time.*

Standard demand

Introduce the investigation students should follow the instructions in the practical. They then complete worksheet question 2 *Measuring respiration rate.*

Explain to the students that RQ values can be calculated from either experiment results or symbol equations. They then complete worksheet question 3 *RQ values.*

Teaching and learning notes: *Students will need to calculate RQ values – this is a new concept for GCSE. The students can use either woodlice or germinating beans in the apparatus.*

High demand

Discuss the link between respiration and metabolic rate. Students complete questions 6–8 on page 19 of the Student Book.

Plenary suggestions

Ask students to represents the elements in oxygen and glucose molecules (you will need 6 oxygen molecules made up of 2 students per molecule). Then ask them to rearrange themselves into the products of respiration.

OR

Provide the students with some symbol equations for respiration using different substances

(e.g. $2C_{51}H_{98}O_6 + 145O_2 \longrightarrow 102CO_2 + 98H_2O$) and ask them to calculate the RQ value.

Assessment opportunities

Worksheet b3_c_01 provides staged opportunities to assess students' learning.

The plenary should provide good checkpoints for students' progress.

Answers

Student Book

Q1 Oxygen • **Q2** Carbon dioxide • **Q3** Maintenance of body temperature, making proteins or contracting muscles • **Q4** Aerobic respiration • **Q5** 1.4 / 2.0 = 0.7 **Q6** Used as an energy store • **Q7** Your metabolic rate is the amount of energy your body needs. Aerobic respiration provides your body with energy. This means that metabolic rate can be estimated by measuring oxygen uptake • **Q8** The process of respiration is controlled by enzymes, which enzymes are more efficient at temperatures around 40 °C, so the lizard needs to warm up as it cannot maintain body temperature

Fig 1 heat (and light) • **Fig 2** respiration • **Fig 3** more energy needed for movement so more respiration and therefore more oxygen needed

Worksheet

Q1a Energy, cells, oxygen • **Q1b** oxygen, water • **Q2c** No – you would need to know the volume of the gas used not just the distance the dye moved • **Q2d** The scale on the ruler is in millimetres, which is not very accurate as it does not measure volume. It is not easy to measure how far the dye moves as it is difficult to judge the end of the dye • **Q2e** Repeat using glass beads or dead mung beans • **Q2f** Ideas to include using a water bath to surround the boiling tube so the process can be repeated at different temperatures • **Q3a** 0.93 • **Q3b** using the idea of 6/6 = 1 aerobic respiration using only glucose has a value of 1

B3c: Respiration

Resources

Student Book pages 20–21 • Equipment for practical
Interactive Book Quick starter: Anaerobic respiration
Files on Teacher Pack CD: b3_c_02_worksheet; b3_c_02_practical; b3_c_0 2_technician

Learning objectives

- Describe an experiment to measure resting pulse rate and recovery time after exercise.
- Explain why anaerobic respiration takes place during hard exercise in addition to aerobic respiration.
- Explain fatigue in terms of lactic acid build up (oxygen debt) and how this is removed during recovery.

Learning outcomes

- Describe how to measure recovery time and explain that breathing rate and pulse rate increases during exercise because the muscles need more oxygen and need to remove more carbon dioxide.
- Recall the word equation for anaerobic respiration and explain that anaerobic respiration occurs when the muscles do not get enough oxygen.
- Explain that lactic acid builds up because of the incomplete breakdown of glucose due to a lack of oxygen in the cells.

Prior knowledge

Students should know how to measure pulse rate.

Some students may know that lactic acid builds up in muscle during exercise.

Key vocabulary

anaerobic respiration • lactic acid • muscle fatigue • oxygen debt • recovery rate

Barriers to learning

Students may confuse the equations for anaerobic reaction with aerobic respiration.

Using cards with all the substrates and products from both reactions on and ask them to arrange them to show the two reactions.

Curiosity and starter suggestions

- Ask students to find their pulse and count the beats for 30 seconds; explain that this value can then be doubled to give them their resting pulse.

OR

- Ask students to describe what happens to their pulse and breathing rate when they exercise.

Learning activities

Worksheet b3_c_02 + Practical b3_c_02

Low demand

Use the starter activity to lead into a discussion about how and why pulse rate changes during exercise. Introduce the investigation; students should follow the instructions in the practical. Ask students to record their results and complete worksheet question 1 *Measuring recovery time.*

Teaching and learning notes: *Students will need to analyse data from a pulse rate experiment, if time is limited they can be given data and still answer the questions on worksheet b3_c_02.*

Standard demand

Introduce the fist-clenching activity; students should follow the instructions in practical. Ask students to record their results on worksheet b3_c_02.

Students should notice that repetitive movements quickly make muscles tired. (In case someone asks, heart muscles are different from body muscles and can keep on working.) Discuss how holding the arm above the head will tire the muscles more quickly. This is because there will be problems getting enough blood (carrying oxygen and glucose) to the muscles.

Students can now be introduced to the scientific terms 'aerobic respiration' and 'anaerobic respiration' and an explanation of why a muscle becomes tired. Students complete worksheet question 2 *Fist-clenching*.

Teaching and learning notes: *Foundation students will need to complete the investigation on recovery time. Therefore, if time is limited the first investigation may have to be missed out. If this is the case, teachers should ensure that the anaerobic respiration theory is covered at some point.*

High demand

Develop the discussion on anaerobic respiration to include idea about oxygen debt. Students complete worksheet question 3 *Muscle fatigue and lactic acid*.

Plenary suggestions

Ask students to describe what will happen to their breathing rate as they walk to another classroom and then sit down.

OR

Using cards with all the substrates and products from both anaerobic and aerobic respiration on and ask them to arrange them to show the two reactions.

Assessment opportunities

Worksheet b3_c_02 provides staged opportunities to assess students' learning. In addition, thoughtful questioning during class discussions may be used to draw out blocks to learning.

Both plenary suggestions provide opportunity for students to demonstrate their understanding.

Answers

Student Book

Q9 Increases • **Q10** Carbon dioxide • **Q11** Muscle cells • **Q12** Anaerobic • **Q13** Lactic acid • **Q14** The lactic acid damages the muscle cells • **Q15** Aerobic respiration uses oxygen and completely breaks down the glucose, anaerobic releases less energy and makes lactic acid • **Q16** replaces oxygen to allow aerobic respiration • **Q17** Lactic acid is taken to the liver where it is broken down using oxygen – breathing rate stays high to take in extra oxygen to do this

Fig 4 breathed it out from the lungs • **Fig 6** his muscle cells are not getting enough oxygen for just aerobic respiration

Worksheet

Q1a–d Will depend on results • **Q1e** The muscle cells are working harder and need more energy; breathing rate increases to take in more oxygen and remove the extra carbon dioxide; pulse rate increases to get more oxygen to the muscles so that respiration rate can increase to release more energy • **Q2b** Should feel pain • **Q2c** Should be harder because becomes painful quicker • **Q2d** Above head arm does not get oxygen as easily so anaerobic respiration used, which makes lactic acid • **Q3** Lack of oxygen to the muscle means anaerobic respiration is used, which produces lactic acid; after exercise the lactic acid is broken down in the liver, which requires extra oxygen to be taken in – this extra oxygen is the oxygen debt

B3d: Cell division

Resources

Student Book pages 22–23 • Equipment for practical • ICT equipment

Interactive Book Quick starter: Specialised cells • Drag and drop: Cells and specialisation • Quick starter: Cell division • Naked Scientist animation: How are new cells formed

Files on Teacher Pack CD: b3_d_01_worksheet; b3_d_01_practical; b3_d_01_technician

Learning objectives

- Describe the difference between unicellular and multicellular organisms. Explain why cell division takes place.
- Explain the advantages of being multicellular.
- Describe DNA replication and mitosis.

Learning outcomes

- Describe difference between unicellular and multicellular organisms and recall that cell division is needed for growth, repair and asexual reproduction.
- Explain the advantages of being multicellular and explain that mitosis produces genetically identical cells needed for an organism to grow.
- Describe the process of DNA replication to include unzipping and complimentary base pairing; they should also be able to describe how chromosomes line up and divide during mitosis.

Prior knowledge

Students should know that cell division is needed for growth.

Some students know that DNA needs to be copied so that it is in all new cells.

Key vocabulary

base pairs • cell division • DNA • DNA replication • mitosis • multicellular • unicellular

Barriers to learning

It is important that higher demand students understand that DNA replication takes place before the cells divide. Some students will think that 'unzipping' occurs when the chromosomes separate.

Using modelling clay to demonstrate the different processes may help, especially if students are asked to describe the stages to another student.

Curiosity and starter suggestions

- Explain to the students that by the time they are 20 years old, they will have replaced all their skin cells 200 times. Ask them to calculate how many times you will have replaced them when you are 60 years old.

OR

- Ask students to work in small groups (perhaps using mini-whiteboards) to write down what they know about DNA and chromosomes.

Learning activities

Worksheet b3_d_01 + Practical b3_d_01

Low demand

Show the class a short video clip of skin cells being grown for skin grafts. Discuss with the class why the body might need new cells. Students complete worksheet question 1 *Cell division.*

Teaching and learning notes: *Students at this level need to be introduced to the terms multicellular and unicellular, this is covered by the activity in standard demand.*

Standard demand

Show the class a photo, diagram or a live specimen of an *amoeba* and explain that the *amoeba* is a unicellular organism. Discuss with the class why unicellular organisms do not need organ systems such as a blood supply. Then explain how the cells of multicellular organisms are differentiated to carry out different jobs. Link this to the idea of cell division and introduce the class experiment. You will need to explain to students that the root tip contains one of the plant's meristems. Meristems are regions of active growth and contain cells that are actively dividing. At any one time, different cells will be in different stages of mitosis, and the object of the experiment is to see at least one of them. The root tip is three-dimensional and individual cells cannot be seen. It therefore is necessary to separate the cells out into a thin layer.

Students complete worksheet questions 2a and 2b *Multicellular organism and mitosis.*

Discuss with the students their observations. Link these into the key terms of mitosis, diploid and genetically identical. Explain that in order for each new cell to contain the same DNA that DNA must be copied before the cell divides. Students complete worksheet questions 2c–f *Multicellular organism and mitosis*. (High demand students also need to answer worksheet question 2g *Multicellular organism and mitosis* at this point.)

Teaching and learning notes: *The root tip practical is difficult and quite often nothing is seen. Students can use the internet instead. Images can be seen on the following website where it is possible for them to identify the stages of mitosis:* *http://www.biology.arizona.edu/cell_bio/activities/cell_cycle/cell_cycle.html*

However, this is a high demand activity and should only be used with the most able.

High demand

Use the images from the practical or the website to discuss what happens during mitosis. Explain that before the cell divides the DNA replicates by forming a double strand using complimentary base pairs.

Students complete worksheet question 3 *DNA replication and mitosis*.

Plenary suggestions

Show students stages of mitosis and ask them to describe what is happening.

OR

Ask the students to match up the key vocabulary with their correct definitions.

Assessment opportunities

Discussion on the practical will provide opportunity to assess students' understanding of the mitosis.

The second plenary provides opportunity to assess students' understanding at high demand.

Answers

Student Book

Q1 Cell division • **Q2** Grow, replace worn out cells, repair damaged tissue • **Q3** Allows organism to be larger, allows for cell differentiation, allow organism to be more complex • **Q4** Red blood cells • **Q5a** Cells have two copies of each chromosome • **Q5b** 23 • **Q6** Because the surface area of their body is not large enough for sufficient gas exchange • **Q7** Single strand unzips then complimentary bases join to form a new double stranded chromosome • **Q8** DNA in original cells are copied to form double stranded chromosomes, the chromosomes line up along the centre of the cell, the chromosomes divide to form single stranded chromosomes, these then move to opposite poles of the cell and a new membrane forms around them

Fig 1 to replace an ear that someone has lost • **Fig 2** to replace worn out skin • **Fig 3** 46 • **Fig 4** so that complimentary bases can be added to copy the DNA • **Fig 5** before the cell starts to divide (stage 2 on diagram)

Worksheet

Answers can be found on Teachers' Resource CD

B3d: Cell division

Resources

Student Book pages 24–25 • ICT equipment

Interactive Book News clip: Embryo testing offers IVF hope • Naked Scientist animation: What is sexual reproduction?

Files on Teacher Pack CD: b3_d_02_worksheet; b3_d_02_technician

Learning objectives

- Describe the role of gametes in sexual reproduction.
- Explain why fertilisation results in genetic variation and how the structure of a sperm cell is adapted to its function.
- Explain why, in meiosis, the chromosome number is halved and each cell is genetically different.

Learning outcomes

- Recall that in sexual reproduction gametes join in fertilisation and that a unique individual forms with half their genes coming from each parent.
- Describe gametes produced by meiosis are haploid and that the joining of gametes to form a diploid zygote results in genetic variation, they should also explain that sperm cells require mitochondria to provide energy and an acrosome that releases enzymes to digest the egg membrane.
- Explain that in meiosis the chromosome number is halved when pairs of chromosomes move to opposite poles and that each new cell is genetically different.

Prior knowledge

Students should know that eggs and sperm join during fertilisation.

Some students know that eggs and sperm are called gametes.

Key vocabulary

acrosome • fertilisation • gamete • genetic variation • haploid • meiosis • mitochondria • sexual reproduction • zygote

Barriers to learning

Many students will confuse mitosis and meiosis.

Ask students to construct a table to show how mitosis and meiosis are similar and how they are different.

Curiosity and starter suggestions

- Show students a video clip of sperm swimming to the egg. There are several examples on the internet.

OR

- Ask students to work in small groups (perhaps using mini-whiteboards) to:
  - describe how cells divide by mitosis.
  - draw series of diagrams to illustrate what happens to the chromosomes during mitosis.

Learning activities

Worksheet b3_d_02

Low demand

Use the starter activity to lead into a discussion about gametes and fertilisation. Students complete worksheet question 1 *Gametes and fertilisation.*

Teaching and learning notes: *Most of this should be recapping KS3 work: the time spent on this depends on the ability of the group.*

Standard demand

Discuss the idea of the sperm cell being produced by meiosis. Talk briefly about the differences between sexual (using meiosis) and asexual (using mitosis) reproduction in terms of the advantages of sexual reproduction in that there is more genetic variation.

Students use the internet and Student Book to complete worksheet question 2a *Making gametes.*

Teaching and learning notes: *If internet access is unavailable students can answer the questions using the Student Book.*

Foundation students may have enough time in the lesson to develop their notes to produce a PowerPoint about gametes and fertilisation.

High demand

Describe how chromosome numbers are halved during meiosis and explain why this results in genetically different cells.

Students use the internet and Student Book to complete question 3a *Meiosis.*

Plenary suggestions

Provide the class with jumbled-up key words. Ask them to identify the words (with or without the Student Book). For examples of words see technician notes.

OR

Divide the class into pairs and ask them to use four pieces of string to show their partner what happens to chromosomes when a cell divides by meiosis.

Assessment opportunities

Worksheet b3_d_02 provides staged opportunities to assess students' learning. In addition, thoughtful questioning during class discussions may be used to draw out blocks to learning.

The second plenary will provide the students with an opportunity to demonstrate their understanding of meiosis.

Answers

Student Book

Q9 Sperm • **Q10** Fertilisation • **Q11** Contains genes from both parents • **Q12** Ovary / testis • **Q13** 92 • **Q14a** Provide energy • **Q14b** Contains enzymes to breakdown egg membrane • **Q15** Chromosomes pair up, one of each pair moves to opposite poles, strands separate and move to opposite poles, four sperm cells form • **Q16** Any two of the following: mitosis – diploid cells form, one division only, no pairing up, two cells form; meiosis – haploid cells form, two divisions involved, chromosomes pair up, four cells form

Fig 6 fertilisation • **Fig 7** so when they join to sperm the new cell has the full number of chromosomes • **Fig 8** to increase the chance of fertilisation • **Fig 9** meiosis • **Fig 10** to provide energy • **Fig 11** stage 2

Worksheet

Q1a Fertilisation – the point when two gametes join; gamete – cells with half the number of chromosomes of body cell, e.g. eggs and sperm; sexual reproduction – reproduction that involves making unique individuals; sperm – male gametes • **Q1b**To increases the chance of fertilisation • **Q2a** Figure 10 page 25 • **Q2b** Contains enzymes to breakdown egg membrane • **Q2c** Meiosis • **Q2d** Diploid • **Q2e** Haploid • **Q2f** When the gametes combine • **Q3a** First division – homologous pairs separate; half go to one pole and the other half to the other pole, which reduces the number of chromosomes. Second division – chromosomes split as in mitosis •

Q3b

mitosis	**meiosis**
daughter cells genetically identical	daughter cells not genetically identical
two daughter cells	four daughter cells
diploid cells form	haploid cells form
homologous pairs do not meet	homologous pairs meet
one division	involves two divisions
body cells form	gametes form
crossing over	no crossing over

B3: Applying your knowledge

Pages 26–27 in the Student Book prepare students for assessment.

When and how to use these pages

This task provides an opportunity for students to apply their science knowledge in a different context.

Ask students to:

- read through the context and tasks, listing any terms that they do not understand
- as a whole class or in small groups, discuss the tasks to ensure all students understand the terminology used and to clarify what is required
- work individually to answer the questions for each task.

If time allows, ask students to mark each other's work using the mark scheme provided.

Notes

The task asks the students to apply their knowledge of genes and mutations to haemophilia in the Royal family. As they work through the tasks the level of demand increases. Students can assess their own learning by using the grade descriptors on page 27.

Answers

This mark scheme is also available on the Teacher Pack CD.

Task	Answer	Notes
1	A change to the DNA or genes	This is a simple recall question
2	DNA Proteins	This is a simple recall question
3	Females will have XX which means if they have the mutation on one X the other X normally has the correct code as with Queen Victoria only one copy of the correct code is needed to make the protein This is why she did not have haemophilia Males have XY – Y chromosomes do not have the protein code if the X has the mutation then they will not have a correct copy and will not be able to make the protein	Standard demand should be able to explain males are XY and females XX A student who shows complete understanding is heading towards grade A
4	Show that during meiosis some gametes have the X with the mutation some have the normal gene Yes but only if her mother is a carrier and her father a haemophiliac	High level answer
5	Mutated gene has the wrong base sequence Protein made by the faulty gene is the wrong shape, this means it will not function	High level answer

Notes

B3e: The circulatory system

Resources

Student Book pages 28–29 • Leaflet-making materials • ICT equipment
Interactive Book Drag and drop: The heart • Matching pairs: Blood vessels • Matching pairs: The blood
Files on Teacher Pack CD: b3_e_01_worksheet; b3_e_01_technician

Learning objectives

- Describe the functions of components of the blood and name the different blood vessels.
- Explain how red blood cells are adapted to their function and describe the role of arteries, veins and capillaries in the transport of blood.
- Describe how haemoglobin is used to transport oxygen.

Learning outcomes

- Recall that blood moves through arteries, veins and capillaries; they should also describe the function of red blood cells, white blood cells and platelets.
- Explain haemoglobin in red blood cells: how their size, shape and lack of nucleus help them carry oxygen. They should also describe the function of plasma in the transport of substances and the role of arteries, veins and capillaries in the transport of blood.
- Describe how haemoglobin reacts with oxygen to form oxyhaemoglobin and they should also be able to explain how arteries, veins and capillaries are adapted to their function

Prior knowledge

Students should know that blood transports substances around the body.

Some students know that white blood cells are part of the immune system.

Key vocabulary

artery • capillary • haemoglobin • oxyhaemoglobin • plasma • platelet • red blood cell • vein • white blood cell

Barriers to learning

Students may be asked about how the structure of red blood cells are adapted to their function. Some students struggle with the terms, structure and function.

Repeated use of these terms and the construction of tables relating structure to function may help.

Curiosity and starter suggestions

- Show an image or animation of blood (http://www.youtube.com/watch?v=6ALyEeBrnRg). Ask students if they can identify the different parts they see.

OR

- Ask students to work in small groups (perhaps using mini-whiteboards) to:
  - list the parts of the blood
  - describe how blood gets from the heart to the liver and back again.

Learning activities

Worksheet b3_e_01

Low demand

Show the class images or a video clip of blood vessels. Use this and the starter to discuss the function of the parts of the blood and the names of the different blood vessels.

Ask the class to answer questions 1 and 2 on page 28 of the Student Book.

Teaching and learning notes: *At this level they only need to name the blood vessels and describe the functions of the different parts, so this should not take long.*

Standard demand

Divide the class into groups. Ask each group to produce a PowerPoint presentation about blood.

Students use the worksheet b3_e_01 to help them.

Teaching and learning notes: *If no internet or computer access is available then the Student Book can be used to produce a poster or leaflet.*

High demand

Ask the class to include the extension section of the worksheet in their PowerPoint presentation.

Plenary suggestions

Draw a red blood cell and write down the ways in which it is different from all other cells in the body.

OR

Ask each group to show their PowerPoint presentation to the rest of the class.

Assessment opportunities

Thoughtful questioning about their PowerPoint presentations may allow students to demonstrate their understanding.

The first plenary might provide good checkpoints for students' progress.

Answers

Student Book

Q1 Red blood cell = transports oxygen, white blood cell = defends against disease, platelet = helps blood to clot • **Q2** Arteries, veins and capillaries • **Q3** One from: contain haemoglobin – allows oxygen to be transported around the body. They do not have a nucleus – this leaves more room to carry oxygen. They are disc-shaped and have a dent on both sides – this helps them to absorb a lot of oxygen. They are very small – they can carry oxygen to all parts of the body • **Q4** Water, hormones, glucose, antibodies and waste products, carbon dioxide • **Q5** So it can flow through the blood vessels • **Q6** Artery • **Q7** It can release its oxygen when needed and then collect more from the lungs • **Q8** Veins have valves to stop backflow of blood; arteries have thick muscle walls to withstand high pressure • **Q9** To allow substances to pass in and out of the capillaries

Fig 1 *100 000 x 365 x age in years* will give an approximate value – for a 15-year-old it is about 5.5×10^8 • **Fig 2** red blood cells • **Fig 3** capillaries • **Fig 4** to increase surface area for gas exchange / so they can absorb more oxygen

Worksheet

Q1 and **Q2** PowerPoint presentations

B3e: The circulatory system

Resources

Student Book pages 30–31 • Equipment for practical • ICT equipment
Interactive Book Naked Scientist animation: How does the circulatory system work?
Files on Teacher Pack CD: b3_e_02_worksheet; b3_e_02_practical; b3_e_02_technician

Learning objectives

- Describe the functions of the heart and explain why blood flows round the body.
- Identify the different parts of the heart and explain why the left ventricle has a thicker wall than the right ventricle.
- Explain the advantage of the double circulatory system in mammals.

Learning outcomes

- Recall that the heart pumps blood to the lungs and the rest of the body and that the blood flows because of pressure differences.
- Label a diagram of the heart and explain that the left ventricle has a thicker muscle wall to pump the blood at higher pressure so that it reaches all parts of the body.
- Explain advantage of the double circulatory system in mammals in that it can produce a higher pressure and increase the rate of flow to the tissues.

Prior knowledge

Students should know that the heart pumps blood around the body.

Some students know the different parts of the heart.

Key vocabulary

atrium • bicuspid valve • double circulatory system • tricuspid valve • ventricle

Barriers to learning

Students find it difficult to transfer the labels of the heart from one diagram to another.

Asking students to label diagrams showing the heart from different angles may help them become more familiar with all the parts of the heart.

Curiosity and starter suggestions

- Show the students images or video clips of blood passing through the heart. (There are several on the internet.) Ask them why the heart has two sides.

OR

- Ask students to write down five things they already know about the heart.

Learning activities

Worksheet b3_e_02 + Practical b3_e_02

Low demand

Show the class a pig or model heart. Discuss with the class the function of the heart. Students complete worksheet question 1 *The function of the heart.*

Teaching and learning notes: *This is just a quick introduction about the heart. It should be used mainly to find out what the students already know.*

Standard demand

Demonstrate or ask the class to dissect a pig or lamb heart. During the dissection, discuss with the class the function of each part and the advantage of the thicker wall of the left ventricle. Students should also be made aware of the function of the heart valves. Instructions for the dissection are in the practical. Students complete worksheet question 2 *The structure of the heart.*

Teaching and learning notes: *It is important that students see an actual heart to get some idea of size and see the difference in the thickness of the muscle wall. It may, however, be more appropriate to do this as a demonstration rather than a class practical.*

High demand

The advantage of double circulation should be discussed with the class during or after the dissection of the heart. Students complete worksheet question 3 *Double circulatory system.*

Plenary suggestions

Ask the class to add labels onto a projected diagram of the heart.

OR

Provide the class with cards showing parts of the heart and ask them to put them in order to show the flow of blood.

Assessment opportunities

Worksheet b3_e_02 provides staged opportunities to assess students' learning. In addition, thoughtful questioning during class discussions may be used to draw out blocks to learning.

The plenary activities might provide good checkpoints for students' progress.

Answers

Student Book

Q10 Right • **Q11** Left • **Q12** Artery • **Q13** Vena cava, right atrium, right ventricle, pulmonary artery, lung, pulmonary vein, left atrium, left ventricle, aorta • **Q14** Has to pump blood further • **Q15** Bicuspid, tricuspid, semi-lunar valves: all prevent backflow • **Q16a** Double circulation blood passes through the heart twice each time it passes round the body • **Q16b** Blood is at higher pressure so the rate of flow to the tissue is higher • **Q17** Blood reaching muscles would be a mixture of oxygenated and deoxygenated blood

Fig 5 right • **Fig 6** their heart has been damaged • **Fig 7** vena cava • **Fig 8** circuit round the body

Worksheet

Q1 Blood, lungs, body, pressure, high, low • **Q2**a See Figure 8 on page 31 of the Student Book • **Q2b** Right ventricle • **Q2c** Left ventricle • **Q2d** Right atrium • **Q2e** Left atrium • **Q2f** Stop the blood flowing back into right ventricle • **Q2g** Has to pump the blood further • **Q3a** double circulation blood passes through the heart twice each time it passes round the body • **Q3b** Blood is at higher pressure so the rate of flow to the tissue is higher

B3f: Growth and development

Resources

Student Book pages 32–33 • Equipment for practical • ICT equipment

Interactive Book Matching pairs: Plant tissues • Matching pairs: Differences in plant a animal growth • News clip: Cells, tissues and organs

Files on Teacher Pack CD: b3_f_01_worksheet; b3_f_01_practical; b3_f_01_technician

Learning objectives

- Describe how to make a stained slide of an onion cell and the functions of the parts of a plant cell.
- Identify simple differences between bacterial cells and plant and animal cells and discuss the use of stem cells.
- Describe the difference between the arrangement of DNA in a bacterial cell and a plant/animal cell.

Learning outcomes

- Describe how to prepare a stained slide using iodine solution; they should also be able to recall that bacteria cells are smaller than plant and animal cells and that cell division is followed by specialisation.
- Recall that bacteria lack a 'true' nucleus mitochondria and chloroplasts; they should also be able to describe uses of stem cells to treat medical conditions and discuss the issues involved.
- Describe bacterial DNA as a single circular strand and explain that embryonic stem cells have the ability to differentiate into many different types of cells.

Prior knowledge

Students should be able to label the parts of an animal cell.

Some students know that bacteria have a different cell structure to plants and animals.

Key vocabulary

bacteria • cell differentiation • cellulose • chloroplast • mitochondria • stem cells • 'true' nucleus • vacuole

Barriers to learning

Some students will find the concept of cell differentiation difficult.

Show students images of as many different types of cells as possible. Ask them to compare the structure of the cells with that of a cheek cell or palisade cell. They should also discuss why the structures are different.

Curiosity and starter suggestions

- Show the students a video of a developing embryo. Discuss how simple cells might turn into blood cells, lever cells, etc.

OR

- Ask students to draw and label an animal and a plant cell (perhaps using mini-whiteboards).

Learning activities — Worksheet b3_f_01 + Practical b3_f_01

Low demand

Use the starter activity to lead into a discussion about how we can use microscopes to see the structure of plant cells.

Students then follow the instructions in the practical. Students then complete worksheet question 1 *Looking at cells.*

Teaching and learning notes: *The worksheet asks students to write up their method and this is because they need to be able to describe how to make a stained slide of an onion cell. Some students find it difficult to do this so you could give them the method in the wrong order and ask them to rewrite it in the correct order.*

Standard demand

Show the students diagrams of animal plant and bacterial cells. Discuss the similarities and differences.

Students then complete worksheet question 2a *Different cells*.

Discuss the idea of growth and the need for cells to divide and differentiate. Explain the importance of stem cells and the issues arising from their use.

Students then complete worksheet questions 2b–d *Different cells*.

Teaching and learning notes: *Students can find out more about stem cells by using the links on the website http://gslc.genetics.utah.edu. This can be done in the lesson or as homework.*

High demand

Develop the discussions on bacteria and stem cells. Students then complete worksheet question 3 *More ideas on cells*.

Plenary suggestions

Show students pictures of cells and ask them to decide if they are plant, animal or bacterial cells.

OR

Debate some of the issues arising from stem cell research.

Assessment opportunities

Worksheet b3_f_01 provides staged opportunities to assess students' learning. In addition, thoughtful questioning during class discussions may be used to draw out blocks to learning

Both plenary suggestions might provide good checkpoints for students' progress.

Answers

Student Book

Q1 Vacuole = contains cell sap and provides support; cell wall = provides support; chloroplast = absorb light energy for photosynthesis • **Q2** Cell wall • **Q3** Cell wall, vacuole, chloroplast • **Q4** Cell membrane, mitochondria, cytoplasm, nucleus • **Q5** E.g. red blood cell, white blood cell, nerve cell, muscle cell • **Q6** Answers depends on students own opinion • **Q7** Embryonic stem cells have the ability to specialise into most cells of the body. Adult stem cells are only able to differentiate into a few different types of cells

Fig 1 putting human stem cells into chicken eggs • **Fig 2** nucleus • **Fig 3** bacteria do not have a 'true' nucleus, mitochondria or chloroplasts • **Fig 4** uses embryonic stem cells that have a right to life

Worksheet

Q1a Chloroplast • **Q1b** Absorb light for photosynthesis • **Q1c** No light underground • **Q1d** Cell wall – support; vacuole – contains cell sap and support • **Q2a** No true nucleus, chloroplasts or mitochondria • **Q2b** Cell differentiation • **Q2c** E.g. used to treat genetic disorders • **Q2d** Ethical issues described • **Q3a** DNA is not in a nucleus and is a single circular strand • **Q3b** Answers will depend on the amount of research but may include – both capable of differentiating, however, embryonic stem cells can differentiate into more types of cells than adult stem cells – both used in treating medical conditions, issues include ideas about embryo's right to life

B3f: Growth and development

Resources

Student Book pages 34–35 • ICT equipment
Files on Teacher Pack CD: b3_f_02_worksheet; b3_f_02 technician

Learning objectives

- Describe how growth can be measured and interpret data on increases in mass.
- Describe and explain why plant growth is different to animal growth.
- Explain the advantages and disadvantages of the different methods of measuring growth.

Learning outcomes

- Describe how to use height, wet mass and dry mass to measure growth and explain that plants grow continually at specific points but all parts of an animal grow during their early stages.
- Recall that dry mass is a better measure of growth and that plant growth is restricted to meristems but unlike animal cells plant cells retain the ability to differentiate.
- Explain that to measure dry mass the organism cannot be living and that different parts of an organism may grow at different rates.

Prior knowledge

Students should know that growth involves cell division.

Some students know that growth can be measured in different ways.

Key vocabulary

cell differentiation • cell enlargement • dry mass • finite size • growth curve • meristems • wet mass

Barriers to learning

It is important that students can interpret growth curves.

Using past exam paper questions allow students to become familiar with such graphs.

Curiosity and starter suggestions

- Show class a growth curve and ask them to describe the pattern.

OR

- Ask students to work in small groups (perhaps using mini-whiteboards) to:
  - say what they know about how organisms grow
  - write down what they know about different ways animals and plants grow.

Learning activities

Worksheet b3_f_02

Low demand

Use the starter activity to lead into a discussion about growth curves and what they show. Discuss with students how growth can be measured and simple ideas about how growth in plants and animals is different. Students complete worksheet question 1 *Growth.*

Teaching and learning notes: *If time is available this lesson would split easily into two. The first lesson could be on measuring growth where students could plan a simple experiment to measure growth in seedlings. Cress seeds could be grown in different conditions and their growth measured as increase in height or mass. The second lesson would look closer at interpreting growth curves and the differences between plant and animal growth.*

Standard demand

Develop the discussions to describe the main phases of a typical growth curve. Use images of growth curves from different organism to show how they are similar and how they are different. There are plenty on the internet if you search using three different search terms – growth curve human, growth curve plant, growth curve animal. Students complete worksheet question 2 *Interpreting growth curves.*

Develop the low demand ideas with the students about how plant and animal growth is different. Students then construct a table showing the differences.

Teaching and learning notes: *The worksheet has been designed to cover the different aspects of the specification. There are other ways to approach them, for example, practical work measuring growth or PowerPoint presentations that cover all the different aspects of growth and measuring growth. The approach used depends on time and equipment available.*

High demand

Students complete worksheet question 3 *Growth rate*.

Plenary suggestions

Describe growth ideas linked to the standard demand specification statement about the differences between plant and animal growth. Ask students to decide if you are describing plant or animal growth. For example, 'only grow to a finite size' would be animals but 'grow continuously' would be plants.

OR

Show students an image of humans growth (Figure 8 on page 35 of Student Book) ask them to explain why the growth of the head may be different to that of the limbs.

Assessment opportunities

Worksheet b3_f_02 provides staged opportunities to assess students' learning. In addition, thoughtful questioning during class discussions may be used to draw out blocks to learning.

Both plenary activities might provide good checkpoints for students' progress.

Answers

Student Book

Q8a 14–16 • **Q8b** Growth stops • **Q8c** Approx. 9–13 • **Q9a** 2 • **Q9b** Lack of space, water or minerals • **Q10** To measure dry mass you need to kill the organism • **Q11** Growth is all over the human body but mainly in the meristems of the tree, tree continues to grow humans reach a finite size • **Q12** May get rounder but not increase in length • **Q13** Water content varies • **Q14** Place it in an oven to dry out, record mass before and after drying

Fig 5 S • **Fig 6** Height, dry or wet mass • **Fig 8** Head

Worksheet

Q1a Phase 3 • **Q1b** Dry mass length or height • **Q2a** 50th • **Q2b** Growth increases up to 75th percentile at 15 months but then drops down and remains on 50th percentile line • **Q2c** 50th • **Q2d** No – remains on or around 50th percentile • **Q2e** 5th • **Q2f** Follows 5th percentile for first 18 months and then falls below the percentile line • **Q2g** Below 5th • **Q2h** Child is underweight as it falls below the 5th percentile • **Q3a** Answer could match table on page 35 of Student Book • **Q3b** Most plant growth occurs at the root and shoot tip so the rate of growth there is faster

B3g: New genes for old

Resources

Student Book pages 36–37 • ICT equipment
Interactive Book Quick starter: Selective breeding • News clip: Cruel breeding debate overshadows Crufts
Files on Teacher Pack CD: b3_g_01_ worksheet; b3_g_01_technician

Learning objectives

- Describe the process selective breeding.
- Discuss the issues involved in selective breeding.

Learning outcomes

- Recall that selective breeding involves selection of characteristics, cross breeding and selection of offspring over many generations.
- Recall that selective breeding can lead to inbreeding and health problems.
- Explain that selective breeding reduces the gene pool which reduces variation and cause the accumulation of harmful recessive characteristics.

Prior knowledge

Students should know that selective breeding involves breeding organisms with the characteristics you want.

Some students know the advantages and disadvantages of selective breeding.

Key vocabulary

characteristic • cross-breed • gene pool • inbred • selective breeding • variation • yield

Barriers to learning

Students need to be able to describe the process of selective breeding even at low demand. They often get the process confused with genetic engineering.

Using cards with the stages of the process on and asking students to put them in the correct order may help consolidate their learning.

Curiosity and starter suggestions

- Show the students images of selectively bred animals. Ask them to suggest why they were bred that way.

OR

- Ask students to work in small groups (perhaps using mini-whiteboards) to list the characteristics they would want to breed into a banana. Encourage them to use their imaginations such as changing flavour or colour.

Learning activities

Worksheet b3_g_01

Low demand

Use the starter activity to lead into a discussion about selective breeding and the processes involved. Students complete worksheet question 1 *Dog breeding*.

Teaching and learning notes: *On the worksheet students are asked to work out the combinations of different crosses. This is an introduction to the idea of selective breeding; the main part of the lesson also covers some of the low demand ideas.*

Standard demand

Ask students to research one example of selective breeding. They should follow the instructions in worksheet question 2 *Selective breeding PowerPoint*.

Teaching and learning notes: *How this is tackled depends on time available. Most of the information is available in the Student Book.*

High demand

Students develop their ideas to complete worksheet question 3 *Selective breeding extension.*

Plenary suggestions

Ask the students to write down some advantages and disadvantages of selectively breeding dogs.

OR

Pair students up and ask them to talk about selective breeding for two minutes to their partner. The partner can then score them on how well they did.

Assessment opportunities

The plenary activities provide opportunity for students to demonstrate their understanding.

The PowerPoint might provide good opportunity for students to demonstrate their progress.

Answers

Student Book

Q1 To get a higher yield so they can make more money • **Q2** So make more profit from each sow • **Q3** Disease resistant, sweet tasting • **Q4** Breed the two together, choose the largest and sweetest plants and keep breeding them • **Q5** Often get deformities / health problems • **Q6** Idea of increased variation / larger gene pool

Fig 1 e.g. lettuce – more leaves; chicken – lays more eggs; cow – makes more milk • **Fig 3** might not be able to see to catch food

Worksheet

Q1a Height – 80 cm or 38 cm; colour – white or grey; coat – curly or rough; ears – small • **Q1b**

parents		**offspring**	
Cairn terrier	Basset Hound	Height – 25 cm Coat – smooth	Colour – fawn Ears – large
Collie	Poodle	Height – 65 cm Coat – curly	Colour – brown and white Ears – small
Irish Wolfhound	Alsatian	Height – 80 cm Coat – medium length hair	Colour – grey Ears – stand up
Doberman	Collie	Height – 66 cm Coat – long hair	Colour – black Ears – medium size
Airedale terrier	Doberman	Height – 60 cm Coat – short length hair	Colour – black and tan Ears – stand up

B3g: New genes for old

Resources

Student Book pages 38–39 • ICT equipment
Interactive Book News Clip: Babies that save lives
Files on Teacher Pack CD: b3_g_02_worksheet; b3_g_02_technician

Learning objectives

- Describe the process of genetic engineering.
- Discuss the issues involved in genetic engineering and gene therapy.

Learning outcomes

- Recall that genetic engineering involves the transfer of genes from one organism to another and that it may be possible to use genetic engineering to cure certain genetic disorders.
- Describe how genetic engineering is used to make golden rice, insulin and disease-resistant plants.
- Use the terms selection, isolation, insertion and replication to describe the principles of genetic engineering and explain why gene therapy using gametes is controversial.

Prior knowledge

Students should know that genetic engineering is used to modify organisms.

Some students may know examples of genetically modified food.

Key vocabulary

genes • genetic engineering • genetically modified • gene therapy • insertion • isolation

Barriers to learning

It is important that students understand the difference between selective breeding and genetic engineering.

Providing them with descriptions of different examples and asking them to decide which one they are may help.

Curiosity and starter suggestions

- Show them images of unusual genetically engineered organisms (use 'genetically engineered animals' or 'genetically engineered plants' as search terms on google images and see what you get) and ask them to decide which ones are real.

OR

- Ask students to work in small groups (perhaps using mini-whiteboards) to write down what they know about the GM crops.

Learning activities

Worksheet b3_g_02

Low demand

Use the starter activity to lead into a discussion about GM crops or ask the class to look at a picture of the square tomato (available on the internet or page 38 of the Student Book).

Discuss the idea of changing things using genetic engineering with the class.

Ask the class to answer questions 7 and 8 on page 38 of the Student Book.

Teaching and learning notes: *This is just a quick introduction for low demand students. Most of the lesson should be spent on the standard demand activity.*

Standard demand

Divide the class into groups. Ask each group to produce a PowerPoint presentation about genetic engineering. Students use the worksheet to help them.

Teaching and learning notes: *As an alternative, ask the class to research the topic using books and to produce an informative poster or leaflet.*

High demand

Ask the students to complete worksheet question 2 *Genetic engineering extension*.

Plenary suggestions

Debate the ethical issues involved in genetic modification.

OR

Pair the students up and ask one to describe to the other how bacteria could be modified to make insulin – using the terms isolation, insertion and replication.

Assessment opportunities

Asking students to talk through their PowerPoint presentations may demonstrate their understanding of genetic engineering.

The second plenary activity provides good checkpoints for students' progress.

Answers

Student Book

Q7a Can spray crops without harming them • **Q7b** Insulin can be made for diabetics • **Q8** Genes, genetic engineering • **Q9** Bacteria • **Q10** Because their diet lacks Vitamin A **Q11** Idea of harmful side effect • **Q12** Gene from insulin is isolated and cut out of human DNA, gene is then inserted into bacterial DNA, the bacteria are then cloned or replicated so the gene gets copied, bacteria start to make insulin • **Q13** Depends on students' own opinions

Fig 4 yes because they would be same shape as bread if used in a sandwich • **Fig 5** yes – provide insulin for diabetics • **Fig 6** provides Vitamin A • **Fig 7** bacteria

Worksheet

Q1 and **Q2** PowerPoint should cover all the points mentioned

B3h: Cloning

Resources

Student Book pages 40–41 • ICT equipment
Interactive Book News clip: Indian twins separated
Files on Teacher Pack CD: b3_h_01_worksheet; b3_h_01_technician

Learning objectives

- Describe the process of cloning that produced Dolly the sheep.
- Discuss the issues involved in cloning.

Learning outcomes

- Recall that cloning produces genetically identical copies and that twins are natural clones.
- Recall cloning Dolly involved the process of nuclear transfer and be able to describe some uses of cloning and discuss the dilemmas concerning human cloning.
- Describe in detail how nuclear transfer involves removing the nucleus from a body cell and placing it in an egg cell; they should also be able to explain the implications of using cloning to supply organs for humans.

Prior knowledge

Students should know that clones are genetically identical copies.

Some students know some of the ethical dilemmas of cloning.

Key vocabulary

asexual reproduction • clones • Dolly • nuclear transfer • stem cells • surrogate

Barriers to learning

It is vital that students understand that clones are genetically identical and not just identical.

Repeated use of the term may help to emphasise the idea.

Curiosity and starter suggestions

- Show the class a newspaper headline or news clip (http://abcnews.go.com/Archives/video/feb-24-1997-dolly-sheep-10615268) about Dolly the sheep. Discuss why it is so important.

OR

- Find the following words on page 40 of the Student Book and write down what they mean: clone, cloning, genetically identical, asexual reproduction.

Learning activities

Worksheet b3_h_01

Low demand

Ask the class to look at a photo of Dolly on page 40 of the Student Book. Discuss why Dolly was so important and explain how clones can form naturally.

Students complete worksheet question 1 *Cloning*.

Teaching and learning notes: *Students need to know that Dolly was the first mammal cloned from an adult. However, there are now many more examples. A suggested activity could be for students to find as many examples as possible (using the internet) in a given time.*

Standard demand

Explain to the students in simple terms how Dolly was cloned, video clips are available on the internet (the news clip from the starter can be used). Extend the discussion to describe different uses of cloning and the ethical dilemmas involved. Students complete worksheet question 2 *Uses of cloning*.

Teaching and learning notes: *How this is tackled depends on time available. Students could produce their own news article or even video about cloning.*

High demand

Explain exactly how nuclear transfer takes place. Students complete worksheet question 3 *Nuclear transfer*.

Plenary suggestions

Hold a debate on the rights and wrongs of human cloning.

OR

True or false statements about cloning – read out five statements. Are they true or false?

Assessment opportunities

Worksheet b3_h_01 provides staged opportunities to assess students' learning. In addition, thoughtful questioning during class discussions may be used to draw out blocks to learning.

The second plenary might provide good checkpoints for students' progress.

Answers

Student Book

Q1 Involves one parent • **Q2** Dolly the sheep • **Q3** Genetically identical • **Q4** They are formed naturally and are genetically identical • **Q5** They will all have the characteristic you want • **Q6** Provide organs for transplants • **Q7** E.g. it may lead to adults being cloned • **Q8** Her DNA came from a different sheep • **Q9** Students' own opinions • **Q10** Students' own opinions

Fig 1 it is a clone • **Fig 2** DNA is not the same – came from different eggs • **Fig 3** nuclear transfer • **Fig 4** DNA came from the cells of B

Worksheet

Q1a Asexual, identical, adult, twins • **Q2** Taking a nucleus from a cell and placing it into an egg cell • **Q2b** Producing large numbers of animals, provide organs for transplants, idea of gene therapy • **Q2c** Sensible ethical issue – not just playing God • **Q3a** Similar to Figure 4 on page 41 of Student Book • **Q3b** E.g. gene therapy, transplants • **Q3c** Low success rate, premature aging • **Q3d** Students' own opinions

B3h: Cloning

Resources

Student Book pages 42–43 • Equipment for practical • ICT equipment
Files on Teacher Pack CD: b3_h_02_worksheet; b3_h_02_practical; b3_h_02_technician

Learning objectives

- Describe how to clone different plants.
- Discuss the advantages and disadvantages of cloning plants.
- Describe how to clone plants using tissue culture.

Learning outcomes

- Recall how to take cuttings and how spider plants, strawberries and potatoes reproduce asexually.
- Describe the advantages of cloning to include mass production and a guarantee of the required characteristics.
- Describe the process of tissue culture to include, selection of characteristics, the use of small pieces of tissue, aseptic techniques and a suitable growth medium.
- Explain that cloning of animals is difficult because animal cells lose the ability to differentiate.

Prior knowledge

Students should know that asexual reproduction produces clones.

Some students will know some advantages and disadvantages of cloning.

Key vocabulary

asexual reproduction • clones • genetically identical • plantlet • tissue culture • variation

Barriers to learning

It is vital that foundation students are able to describe how different plants reproduce asexually. They often mix up the different ideas.

Using diagrams and asking students to annotate them may help.

Curiosity and starter suggestions

- Show the students a plant such as geranium or a potato and ask them how they could turn it into several genetically identical plants.

OR

- Ask students to write down five things they know about cloning.

Learning activities

Worksheet b3_h_02 + Practical b3_h_02

Low demand

Show the class examples of asexual reproduction and discuss how the new plants grow.

Ask students to follow instructions in practical.

Students then answer worksheet question 1 *Asexual reproduction in plants.*

Teaching and learning notes: *Standard demand students should either attempt to take cuttings or clone cauliflower depending on which tier of examination they intend to do. Both these take several weeks so it may be a good idea to have examples already prepared.*

Standard demand

Discuss advantages and disadvantages of cloning plants with the class. Ask students to produce an informative leaflet or poster about the advantages and disadvantages.

Teaching and learning notes: *This may need to be a homework activity if there is not enough time in the lesson.*

High demand

Discuss with students that only small sections of a plant are needed for cloning. Students then follow instructions in practical.

Students then answer worksheet question 2 *Tissue culture*.

Plenary suggestions

Provide the students with sentences about taking plant cuttings in the wrong order and ask them to put them in the correct order.

OR

Ask students to write down two advantages and two disadvantages of cloning plants.

Assessment opportunities

Worksheet b3_h_02 provides staged opportunities to assess students' learning. In addition, thoughtful questioning during class discussions may be used to draw out blocks to learning

The plenary activities may provide good checkpoints for students' progress.

Answers

Student Book

Q11 Sends out runners, buds then grow into plantlets, plantlets put down roots into the soil • **Q12** Cut part of the stem, remove flower and some of the leaves (dip in hormone rooting powder), put into damp soil and cover with a plastic bag • **Q13** Cut the potato into 5 making sure each piece has a bud then plant them • **Q14** E.g. all plants are identical, quicker than seed • **Q15** May not be resistant to disease so all plants would get the disease, reduces genetic variation within the species • **Q16** Making sure it is kept sterile • **Q17** Sterile, growth medium, correct temperature, correct light conditions • **Q18** Most of the sheep's cells have lost the ability to differentiate

Fig 5 sexual reproduction – when tuber grows new shoots • **Fig 6** so it does not get too damp and rot • **Fig 7** in case the environment changes there would be more chance of survival • **Fig 8** so the plants do not get infected and rot

Worksheet

Q1a Strawberry – label runners and plantlets; potato – label tuber; spider plant – label plantlets: see diagram below

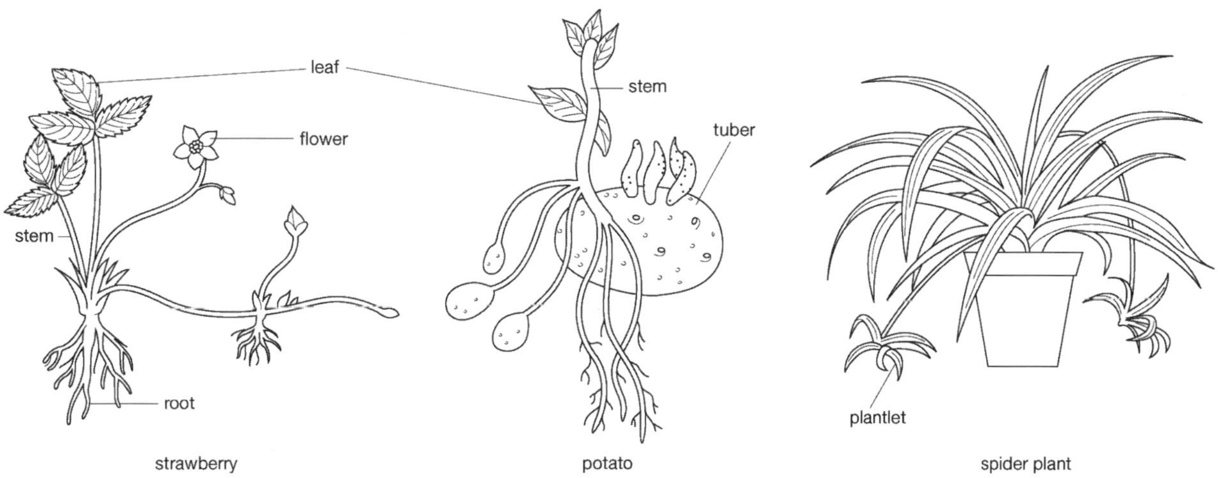

Q1b Strawberry – idea of runners; potato – idea of tubers having buds; spider plant – idea of plantlets • **Q1c** and **Q1d** Answer depends on results • **Q2a** Take small piece of plant and place in sterile growth medium, place them in suitable conditions • **Q2b** Idea of plant cells being able to differentiate

B3: Research and collecting secondary data

Pages 44–45 in the Student Book prepare students for assessment.

When and how to use these pages

This task provides an opportunity to build and assess the skills that students will use when researching and collecting secondary data

Annotated hints and tips guide students through the tasks.

Ask students to:

- read through the context and tasks, listing any terms that they do not understand
- as a whole class or in small groups, discuss the tasks to ensure all students understand the terminology used and to clarify what is required
- work individually to answer the questions for each task.

If time allows, ask students to mark each other's work using the mark scheme provided.

Pages 278–290 provide further guidance on Practical and Enquiry Skills.

Notes

A brief overview of the task highlighting the main skills covered with any helpful hints for the teachers.

Answers

This mark scheme is also available on the Teacher Pack CD.

Question	Answer	Notes
Why does exercise affect heart and breathing rate?	muscles work harder and need more energy so muscles need more oxygen and muscles need more glucose because respiration increases in muscles more carbon dioxide is produced increase in breathing and heart rate means increase in oxygen to muscles also increase in the removal of carbon dioxide	There are lots of ideas not just to get more oxygen to the muscles.
Why do muscles use anaerobic respiration during exercise?	because they cannot get oxygen fast enough or not enough oxygen for just aerobic respiration to take place	Remember there will still be some aerobic respiration.
What is the oxygen debt?	the extra oxygen taken in at the end of exercise it is needed to break down the lactic acid	
Why does it take time to recover heart and breathing rate after exercise?	need to take in extra oxygen to break down the lactic acid	understanding that the extra oxygen is linked to lactic acid is a difficult idea for some

Why do some people have faster recovery times than others, even when they do the same amount of exercise?	they did not produce as much lactic acid to start with less anaerobic respiration took place	other ideas include they have a greater lung volume so took in more oxygen or simply that they are fitter – but this is a low level answer
How can you compare recovery times in the lab?	ask several people to exercise for the same length of time before exercise measure their pulse rate after exercise measure pulse rate until it returns to normal	this is just an outline as preparation for planning an investigation in part 2

B3: Checklist

Pages 46–47 in the Student Book provide a student-friendly checklist for revision.

When and how to use these pages

This checklist is presented in three columns showing progression, based on the grading criteria.

Remind students that they need to be able to use these ideas in various ways, such as:

- interpreting pictures, diagrams and graphs
- applying ideas to new situations
- explaining ethical implications
- suggesting some benefits and risks to society
- drawing conclusions from evidence they have been given.

These pages can be used for individual or class revision using any combination of the suggestions below.

- Ask students to construct a mind map linking the points on this checklist.
- Work through the checklist as a class and note the points that need further class discussion.
- Ask students to tick the boxes on the checklist worksheet (Teacher Pack CD) if they feel confident that they are well prepared for the topics. Students should refer back to the relevant Student Book pages to revise the points that they feel less confident about.
- Ask students to use the search terms to do further research on the different points in the checklist.

Pages 278−299 provide further assessment guidance.

Module summary

In the introduction to this section, students were presented with a number of new ideas. Work through the list below as part of their revision. Ask students to write their own summaries and mind maps, using this list as a starting point.

- how eggs and sperm are adapted for fertilisation
- how cells divide by a process called mitosis
- how eggs and sperm are made by a special type of cell division called meiosis
- how the blood cells are adapted to their function
- the different parts of the heart
- the role of haemoglobin in the transport of oxygen
- how DNA from one organism can be transferred to another organism
- why selective breeding can be harmful
- how organisms like sheep can be cloned
- the two types of respiration
- how DNA is used to make a protein
- the effect of temperature on enzyme activity

Notes

B3: Exam-style questions: Foundation

Pages 48–49 in the Student Book are exam-style questions for Foundation students.

When and how to use these pages

These questions are based on module B3 and cover a range of different types of questions that students will encounter in their written exams.

- Questions could be used as a revision test once you've completed the section.
- Work through the questions as a class as part of a revision lesson.
- Ask students to mark each other's work, using the mark scheme provided.
- As a class, make a list of the questions that most students did not get right. Work through these as a class.

Notes on worked example

The worked example takes students through a six-mark question on growth in animals and plants.

Assessment objectives

These exam-style questions cover the Assessment objectives as described below.

Assessment objectives		Questions
AO1	Recall, select and communicate their knowledge and understanding of science	2ai, 2b, 3a, 3bi, 3c, 4a, 4b
AO2	Apply skills, knowledge and understanding of science in practical and other contexts	1a, 2aii, 3bii
AO3	Analyse and evaluate evidence, make reasoned judgements and draw conclusions based on evidence	1b

Answers

These answers are also supplied on the Teacher Pack CD so that students can mark their own, or their peer's work.

Question number	Answer	Additional notes	Mark
1ai	Longer the length of exercise, the higher the pulse rate		1
aii	Longer exercise, the more oxygen is needed by the muscle Longer exercise, the more carbon dioxide is made Idea that heart beats faster to transport gases to and from lungs		1 1 1
b	repeat the experiment / repeat using different students / measure pulse rate using a monitor	Any one idea	1
			[5]
2ai	cut part of the stem remove flower and or some of the leaves dip in hormone rooting powder put into damp soil	Any three ideas, one mark each	3

	cover with a plastic bag	must be damp or wet soil	
aii	Red all the plants would be genetically identical to the parent plant		1 1
b	**advantage** all the plants will have the characteristic you want **disadvantage** may not be resistant to disease so all plants would get the disease / reduces genetic variation within the species		1 1
			[7]
3a	peel of a small piece of onion skin place skin onto microscope slide add a drop of iodine solution gently place a cover slip on top	Any three ideas	3
bi	support		1
bii	onion is found underground where there is no light		1
c	no 'true' nucleus in bacteria; no mitochondria in bacteria	Any one idea ignore chloroplasts	1
			[6]
4a	choose the fastest offspring breed these over several generations (with other fast horses)		1 1
b	this would be inbreeding inbreeding reduces variation / gene pool could lead to unhealthy horses	Any two ideas	2
			[4]
			[22]

B3: Exam-style questions: Higher

Pages 50–51 in the Student Book are exam-style questions for Higher students.

Important note from the Publisher

In some early printings of the Additional Science B Student Book the B5 version of page 51 page was inserted instead of the B3 version. If this affects you, the correct page 51 can be found on the CD-ROM entitled p3_page51_correction. We apologise for this.

When and how to use these pages

These questions are based on module B3 and cover a range of different types of questions that students will encounter in their written exams.

- Questions could be used as a revision test once you've completed the section.
- Work through the questions as a class as part of a revision lesson.
- Ask students to mark each other's work, using the mark scheme provided.
- As a class, make a list of the questions that most students did not get right. Work through these as a class.

Notes on worked example

The worked example takes students through a six-mark question on urine concentration.

Assessment objectives

These exam-style questions cover the Assessment objectives as described below.

Assessment objectives		Questions
AO1	Recall, select and communicate their knowledge and understanding of science	2a, 2b, 3b
AO2	Apply skills, knowledge and understanding of science in practical and other contexts	1a, 1b, 3a, 3c, 4
AO3	Analyse and evaluate evidence, make reasoned judgements and draw conclusions based on evidence	1c

Answers

These answers are also supplied on the Teacher Pack CD so that students can mark their own, or their peer's work.

Question number	Answer	Additional notes	Mark
1ai	3.7	must be correctly rounded not 3.6	1
aii	correctly labelled axis		1
	correctly plotted points		1
	curve should be U shaped through most points		1
bi	as temperature increases from 20°C to 40°C the time decreases, after this the time increases	need full description for mark	1

bii	as temperature increases from 20°C to 40°C kinetic energy increases enzymes and substrate join more often after 40°C enzyme denatures / changes shape substrate can no longer fit into enzyme	Any three ideas	3
ci	Third attempt at 50°C		1
cii	water bath may have been at wrong temperature may have incorrectly judged the end point		
			[10]
2a	nucleus / mitochondria	ignore chloroplast as not found in animal cells	1
b	DNA unzips idea of complementary bases bases join onto original DNA strands	Any two ideas	2
c	gene is a code for insulin code is used to join the correct sequence of amino acids together DNA is copied onto mRNA mRNA used to join amino acids together on the ribosomes		1 1 1 1
			[7]
3a	only one ventricle only one atrium no left and right side	Any two ideas	2
b	prevent backflow		1
c	pressure of blood is less		1
			[4]
4ai	55/77 = 0.71	2 marks for correct answer 1 mark for 55/77 but wrong answer or incorrect rounding e.g. 0.7142 = 1	2
aii	would be 1		1
aiii	Amount of oxygen used would equal the amount of carbon dioxide produced Or from the equation it would be 6/6 = 1		1
			[4]
			[25]

B4: Introduction

Pages 52–53 in the Student Book provide an introduction to module B4.

When and how to use these pages

These pages summarise what students should already know from KS3 or previous GCSE units and provide an overview of the content that they will learn in this module.

- Use these pages as a revision lesson before you start the first new topic.
- Brainstorm everything that students remember about the different topics using the headings as a starting point. Compare your list with the points in the Student Book.
- Use the questions on the left-hand page as a starting point for class discussions.
- Ask students if they can tell you anything about the topics on the right-hand page.
- Make a note of any unfamiliar / difficult terms and return to these in the relevant lessons.

You can revisit these pages at the following points:

- before the lessons on Leaves and photosynthesis pages 58–65
- before the lessons on Diffusion and osmosis pages 66–69
- before the lessons on Transport in plants and Plants need minerals pages 72–79
- before the lessons on Decay and Farming pages 80–87.

Overview of module

In this section students will learn about important processes that occur in green plants and the implications for farming and food preservation.

The subject of ecology is explored in terms of sampling and mapping the distribution of organisms.

Students will then look at the process of photosynthesis and the adaptations of leaves for this process.

Students will also learn about the basic processes of diffusion and osmosis and how these relate to transport in plants. Mineral nutrition is covered along with the principles of decay and how to prevent it.

Finally, the two different methods of intensive and organic farming are compared.

Barriers to learning

Students may need extra guidance with the following terms and concepts:

Ecology in the local environment

Many students think that organisms live in certain positions in a habitat because the conditions are best suited for them. This may be the case for some situations but it is important to remind students about the topic of competition from B2.

Weeds often grow in unfavourable conditions because there is less competition there and they are able to survive. In more favourable areas the weeds may be out-competed.

The construction of a suitable key is always a challenge to students.

Photosynthesis

Students need to appreciate that the process of photosynthesis only produces sugars. All the other substances that a plant needs are made from this sugar and often need additional minerals to supply other elements.

Many students, even at A level think that plants respire at night and then switch to photosynthesis during the day. The continual nature of respiration need to be emphasised.

Leaves and photosynthesis

The topic of leaf structure is not one that is found particularly interesting by students. By moving fairly swiftly through the topic and introducing practical work, they should stay focussed.

Students have always thought of chlorophyll as being a single chemical substance. For higher tier they must appreciate that it is a combination of pigments.

Transport in plants

Many candidates think that plants just take up water for photosynthesis. It must be emphasised that this only makes up a small part of the water moving through a plant.

Many candidates think that transpiration rate increases if light intensity or temperature increases because it is directly linked to photosynthesis.

Plants need minerals

One of the main misconceptions in this topic is for students to describe fertilisers as 'plant food'. This is accentuated by the use of this term on some fertiliser packaging.

Make sure that students appreciate that plants make their own food in the form of sugars by photosynthesis but minerals are required to convert this sugar into other compounds.

It is difficult to demonstrate the effects of mineral deficient soils in the short term in the laboratory. A long term investigation can be set up, but it will take some time for students to see the results.

Decay

Candidates should appreciate that not all bacteria cause disease and all fungi rot.

It is important to emphasise to students that this item concentrates on decay and decomposers. These microorganisms will spoil food and change the taste and appearance. Pathogenic microorganisms however, can also grow on food and cause food poisoning.

Farming

The terms pesticide and insecticide are thought to mean the same thing. It is important to emphasise to students that insecticides are a subclass of pesticides.

Many candidates will have heard of organic food and may have misconceptions about its merits one way or another. Hopefully presenting them the facts will allow them to see both sides of the argument.

Practicals in this unit

In this unit students will do the following practical work

- Using quadrats
- Gas production by pondweed
- Moving molecules
- Change in length of potato cores
- Stalks and dye
- Decomposers
- Testing leaves for starch
- Stomata practical
- Osmosis in living potato cells
- Osmosis in onion cells
- Measuring transpiration
- Measuring bacterial activity

Key vocabulary covered in this unit

agility • cardiovascular efficiency • diastolic • fitness • health • speed • stamina • strength • stroke • systolic cholesterol • haemoglobin • nicotine • plaques • saturated fat • thrombosis

adipose tissue • carbohydrate • deficiency • fatty acids • fibre • glycerol • glycogen • fat • protein • mineral • vitamin • BMI • EAR • first class proteins • kwashiorkor • obese • second class proteins

benign • host • infectious • malignant • parasite • pathogen • vector

antibiotics • antibodies • antigens • antivirals • immunisation • immunity • memory cells • placebos• toxins • vaccine

accommodation • blind spot • ciliary muscle • cornea • iris • optic nerve • pupil • suspensory ligament • retina

axon • CNS • dendrites • effector • neurone • peripheral • receptor • reflex • sheath • spinal cord • synapse • stimulus • transmitter substance • voluntary response

addiction • depressants • hallucinogens • performance enhancers • painkillers • stimulants • rehabilitation • tolerance • withdrawal symptoms

carbon monoxide • carcinogenic • cirrhosis • emphysema • nicotine • particulates

heat stroke • hypothermia • homeostasis • negative feedback • vasodilation • vasoconstriction

diabetes • hormone • insulin • pancreas • type 1 • type 2

auxins • cell elongation • dormancy • geotropic • phototropic • plant hormones

dormancy • rooting powder • selective weedkillers

chromosomes • fertilisation • gametes • genes • inherited disorders • mutations • sex chromosomes

allele • dominant • genotype • heterozygous • homozygous • monohybrid • phenotype • recessive

B4a: Ecology in the local environment

Resources

Student Book pages 54–55
Files on Teacher Pack CD: b4_a_01_worksheet

Learning objectives

- Use the terms ecosystem, habitat, community and population in the correct context.
- Explain data that shows zonation of organisms.
- Explain differences between biodiversity in different ecosystems.

Learning outcomes

- Explain the differences between ecosystem, habitat, community and population.
- Explain how the distribution of organisms within a habitat is affected by various factors.
- Define biodiversity and compare the biodiversity of natural ecosystems and artificial ecosystems.

Prior knowledge

Organisms do not live at random scattered across the planet. They are adapted to live in particular habitats. Organisms interact with each other for various reasons such as predation and mutualism. These factors may influence where they live.

Key vocabulary

biodiversity • community • ecosystem • habitat • kite diagram • transect • zonation

Barriers to learning

Many students think that organisms live in certain positions in a habitat because the conditions are best suited for them. This may be the case for some situations but it is important to remind students about the topic of competition from B2.

Weeds often grow in unfavourable conditions because there is less competition there and they are able to survive. In more favourable areas the weeds may be out-competed.

Curiosity and starter suggestions

- Show students a photograph of a natural deciduous woodland and one of a conifer plantation. Ask students to work in small groups (perhaps using mini-whiteboards) to write down any differences that they can see.

OR

- Show students photographs of the Eden Project. Ask if anybody has visited the project. Describe the different 'zones' that can be found there.

Learning activities

Worksheet b4_a_01

Low demand

Use the first starter activity to lead into a discussion about natural and artificial habitats. Ask students to think of other habitats that may be natural or artificial. Students answer worksheet question 1a *Different types of habitats*. Ask students which habitats they think have the greatest variety of organisms living there. Introduce the term biodiversity.

Standard demand

Use the example of the Eden Project to explain the term habitat and describe some examples. Then explain the difference between the terms ecosystem and habitat. Then introduce the terms population and community. Ask students to compare the populations and communities in a lake or a deciduous woodland with those in a fish farm or in a conifer plantation. Students can then answer worksheet question 2a *Distribution of organisms*. Explain to students that organisms are not spread at random in a habitat. An example of the plants growing different distances from a road or from a tree can be used as an example. To investigate this we must sample at different distances from the road or tree using a transect line.

Answering worksheet question 2b *Distribution of organisms* will give them some experience of interpreting data from kite diagrams.

Teaching and learning notes: *Depending on the nature of the school grounds and the time of year, it might be possible for students to obtain their own data and construct their own kite diagrams. This may be delayed until the next lesson which includes the use of quadrats.*

High demand

Following on the discussion of the kite diagrams, ask students to suggest why some plants might grow near the road or tree and others further away. The term 'zonation' can then be introduced.

Remind students of the Eden Project and then show a photograph of Biosphere 2. The basic difference between the two 'greenhouses' can be discussed in terms of ecosystems and the enclosed nature of Biosphere 2. Both systems do require an input of energy as do all ecosystems.

Finally, ask students to explain the differences between the biodiversity of different ecosystems. Lakes and fish farms or native woodland and conifer plantations can be used.

Worksheet question 3 *Zonation* tests many of these ideas.

Teaching and learning notes: *If time is permitting, it may be possible for students to search the websites of the Eden Project and Biosphere 2 to find out information using directed questions.*

Plenary suggestions

Distribute a list to the students containing the key vocabulary words and a few extra. Students enter subject-specific terms into a 'Bingo' grid. Read out the definitions, and students cross off terms as they identify terms from the definitions. When a student has a line, s/he shouts 'Bingo!', then reads the terms back, giving the definitions as well.

OR

Discuss why biosphere 2 has that name. What is biosphere 1 (the Earth)? If all the components of an ecosystem are recycled why are people worried about the balance of the materials in biosphere 1?

Assessment opportunities

Worksheet b4_a_01 provides staged opportunities to assess students' learning (afl). In addition, thoughtful questioning during class discussions may be used to draw out blocks to learning.

The second plenary discussion is a good way to make more able students think about balance in ecosystems.

Answers

Student Book

Q1a Natural: pond, woodland, grassland • **Q1b** Artificial: fish farm, plantation, motorway verge • **Q2** Examples include: badger, fox, woodpecker, worm, rabbit, deer • **Q3** Habitat – a place where animals and plants live. Ecosystem – a group of living things and their environment • **Q4** Number of individuals in a certain area • **Q5** Grasses and ferns • **Q6** Temperature or light intensity. Both could limit photosynthesis and growth • **Q7** Little light reaching the floor of the forest so little plant growth. Few insects so few birds

Fig 1 out-competed by the grey squirrel • **Fig 2** trees in a plantation are more regularly planted • **Fig 3** ferns • **Fig 4** provided with food and no competition from other fish

Worksheet

Q1a Artificial: a motorway verge, a conifer plantation, a fish farm, a field of wheat; natural: a lake, a deciduous woodland • **Q1b** The variety of different species in a habitat • **Q1c** For plants: enough sunlight, water, minerals, suitable climate, soil type; for animals: climate, availability of food, predators • **Q2a** A deciduous woodland, a lake, a motorway verge, a conifer plantation, a field of wheat, a fish farm (last three in any order) • **Q2bi** A kite diagram • **Q2bii** A straight line across a habitat along which samples can be taken • **Q2biii** Close to the path it is trampled, away from the path it is outcompeted by ferns • **Q2biv** Eat grasses or mosses, eaten by spiders • **Q3a** Different plants live at different distances from the pond • **Q3b** The soil is too wet • **Q3c** Obtaining enough sunlight and carbon dioxide • **Q3d** Water, minerals, gases are recycled, energy is not.

B4a: Ecology in the local environment

Resources

Student Book pages 56–57 • Equipment for practical
Files on Teacher Pack CD: b4_a_02_worksheet; b4_a_02_practical; b4_a_02_technician

Learning objectives

- Make decisions on the best methods of counting and collecting data.
- Develop practical skills to collect data and use it to estimate population size.
- Understand why estimates and real population sizes may differ.

Learning outcomes

- Describe how to use different collecting and counting methods.
- Use keys to identify plants and animals.
- Use data from collecting and counting methods to calculate an estimate of the population size.
- Explain the effect of sample size on the accuracy of an estimate of population size.
- Explain the need to make certain assumptions when using capture-recapture data.

Prior knowledge

Living organisms show differences. This is called variation. These differences can be used to identify organisms and classify them into groups.

When sampling in biology, the more samples that are taken the more chance that the result will be repeatable.

Key vocabulary

kite diagram • pit-fall trap • pooter • quadrat

Curiosity and starter suggestions

- Ask students which plants or animals live in the school grounds. Make a list.

OR

- Ask students if they know what a dandelion plant looks like. Ask them how they would count how many of them there are on the school football pitch.

Learning activities

Worksheet b4_a_02 + Practical b4_a_02

Low demand

Use the first starter activity to encourage the students to suggest ways of sampling the grounds and counting the plants or collecting the animals. Show the students a quadrat, a sweep net, a pooter and a pit-fall trap.

Then show the students photos of several similar animals or plants and ask them how they could identify what organism they are. Introduce the idea of a key. Students could try and write a simple key to identify a pen, pencil, rubber, ruler and protractor.

Students can then attempt practical b4_a_02. They can then try worksheet question 1 *Examining a pond.*

Teaching and learning notes: *Candidates are only expected to be able to use a key not construct one. However, constructing a simple key does aid understanding of use of keys.*

Standard demand

Use the second starter suggestion to introduce the idea of sampling rather than counting the entire population. The football pitch idea can be extended to explain the importance of sampling at random, not avoiding the goalmouths, etc. Ask students to suggest ways of measuring at random with a quadrat.

Then discuss if this would work with animals and what problems this might present.

Introduce the idea of 'capture and recapture'. This can be easily demonstrated by putting a number of pieces of paper in a bag. The students can take a number out, count them and mark them. Then they put them back into the bag and sample again. They can use the formula to estimate the population of the bag and then see how close they are. Worksheet question 2 *Distribution of organisms* contains an example of this technique.

Teaching and learning notes: *Depending on the nature of the school grounds and the time of year and the time available, it might be possible for students to obtain their own data and estimate the population of dandelions on a field.*

High demand

Students could repeat the 'capture and recapture' experiment but take different size samples. They can see which gives the most accurate estimate of the population size.

Then ask the students how the animals should be marked in the wild and what other precautions should be taken.

Worksheet question 3 *Sampling accuracy* tests many of these ideas.

Plenary suggestions

List some animals and ask the students to suggest how they would catch them. For example: pit-fall trap – ants, snails, slugs; nets – moths, butterflies, dragonflies; pooter – ladybirds, spiders.

OR

Discuss reasons why samples are often not taken at random and why random sampling is important. The idea of random numbers can be discussed.

Assessment opportunities

Worksheet b4_a_02 provides staged opportunities to assess students' learning (afl). In addition, thoughtful questioning during class discussions may be used to draw out blocks to learning.

The second plenary discussion is a good way to make more able students think about reasons why random sampling is often not achieved.

Answers

Student Book

Q8 A = spider; B = butterfly; C = ant • **Q9** b the net • **Q10** c pitfall trap • **Q11a** It would make the moths more conspicuous to predators • **Q11b** 600 • **Q12** Reproduction or immigration • **Q13** A population is all the organisms of one species living in a habitat but a community is all the organisms of any species living in a habitat • **Q14** That area might be unrepresentative of the whole area • **Q15** In choosing an area the plants living there might not be a true sample of the whole area

Fig 9 he threw the quadrat over his shoulder • **Fig 10** to catch the moths as they are flying

Worksheet

Q1a A net • **Q1b** A = annelid; B = cnidarians; C = mollusc; D = arthropod • **Q2a** Area of pond = $5 \times 5 \times 3.14 = 78.5 \times 6 = 471$ • **Q2b** $35 \times 30/3 = 350$ • **Q3a** It must be permanent enough to stay there until sampled again but not make it more likely to die • **Q3b** The second method because he sampled in five different areas whereas in the first method only one area was sampled and it might not be representative

B4b: Photosynthesis

Resources

Student Book pages 58–59 • Equipment for practical

Interactive resources Products of photosynthesis • Matching pairs; This Matching pair activity involves matching half sentences to make up correct facts about the products of photosynthesis

Files on Teacher Pack CD: b4_b_01_worksheet; b4_b_01_practical; b4_b_01_technician

Learning objectives

- Understand that the products of photosynthesis can be used by the plant to produce all the substances that it needs.

Learning outcomes

- Recall and use the word and balanced symbol equation for photosynthesis.
- Recall that glucose can be converted to other substances in plants to be used for different functions.
- Explain why insoluble substances are used for storage.
- Explain how experiments using isotopes have shown that photosynthesis is a two stage process.

Prior knowledge

Plants are the base of all food chains because they are producers and can make their own food using the energy from sunlight.

Key vocabulary

cellulose • chlorophyll • isotope • photosynthesis • starch

Barriers to learning

Students need to appreciate that the process of photosynthesis only produces sugars. All the other substances that a plant needs are made from this sugar but often need additional minerals to supply other elements.

Curiosity and starter suggestions

- Show students photographs of a variety of different plant leaves (all green). Ask them what they all have in common and why.

OR

- Ask students to make a list (perhaps using mini-whiteboards) of the different types of molecules that plants need to make to survive and grow.

Learning activities

Worksheet b4_b_01 + Practical b4_b_01

Low demand

Following on from the first starter activity introduce the term chlorophyll and explain its function in leaves.

Ask the students what else plants need to photosynthesise and make food. Write the word equation for photosynthesis.

Then ask students why photosynthesis is so important for animals like us. Identify the production of oxygen as a waste product and the production of food. Now ask students how plants store this food. If it is as sugar, why are rice and other seeds not sweet? Introduce the idea of starch for storage.

They can then try worksheet question 1 *Light and photosynthesis*.

Teaching and learning notes: *Candidates have probably covered respiration in B3 and so the relationship between the two equations can be emphasised.*

Standard demand

Use the first starter suggestion or lead on from the low demand lesson to ask how we can test for starch in a leaf. Ask students if they can remember the food test for starch. Try dropping iodine solution on to a leaf and ask pupils why it is not going black. This can develop into the correct method and lead into the practical.

Point out to the students that starch is not the only chemical that plants need. Run through a list of other substances and the reason plants need them. Make sure that students can write the word equation for photosynthesis.

They can then try worksheet question 2 *Floating leaf discs*.

High demand

Ask students to look at the balanced symbol equation for photosynthesis. Ask them how we can tell where the oxygen comes from. Is it from the carbon dioxide or the water or both?

Explain that isotopes can be used to follow atoms through biological reactions because they behave the same as the normal atom but are often radioactive and so can be traced.

Explain that isotopes have been used to show that the oxygen comes from the water and that photosynthesis is a two stage process. Outline the two stages.

Worksheet question 3 *Using isotopes* provides an example of the use of isotopes.

Teaching and learning notes: *Isotopes are covered in C4a and so hopefully most students should have met this idea by now.*

Plenary suggestions

Provide the class with word cards (oxygen, carbon dioxide, water, glucose, chlorophyll, sunlight, arrow) and ask them to set the cards out to show the equation for photosynthesis.

OR

Ask students to suggest reasons why our understanding of the reactions of photosynthesis has changed over time. This will lead nicely into the next lesson.

Assessment opportunities

Worksheet b4_b_01 provides staged opportunities to assess students' learning (afl). In particular question 3 *Using isotopes* and the use of isotopes should challenge the more able students.

The second plenary discussion is a good way to make more able students think about developments such as the discovery of oxygen and the increasing knowledge and use of isotopes.

Answers

Student Book

Q1 Plants need carbon dioxide, light and water for photosynthesis • **Q2** Oxygen and glucose • **Q3** Turn it into starch • **Q4** Glucose is a small soluble molecule • **Q5** It is insoluble • **Q6** No energy is available for the reaction • **Q7** Three from: cellulose, fats, protein, chlorophyll, DNA • **Q8** So that it does not draw water into the cell • **Q9** Carbon, hydrogen and oxygen

Fig 2 chlorophyll • **Fig 4** glucose and oxygen

Worksheet

Q1a Cress seedlings without light have grown taller but thinner and are yellow not green • **Q1b** Light is needed for photosynthesis and to produce chlorophyll and other substances for growth • **Q1c** They would die as they would not be able to make any sugar • **Q2a** $6CO_2 + 6H_2O \rightarrow C_6H_{12}O_6 + 6O_2$ • **Q2b** It produces oxygen which makes the discs less dense • **Q2c** No chlorophyll so light is trapped and no photosynthesis. Therefore no oxygen is made • **Q3a** Radioactive carbon dioxide is taken in by the plant and the carbon is made into sugars by photosynthesis. The sugars give out radiation which turns the photographic plate dark • **Q3b** As the plant is left for longer the radioactive sugars are transported to other parts of the plants for different uses so other parts appear dark • **Q3c** The oxygen given off by photosynthesis comes from water not carbon dioxide

B4b: Photosynthesis

Resources

Student Book pages 60–61 • equipment for practical
Interactive Book Quick starter: Photosynthesis limiting factors
Files on Teacher Pack CD: b4_b_02_worksheet; b4_b_02_practical; b4_b_02_technician

Learning objectives

- Appreciate that understanding of the process of photosynthesis has developed over time.
- Use data from photosynthesis experiments to determine limiting factors.
- Explain the relative rates of photosynthesis and respiration in plants.

Learning outcomes

- Describe the development of the understanding of the process of photosynthesis.
- Describe how the rate of photosynthesis can be increased.
- Explain the effects of limiting factors on the rate of photosynthesis.
- Explain why plants take in carbon dioxide and give out oxygen during the day and do the reverse at night.

Prior knowledge

All organisms need to respire to release energy from food to supply important biological processes. Plants are no exception to this.

Key vocabulary

limiting factor • respiration

Barriers to learning

Many students, even at an advanced level think that plants respire at night and then switch to photosynthesis during the day. The continual nature of respiration needs to be emphasised.

Curiosity and starter suggestions

- Show students a photograph of a tropical rain forest. Ask them to think about why the plants grow so fast.

OR

- Show students a plotted plant. Ask them to think about how we could measure how fast it is photosynthesising.

Learning activities — Worksheet b4_b_02 + Practical b4_b_02

Low demand

Following on from the first starter activity ask pupils why plants grow so fast in tropical rainforests.

They can then try worksheet question 1 *Photosynthesis and growth.*

Standard demand

Use the second starter suggestion and run through the reactants and products of photosynthesis. Why is it difficult to measure any of these as an indication of photosynthesis? Students may suggest the use of an aquatic plant. It may be useful to show them some pondweed that has been set up to collect oxygen for several days. The oxygen could be tested with a glowing splint.

Tell the students that the plant respires day and night as well as photosynthesising during the day. Ask them why it is possible to collect oxygen from the plant.

Students can then carry out the practical with *Elodea*. They can then try worksheet question 2 *Gas production by* Elodea.

Students then need to appreciate the changes that have occurred in the understanding of photosynthesis. They can read the section on page 60 of the Student Book.

Teaching and learning notes: *The pondweed* Cabomba *is a good alternative to* Elodea *if it can be sourced. It tends to give a more reliable stream of bubbles.*

High demand

Ask students if the pondweed would photosynthesise faster and faster if the light was made brighter and brighter. They should realise that there is a limit due to some other factor. Introduce the term 'limiting factor'. See if there is any indication that their graph is levelling off and ask them to suggest what might be limiting.

Then see if students can suggest the shape of a graph that shows carbon dioxide intake or output by the plant over 24 hours. They can then test their understanding by trying worksheet question 3 *Limiting factors*.

Teaching and learning notes: *Limiting factors and the balance between respiration and photosynthesis is a difficult concept and so all but the most able students will need to be led slowly through these ideas.*

Plenary suggestions

Try the true or false activity given in the technician's notes.

OR

Ask students to draw a time line covering the breakthroughs in the understanding of photosynthesis.

Assessment opportunities

The second plenary task is a good way to test the students understanding of the process of photosynthesis.

Answers

Student Book

Q10 More sunlight and warmer temperatures • **Q11** To prevent them being killed by frosts • **Q12** To increase the temperature and to provide carbon dioxide for photosynthesis • **Q13** It would die • **Q14** Carbon dioxide concentration, light intensity and temperature **Q15** Similar shaped curve but with a higher plateau • **Q16** Photosynthesis stops so carbon dioxide is only being produced and not used

Fig 6 photosynthesis will be slower • **Fig 7** faster photosynthesis • **Fig 8** plant gained 155 pounds and soil lost 5 ounces • **Fig 9** removed shades from the ceiling • **Fig 10** other factors become limiting • **Fig 11** not enough light

Worksheet

Q1a 65 • **Q1b** June. Temperatures are getting warmer, there is maximum light and also water is available so the grass photosynthesises more and grows more • **Q1c** Temperatures are too low so the grass does not grow • **Q2a** Oxygen • **Q2b** To obtain an average to make the result more repeatable • **Q2c** As the lamp is moved closer, the rate of photosynthesis increases but then levels off • **Q2d** Put the pondweed in a water bath. Vary the temperature but keep other factors constant. Make sure that you wait long enough before counting the bubbles at each temperature • **Q3a** 130 units into the plant • **Q3b** The light intensity is not the limiting factor, some other factor is limiting the reaction • **Q3c** About 200 arbitrary units • **Q3d** They are equal

B4c: Leaves and photosynthesis

Resources

Student Book pages 62– 63 • Equipment for practical
Interactive Book Naked Scientist animation: How do plants live and grow?
Files on Teacher Pack CD: b4_c_01_worksheet; b4_c_01_practical; b4_c_01_technician

Learning objectives

- Explain how light is trapped by plants for photosynthesis.

Learning outcomes

- Name and locate the parts of a leaf.
- Explain how the cellular structure of a leaf is adapted for efficient photosynthesis.
- Recall that chlorophyll pigments in chloroplasts absorb light energy for photosynthesis.

Prior knowledge

Plant cells make up tissues and different tissues make up plant organs, e.g. a leaf. Different plant organs work together in a plant system, e.g. a water transport system.

Key vocabulary

chlorophyll • chloroplasts • epidermis • guard cell • palisade mesophyll • spongy mesophyll • stomata • vascular bundle

Barriers to learning

The topic of leaf structure is not one that is found particularly interesting by students. By moving fairly swiftly through the topic and introducing practical work, they should stay focussed.

Curiosity and starter suggestions

- Give students a selection of leaves. Ask them what they all have in common.

OR

- Try putting a whole leaf under the microscope. Ask students why they cannot see anything clearly.

Learning activities — Worksheet b4_c_01 + Practical b4_c_01

Low demand

From the first starter activity the students should identify that all the leaves are green and broad. Explain that the green colour is chlorophyll and this is found in structures called chloroplasts. The broad shape traps maximum sunlight. Ask students which parts of plants have chloroplasts and why.

They can then try worksheet question 1 *Leaf structure*.

Standard demand

Leading on from the second starter activity introduce students to the idea of making an imprint of the leaf surface using nail varnish. Use the practical to introduce the idea of stomata.

Then ask students why the top of a leaf looks more shiny and greener than the bottom surface. To find out why, it is necessary to look at a section through a leaf. This is shown in worksheet question 2 *Leaf structure*.

Teaching and learning notes: *If the students have difficulties peeling off the nail varnish in the practical, it can be removed by sticking clear tape on the leaf and then pulling it off.*

High demand

Explain how the leaf structure is adapted for photosynthesis by having many different types of specialised cells. Ask the students to list each type of cell and explain how it is adapted.

They can then test their understanding by trying worksheet question 3 *Cellular structure of the leaf*.

Teaching and learning notes: *Limiting factors and the balance between respiration and photosynthesis is a difficult concept and so all but the most able students will need to be led slowly through these ideas.*

Plenary suggestions

Discuss why plant leaves are easily damaged by air pollution.

OR

A text outlining the structure of the leaf containing deliberate errors is given out. Students attempt to spot the errors.

Assessment opportunities

The second plenary task enables teachers to identify misconceptions. It also provides for metacognition.

Answers

Student Book

Q1 Leaves, stem and sometimes the flower • **Q2** The chloroplasts • **Q3** Photosynthesis • **Q4** Light energy • **Q5** Spongy mesophyll, palisade mesophyll and guard cells • **Q6** See if it has made starch by testing it with iodine solution • **Q7** Some cells carry water to the leaf, others take sugar away from the leaf • **Q8** Small pores on the bottom of the leaf that are used to exchange gases • **Q9** They will be able to photosynthesise faster and so grow faster • **Q10** This surface is shaded from the sun and so they do not lose too much water

Fig 2 They contain chlorophyll for photosynthesis • **Fig 3** cell wall • **Fig 4** underside

Worksheet

Q1a Cell labelled correctly • **Q1b** Cell A because it contains chloroplasts • **Q2a** From the top: Palisade mesophyll cell, cell in vascular bundle and guard cell • **Q2b** Spongy mesophyll, palisade mesophyll and guard cells • **Q2ci** The cells with most chloroplasts are closer to the top surface of the leaf • **Q2cii** The top surface has a thicker waxy cuticle • **Q3a** The air is trapped in the air spaces of the leaf • **Q3b** The air gets hot and expands • **Q3c** The air comes out of the stomata which are mainly on the bottom surface • **Q3d** Grass leaves tend to grow straight upwards so there are even numbers of stomata on each surface

B4c: Leaves and photosynthesis

Resources

Student Book pages 64–65
Files on Teacher Pack CD: b4_c_02_worksheet; b4_c_02_technician

Learning objectives

- Explain the structure of a leaf in terms of the needs of photosynthesis.
- Explain the effect of different colours of light on photosynthesis.

Learning outcomes

- Explain how leaves are adapted for efficient photosynthesis.
- Interpret data on the absorption of light by photosynthetic pigments.

Prior knowledge

Plant leaves are the site of most photosynthesis in plants. Leaves trap light which is a mixture of different colours.

Key vocabulary

carotene • chlorophyll a • chlorophyll b • pigments • root hairs • xanthophyll

Barriers to learning

Students have always thought of chlorophyll as being a single chemical substance. For higher tier they must appreciate that it is a combination of pigments.

Curiosity and starter suggestions

Ask pupils to make a list of the substances that plants need for photosynthesis. Then ask them to think about how the plant obtains them.

OR

Discuss whether plants that produced different leaf mutations (sudden genetic changes: for example, with leaves like footballs, leaves with only red pigments, leaves with no stomata or leaves with no veins) would survive and reasons why they would not.

Learning activities

Worksheet b4_c_02

Low demand

Use the starter activity to lead into a discussion about how plants obtain the materials for photosynthesis. Remind the students of the ideas of the Greek scientists and van Helmont's ideas. Describe the entry points of materials required for photosynthesis: water through roots, carbon dioxide through leaf pores. Then describe the exit point of materials produced in photosynthesis: oxygen through leaf pores. Students complete worksheet question 1 *Plants and photosynthesis*

Teaching and learning notes: *Try to emphasise the point that although plants need minerals from the soil, they are not directly used in photosynthesis. They are used to make other substances from the glucose that is produced.*

Standard demand

Explain how leaves are adapted for efficient photosynthesis: broad so large surface area, thin so short distance for gases to travel, contain chlorophyll to absorb light, have a network of veins for support and transport, stomata for gas exchange. The function of chlorophyll in light absorption can be investigated using the practical demonstration. Students complete worksheet question 2 *Chlorophyll and light absorption*.

High demand

From the second starter activity focus on the range of colours that leaves can have. Introduce the idea that chlorophyll is not a single chemical but leaves have a range of coloured chemicals or pigments. Students may be familiar with this idea if they have used chromatography to separate pigments in inks or food colourings.

Show the students absorption spectra for some of these pigments and explain that the combination of these pigments allows the plant to absorb light over a wider range of colours.

Students complete worksheet 3 *Photosynthetic pigments.*

Teaching and learning notes: *If time is available it is possible with a more able group of students to try some chromatography of photosynthetic pigments.*

Plenary suggestions

Ask students about plants with variegated leaves. Why might these plants struggle to compete with other plants and if so, why do they still exist?

OR

Discuss question 18 on page 65 of the Student Book. The different colours of seaweeds are interesting adaptations and should challenge the more able students.

Assessment opportunities

Worksheet b4_c_02 provides staged opportunities to assess students' learning (afl). In particular the idea of different absorption spectra is a good test for more able students.

Answers

Student Book

Q11 Carbon dioxide • **Q12** The leaves, through the stomata • **Q13** The roots take in water from the soil • **Q14** Oxygen • **Q15** To absorb maximum sunlight and carbon dioxide • **Q16** Cells in the vascular bundles • **Q17** To stop them losing too much water • **Q18** Different colours of light penetrate different depths of water. For example, red light does not penetrate very deep, so red seaweed which does not absorb red but absorbs the other colours is adapted to living deeper

Fig 5 water, carbon dioxide and light • **Fig 6** the trees reabsorb the chlorophyll pigments • **Fig 7** they store carbohydrates • **Fig 8** all colours but mostly violet / blue and red • **Fig 9** 550–600 nm

Worksheet

Q1a C • **Q1b** The leaves have a broad surface so that they can trap maximum sunlight • **Q1c** The roots absorb water for photosynthesis through root hairs • **Q1d** Oxygen diffuses out through the stomata • **Q2a** Red, blue, indigo and violet will almost disappear • **Q2b** They are absorbed by the chlorophyll • **Q2c** They are attracted to oxygen. This is produced by photosynthesis and mainly occurs where red and blue light hit the chloroplast • **Q3a** 0.75 • **Q3b** chlorophyll a • **Q3c** So that they can trap a wider range of wavelengths of light to use in photosynthesis

B4d: Diffusion and osmosis

Resources

Student Book pages 66–67 • Equipment for practical
Files on Teacher Pack CD: b4_d_01_worksheet; b4_d_01_practical; b4_d_01_technician

Learning objectives

- Use concentration gradients to explain the direction of diffusion.
- Apply the principles of diffusion to movement of different substances in plants and animals.

Learning outcomes

- Recall that substances move in and out of cells by diffusion through the cell membrane.
- Describe how molecules enter and leave cells by diffusion.
- Explain how the rate of diffusion is increased by various factors.
- Explain how leaves are adapted to increase the rate of diffusion of gases.

Prior knowledge

Plant and animal cells are made up from a number of different parts. The cell membrane controls which substances can leave or enter a cell.

Particles are in constant motion and this movement is more rapid as temperatures increase.

Key vocabulary

diffusion • concentration gradient

Barriers to learning

Students often think that all the particles in diffusion are moving in the same direction. They need to appreciate the random but net movement of the particles.

Curiosity and starter suggestions

- Class demonstration – potassium permanganate. Using forceps, drop a crystal of potassium permanganate (oxidising, harmful) into a beaker of water and ask the class to describe what they see.
- OR
- Ask students to think about setting off a stink bomb. Why does the smell take a while to reach everybody?

Learning activities — Worksheet b4_d_01 + Practical b4_d_01

Low demand

From the first starter suggestion ask students to explain why the purple colour spreads throughout the water. Introduce the idea of a concentration gradient. Give the students a definition of diffusion and explain that it can be responsible for the movement of substances across the cell membrane if the molecules are small enough.

Teaching and learning notes: *Remember to emphasise to students that it is the molecules that are diffusing across the cell membrane.*

Standard demand

Class demonstration – moving molecules. Set up the demonstration shown on b4_d_01_practical. Discuss with the class the relative sizes of the iodine and starch molecules and ask them to predict the direction of movement linked to diffusion and concentration of molecules. Ask the class to answer the prediction questions on the sheet. Leave the apparatus for 10 minutes or use apparatus set up before the lesson.

Discuss the results with the class and link them to the movement of molecules in the body and in plants. Students can attempt worksheet question 2 *Diffusion and concentration.*

Teaching and learning notes: *At standard demand the students should realise that although each particle is moving at random, there is an overall net movement that accounts for diffusion.*

High demand

Following on from the second starter suggestion ask students if they can suggest what factors might determine how quickly it is possible to smell a stink bomb or some perfume from across a room. They should be able to suggest that the concentration of the substance is a factor. They may also suggest temperature which could lead into a discussion about kinetic energy.

The diffusion of molecules from the air into the bloodstream in the lungs is another good example to use. This can lead to the importance of a large surface area and the small distance between the air and the blood.

Students can then attempt worksheet question 3 *Size and shape*.

Plenary suggestions

Ask students to write down **three** places in the body where diffusion takes place. Include the substance diffusing and the direction in which it diffuses.

OR

Show the students the section through a leaf from B4c. Ask them how it is adapted to increase the rate of diffusion.

Assessment opportunities

Worksheet b4_d_01 provides staged opportunities to assess students' learning (afl). In addition the second plenary suggestion will test more able students' understanding of the factors affecting the rate of diffusion.

Answers

Student Book

Q1 It diffuses out through the stomata • **Q2** There are more stomata on the bottom surface of the leaf • **Q3** Metal is impermeable • **Q4a** Respiration • **Q4b** Photosynthesis • **Q5** The plant would not be able to exchange gases and would eventually die • **Q6** So that the plant can be supplied with raw materials for photosynthesis • **Q7** The plant may lose too much water • **Q8** Windy, hot, dry conditions

Fig 1 it is being used up in photosynthesis • **Fig 2** so that the substances leaving one do not enter another

Worksheet

Q1a By diffusion • **Q1b** To increase the surface area for attracting the pheromone • **Q1c** They continue to fly to an area with a higher concentration of pheromone • **Q2a** In case some of the liquid was spilt on the outside of the bag • **Q2b** To make sure that the water did not contain any so that they could see if it diffused through the bag • **Q2c** The glucose can diffuse through the bag but starch cannot as the starch molecules are too big • **Q3a** 1000 • **Q3b** 1000 • **Q3c** Diffusion • **Q3d** Block C. This has the largest surface area but they all have the same volume

B4d: Diffusion and osmosis

Resources

Student Book pages 68–69 • Equipment for practical
Interactive Book Drag and drop: Osmosis • Drag and drop: Water in plant and animal cells
Files on Teacher Pack CD: b4_d_02_worksheet; b4_d_02_practical; b4_d_02_technician

Learning objectives

- Predict the direction of water movement in osmosis.
- Explain why plants wilt.
- Use the effect of osmosis on animal cells to appreciate the need to keep the concentration of the blood constant.

Learning outcomes

- Recognise that water moves in and out of plant cells by osmosis through the cell membrane.
- Explain the term partially permeable.
- Explain how plants are supported by the turgor pressure within cells.
- Describe the effects of the uptake and loss of water on animal cells.

Prior knowledge

Plant cells have a cell wall whereas animal cells do not. The cell wall is freely permeable and supports the cell because it is made of cellulose.

Key vocabulary

crenation • lysis • flaccid • osmosis • partially permeable • turgor • wilting

Barriers to learning

In order to understand how osmosis helps to support plants, students need to understand the different properties of the cell wall and cell membrane in terms of their permeability.

Curiosity and starter suggestions

- Show students a potted plant or a photograph of a plant that has wilted. Ask them why this has happened.

OR

- Tell the students that the Romans used to put salt on the crops of their enemies. What effect might this have?

Learning activities

Worksheet b4_d_02 + Practical b4_d_02

Low demand

Use the first starter activity to lead into a discussion about support in plants. This can be backed up by comparing balloons filled with water or air and a deflated balloon. Balance books on them to show support. Alternatively show how boxes made of paper can support weights. Explain that it is important for plant cells and whole plants to be supported so they can get enough light to photosynthesise.

Explain that the support is provided by the plant cell wall and water can enter the plant cell by a process called osmosis. Students can work in groups to demonstrate osmosis using halves of a potato. One half is boiled. Sugar solution is placed in pits in the potato halves. Both halves of the potato are placed in water and examined after a day. This shows that the membranes in cells are destroyed by boiling and that water is passed from cell to cell. They can attempt worksheet question 1 *Osmosis in living potato cells* as a follow up to the experiment.

Standard demand

Following on from the second starter suggestion, ask students why the crops lose water and wilt. Provide students with a definition of osmosis and explain which direction water moves. Explain the importance of a partially permeable membrane in this process and ask students why it is really a special type of diffusion. Using an explanation of water pressure and turgor pressure as an introduction, students can then work in groups to investigate the change in length of potato cores.

Students then complete worksheet question 2 *Demonstration of osmosis*.

Teaching and learning notes: *It is important to emphasise to students that they need to be clear about whether they are talking about water concentration or solute concentration when discussing osmosis.*

High demand

Students can create a graph from the results of the class experiment on living potato cells, to show which concentration is the same inside and outside the cells.

Then students can examine onion cells or *Elodea* cells in water and in different concentrations of sugar or salt. This can be used to introduce the terms flaccid, plasmolysed and turgid.

Ask students what would happen if the experiment was repeated.

Plenary suggestions

Name **four** fish that live in fresh water and **four** that live in salt water. Now name **two** fish that can live in both fresh and salt water. Why is it difficult for fish to move from salt to fresh water?

OR

With more able students you can ask them 'why do plants not need kidneys but animals do?'

Assessment opportunities

The various practical activities provide numerous opportunities for questioning and discussion.

Worksheet b4_d_02 question 3 *Osmosis and plant cells* provides a good checkpoint for more able students' progress.

Answers

Student Book

Q9 The cell membranes are destroyed and leak • **Q10** The chips will take up water by osmosis • **Q11** They will lose water by osmosis if the salt is concentrated enough • **Q12** It will pass out into the salt solution • **Q13** Sucrose molecules are too large • **Q14** If the salt solution is less concentrated than the contents of the potato cells then water will enter the cells • **Q15** The high temperatures will destroy the cell membrane and make it permeable

Fig 3 water it • **Fig 4** they have taken up water by osmosis • **Fig 6** cell membrane

Worksheet

Q1a In the fresh potato the level of the liquid in the pit will rise, this will not happen in the boiled potato • **Q1b** In the fresh potato water will move by osmosis from the water to the concentrated sucrose solution. In the boiled potato this cannot happen as the cell membranes have been destroyed by the heat • **Q2a** Water has entered the visking sac because the contents have a lower water concentration than the surrounding liquid • **Q2b** The sugar molecules will stay on the right-hand side; some water molecules will have moved from the left to the right, so they are about equal • **Q3a** A = cell wall; B = cell membrane; C = cytoplasm • **Q3b** Concentrated sugar solution • **Q3c** The beetroot cells have lost water by osmosis and so have become flaccid. The cell membrane has come away from the cell wall. This is called plasmolysis

B4: Applying your knowledge

Pages 70–71 in the Student Book prepare students for assessment.

When and how to use these pages

This task provides and opportunity for students to apply their science knowledge in a different context.

Ask students to:

- read through the context and tasks, listing any terms that they do not understand
- as a whole class or in small groups, discuss the tasks to ensure all students understand the terminology used and to clarify what is required
- work individually to answer the questions for each task.

If time allows, ask students to mark each other's work using the mark scheme provided.

Notes

The task is based on items a–d and should be used after these items have been completed. The task places them in an unfamiliar situation and asks them to apply their knowledge. This will provide practice for AO2 questions where students often get confused. This is because they believe they have not covered the work in the question because they have never heard of the organism described. The 'maximise your grade' could be covered to start with so they make an attempt with no help. Then hints can be given depending on the level of the student.

Low demand students may struggle with some of the questions and may need to miss out the last question in steps 1–5.

Answers

This mark scheme is also available on the Teacher Pack CD.

Task	Answer	Notes
1	xylem	This is a simple recall question
2	These are the vascular bundles which contain large numbers of xylem vessels	Standard demand should be able to explain one vascular bundle may contain hundreds of tiny xylem vessels
3	Water evaporating from the leaves sucks the water up	This is due to the water molecules being attracted to each other
4	It evaporates from the flowers	
5	The different coloured inks might move up at different rates causing different coloured flowers	High level answer

Notes

B4e: Transport in plants

Resources

Student Book pages 72–73 • Equipment for practical
Files on Teacher Pack CD: b4_e_01_worksheet; b4_e_01_practical; b4_e_01_technician

Learning objectives

- Describe the arrangement of xylem and phloem in a dicotyledonous root, stem and leaf.
- Describe the structure of xylem and phloem.

Learning outcomes

- Describe how water travels through a plant.
- Describe transpiration as the evaporation and diffusion of water from inside leaves.
- Explain the results of experiments with dyes in terms of transport in xylem.

Prior knowledge

Plants are made up of cells which in turn are made up from tissues.

Different plant tissues form organs, e.g. a leaf.

Different plant organs work together in a plant system, e.g. a water transport system.

Key vocabulary

dicotyledon • phloem • root hairs • transpiration • translocation • xylem

Barriers to learning

Many candidates think that plants just take up water for photosynthesis. It must be emphasised that this only makes up a small part of the water moving through a plant.

Curiosity and starter suggestions

- Show students a photograph of a giant redwood from California. Tell them that they are the tallest trees in the world. The tallest is about 90 m tall. Ask them to write down (perhaps using mini-whiteboards) any problems that being so tall might cause for the plant.

OR

- Ask students to think about the different forces generated on a pipe if water is sucked up from the top or pumped up from below.

Learning activities

Worksheet b4_e_01 + Practical b4_e_01

Low demand

Use the first starter activity to lead into a discussion about where the water comes from that is used by a plant. The fine root system of a seedling can be looked at and the job of root hairs discussed. Explain to students that most of the water is evaporated from the leaves. Students complete worksheet question 1 *Movement of water.*

Teaching and learning notes: *It is important to emphasise that over 90% of the water taken up by the leaves is lost in transpiration. Only a very small percentage is used for photosynthesis.*

Standard demand

The students examine dandelion roots, nettle stems and celery leaf stalks that have been standing in red dye for two days. They examine their cut ends and identify the parts stained red – that is the xylem that carries the red dye in water from roots, stems and leaves. Explain that unlike our blood system there are two different sets of cells in the vascular bundles and they transport different substances. Explain the functions of the two main types of cells – xylem to carry water from roots and phloem to carry dissolved food from leaves. Then discuss how a plant such as a redwood can draw water up a long distance. Students then complete worksheet question 2 *Roots, stems and leaves.*

High demand

From the second starter suggestion, discuss the type of demand placed on xylem by water being sucked up long distances. Liken this to sucking liquid up a thin straw and its tendency to collapse inwards. This can lead onto the structure of xylem vessels and the thickening of the cell walls. Compare this with the structure of phloem which has a tendency to burst outwards rather than collapse inwards. Photographs of xylem and phloem can be looked at.

Plenary suggestions

Ask students why cutting the bark in a circle around a tree can kill the tree.

OR

Ask students why accurately measuring the width of a tree trunk during the day, gives a slightly narrower reading than during the night.

Assessment opportunities

Worksheet b4_e_01 provides staged opportunities to assess students' learning (afl).

Question 3 *Xylem and phloem* is a particularly good summary of the differences between xylem and phloem.

Answers

Student Book

Q1 Root hairs • **Q2** For photosynthesis, support, minerals, cooling • **Q3** It would wilt and maybe die • **Q4** Water, minerals and sugars • **Q5** Xylem and phloem • **Q6** Sugars and amino acids • **Q7** Contain carbohydrates, vitamins and minerals • **Q8** Due to their thickened cell walls • **Q9** Phloem forms only a thin ring and no food would get to the growing points • **Q10** The tree needs plenty of support

Fig 1 so that the path of water can be seen • **Fig 2** the soil

Worksheet

Q1a the water enters from the soil into root hairs, passes up the xylem to the leaves. It diffuses out of the vascular bundles in the leaves and then passes out of the stomata • **Q1b** most of the stomata are found on the bottom surface of the leaf • **Q2a** A = leaf; B = shoot; C = root • **Q2b** xylem shaded • **Q2c** xylem • **Q2di** X on phloem of plant stem • **Q2dii** the phloem contains dissolved food / sugars • **Q3a** answers vertically xylem = dead, yes, continuous, upwards, water + minerals, transpiration phloem = living, no, end walls, both ways, sugars, translocation

B4e: Transport in plants

Resources

Student Book pages 74–75 • Equipment for practical
Files on Teacher Pack CD: b4_e_02_worksheet; b4_e_02_practical; b4_e_02_technician

Learning objectives

- Describe the effect of environmental factors on transpiration rate.
- Explain how the structure of a leaf is adapted to reduce excessive water loss.

Learning outcomes

- Interpret the results of transpiration experiments.
- Explain how plants can cope with hot conditions by having certain adaptations to their leaves.

Prior knowledge

All organisms can respond to changes in their environment. This can be the internal or external environment.

Organisms that live in extreme environments have special adaptations to survive these conditions.

Chemicals can move by diffusion from areas of low concentration to areas of high concentration.

Key vocabulary

humidity • stomatal aperture • transpiration rate

Barriers to learning

Many students think that transpiration rate increases if light intensity or temperature increases because it is directly linked to photosynthesis.

Curiosity and starter suggestions

- Tell students that plants losing water by evaporation is a little like wet clothes or wet hair drying. Ask them to write down the conditions that make clothes or hair dry faster.

OR

- Ask students to think about how plants can reduce water loss if conditions are particularly dry.

Learning activities — Worksheet b4_e_02 + Practical b4_e_02

Low demand

Use the first starter activity to lead into a discussion about how we can measure water loss from a potted plant or a leaf. The idea of leaves on a washing line can be discussed.

Ask students which environmental conditions they could alter and how they could do this. Also remind students what happens if a plant loses more water than it takes in. Students complete worksheet question 1 *Transpiration rate.*

Standard demand

Students can use a potometer to investigate the effects of different conditions. Discuss with students the main precautions that need to be taken when setting up the potometer. Also discuss the fact that it measures water uptake not water loss. Remind students that these figures are very similar. After the practical students then complete worksheet question 2a *Roots, stems and leaves.*

Tell students that a medium size tree can lose about 200 to 400 litres of water in a day. Discuss if this is any use to the plant and how the plant can reduce this to some extent. Students then complete worksheet question 2b *Roots, stems and leaves.*

Teaching and learning notes: There are many different types of potometer. Students find this experiment difficult to set up. Sometimes the plants have been wet, there are air bubbles in the xylem cells or the apparatus leaks. A spare set of results might be useful.

High demand

Discuss with students the reasons why environmental conditions will change the rate of transpiration. This involves consideration of the factors effecting diffusion from the last item.

Then an explanation of how stomata can open and close can be given. The curving of guard cells with increasing turgidity can be demonstrated by inflating a long balloon which has tape stuck on one side. The distribution of stomata can be considered using worksheet question 3 *Stomata distribution*.

Plenary suggestions

Ask students a series of questions (e.g. 'What is the name of the pores through which plant leaves lose water?'). Instead of asking for 'hands-up', students indicate their 'certainty of response' by holding up 1 to 5 fingers (1=very uncertain; 5=certain).

OR

Show a cactus plant and ask how it can survive hot dry conditions.

Assessment opportunities

Worksheet b4_e_02 provides staged opportunities to assess students' learning (afl).

The second plenary suggestion is a useful monitoring tool and often reminds pupils they know more than they believe and builds confidence.

Answers

Student Book

Q11 Evaporation • **Q12** Warm, dry and windy • **Q13a** Transpiration • **Q13b** Wind with a fan, warm with a heater, humid with boiling kettles • **Q14** A small quantity of water is used in photosynthesis and not lost • **Q15** There is very little water available in the soil • **Q16** They lose less water • **Q17** Transplanting breaks roots and under these conditions too much water would be lost which cannot be easily replaced • **Q18** It has leaves with buried stomata surrounded by leaf hairs. The leaves are curled so the stomata are surrounded by high humidity and are not exposed to wind • **Q19** It may need the carbon dioxide

Fig 6 to see if light has an effect on transpiration • **Fig 7** to lose less water • **Fig 9** it will exchange more gasses and lose more water

Worksheet

Q1a Water, transpiration, windy, humid • **Q1b** Temperature, light intensity • **Q2ai** Less water loss because there would be less water uptake • **Q2aii** Less water loss as stomata would be blocked • **Q2bi** So much water is lost that the plant may wilt • **Q2bii** It provides water for photosynthesis / cooling / support / minerals • **Q3** Leaf A is a normal leaf. Leaf B is a grass leaf because it has stomata on both surfaces; there are no upper and lower surfaces in a leaf that grows vertically. Leaf C is a water lily leaf because it has stomata on the upper surface; if they were in the lower surface the leaf would become water logged and unable to transpire. Leaf F is a marram grass leaf because it has special adaptations to reduce water loss, i.e. curled leaves, hairs to trap moisture. Leaf E is a heather leaf because it has sunken stomata to reduce water loss. Leaf D is a cactus leaf because it is shaped as a spine and has few stomata to reduce water loss

B4f: Plants need minerals

Resources

Student Book pages 76–77
Interactive Book Quick starter: The nitrogen cycle
Files on Teacher Pack CD: b4_f_01_worksheet

Learning objectives

- Recall that fertilisers contain minerals.
- Describe how elements obtained from soil minerals are used in the production of compounds in plants.

Learning outcomes

- Understand that converting sugars to other substances requires elements other than carbon, hydrogen and oxygen.

Prior knowledge

Photosynthesis in plants produces sugars. These are carbohydrates containing carbon, hydrogen and oxygen. To survive, plants also need proteins, fats, DNA and chlorophyll.

Key vocabulary

fertiliser • magnesium • minerals • nitrates • NPK • phosphates • potassium

Barriers to learning

One of the main misconceptions in this topic is for students to describe fertilisers as 'plant food'. This is accentuated by the use of this term on some fertiliser packaging.

Make sure that students appreciate that plants make their own food in the form of sugars by photosynthesis but minerals are required to convert this sugar into other compounds.

Curiosity and starter suggestions

- Ask pupils why farmers in some countries cut down rainforest to grow crops but need to move to new areas every several years.

OR

- Show pupils photographs (or containers) for different fertilisers. Ask them why there are different fertilisers for different plants.

Learning activities

Worksheet b4_f_01

Low demand

Use the first starter suggestion and the lesson context on page 76 of the Student Book to explain the problems of early farmers and their solution of 'slash and burn': that is, move to new ground when their crops declined. Ask students what chemicals they think plants took from the ground.

Explain that fertilisers contain elements needed by plants and explain the NPK values given to fertilisers.

Ask the students to complete worksheet question 1 to analyse data about using natural and artificial fertilisers.

Standard demand

Explain to students what plants require minerals for: nitrates for proteins which are needed for cell growth, phosphates for respiration and growth, potassium compounds for respiration and photosynthesis, magnesium compounds for photosynthesis.

Students can complete worksheet question 2.

Teaching and learning notes: *It is important here to emphasise the distinction between minerals and plant food as discussed in the Barriers to learning section above.*

High demand

Explain to students that the production of many important compounds by plants requires elements that are obtained from soil minerals: nitrogen to make amino acids and proteins, phosphorus to make DNA and cell membranes, potassium to help enzymes (in photosynthesis and respiration), magnesium to make chlorophyll.

Students should also appreciate that different crops will need a different balance of minerals and this is reflected in the differing content of fertilisers. Students can complete worksheet question 3.

Plenary suggestions

Organic farmers do not use artificial fertilisers. Ask students to suggest why their foods are more expensive to buy.

OR

Ask students what plants like venus fly traps and pitcher plants might get from the insects that they trap.

Assessment opportunities

Worksheet b4_f_01 provides staged opportunities to assess students' learning (afl). It provides a number of opportunities for quantitative work, which is particularly important in this specification.

Answers

Student Book

Q1 grew low yielding plants / did not have fertilisers • **Q2** nitrogen, phosphorus and potassium • **Q3** to convert sugar into other substances • **Q4** magnesium and potassium • **Q5** phosphates and potassium • **Q6** nitrates and phosphates • **Q7** at this time the plants are growing fast • **Q8** nitrates and potassium • **Q9** they speed up chemical reactions • **Q10** magnesium • **Q11** phosphorus

Worksheet

Q1a natural: cow manure / wood ash / bonemeal / pig manure / horse manure / fishmeal; artificial: superphosphate / ammonium sulfate / ammonium phosphate • **Q1b** wood ash • **Q1c** artificial fertilisers are quicker acting • **Q1di** fishmeal • **Q3dii** 3:4:1 • **Q1e** the phosphorus is very concentrated • **Q2a** 0.7 tonnes/hectare • **Q2b** This uses 'the law of diminishing returns' – by doubling the amount of fertiliser from 0 to 50, the crop increases from 2.5 to 7 tonnes/hectare, almost three times the size. If the amount of fertiliser is again doubled from 50 to 100 tonnes/hectare, the crop only increases from 7 to 8.4 tonnes/hectare. It is tempting to state the highest amount of fertiliser, as this would give the largest crop, however by spending more and more money, the farmer's increase in yield becomes less and less; the correct amount of fertiliser depends partly on its cost. Most farmers would choose 50 kg of fertiliser/hectare • **Q2c** they are used to make amino acids and so proteins • **Q3a** as a control / comparison • **Q3b** potatoes need less nitrogen than wheat • **Q3c** field 4; a fertiliser containing nitrogen, phosphorus and potassium would be expensive – the increase in crop yield may not justify the expense • **Q3d** proteins, chlorophyll, DNA

B4f: Plants need minerals

Resources

Student Book pages 78–79
Files on Teacher Pack CD: b4_f_02_worksheet

Learning objectives

- Explain why gardeners need to provide suitable conditions in the soil for active transport.

Learning outcomes

- Relate mineral deficiencies to the resulting poor plant growth.
- Explain how minerals are taken up into root hair cells by active transport.

Prior knowledge

To grow healthily, plants need proteins, fats, DNA and chlorophyll.

Chemicals can only move by diffusion from areas of low concentration to areas of high concentration.

Key vocabulary

active transport • concentration gradient • mineral deficiency • respiration • root hairs

Barriers to learning

It is difficult to demonstrate the effects of mineral-deficient soils in the short term in the laboratory. A long-term investigation can be set up but it will take some time for students to see the results.

Curiosity and starter suggestions

- Ask students to think about the possibility of growing crops on the moon or another planet. What would happen if we only supplied the plants water and carbon dioxide?

OR

- Ask students why a lack of minerals in plants might have an effect on our health.

Learning activities

Worksheet b4_f_02

Low demand

Use the first starter activity to discuss the need for minerals and ask pupils how they would design an experiment to see what effect the lack of individual minerals would have on plant growth.

Students can then attempt worksheet question 1.

Teaching and learning notes: *Teachers may want to try this experiment as a demonstration but it needs careful preparation and glassware and distilled water that is mineral free.*

Standard demand

Explain to students that mineral deficiencies result in poor plant growth: nitrate – poor growth and yellow leaves, phosphate – poor root growth and discoloured leaves, potassium – poor flower and fruit growth and discoloured leaves, magnesium – yellow leaves.

Students can complete worksheet question 2.

High demand

Explain to students that rainwater contains a very dilute solution of minerals. Ask them why the uptake of minerals cannot be based on diffusion. Explain the process of active transport and why it requires energy.

Ask the students to complete worksheet question 3 *Active transport* to show that oxygen and energy are required.

Plenary suggestions

Ask students if the mineral content of some soils can be too high. They might think back to the lesson on osmosis and salt in soils. Other minerals to think about are heavy metals such as copper or lead.

OR

Revisiting the previous plenary suggestion about venus fly traps and pitcher plants, ask students why living in boggy areas makes it so difficult for these plants to absorb minerals.

Assessment opportunities

Worksheet b4_f_02 provides staged opportunities to assess students' learning (afl).

For more able students the ideas of *mycorrhiza* or lichens can be introduced coupled with questioning.

Answers

Student Book

Q12 to provide the plants with minerals • **Q13** nitrogen, phosphorus, potassium • **Q14a** 1.67 kg • **Q14b** 3.33 kg • **Q14c** 5.0 kg • **Q15** the impurities might provide the plants with minerals • **Q16** lack of phosphates • **Q17** lack of phosphate or lack of potassium • **Q18** plants only need minerals in small quantities • **Q19** it develops deficiency symptoms • **Q20** they compete with the mineral for the carrier • **Q21** it requires energy to take up minerals.

Worksheet

Q1a to act as a control / for comparison • **Q1b** to stop algae growing • **Q1c** height / mass • **Q1d** root hairs • **Q2a** poor growth and yellow leaves • **Q2b** poor fruits and flowers and discoloured leaves • **Q2c** poor root growth and discoloured leaves • **Q3a** more sulfate ions are absorbed when oxygen is present (almost doubles) • **Q3b** respiration • **Q3c** more oxygen so more respiration, which provides the energy for active transport of sulfate ions

B4g: Decay

Resources

Student Book pages 80–81 • Equipment for practical
Interactive Book Drag and drop: Saprophytes
Files on Teacher Pack CD: b4_g_01_worksheet; b4_g_01_practical; b4_g_01_technician

Learning objectives

- Recall the key factors in the process of decay.
- Explain why changing temperature and the amounts of oxygen and water affect the rate of decay.
- Explain how saprophytic fungi digest dead material.
- Explain how detritivores increase the rate of decay.

Learning outcomes

- Explain that bacteria and fungi are the main decomposers and need certain conditions to work.
- Understand the importance of surface area on the rate of decay.

Prior knowledge

Many organisms use aerobic respiration and this requires oxygen. The process is controlled by enzymes and they are affected by changes in temperature.

Key vocabulary

compost • decomposers • decomposition • detritivores • detritus • saprophytes • sewage

Barriers to learning

Candidates should appreciate that not all bacteria cause disease and all fungi rot.

Curiosity and starter suggestions

- Show the students a photograph of Otzi the iceman. Ask pupils why he is so well preserved after several thousand years.

OR

- Ask students to work in small groups (perhaps using mini-white boards) to try and list the conditions needed for decay.

Learning activities

Worksheet b4_g_01 + Practical b4_g_01

Low demand

Use the starter activity about Otzi to lead into a discussion about the conditions needed for decay. Ask pupils what would happen if dead material did not decay. Pasteur's famous experiments with curved neck flasks and broth can be described to highlight the role of microorganisms in the decay process.

Students can now look at the practical demonstration featuring decomposition in soil and try to answer the questions. More details of the demonstration are described on page 80 of the Student Book.

Ask the students to complete worksheet question 1.

Standard demand

Ask students what organisms like worms and woodlice feed on. Introduce the term detritus and detritivore. The idea of increasing surface area for the microorganisms to work on should be fairly familiar to students now as a concept.

Students complete worksheet question 2.

Teaching and learning notes: *If time is available students could try and extract some detritivores from soils using a Tullgren funnel. A key could be used to aid identification.*

High demand

Explain to students how an increased temperature will speed up enzyme action in microorganisms and therefore the digestion of waste. Make sure that they realise that decomposers are aerobic and so a lack of oxygen will prevent decomposition. This may explain the preservation of dead bodies in bogs and swamps. Explain to students the meaning of the term saprophyte and explain how they feed.

Students can then attempt worksheet question 3.

Plenary suggestions

Ask students about the Mary Rose. Why is it so hard to preserve it now that it is above water?

OR

For more able students the idea of a suitable pH can also be discussed. Ask the students to devise an ideal composter.

Assessment opportunities

Students can line up in pairs and discuss the topic of decay with each other for 2 minutes, before moving on to another pupil. Pupils then attempt to teach each other what they already know and what they have just learned.

The teacher can listen to conversations and can draw out excellent points and correct misconceptions afterwards.

Answers

Student Book

Q1 when organisms die or excrete • **Q2** bacteria and fungi • **Q3** water, oxygen, food and a suitable temperature • **Q4** they recycle minerals • **Q5** dead organic material • **Q6** they feed on dead materials and produce living tissue • **Q7** low oxygen / low temperature / microorganisms not mixed in • **Q8** to release minerals for their plants • **Q9** the microorganisms are generating heat • **Q10** to provide the microorganisms with oxygen for respiration • **Q11** so the digested food can dissolve

Worksheet

Q1a to provide the microorganisms with water • **Q1b** to allow oxygen into the compost heap • **Q1c** bacteria and fungi • **Q2a** all the organisms / maggots, woodlice and microorganisms / microorganisms only • **Q2b** bag with 10 mm holes • **Q2c** the more detritivores that can enter the bag then the more decomposition. This is because they increase the surface area for microorganisms to work on • **Q3a** it is slower • **Q3b** the temperature is lower therefore enzyme action is slower • **Q3b** they release enzymes onto the food and then take up the partially digested food

B4g: Decay

Resources

Student Book pages 82–83 • Equipment for practical
Interactive Book Matching pairs: Food preservation • Quick starter: Food preservation
Files on Teacher Pack CD: b4_g_02_worksheet; b4_g_02_practical; b4_g_02_technician

Learning objectives

- Recognise the various food preservation techniques that reduce the rate of decay.
- Explain how food preservation methods reduce the rate of decay.

Learning outcomes

- Appreciate that removing one of the factors needed for decay can preserve food.

Prior knowledge

From the previous spread, students need to appreciate the conditions that are needed for decomposers to decay organic material.

Key vocabulary

canning • drying • food preservation

Barriers to learning

It is important to emphasise to students that this item concentrates on decay and decomposers. These microorganisms will spoil food and change the taste and appearance. Pathogenic microorganisms, however, can also grow on food and cause food poisoning.

Curiosity and starter suggestions

- Show students a selection of food types. Ask them to make a list of the possible methods of food preservation.

OR

- Show students a photograph of Captain Scott's hut. The hut is still full of food supplies, including perfectly preserved Fry's cocoa and Coleman's flour, and treats such as tins of boiled cabbage. Why have they not decayed?

Learning activities

Worksheet b4_g_02 + Practical b4_g_02

Low demand

Use the starter activity to lead into a discussion about the different methods that are available to preserve food. It may be useful to discuss some of the advantages and disadvantages of using each method. Milk is a good example to use as it can be dried or heated in a number of different ways (pasteurised, sterilised or UHT).

Students can attempt worksheet question 1.

Teaching and learning notes: *See the Barrier to learning section concerning the distinction between pathogenic and decomposing microbes.*

Standard demand

Using the second starter activity, students should start to realise that if any of the factors discussed in the last item are removed, then decay cannot occur. A change in pH is one factor that was not covered before and this can be investigated in the practical involving yoghurt.

Each of the methods of preservation can be considered in terms of microbial growth and enzyme action.

Students complete worksheet question 2.

Teaching and learning notes: *The addition of salt or sugar to a food is usually the most difficult to explain. This might need some revision of osmosis.*

High demand

There are no higher tier statements covering this topic.

Plenary suggestions

Ask students which of the preservation methods kill microbes and which stop them reproducing.

OR

Ask students why it can be dangerous to defrost meat and then freeze it again without cooking it.

Assessment opportunities

Worksheet b4_g_02 provides staged opportunities to assess students' learning (afl).

It may also be useful to prepare a list of food preservation methods and ask students to identify them given a series of clues.

Answers

Student Book

Q12 they might contain toxic substances • **Q13** adding sugar / canning • **Q14** fish / meat • **Q15** beans, peas, etc • **Q16** the food is not cooked properly • **Q17** 70 000 • **Q18** improved hygiene • **Q19** microorganisms may have entered

Worksheet

Q1 labels in correct positions • **Q2a** adding vinegar – pH is too low / adding salt – microorganisms are dried out / canning – microorganisms are killed by heat • **Q2bi** they have been dehydrated • **Q2bii** they have a high sugar content • **Q2biii** most fungi • **Q2biv** if the water activity is too low water will be drawn out of the microorganisms by osmosis

B4h: Farming

Resources

Student Book pages 84–85
Interactive Book icould career video: Intensive farming: fish farming
Files on Teacher Pack CD: b4_h_01_worksheet

Learning objectives

- Appreciate that although intensive farming maximises yields it can cause environmental problems.

Learning outcomes

- Recall that intensive farming means trying to produce as much food as possible from the land available.
- Describe how intensive farming methods can increase productivity.
- Explain how intensive food production improves the efficiency of energy transfer.
- Explain the disadvantages of using pesticides.

Prior knowledge

Energy passes along food chains in the form of material that is eaten.

This transfer is never 100% efficient as energy is lost in the form of heat and excretory materials.

Key vocabulary

battery farming • fungicides • herbicides • insecticides • hydroponics • persistent • pesticides

Barriers to learning

The terms pesticide and insecticide are usually thought of to mean the same thing. It is important to emphasise to students that insecticides are a subclass of pesticides.

Curiosity and starter suggestions

- Show students a variety of pesticides, herbicides, insecticides and fungicides from home or garden centres. Why do we use them? Why do we use so much of them?

OR

- Show students a photograph of battery hens or pigs in intensive conditions. Ask pupils to compare this with free range animals. How can we tell which conditions the animals prefer?

Learning activities

Worksheet b4_h_01

Low demand

Following on from the first starter activity, ask students to examine the labels or packets of chemical control products from garden centres and list the different types of chemical control.

Explain what is meant by intensive farming and ask students for some examples of its use. Most will have heard of battery hens and glasshouses but fewer will have any knowledge of hydroponics or fish farms.

Students can then attempt worksheet question 1.

Teaching and learning notes: *See the comment above in Barriers to learning when discussing types of pesticides.*

Standard demand

Explain to students some of the disadvantages of using pesticides such as DDT. Include the dangers of killing natural predators, pollinators and the concept of bioaccumulation. The term persistent should be used when talking about pesticides such as DDT. Students can then attempt worksheet question 2a.

The idea of growing crops on the moon without soil can be used to introduce the idea of hydroponics. This can be followed up by worksheet question 2b.

The ethics of intensive farming and in particular with respect to animals can be discussed. It may be that some members of the class have strong views.

Teaching and learning notes: *If time is available, students could research for an Intensive farming presentation. Divide the class into six groups: three collect information in support of intensive farming and three collect information against intensive farming. The students can use the Internet and information from the Student Book. The groups produce a presentation to report to the whole group (possibly through a short video) or a poster.*

High demand

Explain to students the advantages and disadvantages of hydroponics: better control of mineral levels, better control of disease, lack of support for plant, required addition of fertilisers. They can attempt worksheet question 3.

Ask students why farmers may decide to keep their animals indoors and restrict their movement. Does this make them grow faster? This will need some recapping about energy conversions along food chains.

Plenary suggestions

Take a vote on whether intensive farming should be allowed. Ask students if they might have voted differently if they lived in a different country.

OR

Review the posters, presentations or videos produced by the students in the standard demand class activity. If possible, get one group to give a short presentation created in the standard demand class activity.

Assessment opportunities

Worksheet b4_h_01 provides staged opportunities to assess students' learning (afl). In addition, thoughtful questioning during class discussions may be used to draw out blocks to learning.

The bioaccumulation concept is quite difficult for standard demand and answers will give a good indication of students' ability.

Answers

Student Book

Q1 insecticide • **Q2** to provide a high yield of eggs • **Q3** may be cruel to animals / may cause pollution • **Q4** salmon • **Q5** the bees pollinate flowers and so their would be less seeds and fruit • **Q6** cruelty to animals / toxic and persistent pesticides • **Q7** the concentration was too low • **Q8** for respiration to release energy for active transport • **Q9** they need less food to keep warm • **Q10** high energy / protein plants such as soya

Worksheet

Q1a insecticide • **Q1b** eat the crops decreasing yield / spread disease • **Q1c** from food web • **Q1d** they would decrease in numbers due to lack of food • **Q2a** it is passed along the food chain and increases in concentration because it is persistent until it is in high enough concentration in the polar bear to cause damage • **Q2bi** hydroponics • **Q2bii** barren conditions where there is little soil • **Q3a** minerals • **Q3b** for respiration in roots to release energy for active transport • **Q3c** disadvantage is lack of support / advantage is that insecticides can be added and the minerals can be monitored and adjusted if necessary

B4h: Farming

Resources

Student Book pages 86–87
Files on Teacher Pack CD: b4_h_02_worksheet

Learning objectives

- Appreciate that although intensive farming maximises yields it can cause environmental problems.

Learning outcomes

- Describe organic farming techniques.
- Explain the advantages and disadvantages of organic farming.
- Explain the advantages and disadvantages of biological control.

Prior knowledge

Students should have studied the conditions and advantages of intensive farming techniques covered in the previous lesson.

Key vocabulary

biological control • crop rotation • nitrogen-fixing crops • organic farming

Barriers to learning

Many candidates will have heard of organic food and may have misconceptions about its merits one way or another. Hopefully, presenting them the facts will allow them to see both sides of the argument.

Curiosity and starter suggestions

- Show students some food / labels from major supermarkets showing organic food. Ask them what they think this means.

OR

- Find out how many students prefer foods grown by organic methods, non-organic methods, either or don't know what they eat by a show of hands. Keep a running total of teaching groups.

Learning activities

Worksheet b4_h_02

Low demand

Tell students that organic farmers are not allowed to use artificial fertilisers or chemical pesticides. Ask them what problems this might cause. Why do they think that organic food is dearer?

Ask students to use the internet to find out what the prickly pear is and what happened when it reached Australia. Tell them that Cactoblastis is an example of biological control. Rabbits were also controlled in Australia, this time using a virus.

Students can then attempt worksheet question 1.

Teaching and learning notes: *Students might ask why Australia is often subject to invader pests. This can be discussed in terms of a lack of native predators and its unique flora and fauna as it has been isolated for so long.*

Standard demand

Ask students to use the internet to find out what organic farmers can do as an alternative to using artificial fertilisers or chemical pesticides. Get them to make a list. Do any of these practices explain why organic food is more expensive? Students can then use the internet to investigate why organic produce has become more popular. They may also follow the debate about any health benefits. They can produce a poster, presentation or video.

Returning to biological control, the cases when it has gone wrong can be discussed. The most famous is the cane toad which is covered on worksheet question 2. Students may also want to find out about the mongoose in Hawaii.

Teaching and learning notes: *With more able students other types of biological control can be considered. A good example is the release of sterile male insects into the wild such as the screw worm.*

High demand

There are no higher tier statements in this topic.

Plenary suggestions

Ask students how we can tell if food is 'organic' or not.

OR

Students give presentations or view a display of the posters produced in the Standard demand activities.

Assessment opportunities

Worksheet b4_h_02 provides staged opportunities to assess students' learning (afl).

A game of bingo can test students' knowledge of the two farming lessons. Students enter farming terms (from a list distributed by the teacher) into a 'Bingo' grid. The teacher reads out definitions and pupils cross off terms as they identify terms from the definitions. When a pupil has a line, she/he shouts 'Bingo!', and then reads the terms back, giving the definitions as well.

Answers

Student Book

Q11 chemical pesticides and artificial fertilisers • **Q12** they eat slugs and snails • **Q13** they eat greenfly • **Q14** biological control • **Q15** rice • **Q16** they have root nodules that contain nitrogen-fixing bacteria • **Q17** the yields are not as high • **Q18** to add to the soil instead of fertilisers • **Q19** they have no natural predator there • **Q20** personal choice • **Q21** the yields are not as high and costs are higher

Worksheet

Q1 uses natural fertilisers such as compost to increase the minerals in the soil / weeds the land to avoid competition for crops / uses biological control to eat or kill pests • **Q2a** cane beetle larvae eat sugar cane roots, so an insecticide may not have been effective underground • **Q2b** 300–400 years at the present rate but will actually be a lot less due to the ever-increasing toad population • **Q2c** used a secure trial/pilot to see whether the toads ate the cane beetles and to make sure they didn't cause any other problems • **Q2d** introduce sterile toads to reduce offspring, contain advance and destroy them, try to discover a specific poison or disease

B4: Analysis and evaluation

Pages 88–89 in the Student Book prepare students for assessment.

When and how to use these pages

This task provides an opportunity to build and assess the skills that students will use when analysing and evaluating data.

Annotated hints and tips guide students through the tasks.

Ask students to:

- read through the context and tasks, listing any terms that they do not understand
- as a whole class or in small groups, discuss the tasks to ensure all students understand the terminology used and to clarify what is required
- work individually to answer the questions for each task.

If time allows, ask students to mark each other's work using the mark scheme provided.

Pages 278–290 provide further guidance on Practical and Enquiry Skills.

Notes

This task involves analysing and evaluating a set of data. In the investigation cobalt chloride paper is used to indicate the loss of water from the surface of leaves. This is a simple investigation that could be carried out by the students. This will give them more understanding of the investigation and help improve their practical skills.

Answers

This mark scheme is also available on the Teacher Pack CD.

Question	Answer	Notes
Calculate the mean values.	3.7; 1.1; 12.4; 6.8; 11.0; 11.	Make sure averages are all quoted to one decimal place.
Plot the results as bar charts using the same scales for the axes. Use the *y*-axis for the time taken (in minutes) and the *x*-axis for types of leaves.	axis labelled with units time taken (*y*-axis) against leaf type (*x*-axis). even scale	
Explain the link between the time taken for the cobalt chloride paper to turn pink and the rate of water loss.	The faster the leaf loses water then the quicker the cobalt chloride paper will change colour. This is because water will exit the leaves by transpiration and cause the blue paper to turn pink.	You need to use science to explain the link.
Is there a simple pattern for water loss from the upper and lower surface of all leaves?	In the first two leaves water is lost more rapidly from the lower surface than from the top. In the third leaf these two figures are similar.	
Is there a difference in water loss from the three types of leaves?	The geranium leaves lose water far more rapidly that the laurel leaves.	

Do the results match the hypotheses?	This is because laurel has a much thicker waxy cuticle than geranium and so the leaves lose water more slowly. In dicotyledons, most stomata are on the bottom of leaves and so most water is lost from the lower epidermis of the laurel and geranium leaves. The pampas grass leaves grow straight up so there is little difference between the two surfaces.	The key point here is to explain the link between the number of stomata and the rate of water loss.
What possible sources of error or limitations are there in the experimental technique?	It is difficult to judge by eye the change in colour and the moisture content of the paper may be different to start with. A colour chart giving a standard pink colour could be used for comparison.	No investigation is perfect there are always limitations.
Suggest what further experiments could be done on the leaves to link up water loss with stomatal distribution.	The stomatal distribution could be measured by taking impressions of the leaves with nail varnish and observing under the microscope.	

B4: Checklist

Pages 90–91 in the Student Book provide a student-friendly checklist for revision.

When and how to use these pages

This checklist is presented in three columns showing progression, based on the grading criteria.

Remind students that they need to be able to use these ideas in various ways, such as:

- interpreting pictures, diagrams and graphs
- applying ideas to new situations
- explaining ethical implications
- suggesting some benefits and risks to society
- drawing conclusions from evidence they have been given.

These pages can be used for individual or class revision using any combination of the suggestions below.

- Ask students to construct a mind map linking the points on this checklist.
- Work through the checklist as a class and note the points that need further class discussion.
- Ask students to tick the boxes on the checklist worksheet (Teacher Pack CD) if they feel confident that they are well prepared for the topics. Students should refer back to the relevant Student Book pages to revise the points that they feel less confident about.
- Ask students to use the search terms to do further research on the different points in the checklist.

Pages 278–299 provide further assessment guidance.

Module summary

In the introduction to this section, students were presented with a number of new ideas. Work through the list below as part of their revision. Ask students to write their own summaries and mind maps, using this list as a starting point:

- the parts of a plant cell
- the names and location of different cells and tissues in a leaf and stem
- how the cellular structure of a leaf is adapted for efficient photosynthesis
- the effects of the uptake and loss of water on plant and animal cells
- the use of keys to identify plants and animals
- the variety of organisms in a small area
- the biodiversity of natural and artificial ecosystems
- the advantages and disadvantages of biological decay
- why plant leaves have different arrangements to reduce excessive water loss
- how the distribution of organisms is affected by other living organisms
- how to map the distribution of organisms in a habitat
- why plants wilt when they are short of water
- find out about intensive farming methods
- how intensive farming can cause harm to the environment
- discuss the use of fertilisers and pesticides in farming
- how the overall gaseous exchange in plants shows that they take in carbon dioxide and give out oxygen during the day and do the reverse at night.

Notes

B4: Exam-style questions: Foundation

Pages 92–93 in the Student Book are exam-style questions for Foundation students.

When and how to use these pages

These questions are based on module B4 and cover a range of different types of questions that students will encounter in their written exams.

- Questions could be used as a revision test once you've completed the section.
- Work through the questions as a class as part of a revision lesson.
- Ask students to mark each other's work, using the mark scheme provided.
- As a class, make a list of the questions that most students did not get right. Work through these as a class.

Notes on worked example

The worked example takes students through a nine-mark question based on photosynthesis.

There are three parts to the question – starting with linking the presence of chloroplasts to the function of photosynthesis.

Answers are then given that do not match all the marks. Hints are provided to show students how to produce a higher level answer.

The students could be given the answer with the hints covered up and then they could discuss improvements that should be made.

Assessment objectives

These exam-style questions cover the Assessment objectives as described below.

Assessment objectives		Questions
AO1	Recall, select and communicate their knowledge and understanding of science	1a, 2a–b, 3, 4a, 5b
AO2	Apply skills, knowledge and understanding of science in practical and other contexts	1b, 2c, 3
AO3	Analyse and evaluate evidence, make reasoned judgements and draw conclusions based on evidence	4b, 5a

Answers

These answers are also supplied on the Teacher Pack CD so that students can mark their own, or their peer's work.

Question number	Answer	Additional notes	Mark
1a	the distribution of organisms in a habitat results from a transect line		2
b	no food no shelter		2
			[4]
2a	transpiration		1
b	evaporation of water and diffusion through stomata		3

c	normal leaf no jelly stopping evaporation/diffusion	e.g. as heat, through respiration	2
			[5]
3	Content Identifies gas 1 as carbon dioxide, gas 2 as oxygen Day; plant photosynthesises Using carbon dioxide and produces oxygen Fish respire using oxygen and produce carbon dioxide during day and night; Plants also respire but this is masked by photosynthesis Therefore during day, more oxygen and less carbon dioxide in the water Night; no photosynthesis by plant Both fish and plants respire and use up oxygen releasing carbon dioxide Therefore during night less oxygen and more carbon dioxide		6
			[6]
4a	nitrogen, phosphorus, potassium		1
b	phosphorus 3.32; potassium 4.98		2
			[3]
5a	rice crop C Largest crop when fertilisers not used		2
b	any two biological control crop rotation varying seed planting time use nitrogen fixing crops		2
			[4]
			[22]

B4: Exam-style questions: Higher

Pages 94–95 in the Student Book are exam-style questions for Higher students.

When and how to use these pages

These questions are based on module B4 and cover a range of different types of questions that students will encounter in their written exams.

- Questions could be used as a revision test once you've completed the section.
- Work through the questions as a class as part of a revision lesson.
- Ask students to mark each other's work, using the mark scheme provided.
- As a class, make a list of the questions that most students did not get right. Work through these as a class.

Notes on worked example

The worked example takes students through a ten-mark question based on using a potometer.

There are four parts to the question – which cover the principles of the potometer and some analysis of results.

Answers are then given that do not match all the marks. Hints are provided to show students how to produce a higher level answer.

The students could be given the answer with the hints covered up and then they could discuss improvements that should be made.

Assessment objectives

These exam-style questions cover the Assessment objectives as described below.

Assessment objectives		Questions
AO1	Recall, select and communicate their knowledge and understanding of science	1a, 2b–c, 2a–c, 5
AO2	Apply skills, knowledge and understanding of science in practical and other contexts	3,4a-b,
AO3	Analyse and evaluate evidence, make reasoned judgements and draw conclusions based on evidence	3

Answers

These answers are also supplied on the Teacher Pack CD so that students can mark their own, or their peer's work.

Question number	Answer	Additional notes	Mark
1a	gradual change in an abiotic factor such as lack of water/ trampling		2
b	less biodiversity/ smaller range of species forestry is an artificial ecosystem usually only one type of tree so lack of food /shelter for animals and too much shade for other plants		3
			[5]
2a	Diagram A shows the light energy splitting up water Diagram B shows the light energy splitting up carbon dioxide		2

b	experiments used isotopes of oxygen in water molecule using Chlorella/ green algae isotopes in the oxygen given off		4
c	(light energy) $6CO_2 + 6H_2O \Rightarrow C_6H_{12}O_6 + 6O_2$ (chlorophyll) 1 mark for correct formulae/ numbers	e.g. as heat, through respiration	2
			[8]
3	Level 3 (5/6 marks) Good understanding of osmosis and diffusion, may give diagrams to explain processes. Uses some data from the diagram i.e. measures increase / decrease in length. Information clear and relevant. Precise in use of concentrations. Specialist terms used appropriately. Few, if any, errors in grammar, punctuation and spelling		5/6
	Level 2 (3/4 marks) Sound understanding of osmosis and diffusion. May not use/ little use of mathematical data. Information mainly relevant and coherent. Few specialist terms used. Occasional errors in grammar, punctuation and spelling.		3/4
	Level 1 (1/2 marks) Limited understanding of osmosis. Answer brief and showing some confusion. Errors in grammar, punctuation and spelling prevent communication of the science.		1/2
	Level 0 (0 marks) Insufficient or irrelevant science.		0
			[6]
4a	phosphorus used to make DNA and cell membranes so important in growth and reproduction Potassium important for enzymes to work in photosynthesis and respiration		3
b	oxygen needed for mineral uptake because energy required for transport system diffusion not involved energy from respiration		4
			[4]
5	any four points explains photosynthesis and transpiration leaf adapted for efficient photosynthesis by having stomata to exchange gases having film of water around mesophyll cells therefore water will evaporate points out dangers of losing too much water, e.g. wilting, problems of cooling		4
			[4]
			[27]

C3: Introduction

Pages 96–97 in the Student Book provide an introduction to module C3.

When and how to use these pages

These pages summarise what students should already know from KS3 or previous GCSE units and provide an overview of the content that they will learn in this module.

- Use these pages as a revision lesson before you start the first new topic.
- Brainstorm everything that students remember about the different topics using the headings as a starting point. Compare your list with the points in the Student Book.
- Use the questions on the left-hand page as a starting point for class discussions.
- Ask students if they can tell you anything about the topics on the right-hand page.
- Make a note of any unfamiliar / difficult terms and return to these in the relevant lessons.

You can revisit these pages at the following points:

- before the lesson on Reacting masses pages 110–111
- before the lesson on Energy pages 120–121
- before the lesson on Batch or continuous processes pages 124–125.

Overview of module

In this section students will study the factors affecting reaction rates including temperature, concentration, pressure, surface area and catalysts.

Most of the products we use are manufactured. You will discover how chemists calculate the amount of product they can expect to get from their reactants and how to check the efficiency and sustainability of chemical processes.

You will find out why some reactions release energy, while others absorb it and how these energy transfers can be measured. Many bulk products like ammonia are manufactured on a huge scale in continuous processes. Others, like medicines are manufactured on a smaller scale using batch processes. You will explore how medicines are developed, tested, manufactured, and marketed, and about the factors that affect their cost.

Carbon exists in various forms, including diamond, graphite, buckminsterfullerene and nanotubes. You will learn how their structure gives rise to their properties and why that makes them useful.

Barriers to learning

Students may need extra guidance with the following terms and concepts:

Rates of reaction (1)

Students must recognise that the fastest reaction finishes in the shortest time and that a reaction will stop as soon as one reactant has been used up.

Rates of reaction (2)

Students need to recognise that the rates of reactions are determined by the frequency of successful collisions and need to be able to link short reaction times to fast reaction rates.

Rates of reaction (3)

Students must recognise that gases and aqueous reactants can only collide with the particles on the exposed surface of a solid. They should also recognise that catalysts aren't reactants, they just make it easier for reactions to take place.

Reacting masses

Students must recognise what the subscripts in formulas represent and that mass is conserved during chemical reactions.

Percentage yield and atom economy

Students must recognise that a balanced symbol equation can be used to predict the yield of a reaction and that both the atom economy and the percentage yield determine the mass of product obtained, from a given mass of reactants.

Energy

Students must recognise that reactions like cooking, which need a continuous supply of heat, are endothermic. Different fuels release different amounts of energy. If less fuel is needed, to release the same amount of energy, it must release more energy per gram.

Batch or continuous?

Students must recognise that continuous production methods reduce costs and that the cost speciality chemicals like medicines covers much more than the raw materials they are made from.

Allotropes of carbon and nanochemistry

Students must recognise that the diamond and graphite are giant structures and that the space inside fullerenes is hollow, so other molecules can fit inside it.

Practicals in this unit

In this unit students will do the following practical work:

- Measure a reaction rate
- To compare the volume of carbon dioxide released by different volumes of acid
- Measure the effect of temperature on reaction rate
- Measure the effect of concentration on reaction rate
- Measure the effect of surface area on a reaction rate
- Measure the effect of catalysts on a reaction rate
- Carry out precipitation reactions
- Carry out the decomposition of copper carbonate
- Measure the yield of a reaction
- Preparation of magnesium sulphate
- Decide whether reactions are endothermic or exothermic
- Compare the energy released by different fuels
- Separate pigments from plant material using paper chromatography

Key vocabulary covered in this unit

gradient • rate of reaction • reaction time
directly proportional • limiting reactant • product • reactant
collision theory • concentration • pressure • temperature
extrapolation • interpolation
ignited • surface area
catalyst
relative atomic mass • relative formula mass
conservation of mass • yield
actual yield • percentage yield • predicted yield
atom economy • M_r • A_r
endothermic • exothermic
calorimeter • specific heat capacity
batch • bulk chemical • continuous • pharmaceuticals • speciality chemical
boiled • chromatography • crushed • generic • patent • trials
allotrope • covalent bonding • diamond • Buckminster fullerene • giant structure • graphite
fullerene • nanotube

C3a: Rate of reaction (1)

Resources

Student Book pages 98–99 • Equipment for demonstrations and practical
Interactive Book Naked Scientist animation: What controls the rate of a chemical reaction?
Files on Teacher Pack CD: c3_a_01_worksheet; c3_a_01_practical; c3_a_01_technician

Learning objectives

- Recognise that reactions occur at very different rates.
- Understand that the fastest reaction has the shortest reaction time.
- Interpret data in tabular, graphical or written form.

Learning outcomes

- Recognise that some reactions can be fast and others very slow.
- Describe what is meant by the rate of reaction.
- Recognise that reaction times are shorter for faster reactions.
- Interpret data about the rate of reaction or reaction time.
- Calculate the rate of reaction from the slope of a graph (high demand).
- Extrapolate and interpolate graphs (high demand).

Prior knowledge

Students should recognise that reactions can produce a gas, cause a colour or temperature change or convert an insoluble solid into soluble products.

Key vocabulary

gradient • reaction time • rate of reaction

Barriers to learning

Students must recognise that the fastest reaction finishes in the shortest time.

Curiosity and starter suggestions

- Let off a party popper and explain that a fast chemical reaction inside the popper produced enough gas to blow out the paper streamers. Then display some rusted iron or an image of something rusting and emphasise that some reactions are much slower.

OR

- Show a video clip of an explosion and elicit students' ideas about when it's useful for a reaction to be fast. Suitable suggestions are for fireworks and to blow up car air bags after a crash.

Learning activities — Worksheet c3_a_01 + Practical c3_a_01

Low demand

Students could begin by reading the relevant section of the Student Book and answering questions 1 and 2.

Explain that the reaction between magnesium and hydrochloric acid is fairly fast, but not too fast to measure.

Ask each group to drop a strip of magnesium ribbon into a beaker with 50 cm^3 of acid, and time how long it takes to react completely. Compare their results and elicit ideas about why they are not completely reproducible. They should appreciate that it is difficult to determine exactly when the last piece of magnesium has gone.

Calculate the mean value and explain that this will minimise the effects of random variation between the measurements. Then ask students to predict how long the reaction would take it was twice as fast. Check they understand the connection between the speed of the reaction and the reaction time.

Explain that we can learn more about a reaction by seeing how its speed changes during the reaction. Demonstrate the use of a gas syringe to follow the reaction. Groups should then collect their own results using Practical c3_a_01 as a guide. They plot a graph of their results and consolidate their understanding by completing Section 1a–e from Worksheet c3_a_01.

Teaching and learning notes: *Use strong thread to tie the syringe plunger to its barrel to prevent it being pushed out completely. Advise students to twist the plunger of the gas syringe gently if it seems to be sticking.*

Standard demand

After students have completed the experiment outlined in the previous section, use the *Reaction rates* section of the Student Book to explain the shapes of their graphs. Students should then complete Section 2a–c of Worksheet c3_a_01.

Teaching and learning notes: *As an extension, students could be asked to draw a pale pencil line on their graphs to show what will happen if they use the same volume of acid but half the length of magnesium ribbon. They should then carry out the experiment and plot their second set of results on the same axes to check their prediction. The relationship between the amounts of reactants and products is considered in more detail in the following lesson.*

High demand

After students have completed the activities outlined in the previous sections, use the *Calculating the rate of reaction* section of the Student Book to explain how the exact rate can be calculated from the slope of a graph. Students should then complete Section 3a–b of Worksheet c3_a_01.

Plenary suggestions

Describe a series of graphs and ask students to draw them using mini-whiteboards or an interactive whiteboard, for example at first the reaction releases 10 cm^3 of hydrogen per second but it rapidly slows down and after 5 seconds the reaction has stopped.

OR

Show a selection of reaction rate graphs on the interactive whiteboard. Using mini-whiteboards, students describe what the graphs show and (high demand) what units the reaction rate would be measured in.

Assessment opportunities

Worksheet c3_a_01 provides staged opportunities to assess students' learning.

Answers

Student Book

Q1a Hydrogen, nitrogen • **Q2a** An example of a fast reaction, for example an explosion • **Q2b** An example of a slow reaction such as rusting • **Q3a** Graph correctly plotted • **Q3b** Steepest part of the graph labelled fastest reaction • **Q3c** End time of each reaction read from graph, for example, experiment 1, 3.6–4.0 minutes; experiment 2, 4.4–4.8 minutes • **Q4** Place a beaker of hydrochloric acid on an electronic balance that reads to three decimal places. Add a strip of magnesium ribbon and record the mass every 10 seconds. Subtract each reading from the initial mass to find the mass of hydrogen released so far • **Q5** 1.5 cm^3/s

Figure 1 To break up the rock • **Figure 2** The reaction is faster • **Figure 3** It allows reaction rates to be compared numerically

Worksheet

Q1a Acid, magnesium, side-arm flask and gas syringe, correctly labelled, on the diagram • **Q1b** Steepest section of the graph labelled 'reaction is fastest because the graph is steepest'; flat section of the graph labelled 'graph is flat because the reaction has finished' • **Q1c** 47.5 cm^3 • **Q1d** 44–46 s • **Q1e** faster • **Q2a** The reaction rate is changing • **Q2b** The reaction has finished • **Q2c** 0.83 – 0.53 = 0.30 g, 0.53 – 0.39 = 0.14 g, 0.39 – 0.33 = 0.06 g • **Q3a** The reaction is slowing down • **Q3b** At the start, rate = 60 cm^3 of gas in 12 s = 5.00 cm^3 of gas/s; after 30 s, rate = 32 cm^3 of gas in 60 s = 0.53 cm^3 of gas/s

C3a: Rate of reaction (1)

Resources

Student Book pages 100–101 • Equipment for demonstrations and practical
Files on Teacher Pack CD: c3_a_02_worksheet; c3_a_02_practical; c3_a_02_technician

Learning objectives

- Explain that reactions stop when one reactant is used up.
- Recall that the limiting reactant is the one that is not in excess.
- Explain how the amount of product depends on the amount of the limiting reactant (high demand).

Learning outcomes

- Explain why reactions eventually stop.
- Recognise and use the idea that the amount of product formed is directly proportional to the amount of the limiting reactant because it is all used up at the end of the reaction.
- Explain why the amount of product formed is directly proportional to the amount of limiting reactant used (high demand).

Prior knowledge

Students should recognise that reactions produce new substances.

Key vocabulary

directly proportional • limiting reactant • product • reactant

Barriers to learning

Students must recognise that a reaction will stop as soon as one reactant has been used up.

Curiosity and starter suggestions

- Display a large container of coloured balls. Add a few of a different colour. Explain that the balls represent reactants. They react to make a new substance. Ask what decides how much of the new compound forms. If students aren't sure, ask volunteers to 'react' the two colours together and remove them from the container until one colour is used up.

OR

- Demonstrate the formation of a precipitate between potassium iodide and lead nitrate and explain that you want to find out how to make as much of the yellow pigment as possible. Ask volunteers to put 5 cm^3 of potassium iodide in six separate test tubes and add different volumes of lead nitrate to each: 0.5, 1, 1.5, 2, 3 and 4 cm^3. Spin the tubes in a centrifuge for 2 minutes and then compare the heights of the precipitates. Elicit students' ideas about why the largest amounts of lead nitrate did not produce more yellow pigment.

Learning activities — Worksheet c3_a_02 + Practical c3_a_02

Low demand

Use the *Measuring the rate of reaction* section of the Student Book to remind students what the graph of a reaction shows. Then explain that they are going to compare reactions by measuring the total amount of gas produced. Add some acid to marble chips and remind students that the bubbles produced are carbon dioxide.

Groups follow the instructions on Practical c3_a_02 to compare the volume of carbon dioxide released by different volumes of acid and complete Section 1 of Worksheet c3_a_02.

Teaching and learning notes: *Students could add their results to a whole-class table and averages could be taken to reinforce the need to check that the results are reproducible, to remove anomalous results and to find a mean value to minimise the effects of random errors.*

Standard demand

After students have completed the activities outlined in the previous section, use the *Limiting reactants* section of the Student Book to introduce this term. Link the idea to the starter, where the blue balls or potassium iodide represented a limiting reactant. Explain that doubling the amount of limiting reactant doubles the amount of product, as long as the other reactant is still in excess. Students should then complete Section 2a–c of Worksheet c3_a_02.

Teaching and learning notes: *As an extension, students could be asked to predict how much carbon dioxide they would get if they used 40 cm^3 of the same acid.*

High demand

After students have completed the activities outlined in the previous sections, use the *More on the limiting reactant* section of the Student Book to model the effect a limiting reactant has using particle pictures. Students should then complete Section 3a–d of Worksheet c3_a_02.

Plenary suggestions

Show students the bubbles produced when a spatula of sodium hydrogen carbonate is added to acid. Ask students to identify the limiting reactant and give their reason. Then challenge them to suggest how we could obtain stronger evidence to support their claim. Suggestions could include: use indicator to show that the remaining solution is still acidic; add more sodium hydrogen carbonate to show that more carbon dioxide is produced.

OR

Challenge students to write three sentences using the term 'limiting reactant'.

Assessment opportunities

Worksheet c3_a_02 provides staged opportunities to assess students' learning.

Answers

Student Book

Q6a 21.5 cm^3 • **Q6b** The graph becomes flat • **Q6c** One of the reactants has run out • **Q6d** 65 cm^3 • **Q6e** Steepest/highest • **Q7a** 16.5 cm^3 • **Q7b** Because magnesium is the limiting reactant • **Q7c** Magnesium • **Q8** The reactant that is not present in excess • **Q9** The amount of product would be tripled

Figure 4 Bubbles • **Figure 5** It slows down and eventually stops • **Figure 6** 66 cm^3 • **Figure 7** Blue • **Figure 8** Twice as much product is formed

Worksheet

Q1a Hydrochloric, carbon dioxide, marble chips, more, acid • **Q2a** Accurately plotted graph with a straight line of best fit passing through zero • **Q2b** It doubles • **Q2c** ii • **Q3a** The acid, because the reaction stops when it is all used up • **Q3b** Diagram showing 12 black metal particles surrounded by eight white acid particles • **Q3c** Assuming that one acid particle reacts with each metal particle, only four metal particles can react in the first diagram. In the second diagram, twice as many can react, so twice as much hydrogen is produced • **Q3d** This would make magnesium the limiting factor because there would not be enough to react with acid particles

C3b: Rate of reaction (2)

Resources

Student Book pages 102–103 • Equipment for practical and demonstrations.
Files on Teacher Pack CD: c3_b_01_worksheet; c3_b_01_practical; c3_b_01_technician

Learning objectives

- Describe how temperature, concentration and pressure affect reaction rates.
- Use the collision theory to explain the way temperature, concentration and pressure affect reaction rates.

Learning outcomes

- Recognise that a chemical reaction takes place when reactant particles collide.
- Understand that the rate of reaction depends on the frequency of successful collisions.
- Describe the effect of changing the temperature, concentration or pressure on the rates of chemical reactions.
- Explain, in terms of collisions between reacting particles, why changes in temperature, concentration or pressure change the rate of reaction.

Prior knowledge

Students should be able to use the terms independent, dependent and control variable with confidence.

Key vocabulary

collision theory • concentration • pressure • temperature

Barriers to learning

Students need to recognise that the rates of reactions are determined by the frequency of successful collisions.

Curiosity and starter suggestions

- Pour a solution of sodium hydrogen carbonate into acid to demonstrate a fast reaction. Then ask students to consider how a slow reaction between two solutions could be speeded up and why their method would work. Care must be taken in case of bubbling over beaker sides. Eye protection must be worn.

OR

- Elicit students' ideas about when it is useful to be able to speed up chemical reactions.

Learning activities

Worksheet c3_b_01 + Practical c3_b_01

Low demand

Use the *Collision theory* section of the Student Book to introduce the ideas that chemicals only react when their particles collide, and that they react faster when the concentration, temperature and/or pressure is increased. Students consolidate these ideas by completing Section 1a–e of Worksheet c3_b_01.

Introduce the investigation outlined on Practical c3_b_01 by demonstrating the reaction between sodium thiosulfate and hydrochloric acid. Depending on the students' prior experience, they may need support with the planning section of the investigation. Key points to bring out in discussion are:

- They need results for five different temperatures that cover a good range;
- The main hazards are sulfur dioxide, 2M acid and a Bunsen burner. The risk of breathing difficulties can be minimised by using a well-ventilated room, keeping the reactant temperatures below 55°C, rinsing the reactants away as soon as possible and asking students with severe asthma to leave the laboratory.
- Errors in measuring temperatures can be minimised by heating to just above the target temperature, stirring and cooling to the exact temperature required. Errors in timing can be minimised by using identical crosses. Students should appreciate the need to obtain multiple results at each temperature so that anomalous readings

can be discarded and concordant results averaged to minimise the effects of random errors. A whole-class table should be set up in Excel so that averages can be calculated and plotted as soon as the results are collected. Groups are unlikely to have time to test more than one or two different temperatures.

- Control variables include the shape and size of the flask, the cross, the precise concentrations and volumes used, and the amount of stirring.

Teaching and learning notes: *Classes unfamiliar with the concept of concentration can be shown dilute and concentrated solutions alongside small beakers that illustrate the amounts of solid dissolved in the solutions.*

Standard demand

Use the *More on collision theory* section of the Student Book to introduce the idea that the rate of a reaction is controlled by the rate at which reactant particles collide, and that there are more collisions when the concentration, temperature and/or pressure is increased. Students consolidate these ideas by completing Section 2a–c of Worksheet c3_b_01 before moving on to the investigation outlined above.

High demand

Use the *Even more on collision theory* section of the Student Book to introduce the ideas that the rate of a reaction depends on how frequently particles collide with enough energy to make them react, and that the frequency of successful collisions increases when the concentration, temperature or pressure (for gaseous reactants) is increased. Students summarise the two ways raising the kinetic energy of the particles affects the frequency of effective collisions by completing Section 3 of Worksheet c3_b_01.

Plenary suggestions

Display the class results from the investigation and challenge students to explain why temperature has this effect.

OR

Display a poor explanation and challenge students to improve it, for example hotter particles collide more.

Assessment opportunities

The plenary can be used to assess students' understanding.

Answers

Student Book

Q1 Change the concentration, temperature and/or pressure (if the reactants are gases) • **Q2** Cool the reactants, reduce the concentration of any solutions involved or the pressure if the reactants are gases • **Q3** Gases • **Q4a** A diagram of widely spaced gas particles and a diagram of crowded gas particles • **Q4b** Increasing pressure increases the reaction rate by pushing particles closer together and increasing their collision frequency • **Q5** An increase in temperature increases the average kinetic energy of the particles, so they move faster and collide more frequently. The increase in kinetic energy also makes the collisions more energetic, which means that they are more likely to be successful and lead to a reaction • **Q6** Pressure increases don't affect the movement of solid particles so they have no effect on their collision frequency.

Figure 1 To get the maximum effect, fireworks need to explode when high in the air rather than on the ground when they are immediately lit. This is acts as a safety precaution • **Figure 2** 2, 8 • **Figure 3** Increasing the concentration increases the rate of a reaction by increasing the frequency of collisions between particles • **Figure 4** A temperature increase raises the average kinetic energy of the particles so they move faster and collide more frequently. The increase in kinetic energy also makes the collisions more energetic, which means that they are more likely to be successful

Worksheet

Q1a Every magnesium atom being hit by an acid particle should be coloured in • **Q1b** 12 extra acid particles should be added to the image • **Q1c** It increases the rate of a reaction (because there are more particles in the same volume, which causes more collisions to occur) • **Q1d** Three black gas particles and three white gas particles spread around the large box and squashed closer together in the small box • **Q1e** It increases the average kinetic energy of the particles so they move faster and collide more frequently. • **Q2a** Increasing the concentration increases the rate of a reaction because there are more particles in the same volume, which causes more (frequent) collisions to occur • **Q2b** The increase in temperature increased the average kinetic energy of the particles so they moved around faster • **Q2c** Adding extra acid solution does not affect the concentration of acid particles around the magnesium so it doesn't increase the number collisions between acid and magnesium particles • **Q3** An increase in the average kinetic energy of particles allows them to move faster and collide more frequently. It also makes collisions more energetic, which means that a bigger proportion of the collisions produce a reaction

C3b: Rate of reaction (2)

Resources

Student Book pages 104–105 • Equipment for practical and demonstrations • ICT equipment
Files on Teacher Pack CD: c3_b_02_worksheet; c3_b_02_practical; c3_b_0 2_technician

Learning objectives

- Interpret data in table, graphical and written form involving the effect of temperature, concentration and pressure on the rate of reaction.

Learning outcomes

- Read values from a graph and (high demand) extrapolate or interpolate graphs.
- Compare rates of reaction by comparing reaction times or the gradients of graphs and decide when a reaction has finished.
- Draw sketch graphs to show the effect of changing temperature, concentration or pressure on the rate of reaction or the amount of product formed in a reaction.
- Calculate the rate of reaction from the slope of an appropriate graph (high demand).

Prior knowledge

Students should be able to describe the relationship between the independent and dependent variables shown on a line graph.

Key vocabulary

extrapolation • interpolation

Barriers to learning

Students need to be able to link short reaction times to fast reaction rates.

Curiosity and starter suggestions

- Ask groups to drop an Alka-Seltzer tablet into water and elicit their ideas about what happens. Check they recognise that the tablet is reacting to make soluble products rather than simply dissolving.

OR

- Remind students how they reacted magnesium with hydrochloric acid and collected the hydrogen gas produced and elicit ideas about how else they could measure the rate of reaction.

Learning activities

Worksheet c3_b_02 + Practical c3_b_02

Low demand

Use the *Interpreting data* section of the Student Book to emphasise that reaction rates can be determined by measuring how fast products are made or how fast reactants are used up. Students consolidate these ideas by completing questions 1 and 2.

Introduce the investigation outlined on Practical c3_b_02. Depending on the students' previous experience, it may be necessary to demonstrate how to mix 2M acid with distilled water to make the rest of the acid concentrations needed.

Finally, students should complete Section 1a–c of Worksheet c3_b_02 to practice plotting and describing graphs. Students may need to be shown how to draw lines up to the curve and across to the *y*-axis, from two different concentrations, to provide evidence for their description of the graph.

Teaching and learning notes: *Students should be encouraged to collaborate so that they can obtain more than one result for each concentration. It is best to set up a spreadsheet in Excel to plot students' graphs automatically* *as they collect their results. Ideally, a graph of reaction time against concentration should be displayed alongside a graph of reaction rate against concentration for comparison.*

Standard demand

Use the *Rate of reaction and concentration* section of the Student Book to reinforce the idea that increasing the concentration reduces the reaction time but does not affect the total amount of product formed. Students consolidate this idea by completing questions 3–5. Section 2a–b of Worksheet c3_b_02 can then be used to practice looking for quantitative relationships between variables.

High demand

Use the *Extrapolation and interpolation* section of the Student Book to practice interpolating and extrapolating curves. Students can practice extrapolation by completing Section 3a–c of Worksheet c3_b_02.

Plenary suggestions

Give students a series of relationships, for example the effect of temperature on the reaction rate, and the volume of product against time, at high and low temperatures, and ask them to draw the expected graphs on mini-whiteboards.

OR

Display a poor description of the relationship between the variables shown in their class results and challenge students to improve it, for example 'the graph is a curve'.

Assessment opportunities

The plenary can be used to assess students' understanding.

Answers

Student Book

Q7a 24.5 cm^3 • **Q7b** 40 cm^3 • **Q8a** 0–10 s • **Q8b** 30–50 s • **Q2c** Because gas is escaping and reducing the mass • **Q9** Reducing the concentration cuts the rate of a reaction because there are fewer reactant particles in the same volume, which makes collisions less frequent • **Q10** An increase in temperature increases the average kinetic energy of the particles so they move faster and collide more frequently • **Q11a** Sketch graph showing a straight line or curve that crosses the *y*-axis above zero • **Q11b** Sketch graph showing a horizontal straight line that crosses the *y*-axis above zero • **Q12a** 55 g • **Q12b** 5–20 g • **Q12c** The longer the time, the lower the mass • **Q1d** Draw a tangent to the curve at 2 minutes and calculate the gradient of the line

Figure 5 Quickly, drops • **Figure 6** The graph becomes horizontal/gas volume stops changing • **Figure 7** It has a steeper gradient • **Figure 8** 38 s at 30°C and 58 s at 58°C

Worksheet

Q1a–1c A graph as shown below left with a smooth curve of best fit. The graph should be annotated to show the reaction rate at two different acid concentrations, and these should be used as evidence for the pattern described, that is the higher the acid concentration, the higher the rate of reaction • **Q2a** When the acid concentration doubles, the rate of a reaction between magnesium and hydrochloric acid is multiplied by four • **Q2b** When the acid concentration triples, the rate of a reaction between magnesium and hydrochloric acid is multiplied by nine • **Q3a** A graph as shown below right that has been extrapolated to estimate the rate with 3M acid • **Q3b** 0.108 cm of Mg/second • **Q3c** the reaction will be faster than the estimated rate

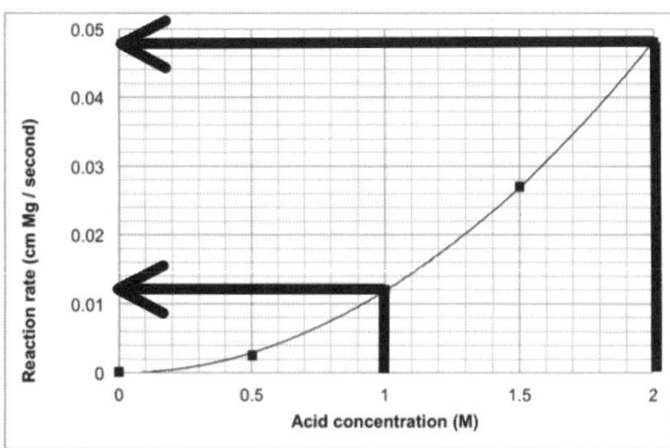

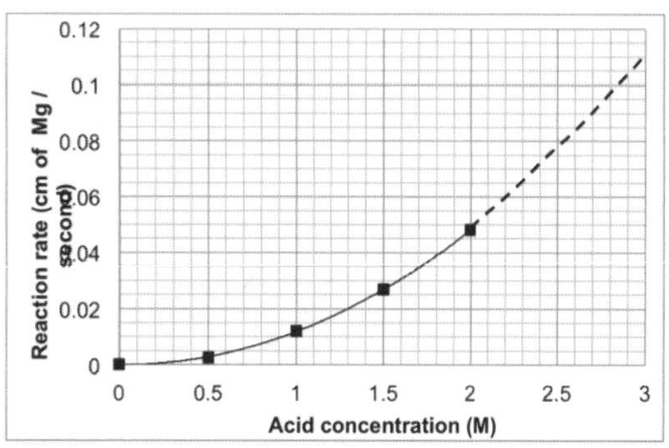

C3c: Rate of reaction (3)

Resources

Student Book pages 106–107 • Equipment for demonstrations and practical
Files on Teacher Pack CD: c3_c_01_worksheet; c3_c_01_practical; c3_c_01_technician

Learning objectives

- Describe how surface area affects reaction rates and why powders can explode.
- Use the collision theory to explain how surface area affects reaction rates.

Learning outcomes

- Recall that the rate of a reaction can be increased by using powdered reactant rather than a lump.
- Describe an explosion as a very fast reaction which releases a large volume of gaseous products.
- Explain, in terms of collisions between reacting particles, the difference in rate of reaction between a lump and powdered reactant.
- Explain the dangers of combustible powders in factories.

Prior knowledge

Students should recognise that particles only react when they collide.

Key vocabulary

gradient • reaction time • rate of reaction

Barriers to learning

Students must recognise that gases and aqueous reactants can only collide with the particles on the exposed surface of a solid.

Curiosity and starter suggestions

- Sprinkle iron filings over a blue Bunsen flame and elicit students' ideas about why things burn better when they are cut into small pieces.

OR

- Carry out the corn flour explosion demonstration or show a video of an explosion.

Learning activities

Worksheet c3_c_01 + Practical c3_c_01

Low demand

Use the *Explosions* section of the Student Book to introduce the lesson. Groups could then compare the reactions of large and small marble chips with hydrochloric acid, using Practical c3_c_01 as a guide. Section 1 of Worksheet c3_c_01 sums up the main points.

Teaching and learning notes: *If datalogging software and a compatible balance are available, the investigation could be done as a whole-class demonstration.*

Standard demand

After students have completed the experiment outlined in the previous section, use centimetre cubes to model the surface areas of large and small chips. Section 2 of Worksheet c3_c_01 structures this activity and the *More on explosions* section of the Student Book consolidates the ideas.

Teaching and learning notes: *Each block should be painted on three sides to make it easy to show that eight separate cubes have twice as much surface area as a 2 × 2 × 2 block.*

High demand

After students have completed the previous sections, use the final section in the Student Book to remind students that reactions are faster when the collision frequency is higher. Students could then complete Section 3 of Worksheet c3_c_01 to check their understanding.

Plenary suggestions

Display the results from the student investigation and challenge students to give a complete conclusion. They should include: what is the same about the graphs, what is different about them, evidence from the graphs to support their assertion and scientific reasons why they would expect these results.

OR

Challenge students to write a scientifically accurate sentence using the phrase: greater surface area.

Assessment opportunities

The plenary is an opportunity to assess students' learning.

Answers

Student Book

Q1 A fast chemical reaction that makes and releases large amounts of gases • **Q2** The reaction is faster • **Q3** It has a large surface area and can catch fire when in contact with oxygen • **Q4** The thin chips have a greater surface area • **Q5** The large surface area of sulfur powder means it can catch fire easily • **Q6** It is difficult to measure the surface area of a marble chip • **Q7** The same amount of reactant is used

Figure 2 Greater effervescence • **Figure 3** It has a greater surface area. The dots represent the reactant particles

Worksheet

Q1 Reactions, gases, outwards, speed, slowly, powders, explosion • **Q2a** 24 cm^3 • **Q2b** 48 cm^3 • **Q2c** Twice as fast because the surface area is twice as big or twice as many collisions can take place • **Q3a** The higher the concentration, the more acid particles in the same volume and the more frequently they collide with the marble chips • **Q3b** The total surface area of the small chips is bigger, so acid particles collide with it more frequently • **Q3c** As soon as any calcium sulfate is formed on the surface of the marble chips, it prevents acid particles from colliding with the marble underneath

C3c: Rate of reaction (3)

Resources

Student Book pages 108–109 • Equipment for demonstrations and practical
Files on Teacher Pack CD: c3_c_02_worksheet; c3_c_02_practical; c3_c_02_technician

Learning objectives

- Describe how catalysts affect reaction rates and why only small amounts are needed.
- Interpret data about the effects of catalysts.

Learning outcomes

- Recall that the rate of a reaction can be increased by the addition of a catalyst, which is a substance that changes the rate of reaction and is unchanged at the end of the reaction.
- Understand why only a small amount of a catalyst is needed to catalyse large amounts of reactants and that a catalyst is specific to a particular reaction.
- Read values from graphs and (high demand) interpret the data about the effects of catalysts.
- Compare rates of reaction by comparing gradients of graphs and calculate the rate of reaction from the slope of an appropriate graph (high demand).
- Decide when a reaction has finished.
- Draw sketch graphs to show the effects of a catalyst on the rate of reaction and the amount of product formed.

Prior knowledge

Students should know that reactions can be speeded up by increasing the temperature of the reactants, their concentration, surface area (for solids) or pressure (for gases).

Key vocabulary

catalyst

Barriers to learning

Students need to recognise that catalysts aren't reactants; they just make it easier for reactions to take place.

Curiosity and starter suggestions

- Add a spatula of manganese dioxide to a flask of hydrogen peroxide solution so that students can witness the bubbles of gas escaping as it decomposes. Demonstrate that this is oxygen by holding a glowing splint inside the flask. It should relight time after time.

OR

- Demonstrate how a car body filler kit uses a small amount of catalyst to speed up the reaction that hardens the filler.

Learning activities

Worksheet c3_c_02 + Practical c3_c_02

Low demand

Demonstrate the decomposition of hydrogen peroxide if this has not been used as a starter. Explain that the effectiveness of catalysts can be compared by measuring the volume of oxygen released in a specific time. Groups should then compare three catalysts using Practical c3_c_02 as a guide. They can then plot a bar chart, identify the best catalyst and complete Section 1a–b of Worksheet c3_c_02. They could consolidate their understanding by completing the *Catalysts* section of the student book.

Teaching and learning notes: *Use strong thread to tie the syringe plunger to its barrel to prevent it being pushed out completely. Advise students to twist the plunger of the gas syringe gently if it seems to be sticking. A small amount of Vaseline will help prevent it sticking.*

Standard demand

After students have completed the experiment outlined in the previous section, use the *Catalysts and rate of reaction* section of the student book to consider the sorts of graphs they would get if the reaction was monitored continuously, with and without a catalyst.

Teaching and learning notes: *As an extension, students could be asked to sketch the shapes of the graphs they would expect if the volume of oxygen collected was plotted against time for each of the catalysts they tested.*

High demand

After students have completed the previous sections, use Section 3 in Worksheet c3_c_02 to consolidate their ideas about catalysts.

Plenary suggestions

Complete Section 2a–c of Worksheet c3_c_02 to test students' understanding in the context of catalytic converters.

OR

Challenge students to explain why using a catalyst to speed up a reaction is usually cheaper in the long term than using high temperatures.

Assessment opportunities

The plenary is an opportunity to assess students' learning.

Answers

Student Book

Q8a Hydrogen • **Q8b** Magnesium chloride • **Q8c** A catalyst • **Q9a** The copper chloride changes colour during the reaction and catalysts are not chemically changed during reactions • **Q9b** To ensure all the zinc reacts • **Q9c** To show that a smaller surface area decreases reaction rate, but does not change the amount of product made • **Q10** The reaction rate will be slower because a lump of zinc is used instead of powder. There is no change to the volume of hydrogen gas made as the acid is in excess • **Q11** $Zn + H_2SO_4 \rightarrow ZnSO_4 + H_2$

Figure 4 The gradient of the graph would be less steep; the same maximum would be reached

Worksheet

Q1a Reactions, product, used, reactions • **Q1b** Manganese dioxide, the same volume of gas is produced more quickly • **Q2a** The catalyst is made of platinum which is expensive • **Q2b** Catalyst are not used up during reactions • **Q2c** To provide a greater surface area

C3d: Reacting masses

Resources

Student Book pages 110–111 • Equipment for demonstrations and practical
Files on Teacher Pack CD: c3_d_01_worksheet; c3_d_01_technician

Learning objectives

- Calculate relative formula masses.

Learning outcomes

- Calculate the relative formula mass of a substance from its formula (with and without brackets) given the appropriate relative atomic masses.

Prior knowledge

Students should recognise that reactions can produce a gas, cause a colour or temperature change, or convert an insoluble solid into soluble products.

Key vocabulary

relative atomic mass • relative formula mass

Barriers to learning

Students must recognise what the subscripts in formulas represent.

Curiosity and starter suggestions

- Use a mini-quiz to introduce the relative atom masses shown in the periodic table. Suitable questions include, what is the lightest element, name two elements with the same relative atomic mass, which element has 12 times the mass of hydrogen, etc.

OR

- Elicit students' ideas about why each element in the periodic table has two numbers.

Learning activities

Worksheet c3_d_01

Low demand

Make sure students can distinguish between the relative atomic mass and the mass number. Then use the *Relative atomic mass* section of the Student Book to explain how to calculate relative formula masses. Students can then use the element cards from page 2 of Worksheet c3_d_01 to practice this. Section 1 of the worksheet structures the activity.

Teaching and learning notes: *It is useful for every student to have their own calculator for this activity.*

Standard demand

Use the *More on relative atomic mass* section of the Student Book to explain how to calculate the relative formula masses for formulas that contain brackets. Students can then use the element cards from page 2 of Worksheet c3_d_01 to practice this. Section 2 of the worksheet structures the activity.

Teaching and learning notes: *If students ask why brackets are used it is useful to explain that some groups of atoms, like the hydroxide group (OH), usually stay together when compounds react. So if a compound contains more than one of these groups the number outside the bracket shows how many groups of atoms there are.*

High demand

After students have completed the activities outlined in the previous sections, use the *History of relative atomic mass* section of the Student Book to explain why the numbers do not have units. Section 3 of Worksheet c3_d_01 provides an extra challenge.

Plenary suggestions

Challenge students to write the formulas of compounds with these formula masses: 18, 40, 44 and 100.

OR

Speed challenge: put these gases in order of mass – CH_4, CO, CO_2, Cl_2, N_2, O_2, SO_2.

Assessment opportunities

The plenary is an opportunity to assess students' learning.

Answers

Student Book

Q1 207 • **Q2** 238 • **Q3** 44 • **Q4** 44 • **Q5a** 35 • **Q5b** 58 • **Q5c** 148 • **Q5d** 342 • **Q6** argon and potassium would swap places which would prevent elements with similar properties from being in the same group

Figure 1 12 • **Figure 3** 7

Worksheet

Q1a 17 • **Q1b** 16 • **Q1c** 64 • **Q1d** 111 • **Q1e** 53.5 • **Q1f** 80 • **Q1g** 36.5 • **Q1h** 98 • **Q1i** 63 • **Q2a** 96 • **Q2b** 164 • **Q2c** 74 • **Q3a** KOH • **Q3b** Li_2O • **Q3c** NO_2 • **Q3d** $Be(OH)_2$

C3d: Reacting masses

Resources

Student Book pages 112–113 • Equipment for demonstrations and practical
Interactive Book Quick starter: % Composition by mass • Quick starter: Formula mass calculation error
Files on Teacher Pack CD: c3_d_0 2_worksheet; c3_d_02_practical; c3_d_0 2_technician

Learning objectives

- Use equations to determine the masses of reactants and products.

Learning outcomes

- Understand that the total mass of reactants at the start of a reaction is equal to the total mass of products made and that this is called the principle of conservation of mass.
- Use the principle of conservation of mass to calculate the mass of reactant or product, including the mass of gaseous product formed during decomposition, and the mass of oxygen that reacts with a known mass of magnesium to make magnesium oxide.
- Use simple ratios to calculate reacting masses and product masses given the mass of a reactant and a product.
- Use relative formula masses and a provided symbol equation (1:1 molar ratio) to show that mass is conserved during a reaction, and (high demand) when not in a 1:1 molar ratio.
- Recognise and use the idea that the mass of product formed is directly proportional to the mass of limiting reactant used.
- Interpret chemical equations quantitatively, and calculate masses of products or reactants from balanced symbol equations using relative formula masses (high demand).

Prior knowledge

Students should recognise that atoms are rearranged during chemical reactions to form new products, but the total number of atoms does not change.

Key vocabulary

conservation of mass • yield

Barriers to learning

Students must recognise that mass is conserved during chemical reactions.

Curiosity and starter suggestions

- Elicit students' ideas about where atoms go when a compound reacts.

OR

- Scientists estimate that cement making adds more than100 million tonnes per year of carbon dioxide to the atmosphere. Ask students to suggest how scientists came up with this value.

Learning activities

Worksheet c3_d_02 + Practical c3_d_02

Low demand

Use the precipitation reaction between copper sulfate and sodium hydroxide to demonstrate that mass is conserved in chemical reactions. Stress that apparent increases in mass can be caused by elements reacting with a gas from the air and apparent decreases can be caused by gases escaping during the reaction. Then use the *Conservation of mass* section of the Student Book to explain how we can use this idea to calculate how much product a reaction will make. Students can use Section 1 of Worksheet c3_d_02 to practice this.

Teaching and learning notes: *For the demonstration, before the lesson set the apparatus up as shown on the technician's sheet. Record the mass of the apparatus, tip it to mix the solutions and then check the mass again.*

Standard demand

Groups decompose known masses of copper carbonate, using Practical c3_d_02 as a guide, and measure the mass of copper oxide produced. Section 2 of Worksheet c3_d_02 provides results for different masses of copper carbonate and prompts them to draw a graph to display the relationship between the mass of product and the mass of reactant. Check that students recognise that the mass of product is directly proportional to the mass of reactant, and that they appreciate that the mass of product doubles when the mass of reactant is doubled.

The *Calculating reacting masses* section of the Student Book consolidates students' understanding.

Teaching and learning notes: *Students may need to be reminded how to use the balance. They should avoid using the tare button. Warn students to let their evaporating basins cool on a heatproof mat before reweighing them. Worksheet c3_d_02 has model answers in case they don't have time to heat until the mass is constant.*

High demand

After students have completed the activities outlined in the previous sections, use Section 3 of Worksheet c3_d_02 to introduce the idea of using relative formula masses to predict the yield of a reaction. The *Predicting the yield of a reaction* section of the Student Book provides extra practice.

Plenary suggestions

Display the equation for the reaction between magnesium and oxygen and challenge students to calculate the mass of magnesium oxide formed, given the masses of one or both of the reactants.

OR

Ask students to explain how chemists are able to predict how much product they will make.

Assessment opportunities

Worksheet c3_d_02 provides staged opportunities to assess students' learning.

Answers

Student Book

Q7 4.4 g • **Q8a** 8.0 g • **Q8b** 1.6 g • **Q9a** Double the amount of CO_2 and CuO would be made • **Q9b** Half the amount of CO_2 and CuO would be made • **Q10** 4 g • **Q11** 1.6 g • **Q12a** 12 g • **Q12b** The acid is in excess • **Q13** 73 g • **Q14a** 72 g • **Q14b** 36 g • **Q14c** 66 g

Figure 4 The total masses on each side are equal

Worksheet

Q1a 36 • **Q1b** 46 • **Q1c** 20 • **Q1d** 44 • **Q1e** 36 • **Q2a** The average mass of copper oxide formed is directly proportional to the mass of copper carbonate heated; 0.65 g of copper oxide is formed for every gram of copper carbonate heated • **Q2b** They may have stopped heating the copper carbonate before its mass became constant • **Q2c** Students should describe how close their results are to the line of best fit • **Q3a** 40, 36.5, 58.5, 18 • **Q3b** 18.25, 29.25, 9 • **Q3c** 100, 56, 44 • **Q3d** 28, 22 • **Q3e** 200 tonnes • **Q3f** 88 tonnes

C3: Applying your knowledge

Pages 114–115 in the Student Book prepare students for assessment.

When and how to use these pages

This task provides an opportunity to build and assess the skills that students will use when planning an investigation.

Annotated hints and tips guide students through the tasks. Ask students to:

- read through the context and tasks, listing any terms that they do not understand
- as a whole class or in small groups, discuss the tasks to ensure all students understand the terminology used and to clarify what is required
- work individually to answer the questions for each task.

If time allows, ask students to mark each other's work using the mark scheme provided.

Notes

The task prompts students to research the differences between batch and continuous processes.

Answers

This mark scheme is also available on the Teacher Pack CD.

Task	Answer	Notes
1	Any reference to ammonia synthesis having benefits and drawbacks Any reference to different people being affected in different ways	Giving one or two explanations is indicative of a student operating at grade F standard
2	Ammonia can be converted to the nitrates plants need in fertilizers Ammonia can be used to make explosives for warfare	
3	Continuous processes are expensive to set up It is not easy to change what / how much the equipment makes The processes can be automated to reduce labour costs Chemicals like ammonia continuous processes because they are needed continuously and in large quantities	Standard demand should be able to explain the reasons why chemicals are made by continuous or batch processes
4	Iron is a catalyst It speeds up the reaction between nitrogen and hydrogen but remains unchanged at the end of the reaction	
5	Nitrogen is inert / contains a triple covalent bond It takes a lot of energy to break the covalent bonds in nitrogen molecules The reaction is reversible Nitrogen + hydrogen $\rightleftharpoons$ ammonia The reaction reaches equilibrium This means that the forward and backward reactions proceed at the same rate The forward reaction is exothermic, so high temperatures reduce the yield / shift the equilibrium to the left The forward reaction cuts the gas volume, so high pressures increase the yield / shift the equilibrium to the right 450°C and 200 atmospheres are the optimum temperature and pressure and give the most economic yield and reaction rate	A student who shows complete understanding is heading towards grade A*

Notes

C3e: Percentage yield and atom economy

Resources

Student Book pages 116–117 • Equipment for demonstrations and practical
Interactive Book Quick starter: Getting a good yield • Practical investigations: Neutralisation
Files on Teacher Pack CD: c3_e_01_worksheet; c3_e_01_practical; c3_e_01_technician

Learning objectives

- Use percentage yields to determine how much product has formed.
- Recognise factors which lower yields.

Learning outcomes

- Understand percentage yield as a way of comparing the amount of product made (actual yield) to the amount expected (predicted yield). 100% yield means that no product has been lost; 0% yield means that no product has been made.
- Recognise possible reasons as to why the percentage yield of a product is less than 100%, such as loss in filtration, loss in evaporation, loss in transferring liquids, not all reactants react to make product.
- Recall and use the formula: percentage yield = (actual yield ÷ predicted yield) × 100.
- Explain why an industrial process wants as high a percentage yield as possible, including reducing the reactants wasted and reducing cost (high demand).

Prior knowledge

Students should recognise the reaction between acids and carbonates.

Key vocabulary

actual yield • percentage yield • predicted yield

Barriers to learning

Students must recognise that a balanced symbol equation can be used to predict the yield of a reaction.

Curiosity and starter suggestions

- Pour lead(II) nitrate solution into sodium iodide solution to demonstrate the formation of a precipitate of lead iodide and then filter the mixture. Introduce the term yield to describe the amount of lead iodide formed.

OR

- Display a range of household products made using chemical reactions, such as medicines, cleaning products, food additives, and introduce the term yield to describe the amount of a chemical produced during a reaction.

Learning activities

Worksheet c3_e_01 + Practical c3_e_01

Low demand

Explain that groups will be using a chemical reaction to make sodium chloride and measuring the yield of the reaction. Then demonstrate how to add hydrochloric acid to sodium hydrogen carbonate a drop at a time until the reaction stops and how to put a Bunsen on its lowest possible setting to evaporate water from the products. Groups should then collect their own results using Practical c3_e_01 as a guide, and consolidate their understanding by completing Section 1a–d from Worksheet c3_e_01 and the *Yield and percentage yield* section from the Student Book.

Teaching and learning notes: *Warn students not to add the acid too quickly and to heat the products gently.*

Standard demand

The *Calculating percentage yield* section of the Student Book explains how to calculate percentage yields and Sections 2a–d of Worksheet c3_e_01 provide further practice.

Teaching and learning notes: *Students will need calculators.*

High demand

The *Calculating predicted yields* section of Worksheet c3_e_01 challenges students to use balanced symbol equations to calculate predicted yields. Students should then round off the topic by completing the final section of the Student Book.

Plenary suggestions

Present a scenario and ask students to identify all the places where product could be lost; for example, you mix two solutions to make a fertiliser, filter out some insoluble impurities, evaporate the solution to dryness and scrape the solid fertiliser into a plastic bag.

OR

Challenge students to explain what it means if a reaction has a 50% yield.

Assessment opportunities

Worksheet c3_e_01 provides staged opportunities to assess students' learning.

Answers

Student Book

Q1 The amount of product we expect to make • **Q2** Amount of product made • **Q3** Loss in the transfer of liquids; loss of solid during filtration • **Q4** 30% • **Q5** Any three from loss in filtration, loss in evaporation, loss in transferring liquids, some of the reactants don't form products • **Q6a** 90% • **Q6b** Lost during filtration; left in the test tube • **Q7** 75% • **Q8** a and d • **Q9** To maximise profits

Worksheet

Q1a 0.7 g • **Q1b** Actual yield • **Q1c** Not all of the reactants are converted into products: some are lost, some get converted into unwanted products • **Q1d** None of the product is lost • **Q2a** Exact answer will depend on students' actual yield obtained • **Q2b** 50% • **Q2c** Some of the magnesium might not have reacted to form magnesium oxide • **Q2d** If it isn't heated for long enough, some copper carbonate could be left and this has a higher mass than that of copper oxide • **Q3a** A_r of 2Mg = 48, 12 g used in the reaction; M_r of 2MgO = 80, 20 g of MgO made in reaction; % yield is therefore 50% • **Q3b** 25% • **Q3c** 100% • **Q3d** 25%

C3e: Percentage yield and atom economy

Resources

Student Book pages 118–119 • Equipment for demonstrations and practical
Interactive Book Practical investigations: How to use chemical equations
Files on Teacher Pack CD: c3_e_02_worksheet; c3_e_02_practical; c3_e_0 2_technician

Learning objectives

- Use atom economy to determine the percentage of reactant atoms converted into useful products.
- Recognise why chemists aim to maximise atom economy.

Learning outcomes

- Understand atom economy as a way of measuring the amount of atoms that are wasted when manufacturing a chemical, appreciating that 100% atom economy means that all atoms in the reactant have been converted into the desired product.
- Understand that the higher the atom economy, the 'greener' the process.
- Recall and use the formula: atom economy = (M_r of desired products/sum of M_r of all products) × 100.
- Calculate atom economy when given balanced symbol equation and appropriate relative formula masses.
- Explain why an industrial process wants as high an atom economy as possible, including to reduce the production of unwanted products and to make the process more sustainable (high demand).
- Be able to interpret complex atom economy and percentage yield data.

Prior knowledge

Students should recognise that reactions that produce unwanted chemicals cause pollution.

Key vocabulary

atom economy • M_r • A_r

Barriers to learning

Students must recognise that both the atom economy and the percentage yield determine the mass of product obtained from a given mass of reactants.

Curiosity and starter suggestions

- Display images of polluted air and water, and elicit students' ideas about what could be done to make the chemical industry 'greener'.

OR

- Show students an empty pack of painkillers containing ibuprofen and explain that when Boots™ first manufactured the painkiller the process produced a lot of waste products that had to be buried in landfill sites. Elicit students' ideas about why the amount of waste produced has been slashed in recent years.

Learning activities

Worksheet c3_e_02 + Practical c3_e_02

Low demand

Introduce the idea that many chemicals can be made from different reactants. Allocate groups to each reactant that can be used to make magnesium sulfate from sulfuric acid, and demonstrate the procedure. Practical c3_e_02 provides instructions. Once the products have been left to crystallise, the *Atom economy* section of the Student Book can be used to introduce the term, and students could summarise the key points by completing Section 1 of Worksheet c3_e_02.

Teaching and learning notes: *Remind students how to evaporate solutions carefully using a small blue Bunsen flame. Depending on the group, they may need to be helped to transfer their hot magnesium sulfate solutions to crystallising dishes.*

Standard demand

After students have completed the activities outlined in the previous section, use the *Calculating atom economy* section of Worksheet c3_e_02 to explain how the methods can be compared. The *Atom economy formula* section of the Student Book provides further practice.

Teaching and learning notes: *Students will need calculators.*

High demand

The *More on atom economy* section of the Student Book, and Section 3 of Worksheet c3_e_02 give students further practice.

Plenary suggestions

Challenge students to explain what makes a chemical reaction more sustainable.

OR

Show word equations for the production of ethanol from glucose by fermentation and from ethene by the addition of water. Ask students to explain which reaction has the highest atom economy and why.

Assessment opportunities

Worksheet c3_e_02 provides staged opportunities to assess students' learning.

Answers

Student Book

Q10a magnesium + oxygen → magnesium oxide • **Q10b** magnesium + oxygen → magnesium oxide • **Q11** A higher atom economy makes a reaction 'greener' and is more environmentally friendly, and there is less wastage of reactants • **Q12a** Method 1: 89%; Method 2: 91% • **Q12b** Method 2 • **Q12c** It has a higher atom economy, so fewer atoms are wasted and the process is 'greener' • **Q13a** iii, i, ii • **Q13b** Atom economies: *iii* has 100%; *i* has 99%; *ii* has 1.4% • **Q14** If no waste products are produced because there is only one product

Figure 2 Carbon dioxide; the gas turns limewater milky/cloudy • **Figure 3** For example, to soften skin, improve cleanliness, prevent skin wrinkling in water • **Figure 4** Increasing pressure decreases volume, so more hydrogen can be stored; don't smoke near the dispenser, don't set fire to the dispenser, don't use a mobile phone near the dispenser

Worksheet

Q1 reactants, smallest, product, atoms, desired, waste, sustainable, desired • **Q2** M_r of $MgSO_4$, 120; M_r of H_2, 2; so total M_r of products is 122. Atom economy is 98.4% • **Q3a** 4.35% • **Q3b** 17.6% • **Q3c** 6.67% • **Q3d** 15.38% • **Q3e** The percentage yield measures the actual yield as a percentage of the predicted yield, even if a reaction has a high atom economy; if the percentage yield is low, little product will form • **Q3f** It would be better if carbon monoxide was not produced, as it is toxic, and carbon dioxide can be separated from the hydrogen more easily

C3f: Energy

Resources

Student Book pages 120–121 • Equipment for demonstrations and practical
Interactive Book Naked Scientist animation: What are catalysts? • Quick starter: Activation energy graph
Files on Teacher Pack CD: c3_f_01_worksheet; c3_f_01_practical; c3_f_01_technician

Learning objectives

- Distinguish between exothermic and endothermic reactions.
- Explain why reactions involve energy changes.

Learning outcomes

- Recall that an exothermic reaction is one in which energy is transferred into the surroundings (releases energy).
- Recall that an endothermic reaction is one in which energy is taken from the surroundings (absorbs energy).
- Recognise exothermic and endothermic reactions using temperature changes.
- Recall bond making as an exothermic process and bond breaking as an endothermic process.
- Explain why a reaction is exothermic or endothermic using the energy changes that occur during bond breaking and bond making (high demand).

Prior knowledge

Students should recognise that many reactions release heat energy.

Key vocabulary

endothermic • exothermic

Barriers to learning

Students must recognise that reactions like cooking, which need a continuous supply of heat, are endothermic.

Curiosity and starter suggestions

- Show a video of an explosion and ask students to spot evidence that the reaction releases energy.

OR

- Demonstrate some exothermic reactions: the pop test for hydrogen, burning methanol and the reaction between anhydrous copper sulfate and water.

Learning activities

Worksheet c3_f_01 + Practical c3_f_01

Low demand

Students could begin by reading the relevant section of the Student Book and answering questions 1–4. Stress that reactions like cooking, which need a continual supply of energy, and reactions that cause a temperature drop are both endothermic.

Introduce Practical c3_f_01 and stress the need to keep the polystyrene cup in a beaker to stop it tipping. Demonstrate how to hold it at an angle when measuring the temperature, to make sure the thermometer bulb is completely covered. Students could consolidate their understanding by completing Section1 of Worksheet c3_f_01.

Teaching and learning notes: *Have a large bowl or bucket available near the sink and instruct students to tip used reactants into this before rinsing their polystyrene cups.*

Standard demand

After students have completed the experiment outlined in the previous section, use Section 2 of Worksheet c3_f_01 to introduce the ideas in the *Making and breaking bonds* section of the Student Book.

Teaching and learning notes: *If Molymod molecular models are available students could use them to model the reactions between hydrogen and oxygen and between methane and oxygen.*

High demand

Use the *'Make or break'* section of Worksheet c3_f_01 to explain how the amounts of energy absorbed and released determine the overall energy change. The final section of the Student Book consolidates this idea.

Plenary suggestions

Ask students to classify processes as exothermic or endothermic, for example a fuel burning, a new bond forming, mercury oxide decomposing into mercury and oxygen and respiration.

OR

Challenge students to write three sentences about exothermic reactions.

Assessment opportunities

The plenary is an opportunity to assess students' learning.

Answers

Student Book

Q1 Products • **Q2** Energy changes make the temperature rise or fall, or produce light, sound or movement • **Q3** degrees Celsius • **Q4** Exothermic • **Q5** Energy is released • **Q6** Energy needs to be transferred to the chemicals to break bonds • **Q7** Compare the energy required for bond breaking with the energy given out when new bonds are formed • **Q8** Bond breaking • **Q9** Bond making • **Q10** Exothermic reaction • **Q11** Diagram as shown

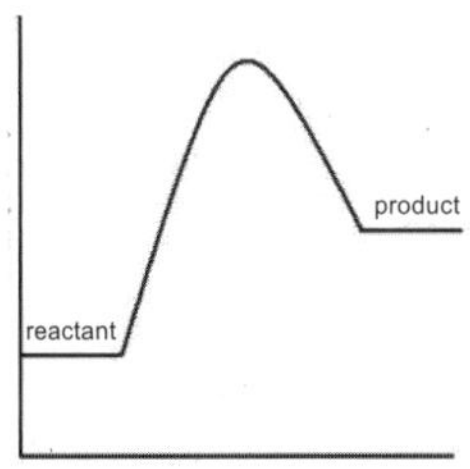

Figure 2 Energy is transferred to the surroundings • **Figure 3** Energy is absorbed from the surroundings • **Figure 4** More energy is released in bond making than is required for bond breaking

Worksheet

Q1a Exothermic • **Q1b** Exothermic • **Q1c** Endothermic • **Q1d** Endothermic • **Q1e** Endothermic • **Q2a** Endothermic, as energy is required to break the bonds in the copper carbonate • **Q2b** Diagram as shown below •

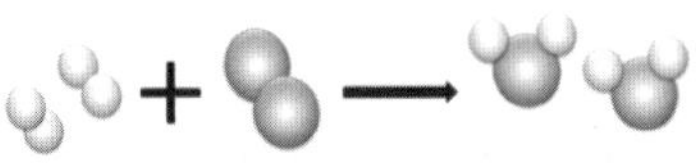

Q3a Bonds between the carbon and hydrogen atoms in methane should be blue; bonds between oxygen atoms should be blue; bonds between carbon and oxygen atoms in carbon dioxide should be red; bonds between oxygen and hydrogen atoms in water should be red • **Q3b** Completed table as shown below • **Q3c** Exothermic •

Bonds broken	Number	Bonds formed	Number
between carbon and hydrogen	4	between carbon and oxygen	2
between oxygen atoms	2	between hydrogen and oxygen	4

Q3d The new bonds formed • **Q3e** Diagram as shown

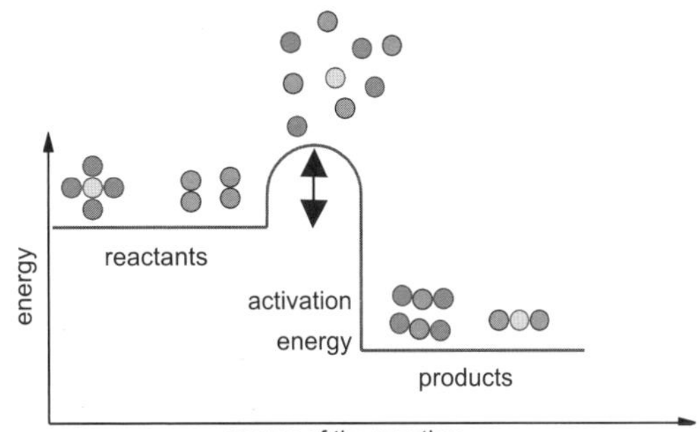

C3f: Energy

Resources

Student Book pages 122–123 • Equipment for demonstrations and practical
Files on Teacher Pack CD: c3_f_02_worksheet; c3_f_02_practical; c3_f_02_technician

Learning objectives

- Compare the amounts of energy transferred when different fuels burn.

Learning outcomes

- Describe a simple calorimetric method for comparing the energy transferred in combustion reactions, including using a spirit burner or a bottled gas burner, heating water in a copper calorimeter, measuring mass of fuel burnt and measuring the temperature change.
- Describe fast and reliable calorimetric methods. Interpret and use data from simple calorimetric experiments related to the combustion of fuels to compare which fuel releases the most energy.
- Use the formula energy transferred (in J) = $m \times c \times \Delta T$ to calculate the amount of energy transferred and (high demand), the mass of water heated (m) and temperature change (ΔT).
- Recall bond making as an exothermic process and bond breaking as an endothermic process.
- Calculate the energy output of a fuel in J/g by recalling and using the formula: energy per gram = energy released in J/mass of fuel burnt in g (high demand).

Prior knowledge

Students should recognise that fuels are chemicals that release energy when they burn.

Key vocabulary

calorimeter • specific heat capacity

Barriers to learning

Students must recognise that if less fuel is needed, it must release more energy per gram.

Curiosity and starter suggestions

- Have two copper calorimeters clamped above the Bunsen burners, with 100 cm^3 of water in each. Place a thermometer, or temperature sensor connected to data-logging software, in each. Light two Bunsen burners. Put one on a yellow flame and one on a blue flame. Start the clock or data-logging software and put one Bunsen under each calorimeter. The blue flame should heat the water twice as fast as the yellow one. Remind students that the flame is yellow because of incomplete combustion, so it releases less energy.

OR

- Show students two spirit burners containing different fuels and elicit their ideas about how the fuels could be compared to see which transfers most energy when it burns.

Learning activities

Worksheet c3_f_02 + Practical c3_f_02

Low demand

Use Section 1 of Worksheet c3_f_02 to introduce the method groups will use to compare fuels. Demonstrate the experiment and stress the need for every group to use the same control variables to make their results comparable. They should agree about how far above the spirit burner to clamp the calorimeter. Groups should then collect their own results using Practical c3_f_02 as a guide. Each group could obtain values for one fuel and contribute them to a class database.

Teaching and learning notes: *Ideally, a spreadsheet should be set up to display the students' results and plot a bar chart to display the average results for each fuel.*

Standard demand

After students have completed the experiment outlined in the previous section, use the *Energy transfer* section of Worksheet c3_f_02 to explain how the energy each gram of fuel transfers can be calculated.

***Teaching and learning notes:** As an extension, students could calculate how much energy their own fuel released per gram and compare it with the standard values: methanol, 22.7 kJ/g; ethanol, 29.7 kJ; propanol, 33.4 kJ/g; butanol, 36.1 kJ/g. If time allows they could evaluate their working methods to deduce where the missing energy has gone.*

High demand

The final section of Worksheet c3_f_02 prompts students to rearrange the equation they have been using to make it more useful for other calculations.

Plenary suggestions

Students could consolidate their understanding by completing the questions from the relevant sections of the Student Book.

OR

Show a fuel burning with a smoky flame and ask students to explain why the fuel transfers less energy than expected.

Assessment opportunities

The plenary is an opportunity to assess students' learning.

Answers

Student Book

Q12 Carbon dioxide and water • **Q13a** Methanol, 10°C; ethanol, 20°C; propanol, 29°C • **Q13b** Propanol • **Q14** If the results are very similar they are precise • **Q15** 6.72 kJ • **Q16** Use the same size and type of calorimeter, measure out the same volume of water, make sure the water starts at the same temperature, keep the flame the same distance from the calorimeter, burn the same mass of each fuel • **Q17** 5040 J/g • **Q18a** 77.62 g • **Q18b** 2445 J.

Figure 5 To find out the energy released by a fuel.

Worksheet

Q1a Methanol, 31°C; ethanol, 35°C; propanol, 37°C; butanol, 40°C, so butanol releases the most energy per gram • **Q1b** Methanol, 3.6 g; ethanol, 2.8 g; propanol, 2.4 g; butanol, 2.2 g, so butanol releases the most energy per gram • **Q1c** Repeat their measurements and show their results are concordant • **Q1d** Yes – these students used two different methods and both illustrate that butanol releases the most energy per gram • **Q2a**

Fuel	Temperature before in °C	Temperature before in °C	Temperature difference in °C	Energy transferred in J	Mass of fuel used in g	Energy per gram in J/g
A	20	56	36	15 120	3.2	4725
B	21	64	43	18 060	4.3	4200
C	19	52	33	13 860	3.6	3850
D	20	61	41	17 220	3.9	4415

• **Q3a** Temperature change = energy transferred/(mass of water × 4.2) • **Q3b** Mass of water heated = energy transferred/(4.2 × temperature change).

C3g: Batch or continuous?

Resources

Student Book pages 124–125 • Equipment for demonstrations
Interactive Book Drag and drop: Batch and continuous processes
Files on Teacher Pack CD: c3_g_01_worksheet; c3_g_01_technician

Learning objectives

- Compare batch and continuous industrial processes.

Learning outcomes

- Describe the differences between a batch and a continuous process.
- Explain why batch processes are often used for the production of pharmaceutical drugs, but continuous processes are used to produce chemicals such as ammonia.
- Evaluate the advantages and disadvantages of batch and continuous manufacturing processes given relevant data and information (high demand).

Prior knowledge

Students should recognise that some chemicals, like ammonia, are manufactured in huge amounts but others, like medicines, are needed in much smaller quantities.

Key vocabulary

batch • bulk chemical • continuous • pharmaceuticals • speciality chemical

Barriers to learning

Students must recognise that continuous production methods reduce costs.

Curiosity and starter suggestions

- Display images of chemical plants on the whiteboard and elicit students' ideas about why some are huge and why they have so many pipes.

OR

- Show an animation of a continuous process like the production of ammonia and challenge students to suggest ways in which industrial processes such as this are different from making chemicals in the lab.

Learning activities

Worksheet c3_g_01

Low demand

Use page 124 in the Student Book to explain the advantages of continuous manufacturing processes. Then talk students through a virtual tour of a chemical plant on the whiteboard. Section 1 of Worksheet c3_g_01 summarises the main differences between batch and continuous processes.

Teaching and learning notes: *It is useful for students to see that a manufacturing plant looks very different from a laboratory. A short tour of a pilot plant using a batch process can be found at www.atworkwithscience.com.*

Standard demand

Students should complete the *Batch or continuous?* section of Worksheet c3_g_01 using the Student Book for reference.

High demand

After students have completed the activities outlined in the previous sections, use the *Choosing the right process* section of the Student Book to evaluate the advantages and disadvantage of batch and continuous processes.

Plenary suggestions

Present students with a list of chemicals and ask them whether a batch or continuous process would be used to make each product, for example ammonia, blue food colouring, a new anticancer drug, sulfuric acid, aspirin.

OR

Give a series of statements and challenge students to decide whether they apply to batch or continuous processes, for example operates continually, can make a different chemical every week, more automated, needs more skilled workers.

Assessment opportunities

Worksheet c3_g_01 provides staged opportunities to assess students' learning.

Answers

Student Book

Q1 A pharmaceutical (or named example) • **Q2** Ammonia or sulfuric acid • **Q3** Add flour, water and yeast, and mix into a dough, knead the dough, put the dough into the oven; in a batch process, the bread is only made when it is needed • **Q4** Different types of bread • **Q5** For any chemical needed in bulk • **Q6** The process is not at the optimum conditions; it is less efficient • **Q7a** Aspirin: advantages – any suitable suggestion, such as batch processes only make what is needed, can match supply to demand; disadvantages – any suitable suggestion, for example the plant is idle for a period, it needs to be cleaned if a different drug is made, labour costs are high, lots of documentation is needed • **Q7b** Sulfuric acid: advantages – any suitable suggestion, for example it is made efficiently, orders are known in advance, labour costs are low; disadvantages – any suitable suggestion, such as it is difficult and expensive to change the amount made, it cannot made anything else

Figure 1 The reaction vessel never stops; nitrogen and hydrogen are constantly added and ammonia is constantly removed

Worksheet

Q1a Diagram highlighted to show the direct path through the apparatus • **Q1b** Diagram labelled: speciality chemicals/medicines • **Q1c** Reaction, products, product • **Q2a** Continuous • **Q2b** Batch • **Q2c** Continuous • **Q2d** Continuous • **Q2e** Continuous • **Q2f** Batch • **Q2g** Batch • **Q2h** Continuous • **Q2i** Continuous • **Q2j** Batch • **Q3a** Batch: high, high, high, low, low; continuous: low, low, low, high, high • **Q3b** Batch: not enough product to justify the expense of setting up a continuous process; grapes may not be available all year; having a batch number for each lot allows them to monitor the quality of the wine

C3g: Batch or continuous?

Resources

Student Book pages 126–127 • Equipment for demonstrations and practical
Files on Teacher Pack CD: c3_g_02_worksheet; c3_g_02_practical; c3_g_02_technician

Learning objectives

- Explain why pharmaceutical drugs are often expensive.

Learning outcomes

- List the factors that affect the cost of making and developing a pharmaceutical drug, including research and testing, labour costs, energy costs, raw materials, time taken for development and marketing.
- Explain why pharmaceutical drugs need to be thoroughly tested before they can be licensed for use.
- Explain why it is difficult to test and develop new pharmaceutical drugs that are safe to use (high demand).
- Recall that the raw materials for speciality chemicals, such as pharmaceuticals, can be either made synthetically or extracted from plants, and describe how chemicals can be extracted from plant sources, including crushing, boiling and dissolving in a suitable solvent, and chromatography.
- Explain why it is important to manufacture pharmaceutical drugs to be as pure as possible.
- Explain why it is often expensive to make and develop new pharmaceutical drugs.
- Interpret melting point, boiling point and chromatographic data relating to the purity of a substance.

Prior knowledge

Students should recognise that new medicines are continually being developed.

Key vocabulary

boiled • chromatography • crushed • generic • patent • trials

Barriers to learning

Students must recognise that the cost of a medicine covers much more than the raw materials it is made from.

Curiosity and starter suggestions

- Display images of a purple foxglove and a heart and ask students to deduce the connection between them.

OR

- Ask students if they have heard anything about new medicines in the news lately. Introduce the idea that each new medicine takes about 10 years to develop and can cost thousands of millions of pounds. Many of our medicines were originally found in plants.

Learning activities

Worksheet c3_g_02 + Practical c3_g_02

Low demand

Groups extract pigments from plant material and separate them using paper chromatography. Practical c3_g_02 provides instructions for the practical work and Section 1 of Worksheet c3_g_02 sums up the key points. Students should also complete the *Factors that affect the costs of medicines* section of the Student Book.

Teaching and learning notes: *It is a good idea to demonstrate how to put a sample onto the chromatography paper. Stress the need to keep the spot as small as possible. A thin layer chromatography plate could also be shown.*

Standard demand

After students have completed the extraction outlined in the previous section, use the *Using chromatography* section of Worksheet c3_g_02 to check that they understand what we can tell from the chromatogram. Students should then complete the *Why are medicines so expensive?* section of the Student Book.

High demand

After students have completed the activities outlined in the previous sections, use the *Developing new medicines* section of Worksheet c3_g_02 to outline the processes involved. Students should then complete the *Drug development* section of the Student Book.

Plenary suggestions

Challenge students to come up with six reasons why new medicines are expensive, for example research, development, testing, raw materials, labour, energy and marketing costs.

OR

Artemisinin, which is the most effective treatment for malaria, is extracted from a Chinese herb. Ask students to come up with one advantage and one disadvantage of relying on a medicine extracted from plants.

Assessment opportunities

Worksheet c3_g_02 provides staged opportunities to assess students' learning.

Answers

Student Book

Q8 Labour costs, research and testing, raw materials, energy costs, development time, marketing and legal costs • **Q9** Some drugs are made from chemicals extracted from plants • **Q10** The pure chemical should melt and boil at a fixed temperature, and give the same result when tested with thin layer chromatography • **Q11** By crushing them to break the cell walls, boiling so the chemicals dissolve and using chromatography to separate the compounds • **Q12** Chromatography can separate the chemical compound from any impurities mixed with it • **Q13** Impure substances do not have fixed melting and boiling points, and in chromatography would not move the same distance in the same time as a pure form of the substance • **Q14** Generic drugs are based on existing medicines so don't have to undergo clinical trials • **Q15** To ensure the drug is safe and effective before being released into the market • **Q16** Long-term trials are needed to identify possible side effects

Figure 3 Lots of wild plants are used to make current medicines and some plants could potentially be used for medicines in the future • **Figure 5** Different chemicals move at different speeds in specific solvents, so compounds can be separated from mixtures and impurities spotted

Worksheet

Q1 Chemists, plants, separated, impurities • **Q2** A, the sample contains small amounts of an impurity; B, the sample does not contain the same chemical as the pure sample • **Q3** 1d, 2e, 3a, 4c, 5b

C3h: Allotropes of carbon and nanochemistry

Resources

Student Book pages 128–129 • Equipment for demonstrations
Interactive Book Naked Scientist animation: Why are diamonds hard but graphite soft?
Files on Teacher Pack CD: c3_h_01_worksheet; c3_h_01_technician

Learning objectives

- Recall the properties of diamond and graphite and explain why they are so different.

Learning outcomes

- Explain why diamond and graphite are allotropes of carbon.
- Recognise the structures of diamond and graphite and explain why they have a giant molecular structure.
- List the following physical properties of diamond: lustrous, colourless and clear (transparent), hard and has a high melting point, insoluble in water, does not conduct electricity.
- Explain, in terms of properties, why diamond is used in cutting tools and in jewellery.
- Explain, in terms of structure and bonding, why diamond does not conduct electricity, is hard and has a high melting point (high demand).
- Explain, in terms of properties, why graphite is used in pencil leads and in lubricants.
- Explain, in terms of structure and bonding, why graphite conducts electricity, is slippery and has a high melting point (high demand).
- List the following physical properties of graphite: black, lustrous and opaque, slippery, insoluble in water, conducts electricity.
- Predict and explain the properties of substances that have a giant molecular structure (high demand).

Prior knowledge

Students should recognise that atoms can link together by forming covalent bonds.

Key vocabulary

allotrope • covalent bonding • diamond • buckminsterfullerene • giant structure • graphite

Barriers to learning

Students must recognise that the diamond and graphite are giant structures.

Curiosity and starter suggestions

- Display images of diamonds, the sharpened ends of pencils and soot, and elicit students' ideas about what they have in common.

OR

- Pass around large chunks of graphite and ask students to describe its properties and suggest what it might be.

Learning activities

Worksheet c3_h_01

Low demand

Use images of diamonds and buckminsterfullerene, and samples of graphite, to compare and contrast their properties. Students can summarise the main points by completing Section 1 of Worksheet c3_h_01.

Teaching and learning notes: *Students could test the softness of the graphite by using it to write on scrap paper. Its conductivity could also be demonstrated.*

Standard demand

Use models of diamond and graphite to emphasise that diamond is the hardest natural substance, while graphite feels slippery, and link these properties to their main uses. Students could annotate the diagrams in Section 2 of Worksheet c3_h_01 to show these.

High demand

Display models of diamond and graphite and ask them to suggest why diamond is hard and graphite slippery, and why only graphite conducts. Lead discussion to the idea that the way the atoms are bonded controls their properties. Students could then complete Section 3 of Worksheet c3_h_01.

Plenary suggestions

Complete questions from the relevant sections of the Student Book.

OR

Describe silicon dioxide as being very similar to diamond. Challenge students to list or explain its properties before revealing that silicon dioxide is sand.

Assessment opportunities

The plenary is an opportunity to assess students' learning.

Answers

Student Book

Q1 Carbon • **Q2** Diamond doesn't conduct electricity, but graphite does; diamond is hard, but graphite is soft and slippery; diamond is transparent, but graphite is opaque; diamond is colourless, but graphite is black • **Q3** Energy is released as heat when materials are cut, particularly when cutting very hard materials in industry, so it is important for the blade to have a high melting temperature so it doesn't melt during use • **Q4** Graphite is slippery, which allows it to slide onto the paper and, as graphite is black, this is seen as black marks • **Q5** A solid lubricant, like graphite, can be used at higher temperatures and pressures than can oil • **Q6** In diamond, every carbon atom is joined to four others in a three-dimensional lattice; the carbons are joined by strong covalent bonds in all directions • **Q7** Each carbon atom is joined to only three others, so each atom has an unpaired electron; these electrons are free to move between the layers • **Q8** The carbon atoms in diamond and graphite are joined by strong covalent bonds to form a giant structure

Figure 1 Jewellery is cut and polished to make it sparkle • **Figure 2** Industrial diamonds are often opaque and brown or black, whereas diamonds used for jewellery are transparent

Worksheet

Q1a Graphite • **Q1b** Diamond • **Q1c** Graphite • **Q1d** Diamond • **Q1e** Both • **Q1f** Graphite • **Q1g** Graphite • **Q1h** Both • **Q2a** Graphite, because it conducts electricity • **Q2b** Diamond, because it is hard • **Q3a** No, because their atoms take too much energy to separate • **Q3b** The weak forces between the layers let them slide over each other • **Q3c** The free electrons make graphite a conductor

C3h: Allotropes of carbon and nanochemistry

Resources

Student Book pages 130–131 • Computers with internet access and presentation software
Files on Teacher Pack CD: c3_h_02_worksheet

Learning objectives

- Explain why fullerenes are allotropes of carbon and explain why they are useful.

Learning outcomes

- Explain why fullerenes are allotropes of carbon.
- Recognise the structure of buckminsterfullerene.
- Recall that nanotubes are used to reinforce graphite in tennis rackets because nanotubes are very strong.
- Recall that nanotubes are used as semiconductors in electrical circuits.
- Explain why fullerenes can be used in new drug-delivery systems.
- Explain how the structure of nanotubes enables them to be used as catalysts (high demand).

Prior knowledge

Students should recognise that fullerenes and carbon nanotubes are allotropes of carbon.

Key vocabulary

fullerene • nanotube

Barriers to learning

Students need to recognise that the space inside fullerenes is hollow, so other molecules can fit within it.

Curiosity and starter suggestions

- Display images of carbon nanotubes and buckminsterfullerene, and ask students to suggest what properties they might have.

OR

- Display images of carbon nanotubes and buckminsterfullerene and elicit students' ideas about what they might be used for.

Learning activities

Worksheet c3_h_02

Low demand

Students will be researching possible uses of carbon nanotubes or fullerenes, and preparing a 1 minute presentation.

Teaching and learning notes: *To avoid wasted time make links to a suitable selection of websites available to students as a starting point. Students could work in pairs or threes. To help maintain concentration during the presentations, students could note down one thing they have learned from each presentation or feedback one good thing about each presentation and one thing that could be improved.*

Standard demand

Students will be researching possible future uses of carbon nanotubes or buckminsterfullerene, and preparing a 1 minute presentation.

High demand

Students will be researching uses of nanotubes that involve combining them with other materials, and preparing a 1 minute presentation.

Plenary suggestions

Complete the questions from the Student Book.

OR

Give students a list of statements and ask whether they refer to buckminsterfullerene, nanotubes or both, for example resembles a football, used to hold catalysts, high tensile strength, conducts electricity, black, can act as a cage to carry medicines around the body, has the formula C_{60}.

Assessment opportunities

The plenary and presentations are opportunities to assess students' learning.

Answers

Student Book

Q9 Diamond, graphite, carbon nanotubes • **Q10** Any two from industrial catalysts, reinforcing graphite in tennis rackets, semiconductors in electrical circuits • **Q11** Allotropes are made up of the same element, but have different structures • **Q12** They are hollow, so could carry drug molecules inside them • **Q13** Buckminsterfullerene exists as discrete 60-carbon structures, whereas diamond contains many carbon atoms covalently joined in a three-dimensional giant structure; more energy is required to break apart the atoms in diamond • **Q14** Giant covalent structures have high melting points and do not usually conduct electricity • **Q15** Nanotubes have a large surface area so this means that the reactant is more likely to bind to the catalyst, which increases the reaction rate.

Figure 4 Six.

C3: Planning and collecting primary data

Pages 132–133 in the Student Book prepare students for assessment.

When and how to use these pages

This task provides an opportunity to build and assess the skills that students will use when planning an investigation.

Annotated hints and tips guide students through the tasks.

Ask students to:

- read through the context and tasks, listing any terms that they do not understand
- as a whole class or in small groups, discuss the tasks to ensure that all students understand the terminology used and to clarify what is required
- work individually to answer the questions for each task.

If time allows, ask students to mark each other's work using the mark scheme provided.

Pages 278–290 provide further guidance on Practical and Enquiry Skills.

Notes

The worked example takes students through a typical planning task. Students are required to formulate a hypothesis, plan an experiment, provide a risk assessment of their plan and carry out the experiment they have planned. They should work in groups of no more than three.

A group discussion could be used to help students formulate a testable hypothesis based on their scientific understanding of what happens when a fuel burns.

Remind students that in order to test their hypothesis, they need to:

1. *Identify the independent variable they need to change to provide evidence to support their hypothesis*
2. *Find a dependent variable they can measure to determine the effect of changing the independent variable*
3. *Choose appropriate equipment and techniques to allow the dependent variable to be measured*
4. *Identify the variables they need to control to make it a fair test*
5. *Choose values for the variables they need to control and account for variables which cannot be controlled*
6. *Decide on a suitable range and number of data points for the independent variable*
7. *Plan how to make the measurements of the dependent variable as accurate as possible*
8. *Decide how to minimise errors*
9. *Carry out a risk assessment and plan how to minimise the risks involved*
10. *If necessary, adapt their plan after their initial tests to improve the quality of the data collected.*

In this practice activity, steps 1–3 have been done for them but it is worth going through the information given and ensuring that students recognise each type of variable and know how to use the equipment suggested. The questions on page 132 take students through the remaining steps.

Answers

Planning your investigation

Q1 The mass of the fuel burner and the temperature of a known mass of water will need to be measured before and after each test.

Q2 The amount of fuel burnt can be varied by changing how long the burner is used for.

Q3 The calorimeter, volume of water, starting temperature and distance between burner and calorimeter need to be kept the same.

Q4 At least four results will be needed to identify a trend.

Q5 Readings need to be repeated until concordant results are obtained – two or three times.

Q6 Use eye protection; tie back long hair/loose clothes; keep the burner lid screwed on tightly; avoid touching hot calorimeters; avoid having excess fuel in the lab.

Q7 Measure 100 cm^3 of water into a calorimeter using a measuring cylinder; measure the initial mass of the burner using a top pan balance that reads to at least one decimal place, and the initial temperature of the water using a thermometer with a resolution of at least 1°C; light burner and heat for 1 minute; stir the water and record the new burner mass and water temperature; find the mass of fuel burnt and the temperature rise of the water by difference; repeat with fresh water until concordant results are obtained; repeat the process using longer heating times.

Give extra credit for:

- *a suitable range of values (1–5 minutes) and suitable intervals between the values chosen*
- *modifying the plan to make it safer, if the initial plan specified times that would make the calorimeter too hot, which could be hazardous*
- *modifying the plan to increase the mass of fuel burnt, if the initial plan specified short times, which might make it too difficult to measure the mass of fuel used accurately*
- *suggesting that anomalous results should be repeated and ignored when average results are calculated*
- *suggesting collaboration with other groups using the same method in order to obtain sufficient repeats*
- *getting every step in a logical order*
- *having no grammar, punctuation or spelling mistakes*

Performing the investigation

Q1 The table must show all the fuel mass measurements.
Give extra credit for:
putting the units only in the heading, not next to each value

Q2 The table must show all the temperature measurements.
Give extra credit for:
omitting anomalous results when calculating averages

Q3 There should be a clear table of results
Give extra credit for:
having all the results in one table

Q4 A line graph; *x*-axis – mass of fuel burnt (g), *y*-axis – temperature rise of the water (°C); a straight line graph through zero would show that the temperature rise is directly proportional to the mass of fuel burnt.

Q5 Any suggestion for improving the method used, e.g. by using draught excluders to reduce heat loses to the surroundings.
Give extra credit for:

- *an explanation of why the improvements are needed.*
- *a detailed description of the improvements that could be carried out.*
- *an explanation of how or why the suggestions would work.*

Q6 The greater the mass of fuel burnt, the greater the temperature rise.
Give extra credit for:
describing the exact relationship between the mass of fuel burnt and the temperature rise.

C3: Checklist

Pages 134–135 in the Student Book provide a student-friendly checklist for revision.

When and how to use these pages

This checklist is presented in three columns showing progression, based on the grading criteria.

Remind students that they need to be able to use these ideas in various ways, such as:

- interpreting pictures, diagrams and graphs
- applying ideas to new situations
- explaining ethical implications
- suggesting some benefits and risks to society
- drawing conclusions from evidence they have been given.

These pages can be used for individual or class revision using any combination of the suggestions below.

- Ask students to construct a mind map linking the points on this checklist.
- Work through the checklist as a class and note the points that need further class discussion.
- Ask students to tick the boxes on the checklist worksheet (Teacher Pack CD) if they feel confident that they are well prepared for the topics. Students should refer back to the relevant Student Book pages to revise the points that they feel less confident about.
- Ask students to use the search terms to do further research on the different points in the checklist.

Pages 278–299 provide further assessment guidance.

Module summary

In the introduction to this section, students were presented with a number of new ideas. Work through the list below as part of their revision. Ask students to write their own summaries and mind maps, using this list as a starting point.

- reaction rates and how they can be changed
- comparing reaction rates using graphs and gradients
- collision theory
- factors affecting reaction rates
- relative atomic mass and relative formula mass
- calculating the mass of reactants needed and products formed
- percentage yield
- atom economy
- the UK chemical industry
- sustainable use of resources
- energy changes in reactions – exothermic and endothermic
- calculating energy transfer
- testing for purity
- batch and continual processes
- factors affecting the cost of chemical manufacture
- allotropes of carbon and their uses – diamond, graphite and buckminsterfullerene
- nanochemistry and its uses.

Notes

C3: Exam-style questions: Foundation

Pages 136–137 in the Student Book are exam-style questions for Foundation students.

When and how to use these pages

These questions are based on module C3 and cover a range of different types of questions that students will encounter in their written exams.

- Questions could be used as a revision test once you've completed the section.
- Work through the questions as a class as part of a revision lesson.
- Ask students to mark each other's work, using the mark scheme provided.
- As a class, make a list of the questions that most students did not get right. Work through these as a class.

Notes on worked example

The worked example takes students through a typical question about the rate of the reaction between marble chips and acid. Students must apply what they know about the reacting particles model and the factors that affect the frequency of collisions.

Assessment objectives

These exam-style questions cover the Assessment objectives as described below.

Assessment objectives		Questions
AO1	Recall, select and communicate their knowledge and understanding of science	1a, 1biv, 4b, 5a, 6a–b, 7, 8
AO2	Apply skills, knowledge and understanding of science in practical and other contexts	1bi–iii, 2a–b, 3a–c, 4a
AO3	Analyse and evaluate evidence, make reasoned judgements and draw conclusions based on evidence	1bv, 5b

Answers

These answers are also on the Teacher Pack CD so that students can mark their own, or their peer's work.

Question number	Answer	Additional notes	Mark
1a	Any three from: increase temperature, increase concentration; increase pressure if gases are involved; increase surface area of any solids; use a catalyst.		3
bi	Answer in range 70– 72 cm^3	Units must be given	1
bii	80 cm^3	Units must be given	1
biii	Between 0 and 20 seconds	Reject answer if more than one box is ticked	1
biv	One of the reactants is used up		1
bv	No: If it did the graph would be a straight line/the gradient changes	A reason must be given	1
			[8]
2a	80		1

b	0.8 g		1
			[2]
3a	sulfuric acid		1
b	percentage yield = 1.5 x 100/ 2 = 75%	Award a mark for the correct answer if the working is not shown	1
c	Product left in the filter paper/glassware Reaction incomplete/other products made		1 1
			[4]
4a	A		1
b	A		1
			[2]
5a	Diagram / description of calorimeter; containing water; thermometer in water; crisp held underneath		1 1 1 1
5b	It is impossible to say; The differences could be random variation or reflect real differences; There is no evidence of repeatability; and no mention of the resolution of the measuring equipment		1 1 1 1
			[8]
6a	Any five from: research; testing; labour; raw materials; time needed for development; marketing		5
b	(Measure their): melting point; boiling point; use chromatography to detect impurities		1 1 1
			[8]
7	Diamond / Graphite Clear / Black Transparent / Opaque Non-conductor / Conducts Hard / Soft / slippery	1 mark for each difference – the relevant property e.g. ability to conduct electricity for both must be given to be awarded a mark	4
			[4]
8	Strengthening plastics; Semi -conductors		1 1
			[2]
			[38]

C3: Exam-style questions: Higher

Pages 138–139 in the Student Book are exam-style questions for Higher students.

When and how to use these pages

These questions are based on module C3 and cover a range of different types of questions that students will encounter in their written exams.

- Questions could be used as a revision test once you've completed the section.
- Work through the questions as a class as part of a revision lesson.
- Ask students to mark each other's work, using the mark scheme provided.
- As a class, make a list of the questions that most students did not get right. Work through these as a class.

Notes on worked example

The worked example takes students through a sequence of exam questions about the production of a bulk chemical, ammonia.

Assessment objectives

These exam-style questions cover the Assessment objectives as described below.

Assessment objectives		Questions
AO1	Recall, select and communicate their knowledge and understanding of science	3c, 4a, 5a–b, 6a–b
AO2	Apply skills, knowledge and understanding of science in practical and other contexts	1a–b, 2a–b, 3a–b, 4b
AO3	Analyse and evaluate evidence, make reasoned judgements and draw conclusions based on evidence	1c

Answers

These answers are also supplied on the Teacher Pack CD so that students can mark their own, or their peer's work.

Question number	Answer	Additional notes	Mark
1ai	temperature		1
aii	final volume of gas		1
b	36 cm^3 at 24°C	Accept 36 cm^3 without reference to the row of the table it came from	1
c	Rates calculated from the average results: 20°C 3.4 cm^3/s 25°C 4.3 cm^3/s 30°C 5.4 cm^3/s 35°C 6.8 cm^3/s Uses evidence to oppose the claim, or states that a 10°C rise increases the rate but does not double it. Gives some indication that there is insufficient evidence to be confident whether the claim is correct or incorrect (for all reactions or temperature ranges).	Deduct 1 mark if there are errors in the calculations Give credit for the deduction that a doubling of the rate would double the volume of gas collected in 10 seconds.	1 1 1
			[6]
2a	120		1

b	400		1
c	$Fe_2(SO_4)_3$ + 6Na → $3Na_2SO4$ + 2Fe 400 + 138 → 426 + 112 538 → 538	1 mark for balanced equation ; 1 mark for showing that total mass is the same on both sides of the equation	1 1
			[4]
3a	% = (38 ÷ 40) x100 = 95%	1 mark for correct answer; 1 mark for correct working	1 1
b	Atom economy = M_r of wanted product (56) x 100 ÷ total mass of products (56+44) = 56%	1 mark for correct answer; 2 marks for correct working	1 2
c	reduce unwanted products make the process more sustainable.		1 1
			[7]
4a	measure out 1 g of fuel put a measured volume of water in a copper calorimeter measure water temperature at the start; burn the fuel re-measure temperature	Credit idea the idea of using a difference in mass to find the mass of fuel used and calculating the energy that would be released by 1 gram. 1 QWC for logical order	5 1 QWC
b	50 × 36 × 4.2 = 7560 J	1 mark for correct answer; 1 mark for correct working	1 1
c	1 g = 25 704 ÷ 3 = 8568 J Mass of water heated = 8568 ÷ (60 × 4.2) = 34g	1 mark for correct amount of energy from 1 g; 1 mark for correct working 1 mark for correct answer for mass of water heated 1 mark for correct working	1 1 1 1
			[12]
5a	only small amounts needed products not needed all the time reactants not available all the time the same equipment can be used to make different products		1 1 1 1
b	Any 5 from: takes years to develop few compounds actually work some are toxic they must pass safely tests raw materials hard to find / extract long term trials to look for side effects	1 QWC for spelling punctuation and grammar	5 1QWC
			[10]
6a	layers slide over each other so colour rubs off on paper		1 1
6b	there are free electrons between the layers		1 1
			[4]
			[43]

C4: Introduction

Pages 140–141 in the Student Book provide an introduction to module C4.

When and how to use these pages

These pages summarise what students should already know from KS3 or previous GCSE units and provide an overview of the content that they will learn in this module.

- Use these pages as a revision lesson before you start the first new topic.
- Brainstorm everything that students remember about the different topics using the headings as a starting point. Compare your list with the points in the Student Book.
- Use the questions on the left-hand page as a starting point for class discussions.
- Ask students if they can tell you anything about the topics on the right-hand page.
- Make a note of any unfamiliar / difficult terms and return to these in the relevant lessons.

You can revisit these pages at the following points:

- before the lesson on The group 1 elements pages 154–155
- before the lesson on The group 7 elements pages 160–161
- before the lesson on Metal structure and properties pages 168–169.

Overview of module

In this section students will study atomic structure and learn how this underpins the chemical and physical properties of the elements and their positions in the periodic table. They learn how atoms are held together by ionic, covalent and metallic bonding and how this influences their properties.

Students will learn about the patterns and trends in the properties of the elements by studying the reactive metals in group 1, the non-metals in group 7, and the transition metals. They will find out why metals are so useful and how new technologies use superconductors.

Finally, students will learn how to detect dissolved ions and learn how water is treated to make it safe to drink.

Barriers to learning

Students may need extra guidance with the following terms and concepts:

Atomic structure

Students must recognise that the properties of an element depend on its atomic structure and that scientific theories may need to be modified when more evidence becomes available.

Ions

Students must recognise that protons and electrons have equal and opposite charges. If their numbers become unequal, a charged ion forms. The stronger the force between its ions, the harder a substance is to melt.

Covalent bonding

Students must recognise that shared electrons contribute to each atom's outer shell of electrons. They must also recognise that scientific ideas are provisional and may need to be modified as more evidence becomes available.

Group 1

Students must recognise that the patterns and trends in the periodic table allow the properties of unknown elements to be deduced and that elements with the same number of outer electrons have similar chemical properties.

Group 7

Students must recognise that although group 7 elements form coloured diatomic molecules, they lose their colour when they react to form separate negative ions.

Transition elements

Students must recognise that the usefulness of metals depends on their physical and chemical properties and that thermal decomposition is different from burning because it splits substances up.

Metals

Students must recognise that the physical properties of metals suit them to different roles and that new technology has benefits and drawbacks.

Purifying and testing water

Students must recognise that water may contain dissolved pollutants even when it looks clean and that ionic compounds split into separate ions when they dissolve.

Practicals in this unit

In this unit students will do the following practical work:

- Observe sodium chloride under the microscope
- Carry out flame tests
- Testing for transition metal ions in solution
- Compare the ease of decomposition of carbonates
- Testing the nitrate concentration in water samples
- Testing for non-metal ions in solution

Key vocabulary covered in this unit

atomic number • electrons • isotopes • mass number • negative charge • neutrons • nucleus • periodic table • positive charge • protons • symbol

confirmed • evidence • model • provisional

atom • bond • charge • dot and cross • lattice • metal • negative • non-metal • positive • stable electronic structure • transfer

conducts electricity • giant ionic lattice • high melting point • stable octet

covalent • covalent bonding • electrons • ionic bonding • metals • non-metals • share • transferring

chemical properties • column • elements • group • period • row

alkali • balanced • density • hydroxide • reactivity

ion • ionic equation • oxidation • stable electronic structure

alkali metals • halogens • metal halide • reactants • trend

displacement • reactivity • reduction

catalyst • ductile • lustrous • malleable metals • periodic table • sonorous • transition metal

carbonates • gelatinous • iron (II) • iron (III) • limewater • milky • precipitation • thermal decomposition

conductor • density • delocalised electrons • ductile • lustrous • malleable • metallic bonds • tensile strength • thermal conductivity

crystals • delocalised electrons • metal grains • resistance • superconductors • superconductivity

aquifer • borehole • chlorination • coolant • filtration • nitrate • pesticide • reservoir • residue • sedimentation

barium chloride • barium ions • chlorides • ions • precipitate • silver ions • silver nitrate • sulfates

C4a: Atomic structure

Resources

Student Book pages 142–143 • Equipment for demonstrations

Interactive Book Quick starter: Atomic odd one out • Naked Scientist animation: How does atomic structure affect how a metal will behave? • Quick starter: Can you unjumble the sentences to find out about the particles in an atom? • Matching pairs: Isotopes

Files on Teacher Pack CD: c4_a_01_worksheet; c4_a_01_technician

Learning objectives

- Describe the structure of atoms.
- Use ideas about atoms to compare elements and their isotopes.

Learning outcomes

- Recall that an atom has a nucleus made of protons and neutrons, surrounded by electrons.
- Recall the relative charge of electrons is –1 and they have a mass of 0.0005, protons have a charge of +1 and mass 1, neutrons have a charge of 0 and mass 1 and (high demand) explain why that makes atoms neutral.
- Understand that atoms have a very small mass, 10^{-23} g, and a very small size, 10^{-10} m (high demand).
- Identify the atomic number of an element or vice versa by using a periodic table.
- Recall that the atomic number is the number of protons in an atom.
- Recall that the mass number is the total number of protons and neutrons in an atom.
- Describe isotopes as varieties of an element that have the same atomic number but different mass numbers.
- Deduce the number of protons, electrons and neutrons in a charged particle given its atomic number, mass number and the charge on the particle using data in a table and using the conventional symbolism, for example carbon-12.
- Identify isotopes from data about the number of electrons, protons and neutrons in particles.

Prior knowledge

Students should recognise that atoms are the smallest particles of an element.

Key vocabulary

atomic number • electrons • isotopes • mass number • negative charge • neutrons • nucleus • periodic table • positive charge • protons • symbol

Barriers to learning

Students must recognise that the properties of an element depend on the atomic structure of its atoms.

Curiosity and starter suggestions

- Give students samples of aluminium foil and graphite. Check they can identify the elements and locate them in the periodic table, and elicit students' ideas about why these elements are so different.

OR

- Point out the number of elements in the periodic table and ask groups to suggest what's different about each sort of atom.

Learning activities

Worksheet c4_a_01

Low demand

Show the class a hula-hoop model of the hydrogen atom and point out the positive proton in the middle and the negative electron orbiting it. Stress that real atoms are spherical, not two-dimensional like the model. Point out hydrogen in the periodic table and explain the link between an element's atomic number and the number of protons.

Show a hula-hoop model of the helium atom and introduce neutrons. Students should complete Section 1 of Worksheet c4_a_01 to check their understanding.

Teaching and learning notes: *Emphasise that real atoms do not have a solid boundary like the hula-hoop models – just a space where the electron can orbit.*

Standard demand

Use examples from the periodic table to explain how to work out the numbers of protons, neutrons and electrons in an atom and introduce isotopes. Section 2 of Worksheet c4_a_01 checks students' understanding.

Teaching and learning notes: *Stress that not all isotopes are radioactive.*

High demand

Ask groups to suggest a strength and a weakness of the hula-hoop models of the atom. Key strengths are that they show that most of an atom is empty space and show the sub-atomic particles atoms contain.

Show a video sequence or image of sodium reacting with chlorine and explain that in reactions like this, electrons can move from the metal to the non-metal. When this happens the charges on the protons and electrons no longer cancel each other out. The new particles formed are charged ions.

Section 3 of Worksheet c4_a_01 checks students' understanding.

Plenary suggestions

Complete questions from the relevant sections of the student book.

OR

Distribute scrap paper or mini whiteboards and pens and organise a quick quiz about the elements, for example how many electrons does argon have, find a metal with 20 protons, find a non-metal with 10 neutrons, and so on.

Assessment opportunities

The plenary is an opportunity to assess students' understanding.

Answers

Student Book

Q1 A positive charge – the magnitude of the charge depends on the number of protons • **Q2** –1 • **Q3** None • **Q4** Sulfur • **Q5** Nine • **Q6** One • **Q7** +1 • **Q8** Atoms of the same element with the same atomic number but different mass numbers • **Q9** See table below • **Q10** 19 protons, 19 electrons, 20 neutrons • **Q11** Chlorine-35

	Atomic number	**Mass number**	**Number of protons**	**Number of electrons**	**Number of neutrons**
carbon-14	6	14	6	6	8

Figure 2 –1 • **Figure 3** 12 • **Figure 4** 4 • **Figure 5** The number of neutrons is different, so they have different mass numbers

Worksheet

Answers to worksheet can be found on the Teacher's Pack CD.

C4a: Atomic structure

Resources

Student Book pages 144–145 • Equipment for demonstrations
Files on Teacher Pack CD: c4_a_02_worksheet; c4_a_02_technician

Learning objectives

- Distinguish formulas of elements and compounds.
- Use electronic structures to identify elements.
- Explain how ideas about atomic structure developed.

Learning outcomes

- Explain why a substance is an element or a compound given its formula.
- Deduce the number of occupied shells or the number of electrons from the electronic structure of an element.
- Describe and explain the significance of Dalton's atomic theory and how the work of J. J. Thomson, Rutherford and Bohr contributed to the development of the theory of atomic structure, noting how the atomic theory changed as new evidence was found and that science explanations are more convincing when predictions are later confirmed, and (high demand) how unexpected results led to the theory of a nuclear atom.
- Describe the arrangement of elements in the periodic table.
- Explain how the identity of an element can be deduced from its electronic structure and (high demand) deduce the electronic structure of the first 20 elements in the periodic table.

Prior knowledge

Students should recognise that elements form compounds when they react and that atoms contain protons, neutrons and electrons.

Key vocabulary

confirmed • evidence • model • provisional

Barriers to learning

Students must recognise that scientific theories may need to be modified when more evidence becomes available.

Curiosity and starter suggestions

- Show a video or image of sodium reacting with chlorine and check that students can explain why the product formed is a compound. Then display a jar of salt with a large label NaCl and ask how we could tell from the formula that it's a compound.

OR

- Display three jars with labels Co, CO and CO_2 and ask students to deduce everything they can about the contents from the labels.

Learning activities

Worksheet c4_a_02

Low demand

Remind students that all the substances in the periodic table are elements and that they react to form compounds. Point out that the symbols for elements start with capitals and subscripts show when more than one atom of an element is present. Students can check their understanding by completing page 1 of Worksheet c4_a_02.

Use the models to remind students that electrons orbit the nucleus. Explain that the first shell can only hold two electrons, so lithium needs to start filling another shell, further from the nucleus. Issue electronic structure cards, and model electrons, and point out the link between an element's position in the periodic table, the number of electron shells and the number of electrons in the outer shell. Practice constructing the electronic structures of randomly chosen atoms from hydrogen to calcium.

Explain that many scientists worked for years to discover the structure of the atom. Use molecular models to demonstrate that Dalton's model of the atom as an indivisible sphere is still useful for showing the shapes of molecules, but doesn't explain all the evidence we have about atoms. As new evidence has been discovered our model of the atom has become more detailed. Students could sum up by completing Section 2 of Worksheet c4_a_02.

Teaching and learning notes: *Students need to recognise that the formula shows what atoms are present in the smallest piece of a compound, which for chlorine is a* Cl_2 *molecule.*

Standard demand

Explain that the periodic table was constructed before electrons were discovered, but it reflects patterns in the electronic structures of the elements, for example all group 1 elements have one electron in their outer shell. Use Section 2 of Worksheet c4_a_02 to check that students can recognise the connection between an atom's electronic structure and its period and group.

Teaching and learning notes: *It is essential for students to recognise that the elements in each period are filling the same level of outer shell and that the number of electrons in their outer shells is the same as the group number.*

High demand

After students have completed the activities outlined in the previous sections, use Section 3 of Worksheet c4_a_02 to explain the evidence Rutherford used to support his model of the atom. Explain that Rutherford was convinced that neutrons existed, but his theory became more convincing when another scientist found evidence for them.

Plenary suggestions

Complete questions from the relevant sections of the Student Book.

OR

Point to an element in the periodic table and challenge students to tell you as much about it as they can.

Assessment opportunities

Worksheet c4_a_02 provides staged opportunities to assess students' learning.

Answers

Student Book

Q12 Cu is the only element; $CuCl_2$ and $CuSO_4$ are compounds – the element only has one type of atom and the compounds have atoms of more than one type • **Q13** 12 • **Q14** 3 • **Q15** It proved that atoms were not solid; Dalton's model was too simple • **Q16** 11 • **Q15** 11 • **Q16** Diagram should show two electrons in the inner shell, eight in the middle shell and one in the outer shell • **Q19** 2.7 • **Q20** 2.8.2 • **Q21** 2.8.8.1 • **Q22** Aluminium

Figure 6 Elements are made up of only one type of atom • **Figure 8** 2 • **Figure 9** 2

Worksheet

Q1a It contains two elements that have reacted together • **Q1b** Co, 1; CO, 2; CO_2, 3; $CaCO_3$, 5; $CuSO_4$, 6; Na_2CO_3, 6; $Ca(OH)_2$, 5; NH_4Cl, 6; $(NH_4)_2SO_4$, 15 • **Q1c** Diagram should show two electrons in the inner circle, four in the outer circle • **Q1d** Diagram should show two electrons in the inner circle, eight in the middle circle and two in the outer circle • **Q1ei** Rutherford's model • **Q1eii** Thomson's model • **Q1eiii** Dalton's model • **Q1eiv** Bohr's model • **Q2a** Both have one electron in their outer shell • **Q2b** Calcium: group 2, period 4; oxygen: group 6, period 2; chlorine: group 7, period 3 • **Q2c** Potassium, fluorine, carbon, aluminium, argon • **Q3a** The gold foil only has a few layers of atoms and most of an atom's volume is empty space • **Q3b** The tiny positive nuclei in the gold atoms were repelling the positively charged alpha particles and causing them to change course • **Q3ci** Ne: 2.8 • **Q3cii** P: 2.8.5 • **Q3ciii** Be: 2.2 • **Q3civ** Ar: 2.8.8 • **Q3cv** K: 2.8.8.1 • **Q3cvi** O: 2.6

C4b: Ionic bonding

Resources

Student Book pages 146–147 • Equipment for demonstrations

Interactive Book Quick starter: Predicting the formula of calcium fluoride • Naked Scientist animation: What is ionic bonding? • Practical investigations: Making salt in space

Files on Teacher Pack CD: c4_b_01_worksheet; c4_b_01_technician

Learning objectives

- Explain how and why ions form.
- Deduce the formulae of ionic compounds.

Learning outcomes

- Recall that an ion is a charged atom or group of atoms.
- Recognise an ion, an atom and a molecule from given formulae.
- Understand that atoms with an outer shell of eight electrons have a stable electronic structure.
- Explain how and why metal atoms form positive ions.
- Explain how and why non-metal atoms form negative ions.
- Understand that, in ionic bonding, a metal and non-metal combine by transferring electrons to form positive ions and negative ions that then attract one another.
- Deduce the formula of an ionic compound from the formula of the positive and negative ions.
- Explain, using the 'dot and cross' model, the ionic bonding in simple binary compounds (high demand).

Prior knowledge

Students should recognise which elements are metals and which are non-metals.

Key vocabulary

atom • bond • charge • dot and cross • lattice • metal • negative • non-metal • positive • stable electronic structure • transfer

Barriers to learning

Students must recognise that protons and electrons have equal and opposite charges. If their numbers become unequal, a charged ion forms.

Curiosity and starter suggestions

- Point to elements in the period table and challenge students to say whether they are metals or non-metals. If there is any confusion, students should mark the dividing line between metals and non-metals on their periodic tables.

OR

- Elicit students' ideas about how a neutral atom can turn into a positive or negative ion.

Learning activities

Worksheet c4_b_01

Low demand

Use Section 1 of Worksheet c4_b_01 to clarify the difference between atoms, ions and molecules.

Teaching and learning notes: *Models help to show the difference between the solid lattices in a metal or salt and the separate molecules in non-metal compounds. These molecules can be hung from the ceiling to emphasise that they are small and separate.*

Standard demand

Point out the noble gases in the periodic table and explain that they don't react and don't make molecules. They have stable electronic structures because they have full outer shells.

Contrast the noble gases with fluorine, the most violently reactive non-metal. If no video is available, describe how other elements burst into flames as soon as they come into contact with fluorine. Use the periodic table to show that fluorine only needs to gain one electron to get a full outer shell.

Use coloured balls to show that gaining an electron gives fluorine 10 negative electrons. As it only has nine positive protons to balance them, it will form a negative ion when it reacts. Contrast fluorine with sodium. Show how it can get a full outer shell by losing one electron and explain how this produces a positive ion.

Show how sodium and fluorine ions attract each other to form a crystal lattice and how the formula of a compound depends on the charges on its ions.

Students should complete Section 2 of worksheet c4_b_01 to check their understanding.

High demand

After students have completed the activities outlined in the previous sections, use the section *Describing ionic bonding* of the Student Book to explain Section 3 of Worksheet c4_b_01 to explain how to draw 'dot and cross' diagrams to model ionic bond formation.

Plenary suggestions

Name two elements and ask students to work out the formula of the compound they would form.

OR

Complete the questions from the relevant sections of the Student Book.

Assessment opportunities

Worksheet c4_b_01 provides staged opportunities to assess students' learning.

Answers

Student Book

Q1 O • **Q2** Mg^{2+} • **Q3** H_2 • **Q4** 3 • **Q5** Metal atoms have between one and three outer electrons, which they lose when they react; non-metal atoms gain electrons to fill their outer shell • **Q6** When an atom loses an electron, there are more positive charges than negative charges in the atom • **Q7** Metals transfer their electrons to the 'spaces' in the electron shells of non-metals • **Q8** Aluminium makes a 3+ ion and chlorine makes a 1– ion, so three chloride ions are needed to bond to one aluminium ion • **Q9**

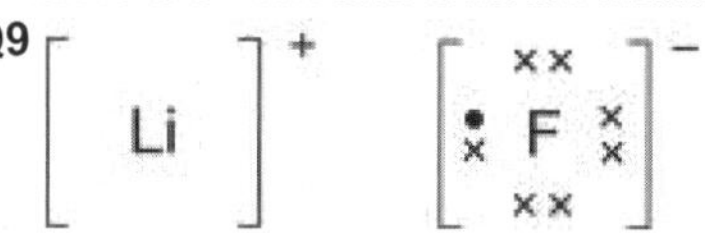

Figure 1 An atom of sodium that has lost one electron so is positively charged • **Figure 2** 8 • **Figure 3** Only the outer shell is shown and the sodium atom transferred its only outer electron to chlorine • **Figure 4** 8 • **Figure 5** To illustrate that they came from the magnesium atom

Worksheet

Q1a Atoms: H, O, F, Mg, Zn; ions: Ca^{2+}, Cl^{-}, NH_4^{+}, SO_4^{2-}; molecules: CO_2, H_2O, CH_4 • **Q1bi** Molecule • **Q1bii** Ions • **Q1biii** Ions • **Q1biv** Molecule • **Q2a** Because their outer shell is full • **Q2b** O^{2-}; F^{-} • **Q2c** Na^{+}; Mg^{2+}; Al^{3+} • **Q2di** Li^{+} • **Q2dii** Cl^{-} • **Q2diii** Ca^{2+} • **Q2div** S^{2-} • **Q2dv** Br^{-} • **Q2dvi** K^{+} • **Q2e** $MgBr_2$; K_2O; AlI_3; NaBr; CaO; $MgCl_2$ • **Q3a, b, c** and **d** are on the Teachers Pack CD

C4b: Ionic bonding

Resources

Student Book pages 148–149 • Equipment for demonstrations
Interactive Book Matching pairs: Identifying ionic compounds
Files on Teacher Pack CD: c4_b_02_worksheet; c4_b_02_technician

Learning objectives

- Compare the properties of ionic compounds.
- Relate the structures of ionic compounds to their properties.

Learning outcomes

- Compare the electrical conductivity of sodium chloride in solid, molten liquid and solution.
- Compare the melting points of sodium chloride and magnesium oxide.
- Recall that sodium chloride solution conducts electricity.
- Recall that magnesium oxide and sodium chloride conduct electricity when molten.
- Describe the structure of sodium chloride or magnesium oxide as a giant ionic lattice in which positive ions are strongly attracted to negative ions.
- Explain, in terms of structure and bonding, some of the physical properties of sodium chloride, including its high melting point and its electrical conductivity as a solid, a molten liquid and in solution (high demand).
- Explain, in terms of structure and bonding, why the melting point of sodium chloride is lower than that of magnesium oxide (high demand).
- Predict and explain the properties of substances that have a giant ionic structure (high demand).

Prior knowledge

Students should recognise that ions of opposite charge form when metals react with non-metals.

Key vocabulary

conducts electricity • giant ionic lattice • high melting point • stable octet

Barriers to learning

Students must recognise that the stronger the forces between a substance's particles, the harder it is to melt.

Curiosity and starter suggestions

- Pass round large crystals of rock salt.

OR

- Elicit students' ideas about the properties of salt. Will it melt or conduct electricity?

Learning activities

Worksheet c4_b_02

Low demand

Demonstrate that even a roaring Bunsen flame cannot melt sodium chloride or magnesium oxide and reveal that all ionic compounds have high melting points. Show that neither compound conducts electricity when solid, but sodium chloride does in solution, when its ions are free to move.

Use models to show the difference between a solid ionic compound and a molten one and reveal that all molten ionic compounds will conduct because their ions are free to move. Students sum up by completing Section 1 of Worksheet c4_b_02.

Standard demand

After students have completed the activities outlined in the previous section, let them look at sodium chloride under the microscope. Emphasise that the crystals have regular shapes because ions of opposite charge attract each other in every direction. Students should complete the diagram on Section 2 of Worksheet c4_b_02 to illustrate this.

High demand

Discuss the links between the structures of ionic compounds and their properties and use Section 3 of Worksheet c4_b_02 to check students' understanding.

Plenary suggestions

Ask groups to role play the changes in the properties of ionic compounds that take place when they are heated.

OR

Complete questions from the relevant sections of the Student Book.

Assessment opportunities

Worksheet c4_b_02 provides staged opportunities to assess students' learning.

Answers

Student Book

Q10 Its melting point is high, 804°C, because of its giant ionic lattice structure • **Q11** Soluble • **Q12** When solid • **Q13** Its melting point is very high, 2800°C, because of its giant ionic lattice structure • **Q14** When molten or dissolved in water • **Q15** Sodium chloride forms a cubic lattice with alternate positive sodium and negative chloride ions • **Q16** An outer shell filled with eight electrons • **Q17**

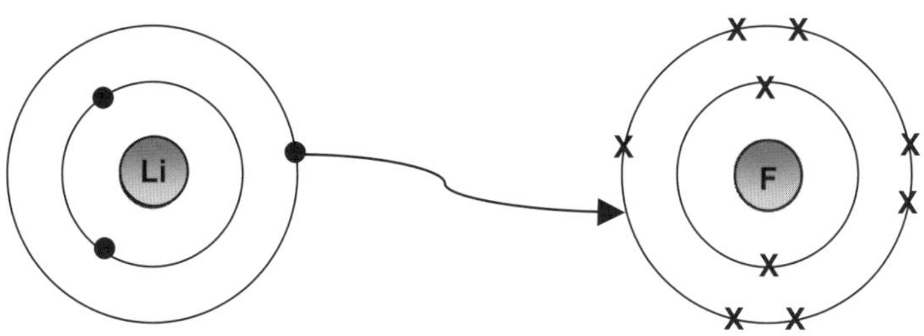

• **Q18**

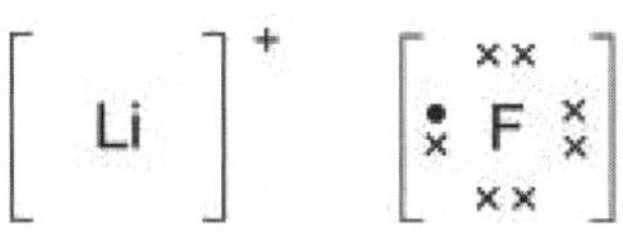

• **Q19**

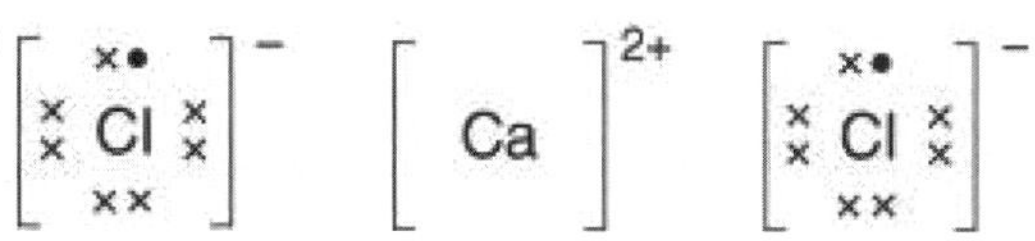

• **Q20** Each magnesium atom donates two electrons to an oxygen atom, which means that stronger ionic bonds exist between magnesium and the oxide than if only one electron was transferred; magnesium ions have a small radius so can get very close to oxygen atoms, which makes the bonds between magnesium and the oxide ion stronger • **Q21** The ions are not free to move • **Q22** The ions are free to move

Figure 6 The crystals in sodium chloride have a cubic shape • **Figure 7** It has evaporated. • **Figure 8** Chlorine • **Figure 9** It is cubic in shape • **Figure 10** For every one oxide ion, two sodium ions must bind • **Figure 11** For every one magnesium ion, two chlorines must bind

Worksheet

Q1 Magnesium oxide, electricity, high, conduct, dissolved • **Q2** Diagram should show alternating positive and negative ions throughout the lattice • **Q3a** 1C; 2D; 3B: 4A • **Q3b** The missing data is 2, $CaCl_2$, CaO, giant ionic lattice, does not conduct, conducts

C4c: The periodic table and covalent bonding

Resources

Student Book pages 150–151 • Equipment for demonstrations
Interactive Book Naked Scientist animation: What is covalent bonding? • Quick starter: How do we know sugar isn't ionic?
Files on Teacher Pack CD: c4_c_01_worksheet; c4_c_01_technician

Learning objectives

- Describe how non-metals combine by sharing electron pairs.

Learning outcomes

- Recall that there are two types of bonding – ionic bonding between metals and non-metals, and covalent bonding between non-metals.
- Recall that non-metals combine together by sharing electron pairs and that this is called covalent bonding.
- Describe carbon dioxide and water as simple molecules with weak intermolecular forces between molecules.
- Explain, using the 'dot and cross' model, the covalent bonding in simple binary compounds or molecules containing single and double covalent bonds (high demand).

Prior knowledge

Students should recognise that non-metals react to form compounds made of molecules.

Key vocabulary

covalent • covalent bonding • shared electrons • ionic bonding • metals • non-metals • transferring

Barriers to learning

Students must recognise that shared electrons contribute to each atom's outer shell of electrons.

Curiosity and starter suggestions

- Review ionic bonding by asking volunteers to role play the reaction between sodium and chlorine.

OR

- Elicit students' ideas about what holds the atoms in a molecule together.

Learning activities

Worksheet c4_c_01

Low demand

Challenge students to use molecular models to make H_2, Cl_2, CH_4, CO_2 and H_2O.

Pour out the beaker of model water molecules and explain that it takes very little energy to pull small molecules apart. Their boiling points are very low, so they are gases, or liquids like water. The molecules are not charged like ions, so they also do not conduct. Students sum up by completing Section 1 of Worksheet c4_c_01.

Teaching and learning notes: *If molecular models are unavailable use laminated circles of coloured card to make two-dimensional models.*

Standard demand

Use the model water molecules to contrast the weak intermolecular forces between covalent molecules with the strong bonds that hold the atoms together. Use the model hydrogen atoms to show how electron shells can overlap so that the electrons in them can be shared. Students should check their understanding by completing Section 2 of Worksheet c4_c_01.

Teaching and learning notes: *Make sure students understand the link between the number of outer electrons an atom has and the number of bonds it can form.*

High demand

After students have completed the activities in the previous sections, they should practice drawing dot and cross diagrams to model covalent bonding using Section 3 of Worksheet c4_c_01.

Plenary suggestions

Complete questions from the relevant sections of the Student Book.

OR

Show a space-filling model of a hydrogen sulfide molecule and challenge students to predict as much as they can about this chemical.

Assessment opportunities

Worksheet c4_c_01 provides staged opportunities to assess students' learning.

Answers

Student Book

Q1 Six • **Q2** Three • **Q3** Seven • **Q4** Five • **Q5** Covalent bonding • **Q6**

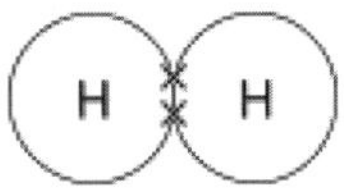

• **Q7** O=C=O • **Q8**

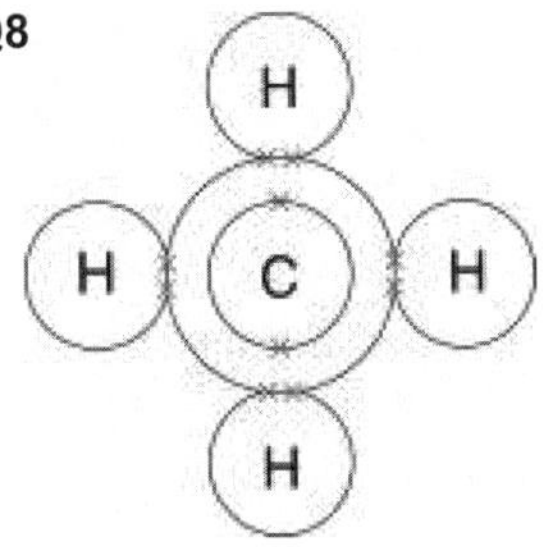

• **Q9**

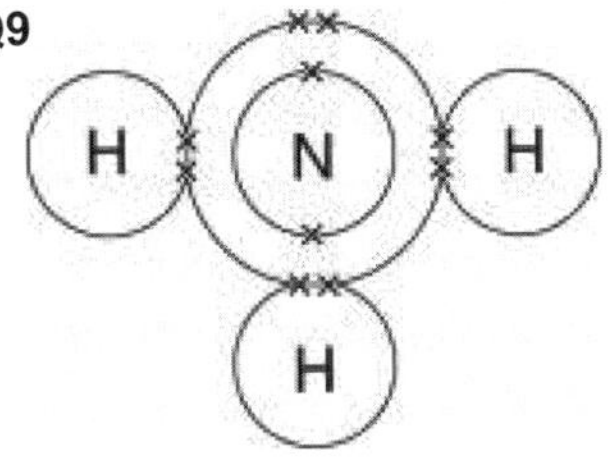

Figure 1 Both often contain sulfur compounds • **Figure 2** No • **Figure 3** Diatomic • **Figure 4** One – the hydrogen atoms each share one of their electrons with the oxygen atom • **Figure 5** Two – each oxygen gives two electrons to the carbon atom.

Worksheet

Q1 Covalent, oxygen, carbon dioxide, carbon dioxide, liquids, melting/boiling, boiling/melting, covalent • **Q2a** Carbon dioxide • **Q2b** See diagram below

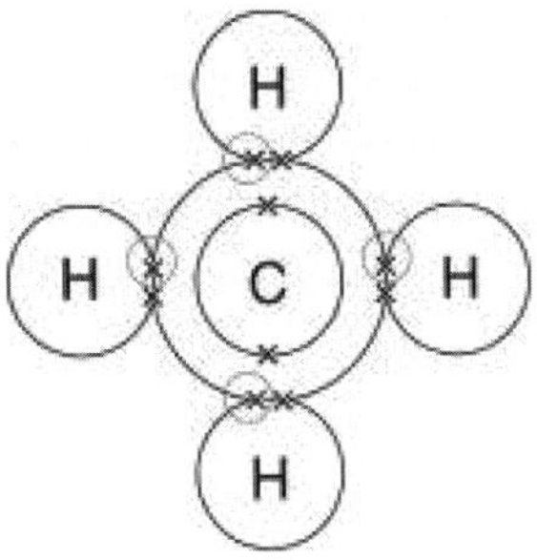

• **Q2**

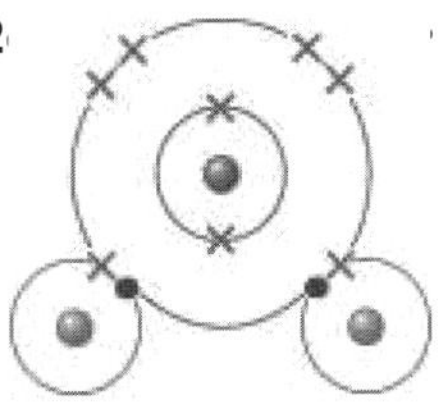

• **Q3a**

• **Q3b**

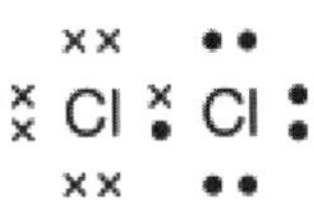

• **Q3c**

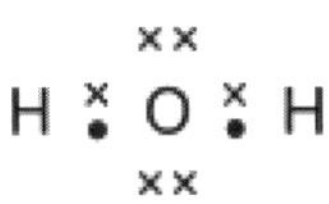

C4c: The periodic table and covalent bonding

Resources

Student Book pages 152–153 • Equipment for demonstrations
Interactive Book Drag and drop: Elements and compounds • Drag and drop: Classifying elements in the periodic table
Files on Teacher Pack CD: c4_c_02_worksheet; c4_c_02_technician

Learning objectives

- Relate an element's position in the periodic table to its atomic structure.
- Describe how the periodic table came to be developed.

Learning outcomes

- Recall that carbon dioxide and water do not conduct electricity.
- Deduce, using a periodic table, elements that are in the same group.
- Describe a group of elements as all the elements in a vertical column of the periodic table and that the elements have similar chemical properties.
- Deduce, using a periodic table, elements that are in the same period.
- Describe a period of elements as all the elements in a horizontal row of the periodic table.
- Describe the main stages in the development of the classification of elements, including Dobereiner, Newlands and Mendeleev, and understand that classification of elements was provisional, based on evidence gathered at that time.
- Recognise that the group number is the same as the number of electrons in the outer shell.
- Deduce the group to which an element belongs from its electronic structure (limited to the s and p blocks).
- Recognise that the period to which the element belongs corresponds to the number of occupied shells in the electronic structure.
- Deduce the period to which the element belongs from its electronic structure.
- Explain, in terms of structure and bonding, some of the physical properties of carbon dioxide and water, such as low melting points and inability to conduct electricity (high demand).
- Predict and explain the properties of substances that have a simple molecular structure (high demand).
- Describe the evidence or observations that caused Newlands and Mendeleev to develop new models of periodic classification of elements, and (high demand only) explain how further evidence confirmed Mendeleev's ideas about the periodic table, including confirmation of his predictions about unknown elements, and how the results of investigations on atomic structure (mass number and electronic structure) agreed with his ideas.

Prior knowledge

Students should recognise the modern periodic table.

Key vocabulary

chemical properties • column • elements • group • period • row

Barriers to learning

Students must recognise that scientific ideas are provisional and may need to be modified as more evidence becomes available.

Curiosity and starter suggestions

- Elicit students' ideas about what is the same about the elements in a vertical group and what the elements in a horizontal period have in common.

OR

- Play a recording of Tom Lehrer's song 'The periodic table'.

Learning activities

Worksheet c4_c_02

Low demand

Use page 152 of the Student Book to remind students what a group and a period are and check that they can name the period and group for any element. Then explain how the periodic table was gradually put together. Students can summarise these points by completing Section 1 of Worksheet c4_c_02.

Teaching and learning notes: *A video about Mendeleev's work or the patterns in the periodic table would be useful at this point.*

Standard demand

Use the Group numbers section in the Students Book to remind students what is the same about the electronic structures of the elements in each group and period. Students should check their understanding by completing Section 2 of Worksheet c4_c_02.

Teaching and learning notes: *Students often find it helpful to count out the electronic structures of elements on the periodic table. They should start at hydrogen and restart from 1 at the end of each period.*

High demand

Discuss Mendeleev's contribution to the development of the periodic table and draw out the general point that scientific theories are more likely to be accepted if they make predictions that are later proved to be correct. Students should complete Section 3 of Worksheet c4_c_02 to check their understanding.

Plenary suggestions

Complete questions from the relevant sections of the Student Book.

OR

Challenge students to come up with arguments for and against putting hydrogen in group 1.

Assessment opportunities

The plenary assesses students' understanding.

Answers

Student Book

Q10 Beryllium, magnesium, calcium • **Q11** Lithium, beryllium, boron, carbon, nitrogen, oxygen, fluorine, neon • **Q12** Group 1 • **Q13** Lithium has only one electron in its outer shell • **Q14** Group 2 • **Q15** Nitrogen has electrons in two shells • **Q16** There are weak intermolecular forces between carbon dioxide molecules • **Q17** Water does not have free electrons • **Q18** Group 5, period 3

Figure 6 Lithium, sodium, potassium • **Figure 7** Sodium, magnesium, aluminium, silicon, phosphorus, sulfur, chlorine, argon • **Fig 11** The molecules are easier to separate so they have low melting and boiling points

Worksheet

Q1a–d Diagram labelled to show group and period numbers and the symbols of the elements in groups 1, 7 and 8 • **Q1e** Properties, eight, elements, similar, predicted, strengthened • **Q2a** 2.4; period 2, group 4 • **Q2b** 2.8.7; period 3, group 7 • **Q2c** 2; period 1, group 8 • **Q2d** 2.8; period 2; group 8 • **Q2e** 2.6; period 2; group 6 • **Q3a** Group 8 • **Q3b** One of gallium, indium, thallium • **Q3c** Gallium matches all of Mendeleev's predictions • **Q3d** The row (period) an element is in indicates the number of its shells that contain electrons; the column (group) an element is in indicates the number of electrons in its outer shell

C4d: The group 1 elements

Resources

Student Book pages 154–155 • Equipment for demonstrations
Interactive Book Matching pairs: Alkali metals • Practical investigations: Acids, alkalis and bases
Files on Teacher Pack CD: c4_d_01_worksheet; c4_d_01_technician

Learning objectives

- Describe the physical and chemical properties of group 1 elements.
- Write equations for their reactions with water.

Learning outcomes

- Recognise sodium, lithium and potassium as group 1 elements.
- Explain why the group 1 elements are known as the alkali metals.
- Explain why group 1 elements are stored under oil.
- Describe the reactions of lithium, sodium and potassium with water, noting that hydrogen is formed and an alkali is formed, which is the hydroxide of the reacting metal.
- Construct the word equation for the reaction of a group 1 element with water.
- Predict the physical properties of rubidium and caesium and how they react with water.
- Construct a balanced symbol equation for the reaction of a group 1 element with water (high demand).

Prior knowledge

Students should recognise that the group 1 metals have similar chemical and physical properties.

Key vocabulary

alkali • balanced • density • hydroxide • reactivity

Barriers to learning

Students must recognise that the patterns and trends in the periodic table allow the properties of unknown elements to be deduced.

Curiosity and starter suggestions

- Show bottles of group 1 metals and elicit students' ideas about why they are stored under oil and why the pieces are so small.

OR

- Drop nails into water and ask students if a solid lump of metal could ever float on water.

Learning activities

Worksheet c4_d_01

Low demand

Demonstrate the reactions of lithium, sodium and potassium with water and emphasise the similarities between them, the way they get softer and less dense going down the group and the way their reactivity increases going down the group. Students sum up by completing Section 1 of Worksheet c4_d_01.

Teaching and learning notes: *Do make sure everything needed for the demonstration is set up before the lesson and check the safety precautions listed on the technicians guide (Technician c4_d_01). It is helpful to follow up the demo with a video so students can see close-ups of the metals and their reactions with water.*

Standard demand

Use Section 2 of Worksheet c4_d_01 to explain how patterns and trends in the properties of the elements let us predict what the rest of the group will be like. Check that students appreciate that chemicals with hydroxide groups in them make alkaline solutions when they dissolve.

Teaching and learning notes: *A video of rubidium and caesium reacting is useful to confirm the trends students have identified.*

High demand

After students have completed the activities in the previous sections, they should use Section 3 of Worksheet c4_d_01 to practice interpolating and extrapolating graphs in order to estimate unknown values.

Plenary suggestions

Present the scenario that a new element, explosium, has been discovered. Its atomic number places it below francium in the periodic table. Challenge the students to predict as much as they can about the element.

OR

Complete the questions from the relevant sections of the Student Book.

Assessment opportunities

Worksheet c4_d_01 provides staged opportunities to assess students' learning.

Answers

Student Book

Q1 Any three of lithium, sodium, potassium, rubidium, caesium, francium • **Q2** Silver and shiny • **Q3** They react easily with oxygen and water • **Q4** Lithium • **Q5** Lithium + water → lithium hydroxide + hydrogen • **Q6** Its density is less than that of water • **Q7** They react with water to form alkalis • **Q8** Reactivity increases down the group • **Q9** More vigorous than that with sodium • **Q10** Lower than lithium's melting point • **Q11** $2K + 2H_2O \rightarrow 2KOH + H_2$ • **Q12** Caesium hydroxide

Figure 1 Shiny and silver • **Figure 2** Alkali metals • **Figure 3** Potassium • **Figure 4** Hydrogen

Worksheet

Q1a Alkali metals, water/oxygen, oxygen/water, hydrogen, sodium hydroxide, hydrogen, lilac • **Q1b** Reactivity increases down the group • **Q1c** Observations to illustrate the reactivity of the metals, for example potassium produces a lilac flame when it reacts, lithium releases fewer bubbles than both lithium and sodium • **Q2a** They will react more violently with water than with potassium, because the reactivity of group 1 metals increases going down the group • **Q2b** A, sodium; B, oxygen; C, hydrogen • **Q2c** $2Na + 2H_2O \rightarrow 2NaOH + H_2$ • **Q2d** $2K + 2H_2O \rightarrow 2KOH + H_2$, $2Rb + 2H_2O \rightarrow 2RbOH + H_2$ • **Q2e**The hydroxide ions formed are alkaline • **Q3** Potassium melting point, 55–65°C; francium melting point, 26–30°C; the students' graph should show points correctly plotted, with labelled axes and a curve of best fit

melting point trends in group 1

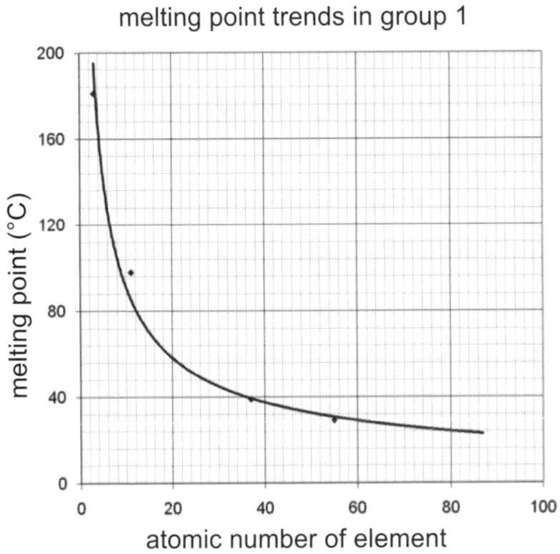

C4d: The group 1 elements

Resources

Student Book pages 156–157 • Equipment for demonstrations and practical
Interactive Book Matching pairs: Testing for ions • Practical investigations: Flame tests
Files on Teacher Pack CD: c4_d_0 2_worksheet; c4_d_02_technician.

Learning outcomes

- Use flame test results to identify group 1 metal ions.
- Use ideas about ion formation to explain the similarities and differences between group 1 metals.
- Use ionic equations to deduce when oxidation is taking place.

Learning outcomes

- Note that the reactivity of group 1 metals with water increases down group 1 and that potassium gives a lilac flame.
- Recall the flame test colours for lithium, sodium and potassium compounds.
- Interpret information about flame tests, for example deduce the alkali metal present from flame colours.
- Describe how to use a flame test to identify the presence of lithium, sodium and potassium compounds, namely the use of moistened flame test wire dipped into a solid sample and then put into blue Bunsen flame.
- Explain why group 1 elements have similar properties in terms of forming positive ions with stable electronic structures (high demand).
- Construct a balanced symbol equation to show the formation of an ion of a group 1 element from its atom (high demand).
- Explain, in terms of electron loss, the trend in reactivity of the group 1 elements with water (high demand).
- Recall the loss of electrons as oxidation and use the ionic equation of a process to explain why it is oxidation (high demand).

Prior knowledge

Students should recognise that group 1 compounds contain ions.

Key vocabulary

ion • ionic equation • oxidation • stable electronic structure

Barriers to learning

Students must recognise that elements with the same number of outer electrons have similar chemical properties.

Curiosity and starter suggestions

- Elicit students' ideas about what makes fireworks coloured.

OR

- Carry out the flame test demonstration using the spray bottles without revealing the chemical in each spray.

Learning activities

Worksheet c4_d_02

Low demand

Explain that all the group 1 metals form white compounds which look very similar, but each metal ion gives a different colour in a Bunsen flame. Demonstrate how to carry out a flame test and ask students to find out which colour each metal ion gives. They can record their results by completing Section 1 of Worksheet c4_d_02.

Teaching and learning notes: *To avoid contamination of the samples, give each group a different metal compound and allow the groups to swap places to see the other compounds. Keep the room well ventilated during the practical and ensure that eye protection is worn at all times.*

Standard demand

Students complete Section 2 of Worksheet c4_d_02 to record how they carried out the test.

Teaching and learning notes: *If the potassium becomes contaminated with sodium, blue glass can be used to filter out the sodium's colour and make the lilac visible.*

High demand

Section 3 of Worksheet c4_d_02 explains where the colour comes from. Students do not need to know this but it is a useful introduction to the fact that moving an electron further from the nucleus takes energy.

Remind students that the metal ions identified by the flame tests were all formed during reactions with non-metals. Their outer electrons were removed completely to leave 1+ ions, which is oxidation. Use page 157 of the Student Book to explain how to write an equation for the process and why the outer electron is harder to remove when there are fewer electron shells.

Teaching and learning notes: *Stress that the group 1 elements react in the same way because they all have one electron in their outer shell, but their reactivity increases as the number of electron shells increase because the outer electrons become easier to remove.*

Plenary suggestions

Complete questions from the relevant sections of the Student Book.

OR

Display images of lithium and potassium atoms and challenge students to note down as many things as possible that are the same about them and also their major differences.

Assessment opportunities

The plenary is an opportunity to assess students' learning.

Answers

Student Book

Q13 Yellow • **Q14** Lilac • **Q15** Lithium • **Q16** Hydrochloric acid • **Q17** A blue Bunsen flame • **Q18** Potassium • **Q19** One • **Q20** To form a full outer shell – this gives them a stable electronic structure • **Q21** Sodium loses the electron from its third electron shell, lithium loses the electron from its second electron shell; sodium's outer electron is further away from the attractive pull of the nucleus than lithium's outer electron, so it is more easily lost • **Q22** Oxidation • **Q23** $Li - e^- \rightarrow Li^+$

Figure 9 Sodium

Worksheet

Q1 Potassium, blue, metal, lithium, lilac, sodium • **Q2** Bunsen, acid, wire

C4: Applying your knowledge

Pages 158–159 in the Student Book prepare students for assessment.

When and how to use these pages

This task provides an opportunity to build and assess the skills that students will use when planning an investigation.

Annotated hints and tips guide students through the tasks. Ask students to:

- read through the context and tasks, listing any terms that they do not understand
- as a whole class or in small groups, discuss the tasks to ensure all students understand the terminology used and to clarify what is required
- work individually to answer the questions for each task.

If time allows, ask students to mark each other's work using the mark scheme provided.

Notes

The task is based on item d – The group 1 elements and should be used after this item is completed.

Answers

This mark scheme is also available on the Teacher Pack CD.

Task	Answer	Notes
1	Hold a lit splint over a tube of the gas If hydrogen is present, it burns with a 'squeaky pop'	This is a simple recall question
2	Potassium	This is a simple recall question
3	Purple Potassium hydroxide Group 1 metals are called alkali metals because they produce alkalis when they react with water The reaction is very exothermic and produces a flame and a corrosive alkaline solution so the experimenter should stand behind a safety screen to protect themselves from splashes or pieces of potassium	Standard demand should be able to recall the product of the reaction, realise that it is alkali and state the colour change with Universal Indicator A student who shows complete understanding is heading towards grade A*
4	$2K + 2H_2O \rightarrow 2KOH + H_2$ potassium + water → potassium hydroxide + hydrogen	
5	Table salt is sodium chloride, NaCl a compound of sodium and chlorine Chlorine	

Notes

C4e: The group 7 elements

Resources

Student Book pages 160–161 • Equipment for demonstrations
Files on Teacher Pack CD: c4_e_01_worksheet; c4_e_01_technician

Learning objectives

- Describe the physical and chemical properties of group 7 elements.
- Write equations for their reactions with group 1 elements.

Learning outcomes

- Recall that the group 7 elements are known as the halogens.
- Recognise fluorine, chlorine, bromine and iodine as group 7 elements.
- Describe the physical appearance of the group 7 elements at room temperature – for example, chlorine is a green gas, bromine is an orange liquid and iodine is a grey solid.
- Describe the uses of some group 7 elements, including that chlorine is used to sterilise water and to make pesticides and plastics, and iodine is used to sterilise wounds.
- Recognise that group 7 elements react vigorously with group 1 elements.
- Identify the metal halide formed when a group 1 element reacts with a group 7 element.
- Construct the word and symbol equations for the reaction between a group 1 element and a group 7 element.

Prior knowledge

Students should expect the group 7 elements to show patterns and trends in their properties.

Key vocabulary

alkali metals • halogens • metal halide • reactants • trend

Barriers to learning

Students must recognise that, although group 7 elements form diatomic molecules, they react to form separate negative ions.

Curiosity and starter suggestions

- Show a video of sodium reacting with chlorine if this won't be carried out as a demonstration later.

OR

- Read lines 9–14 of the Wilfred Owen poem *Dulce et Decorum Est* and ask students what gas the author is referring to. Stress that the gas is toxic at high concentrations, but only kills bacteria at the concentrations found in swimming pools.

Learning activities

Worksheet c4_e_01

Low demand

Demonstrate the appearance of chlorine, bromine and iodine or show images of the elements. Stress that bromine is a very volatile liquid, rather than a gas at room temperature. Sealed tubes of iodine could be passed around the class. The colour of iodine vapour can be demonstrated by warming the iodine crystals in hot water.

Demonstrate the reaction between sodium and chlorine, or show a video of it. Stress that every group 1 element reacts with every group 7 element. Students can practice writing word equations for the reactions using Section 1 of Worksheet c4_e_01.

Teaching and learning notes: *If the appearance and reactivity of the halogens are demonstrated, everything should be prepared before the lesson and kept in the fume cupboard. See Technician c4_e_01 for guidance.*

Standard demand

Remind students that not only do elements in a group have similar chemical reactions, but also they show trends in their physical properties and reactivity. Students should complete Section 2 of Worksheet c4_e_01.

Teaching and learning notes: *Make sure students understand that the formula shows the number of each atom in the smallest piece of the compound, so we write 2NaCl rather than* Na_2Cl_2 *if we have twice as much.*

High demand

Remind students how to use the charges on ions to work out the formula of a compound, then write the formulae in their equation and finally balance it.

Section 3 of Worksheet c4_e_01 can be used to practice extrapolating graphs in order to make predictions.

Teaching and learning notes: *Make sure students understand where to put the x-axis when they need to plot negative numbers.*

Plenary suggestions

Complete questions from the relevant sections of the Student Book.

OR

Name a halogen and challenge students to write five things they know about it.

Assessment opportunities

Worksheet c4_e_01 provides staged opportunities to assess students' learning.

Answers

Student Book

Q1 Sterilising water • **Q2** Sterilising wounds • **Q3** Alkali metals • **Q4** Bromine • **Q5** Grey solid • **Q6** Potassium bromide • **Q7** Sodium + chlorine → sodium chloride • **Q8** Chlorine is a diatomic molecule • **Q9** There is only one chloride ion with each potassium ion • **Q10** $2Li + Cl_2 \rightarrow 2LiCl$

Figure 2 The halogens • **Figure 6** Orange • **Figure 7** Sodium chloride • **Figure 8** 1871

Worksheet

Q1a Halogens, green, liquid, solid, purple, metals, sodium/potassium/lithium, down, sodium chloride • **Q1b** Lithium chloride • **Q1c** Potassium bromide • **Q1d** Sodium iodide • **Q1e** Lithium iodide • **Q1f** Potassium fluoride • **Q1g** Sodium bromide • **Q2a** Chlorine, green, gas; bromine, orange, liquid, iodine, grey, solid • **Q2b** Black solid • **Q2c** $2Na + Cl_2 \rightarrow 2NaCl$ • **Q2d** $2K + Br_2 \rightarrow 2KBr$ • **Q2e** $2Li + I_2 \rightarrow 2LiI$ • **Q2f** $2K + F_2 \rightarrow 2KF$ • **Q2g** $2Na + As_2 \rightarrow 2NaAs$ • **Q2h** $2Li + Br_2 \rightarrow 2LiBr$ • **Q3** 290–300°C

C4e: The group 7 elements

Resources

Student Book pages 162–163 • Equipment for demonstrations and practical
Files on Teacher Pack CD: c4_e_02_worksheet; c4_e_02_technician

Learning objectives

- Use ideas about ion formation to explain the similarities and differences between group 7 metals.
- Use ionic equations to deduce when reduction is taking place.

Learning outcomes

- Recall that the reactivity of the group 7 elements decreases down the group.
- Construct the word and symbol equations for the reaction between a group 7 element and a metal halide.
- Predict the properties of fluorine or astatine given the properties of the other group 7 element, for example physical properties, melting point, boiling point and displacement reactions.
- Describe the displacement reactions of group 7 elements with solutions of metal halides – chlorine displaces bromides and iodides, and bromine displaces iodides.
- Predict the feasibility of displacement reactions, for example will bromine react with sodium astatide solution (high demand).
- Explain why group 7 elements have similar properties in terms of forming negative ions with stable electronic structures (high demand).
- Construct an equation to show the formation of a halide ion from a halogen molecule (high demand).
- Explain, in terms of electron gain, the trend in reactivity of the group 7 elements (high demand).
- Recall the gain of electrons as reduction, and explain why a process is reduction from its ionic equation (high demand).

Prior knowledge

Students should recognise that non-metals react to form compounds made of molecules.

Key vocabulary

displacement • reactivity • reduction

Barriers to learning

Students must recognise that group 7 elements are coloured, but the ions present in their compounds are not.

Curiosity and starter suggestions

- Name that halogen quiz: call out facts about a halogen and ask students to write down the correct symbol.

OR

- Show students a solution of iodine and ask them which halogen is dissolved in the water. Explain that iodine forms a purple vapour, but it makes red–brown solutions.

Learning activities

Worksheet c4_e_02

Low demand

Demonstrate the reaction between chlorine water and potassium bromide and prompt groups to come up with a hypothesis to explain the colour change. Use the term 'displacement' to describe this sort of reaction.

Students should use their hypothesis to predict what will happen if chlorine water is added to potassium iodide. Demonstrate this reaction and add hexane to the products to prove that iodine has been displaced. Check their understanding by asking them to predict what will happen when bromine is added to potassium chloride. Students could then complete Section 1 of Worksheet c4_e_02.

Teaching and learning notes: *It is helpful to display the names of the reactants to help students predict what the product must be. Students may need to be reminded that the products must contain the same atoms as the reactants, just in a different arrangement.*

Standard demand

Remind students that the halogens have similar chemical reactions, because they all have seven electrons in their outer shell, but show trends in their physical properties and reactivity. Students practice writing symbol equations for the reactions by completing Section 2 of Worksheet c4_e_02.

Teaching and learning notes: *Emphasise that the trend in reactivity is the opposite of that shown by group 1 elements. Those with smaller atoms, at the top of the group, are more reactive.*

High demand

Use Section 3 of Worksheet c4_e_02 to remind students that the group 7 halides are ionic compounds. So during a displacement reaction the more reactive element gains electrons and forms ions, which is oxidation.

Stress that it is easier for small non-metal atoms to form ions because the shell the electron fits into is closer to the nucleus. This explains why the trend in reactivity is the opposite of that shown by the group 1 metals, which react by losing electrons.

Teaching and learning notes: *Make sure students understand that no charges are shown when the formulae of ionic compounds are written, because the charges on the ions cancel each other out, but the compounds are made of ions rather than molecules.*

Plenary suggestions

Complete questions from the relevant sections of the Student Book.

OR

Role-play the displacement reaction between chlorine and potassium bromide.

Assessment opportunities

Worksheet c4_e_02 provides staged opportunities to assess students' learning.

Answers

Student Book

Q11 Fluorine • **Q12** Iodine • **Q13** Iodine • **Q14** Chlorine • **Q15** Reactivity decreases down the group • **Q16** Lithium chloride • **Q17** Solid • **Q18** One • **Q19** Reduction • **Q20** $I_2 + 2e^- \rightarrow 2I^-$ • **Q21** $F_2 + 2KI \rightarrow 2KF + I_2$

Worksheet

Q1a Chlorine, green; potassium bromide, colourless; potassium chloride, colourless; bromine, orange • **Q1b** Displacement • **Q1c** Potassium chloride + iodine • **Q1d** No reaction • **Q1e** Potassium bromide + iodine • **Q1f** Potassium iodide + astatine • **Q1g** Potassium fluoride + chlorine • **Q2a** $Cl_2 + 2KBr \rightarrow 2KCl + Br_2$ • **Q2b** $Cl_2 + 2KI \rightarrow 2KCl + I_2$ • **Q2c** $Br_2 + 2KI \rightarrow 2KBr + I_2$ • **Q2d** A more reactive non-metal, from higher in the group, displaces a less reactive one from its compounds • **Q2e** All halogens have seven electrons in their outer shells • **Q3a** They lose electrons and become atoms/molecules, which is oxidation • **Q2g** The shell the electron fits into is closer to the nucleus so the electron is attracted more strongly

C4f: Transition elements

Resources

Student Book pages 164–165 • Equipment for optional display • Computers with internet access and printing facilities
Files on Teacher Pack CD: c4_f_01_worksheet; c4_f_01_technician

Learning objectives

- Describe the properties and uses of transition elements and their compounds.

Learning outcomes

- Identify whether an element is a transition element from its position in the periodic table.
- Recognise that all transition elements are metals and have typical metallic properties.
- Deduce the name or symbol of a transition element using the periodic table.
- Recall that copper and iron are transition elements.
- Recall that compounds of transition elements are often coloured, such as copper compounds are often blue, iron(II) compounds are often light green and iron(III) compounds are often orange/brown.
- Recall that transition elements and their compounds are often used as catalysts – iron in the Haber process and nickel in the manufacture of margarine.

Prior knowledge

Students should be able to identify the transition metals in the periodic table.

Key vocabulary

catalyst • ductile • lustrous • malleable metals • periodic table • sonorous • transition metal

Barriers to learning

Students must recognise that the usefulness of metals depends on both their physical and chemical properties.

Curiosity and starter suggestions

- Ask students to list as many differences as possible between the transition metals on display and the group 1 metals they have seen earlier. Collate their ideas into a concise summary. Then ask what both groups have in common. These are the properties that all metals share.

OR

- Display a range of coloured compounds and elicit students' ideas about what they have in common.

Learning activities

Worksheet c4_f_01

Low demand

Section 1 of Worksheet c4_f_01 sets out the task. Ideally, each student should have their own computer.

Teaching and learning notes: *Before the lesson it is useful to prepare a list of suitable web links for the uses of iron and copper.*

Standard demand

Students extend their research to the colours of transition metal compounds, and their use as catalysts, following Section 2 of Worksheet c4_f_01.

Teaching and learning notes: *Again, make sure students have some useful links to start them off.*

High demand

Section 3 of Worksheet c4_f_01 is an optional extension activity to consolidate students understanding of the link between the charges on ions and the formulas of the compounds they make.

Plenary suggestions

Complete questions from the relevant sections of the Student Book.

OR

Students could swap places and peer-mark each other's research notes.

Assessment opportunities

The plenary is an opportunity to assess students' learning.

Answers

Student Book

Q1 Mn, Cr • **Q2** Any three from lustrous/shiny, can conduct electricity, are sonorous, conduct heat, are malleable, are ductile • **Q3** Blue • **Q4** Either iron is used in the Haber process or nickel is used in margarine manufacture • **Q5** There is a large amount of nitrogen in the air, which cannot be used by plants in its gaseous form; fertilisers convert nitrogen into ammonia and then into nitrates, so the nitrogen compounds can be taken up by plants

Figure 1 Copper, titanium, zinc and iron • **Figure 2** Co • **Figure 3** Blue, copper; turquoise, copper or nickel; orange/brown, iron(III); dark green, iron(II); red, cobalt

Worksheet

Q1 Students should list the names and symbols of five elements, including iron and copper, images of each element in use and a list of the properties that make it right for that job • **Q2a** Students should list the names and symbols of five elements, including iron and copper, and the names and colours of their compounds; they should also note that iron catalyses the Haber process for the production of ammonia, which is important for making fertilisers, and nickel catalyses the hydrogenation of vegetable oils, which is important for the manufacture of margarine, considered a healthier alternative to butter • **Q2b** Students should list the formula of each compound mentioned in Section 2, and the symbols of the ions it contains

C4f: Transition elements

Resources

Student Book pages 166–167 • Equipment for demonstrations and practical
Files on Teacher Pack CD: c4_f_02_worksheet; c4_f_02_practical; c4_f_02_technician

Learning objectives

- Describe the thermal decomposition of transition metal carbonates and write equations for the reactions.
- Describe the precipitation of transition metal hydroxides and write equations for the reactions.

Learning outcomes

- Describe thermal decomposition as a reaction in which a substance is broken down by heat into at least two other substances.
- Describe the thermal decomposition of carbonates of transition elements, including $FeCO_3$, $CuCO_3$, $MnCO_3$ and $ZnCO_3$, noting that a metal oxide and carbon dioxide is formed and that a colour change occurs.
- Construct word equations and (high demand) balanced symbol equations for the thermal decomposition of $FeCO_3$, $CuCO_3$, $MnCO_3$ and $ZnCO_3$.
- Recall that the test for carbon dioxide is that it turns limewater milky.
- Describe precipitation as a reaction between solutions that makes an insoluble solid.
- Describe the use of sodium hydroxide solution to identify the presence of transition metal ions in solution, where Cu^{2+} gives a blue solid, Fe^{2+} gives a grey/green solid and Fe^{3+} gives an orange/brown solid, and note that the solids are called precipitates.
- Construct balanced symbol equations for the reactions between Cu^{2+}, Fe^{2+} and Fe^{3+} with OH^{-} (without state symbols) given the formulae of the ions (high demand).

Prior knowledge

Students should recognise from their earlier work with limestone that carbonates decompose when heated.

Key vocabulary

carbonates • gelatinous • iron(II) • iron(III) • limewater • milky • precipitation • thermal decomposition

Barriers to learning

Students must recognise that thermal decomposition is different from burning because it splits substances up.

Curiosity and starter suggestions

- Heat copper carbonate in an evaporating basin so that students can observe the surface bubbling and turning black as carbon dioxide escapes. Elicit students' ideas about what is happening during the reaction.

OR

- Display two sentences and ask students to decide what is wrong with each statement: transition metals are often coloured; when a compound decomposes it breaks up into separate atoms.

Learning activities

Worksheet c4_f_02 + Practical c4_f_02

Low demand

Explain that transition metal carbonates decompose when they are heated, discuss how we can tell this from their colours and by detecting the carbon dioxide produced and demonstrate the apparatus they will use. Students should test copper carbonate and, if time, another carbonate of their own choice. Set up an area where students can collect their results together to allow their reproducibility to be checked and a class average to be determined for each carbonate. Agree the values of the control variables that groups need to keep the same so that valid comparisons can be made between their results.

Once the results have been collected, comment on their reproducibility and suggest ways to improve the precision of the measurement of the time taken, for example by comparing each sample of limewater with a standard milky sample. Students could complete Section 1a–c of Worksheet c4_f_02 to practice writing word equations.

Show students samples of copper(II) sulfate, iron(II) sulfate and iron(III) sulfate and ask them to deduce which metals they contain. Introduce precipitation reactions as a way of confirming which metal is present.

Demonstrate how to add a few drops of sodium hydroxide to each test solution to form a precipitate. Students should then complete Section 1 of Worksheet c4_f_02.

Teaching and learning notes: *Make sure students are aware of the need to avoid 'suck-back' into the delivery tube when they heat carbonates. They must remove the delivery tube from the limewater before they stop heating. They must not touch any spilt solids and must take care dismantling the apparatus, as it may be very hot.*

Before the lesson, it is useful to set up a spreadsheet to calculate the average and the maximum and minimum values for each carbonate as a guide to the reproducibility of the results.

When they are making precipitates, warn students that each pipette must only be used for one solution.

Standard demand

After the practical activities detailed in the previous section, use Section 2 of Worksheet c4_f_02 to look at decomposition and precipitation reactions in more detail.

High demand

Use Section 3 of Worksheet c4_f_02 to look at what happens to transition metal ions when their compounds decompose or take part in precipitation reactions.

Plenary suggestions

Complete questions from the relevant sections of the Student Book.

OR

Role-play a decomposition or precipitation reaction.

Assessment opportunities

Worksheet c4_f_02 provides staged opportunities to assess students' learning.

Answers

Student Book

Q6 A reaction in which a substance is broken down by heat into two or more substances • **Q7** Pass the gas through limewater; if carbon dioxide is present the solution will turn milky • **Q8** A reaction in which two solutions form an insoluble solid • **Q9** Copper carbonate → copper oxide + carbon dioxide • **Q10** Carbon dioxide • **Q11** Zinc carbonate → zinc oxide + carbon dioxide • **Q12** Sodium hydroxide • **Q13** Copper • **Q14** Add sodium hydroxide to both solutions; the solution containing copper should form a blue precipitate, the solution containing iron should form a pale green precipitate if iron(II) is present or an orange/brown precipitate if iron(III) is present • **Q15** $NiCO_3 \rightarrow NiO + CO_2$ • **Q16** To balance the charge on the Cu^{2+} ion • **Q17** To balance the charge on the Fe^{3+} ion

Figure 5 Potassium chromate and silver nitrate • **Figure 6** From left to right: iron(II) hydroxide, iron(III) hydroxide, copper hydroxide

Worksheet

Q1a Copper carbonate, green; copper oxide, black; carbon dioxide, colourless • **Q1b** Thermal decomposition • **Q1c** Iron(II) oxide + carbon dioxide; manganese(II) oxide + carbon dioxide • **Q1d** Copper(II) sulfate, blue; iron(II) sulfate, pale green: iron(III) nitrate, orange/brown • **Q1e** Shake the soil with water, filter, add sodium hydroxide to the filtrate • **Q2a** A, zinc; B, carbon; C, oxygen • **Q2b** Zinc carbonate → zinc oxide + carbon dioxide • **Q2c** The carbonate breaks down into an oxide and carbon dioxide • **Q2d** Sodium, hydroxide • **Q2e** Copper hydroxide • **Q2f** The precipitate is always iron(III) hydroxide • **Q3a** The charges on their ions cancel out • **Q3b** $CuCO_3 \rightarrow CuO + CO_2$ • **Q2c** $MCO_3 \rightarrow MO + CO_2$, where M can be any metal tested • **Q2d** $Fe^{2+} + 2OH^- \rightarrow Fe(OH)_2$, $Fe^{3+} + 3OH^- \rightarrow Fe(OH)_3$

C4g: Metal structure and properties

Resources

Student Book pages 168–169 • Equipment for optional demonstration
Files on Teacher Pack CD: c4_g_01_worksheet; c4_g_01_technician

Learning objectives

- Relate the properties of metals to their most important uses.

Learning outcomes

- Explain why iron is used to make cars and bridges.
- Explain why copper is used to make electrical wiring.
- List the physical properties of metals, including: lustrous, hard, high density, high tensile strength, high melting and boiling points, good conductors of heat and electricity.
- Interpret data about the properties of metals, for example hardness, density and electrical conductivity.
- Suggest properties needed by a metal for a particular given use.
- Explain why metals are suited to a given use (data will be provided).
- Recognise that the particles in a metal are held together by metallic bonds.
- Explain, in terms of structure, why metals have high melting points and boiling points and conduct electricity.
- Describe metallic bonding as the strong attraction between a sea of delocalised electrons and close-packed positive metal ions (high demand).

Prior knowledge

Students have compared iron and aluminium in the context of designing cars and have researched the properties and uses of transition metals.

Key vocabulary

conductor • density • delocalised electrons • ductile • lustrous • malleable • metallic bonds • tensile strength • thermal conductivity

Barriers to learning

Students must recognise that the physical properties of metals suit them to different roles.

Curiosity and starter suggestions

- Display a sample of iron and a sample of copper and ask which is the most expensive, softest, least reactive, most dense or best conductor. In every case it is copper.

OR

- Challenge students to come up with the best explanation of what these descriptions mean: lustrous, high tensile strength, high density.

Learning activities

Worksheet c4_g_01

Low demand

If students completed the *Useful metals* activity in Worksheet c4_f_01 it would be useful to display their findings as a starting point for this activity. Otherwise, display images of the main uses of copper and iron.

Use Section 1 of Worksheet c4_g_01 to reinforce the relationship between a metal's properties and uses.

Standard demand

Use Section 2 of Worksheet c4_g_01 to emphasise that the properties of metals are related to their structures. Also, explain how the atoms are bonded in metals.

Teaching and learning notes: *Make sure students understand that strong bonds lead to high melting points.*

High demand

Section 3 of Worksheet c4_g_01 extends the model introduced in section 2.

Plenary suggestions

Complete questions from the relevant sections of the Student Book.

OR

Which property quiz: call out uses of metals and ask students what property makes a metal right for that use, for example weights, wiring, mirrors, lift cables, bridges, nails and saucepans.

Assessment opportunities

The plenary is an opportunity to assess students' learning.

Answers

Student Book

Q1 Better conductor • **Q2** Strong **Q3** 3 mohs • **Q4** Gold is lustrous, soft, unreactive and too expensive for bulk uses • **Q5** It has strong metallic bonds • **Q6** By electrostatic forces of attraction between the delocalised electrons and positive metal ions • **Q7** By producing strong metallic bonding • **Q8** When heated, the atoms in a metal move further apart

Figure 2 Good conductor • **Figure 3** By metallic bonds • **Figure 4** Low density • **Figure 5** Delocalised electrons

Worksheet

Q1a Copper: high conductivity • **Q1b** Aluminium: low density • **Q1c** Tungsten: hardness • **Q1d** Tungsten: high melting point • **Q1e** Iron: hardness/low cost • **Q1f** High thermal conductivity • **Q1g** High tensile strength • **Q1h** Lustrous • **Q2a** Tungsten • **Q2b** It takes a lot of heat energy to break strong bonds • **Q2c** Copper, silver • **Q3** Tungsten and iron because they have high melting points

C4g: Metal structure and properties

Resources

Student Book pages 170–171 • Equipment for optional demonstrations • Computers with internet access
Files on Teacher Pack CD: c4_g_02_worksheet; c4_g_02_technician

Learning objectives

- Relate the uses of superconductors to their properties.

Learning outcomes

- Describe what is meant by the term superconductor.
- Recall that at low temperatures some metals can be superconductors.
- Describe the potential benefits of superconductors, including loss-free power transmission, super-fast electronic circuits and powerful electromagnets.
- Explain some of the drawbacks of superconductors (high demand).

Prior knowledge

Students have already been introduced to the structure of metals.

Key vocabulary

crystals • delocalised electrons • metal grains • resistance • superconductors • superconductivity

Barriers to learning

Students must recognise that new technology has benefits and drawbacks.

Curiosity and starter suggestions

- Show images of a magnetic resonance imaging (MRI) machine and a Maglev train and elicit ideas about what they have in common.

OR

- Show images of objects being levitated by powerful electromagnets and ask students what apparatus they would need to replicate the experiment.

Learning activities

Worksheet c4_g_02

Low demand

Section 1 of Worksheet c4_g_02 sets the task. Students must find out how superconductors are used in Maglev trains and consider positive and negative consequences of their introduction.

Standard demand

Use Section 2 of Worksheet c4_g_02 to extend students' research to include the use of superconductors in MRI machines.

Teaching and learning notes: *In each case, details of the way superconductors are used are not part of the specification. They are just a context for considering the benefits and drawbacks of new technology.*

High demand

Section 3 of Worksheet c4_g_02 extends the task introduced in Section 2 by getting students to look more closely at the drawbacks of using MRI machines.

Plenary suggestions

Use the optional demonstrations to show that metals are made of crystals and complete questions from the relevant sections of the Student Book.

OR

Collate the benefits and drawbacks of each of the new technologies students have considered.

Assessment opportunities

The reports of their research can be used to assess students' learning.

Answers

Student Book

Q9 Crystals • **Q10** Regular **Q11** At low temperatures • **Q12** Superconductors can make powerful electromagnets, that levitate the train above the track to cut friction • **Q13** Its resistance drops to zero • **Q14** The temperature at which a material becomes a superconductor • **Q15** Using a superconductor • **Q16** Students should discuss uses of loss-free power transmission, super-fast electronic circuits or powerful electromagnets • **Q17** Only metals (and some allotropes of carbon) have delocalised electrons • **Q18** Superconductors allow new technologies that require fast circuits, loss-free power transmission or powerful electromagnets, but the technologies are explosive because liquid nitrogen or helium needs to be used to cool the circuits • **Q19** MRI machines use superconductors to generate powerful magnetic fields, which allow detailed images of soft tissues to be made

Figure 8 Delocalised electrons

Worksheet

Q1 Students should describe (a) how superconductors are used in Maglev trains, (b) say who would benefit from the technology and (c) describe any disadvantages or risks of the technology • **Q2** Students should describe (a) what an MRI scanner does, and (b) what major drawbacks the powerful electromagnets in MRI machines have • **Q3** Students should describe (a) how superconductors are kept cool, and (b) suggest at least one argument for and one against their use

C4h: Purifying and testing water

Resources

Student Book pages 172–173 • Equipment for optional demonstration
Interactive Book icould career video: Eutrophication • Quick starter: Ranking water purification steps
Files on Teacher Pack CD: c4_h_01_worksheet; c4_h_01_technician

Learning objectives

- Explain why clean water is essential.
- Explain how and why water is purified.
- Explain why purification leaves soluble salts in water.

Learning outcomes

- Interpret simple data about water resources in the United Kingdom (no recall is expected).
- Recall different types of water resources found in the United Kingdom, including lakes, rivers, aquifers and reservoirs.
- Explain why water is a significant resource for many important industrial chemical processes, and why it must be conserved.
- List some of the pollutants that may be found in domestic water supplies, including nitrate residues, lead compounds and pesticide residues, and explain why water may contain some of these.
- List the types of substances present in water before it is purified, for example dissolved salts and minerals, microbes, pollutants, insoluble materials.
- Recall that chlorination kills microbes in water.
- Describe the water purification process to include filtration, sedimentation and chlorination.
- Explain why some soluble substances are not removed from water during purification (high demand).
- Explain the disadvantages of using the distillation of seawater to make large quantities of fresh water (high demand).

Prior knowledge

Students should recognise that filtration removes insoluble impurities from water, but only distillation will remove dissolved salt.

Key vocabulary

aquifer • borehole • chlorination • coolant • filtration • nitrate • pesticide • reservoir • residue • sedimentation

Barriers to learning

Students must recognise that water may contain dissolved pollutants even when it looks clean.

Curiosity and starter suggestions

- Display a sample of obviously dirty water from a local pond or stream and elicit students' ideas about what it might contain and how these contaminants could be removed.

OR

- Run a tap and ask students where the water is coming from and where it is going to.

Learning activities

Worksheet c4_h_01

Low demand

Show students the amount of residue left behind when tap water is evaporated to demonstrate that even water that looks clean contains dissolved solids. Explain that nitrates from fertiliser run-off are a common pollutant. Students could use nitrate-test strips to estimate this pollutant's concentration in tap water and a simulated river water sample. They should complete Section 1 of Worksheet c4_h_01 using page 172 of the Student Book for reference.

Standard demand

Use a video to show the main steps in the purification of water. A sand filter could be demonstrated at this point. Students could then complete Section 2 of Worksheet c4_h_01 using page 173 of the Student Book as a guide.

Teaching and learning notes: *For a suitable video on water purification visit www.southeastwater.co.uk and select 'Water treatment' from the 'Education' menu. If possible, arrange a visit to a water-treatment plant.*

High demand

Demonstrate that salty water gives a white precipitate with silver nitrate. Remind students what distillation involves and demonstrate that the distilled water produced does not give a precipitate with silver nitrate because the salt is left behind. Discuss the fact that using a fuel to distil the water would make it far too expensive, but distillation is a useful way of purifying water in places where solar energy can be used to evaporate it.

Plenary suggestions

Complete questions from the relevant sections of the Student Book.

OR

Name the pollutant: call out clues and ask students to identify the pollutants.

Assessment opportunities

The plenary is an opportunity to assess students' learning.

Answers

Student Book

Q1 It goes back into rivers • **Q2** Rain seeping through porous rocks **Q3** Nitrate residues, lead compounds, pesticide residues • **Q4** Nitrate and pesticide residues • **Q5** Students should state where their nearest water source is and whether anyone is likely to have drunk it before them • **Q6** Evaporating water, which takes huge amounts of energy • **Q7** Bacteria help to remove organic material from the water, so they are killed in the final stage in the purification process

Figure 2 Rivers, reservoirs, bore holes, aquifers and lakes • **Figure 3** To destroy microbes • **Figure 4** Farms

Worksheet

Q1a Clockwise from the top left, the labels are: rivers, reservoirs, bore holes, aquifers and lakes • **Q1b** Solvent, coolant, raw material • **Q1c** Dissolved salts and minerals, microbes, pollutants, insoluble materials • **Q1d** Nitrates, insecticides, lead • **Q1e** To destroy microbes • **Q2a** Filtration • **Q2b** Sedimentation • **Q2c** Chlorination • **Q3a** It makes water purification more expensive • **Q3b** The energy costs for evaporating the water would make it too expensive

C4h: Purifying and testing water

Resources

Student Book pages 174–175 • Equipment for demonstration and practical
Interactive resources Matching pairs: Identifying anions
Files on Teacher Pack CD: c4_h_02_worksheet; c4_h_02_practical; c4_h_02_technician

Learning objectives

- Describe how the soluble salts in water can be identified.

Learning outcomes

- Understand that the reactions of barium chloride with sulfates and silver nitrate with halides are precipitation reactions.
- Recall that barium chloride solution is used to test for sulfate ions and gives a white precipitate.
- Recall that silver nitrate solution is used to test for halide ions, and that chloride ions give a white precipitate, bromide ions give a cream precipitate and iodide ions give a pale yellow precipitate.
- Interpret data about the testing of water with aqueous silver nitrate and barium chloride solutions.
- Construct equations for the reactions of barium chloride with sulfates and silver nitrate with halides.

Prior knowledge

Students should recognise that precipitate reactions occur when insoluble compounds form in solution.

Key vocabulary

barium chloride • barium ions • chlorides • ions • precipitate • silver ions • silver nitrate • sulfates

Barriers to learning

Students must recognise that ionic compounds split into separate ions when they dissolve.

Curiosity and starter suggestions

- Demonstrate the precipitation reaction between lead nitrate and potassium iodide and elicit students' ideas about where the bright yellow solid comes from.

OR

- Display sodium sulfate and barium chloride and ask what products they might form when they react.

Learning activities

Worksheet c4_h_02 + Practical c4_h_02

Low demand

Groups complete Practical c4_h_02 and Section 1 of Worksheet c4_h_02.

Teaching and learning notes: *It is a good idea to demonstrate the difference between a drop of liquid and a squirt from a pipette before students begin work. Emphasise the importance of keeping one pipette for each solution.*

Standard demand

Students could then complete Section 2 of Worksheet c4_h_02 to gain practice at writing word equations.

Teaching and learning notes: *It is helpful to show students that ions appear to swap partners during precipitation reactions and let groups of four role play the process.*

High demand

Remind students how to use ionic charges to deduce the formulas of compounds. Then use Section 3 of Worksheet c4_h_02 to practice writing symbol equations.

Plenary suggestions

Complete questions from the relevant sections of the Student Book.

OR

Display pairs of solutions and ask students to describe what will happen when they mix.

Assessment opportunities

The plenary is an opportunity to assess students' learning.

Answers

Student Book

Q8 Silver nitrate • **Q9** White • **Q10** It takes energy to pump it from its source and to purify it • **Q11** A yellow precipitate • **Q12** A white precipitate • **Q13** Chlorine is added to water supplies to destroy microbes • **Q14** $AgNO_3 + KI \rightarrow KNO_3 + AgI$ • **Q15** $2AgNO_3 + CaCl_2 \rightarrow Ca(NO_3)_2 + 2AgCl$

Figure 6 Yellow

Worksheet

Q1a Barium chloride • **Q1b** A white precipitate of barium sulphate forms • **Q1c** Barium, ammonium • **Q1d** Silver nitrate • **Q1e** A white precipitate of silver chloride • **Q1f** Silver, sodium • **Q2a** Silver iodide + lithium nitrate • **Q2b** Barium sulfate + sodium chloride • **Q2c** Silver chloride + magnesium nitrate • **Q3a** $AgNO_3 + LiI \rightarrow LiNO_3 + AgI$ (yellow precipitate) • **Q3b** $BaCl_2 + Na_2SO_4 \rightarrow 2NaCl + BaSO_4$ (white precipitate) • **Q3c** $2AgNO_3 + MgCl_2 \rightarrow Mg(NO_3)_2 + 2AgCl$ (white precipitate)

C4: Research and collecting secondary data

Pages 176–177 in the Student Book prepare students for assessment.

When and how to use these pages

This task provides an opportunity to build and assess the skills that students will use when planning an investigation.

Annotated hints and tips guide students through the tasks.

Ask students to:

- read through the context and tasks, listing any terms that they do not understand
- as a whole class or in small groups, discuss the tasks to ensure that all students understand the terminology used and to clarify what is required
- work individually to answer the questions for each task.

If time allows, ask students to mark each other's work using the mark scheme provided.

Pages 278–290 provide further guidance on Practical and Enquiry Skills.

Notes

The worked example takes students through a planning task. Students are required to plan an investigation into the best site for a new reservoir. A group discussion could be used to help students consider where our water comes from and why reservoirs are needed.

In this practice activity, the data they need to find have already been selected for them but it is worth going through the information given and ensuring that students recognise why the information would be useful. The questions on page 177 take students through the remaining steps.

Answers

Research and collecting secondary data

Q1 Students should suggest a reputable source, e.g. drinking dater Inspectorate or the regional water boards.

Q2 The regional water boards.

Q3 The regional water boards.

Q4 The regional water boards, Ofwat or Department of the environment.

Q5 Met office.

Q6 Met office.

Q7 The regional water boards or Department of the environment.

Q8 To justify building a new reservoir, the demand in the area must exceed the expected supply.

Q9 In tables and charts.

Q10 Recommend where the new reservoir needs to be built. Recommend ways of reducing demand so that the new reservoir is not needed.

Notes

C4: Checklist

Pages 178–179 in the Student Book provide a student-friendly checklist for revision.

When and how to use these pages

This checklist is presented in three columns showing progression, based on the grading criteria.

Remind students that they need to be able to use these ideas in various ways, such as:

- interpreting pictures, diagrams and graphs
- applying ideas to new situations
- explaining ethical implications
- suggesting some benefits and risks to society
- drawing conclusions from evidence they have been given.

These pages can be used for individual or class revision using any combination of the suggestions below.

- Ask students to construct a mind map linking the points on this checklist.
- Work through the checklist as a class and note the points that need further class discussion.
- Ask students to tick the boxes on the checklist worksheet (Teacher Pack CD) if they feel confident that they are well prepared for the topics. Students should refer back to the relevant Student Book pages to revise the points that they feel less confident about.
- Ask students to use the search terms to do further research on the different points in the checklist.

Pages 278–299 provide further assessment guidance.

Module summary

In the introduction to this section, students were presented with a number of new ideas. Work through the list below as part of their revision. Ask students to write their own summaries and mind maps, using this list as a starting point.

- The structure of the atom
- How isotopes have different mass numbers
- How to recognise an ion from its formula
- How sodium chloride is a giant ionic lattice
- How elements in the same group have similar properties
- How elements in group 7 have seven outer electrons
- Why potassium reacts in a similar way to sodium
- How to predict the properties of group 1 elements
- How chlorine is used to sterilise water
- How to predict some reactions of group 7 elements
- Why compounds of transition metals are often coloured
- How to identify ions of copper using sodium hydroxide
- How to interpret data on the physical properties of metals
- Metals that conduct electricity by delocalised electrons
- Where important water resources are found
- The important stages in the water purification process.

Notes

C4: Exam-style questions: Foundation

Pages 180–181 in the Student Book are exam-style questions for Foundation students.

When and how to use these pages

These questions are based on module C4 and cover a range of different types of questions that students will encounter in their written exams.

- Questions could be used as a revision test once you've completed the section.
- Work through the questions as a class as part of a revision lesson.
- Ask students to mark each other's work, using the mark scheme provided.
- As a class, make a list of the questions that most students did not get right. Work through these as a class.

Notes on worked example

The worked example takes students through a structured question in which students are expected to recall the properties of transition metals.

Assessment objectives

These exam-style questions cover the Assessment objectives as described below.

Assessment objectives		Questions
AO1	Recall, select and communicate their knowledge and understanding of science	1a–b, 3a–b, d, 4a–d, 7
AO2	Apply skills, knowledge and understanding of science in practical and other contexts	2a–b, 7
AO3	Analyse and evaluate evidence, make reasoned judgements and draw conclusions based on evidence	6

Answers

These answers are also supplied on the Teacher Pack CD so that students can mark their own, or their peer's work.

<table>
<tr><th>Question number</th><th>Answer</th><th>Additional notes</th><th>Mark</th></tr>
<tr><td>1a</td><td><table><tr><td>Name of particle</td><td>Charge</td><td>Mass</td></tr><tr><td>proton</td><td>1</td><td>1</td></tr><tr><td>neutron</td><td>0</td><td>1</td></tr><tr><td>electron</td><td>-1</td><td>0</td></tr></table></td><td></td><td>3</td></tr>
<tr><td>b</td><td>Neutrons, atomic, protons, mass, isotopes, electrons</td><td></td><td>6</td></tr>
<tr><td colspan="3"></td><td>[9]</td></tr>
<tr><td>2a</td><td>13, 27, 13, 13, 14</td><td></td><td>5</td></tr>
<tr><td>b</td><td>2</td><td></td><td>2</td></tr>
<tr><td colspan="3"></td><td>[7]</td></tr>
<tr><td>3a</td><td>B</td><td></td><td>1</td></tr>
<tr><td>b(i)</td><td>Positive and negative ions held together in a crystal / lattice</td><td></td><td>2</td></tr>
</table>

b(ii)	Magnesium oxide		1
b(iii)	Solid sodium chloride: non-conductor Molten liquid sodium chloride and sodium chloride in solution: good conductors		2
			[6]
4a	Lithium hydroxide and hydrogen		2
b	More		1
c	Purple		1
d	They all have 1 electron in their outer shell		2
			[6]
5a	(see table below)		4
			[4]
6	C Yellow precipitate with silver nitrate shows iodide ions are present White precipitate with barium chloride shows sulfate ions are present		1 1 1
			[3]
7	Atoms are listed in order of atomic number / number of protons so that elements with the same number of outer electrons are in the same vertical column / group Dalton said that each element was made of indivisible atoms J. J. Thomson discovered electrons Rutherford discovered that atoms had a small positive nucleus Bohr, that electrons are in shells	Any 3 Allow 1 mark for quality of written communication	1 1 1 1 1 1
			[6]
			[41]

5a:

	Colour	State
chlorine	Green	gas
bromine	Brown/orange	Liquid
iodine	Purple/grey	Solid

C4: Exam-style questions: Higher

Pages 182–183 in the Student Book are exam-style questions for Higher students.

When and how to use these pages

These questions are based on module C4 and cover a range of different types of questions that students will encounter in their written exams.

- Questions could be used as a revision test once you've completed the section.
- Work through the questions as a class as part of a revision lesson.
- Ask students to mark each other's work, using the mark scheme provided.
- As a class, make a list of the questions that most students did not get right. Work through these as a class.

Notes on worked example

The worked example takes students through a structured question in which students are expected to recall and explain the properties of transition metals.

Assessment objectives

These exam-style questions cover the Assessment objectives as described below.

Assessment objectives		Questions
AO1	Recall, select and communicate their knowledge and understanding of science	1a, 3a–b(iii), 4d, 5, 7
AO2	Apply skills, knowledge and understanding of science in practical and other contexts	1b, 2a–b, 3b(iii), 4a–c, 7
AO3	Analyse and evaluate evidence, make reasoned judgements and draw conclusions based on evidence	6

Answers

These answers are also supplied on the Teacher Pack CD so that students can mark their own, or their peer's work.

<table>
<tr><th>Question number</th><th>Answer</th><th>Additional notes</th><th>Mark</th></tr>
<tr><td>1a</td><td><table><tr><td>Name of particle</td><td>Charge</td><td>Mass</td></tr><tr><td>proton</td><td>1</td><td>1</td></tr><tr><td>neutron</td><td>0</td><td>1</td></tr><tr><td>electron</td><td>-1</td><td>0</td></tr></table></td><td></td><td>3</td></tr>
<tr><td>b</td><td>Neutrons, isotopes
Carbon
6 protons, 6 electrons, 8 neutrons</td><td></td><td>2
1
1</td></tr>
<tr><td colspan="3"></td><td>[7]</td></tr>
<tr><td>2a</td><td>13, 27, 13, 13, 14</td><td></td><td>5</td></tr>
<tr><td>b</td><td>2.8.8.1</td><td></td><td>2</td></tr>
<tr><td colspan="3"></td><td>[7]</td></tr>
<tr><td>3a</td><td>A, C, D</td><td></td><td>3</td></tr>
<tr><td>b(i)</td><td>Positive and negative ions held together by</td><td></td><td>2</td></tr>
</table>

<table>
<tr><td></td><td>strong electrostatic forces</td><td></td><td></td></tr>
<tr><td>b(ii)</td><td>The (electrostatic) forces between the ions in magnesium oxide are stronger</td><td></td><td>2</td></tr>
<tr><td>b(iii)</td><td>Lithium donates its outer electron to fluorine
Diagram showing the outer shells of lithium and fluorine before and after the reaction
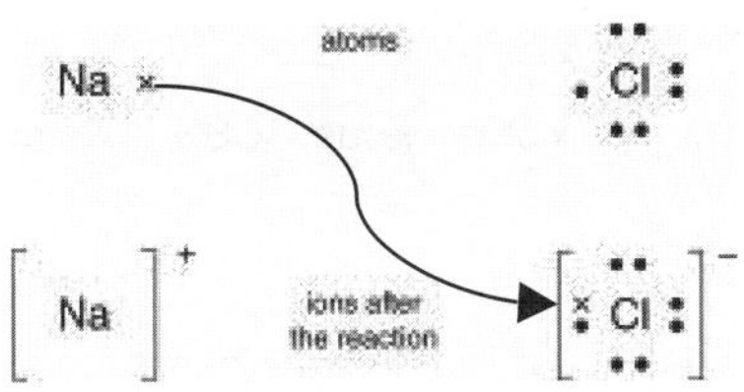
</td><td>The charges must be shown after the reaction.</td><td>1
1</td></tr>
<tr><td colspan="3"></td><td>[9]</td></tr>
<tr><td>4a</td><td>Caesium hydroxide and hydrogen</td><td></td><td>2</td></tr>
<tr><td>b</td><td>More reactive</td><td></td><td>1</td></tr>
<tr><td>c</td><td>Dull grey metal</td><td></td><td>1</td></tr>
<tr><td>d</td><td>They all have 1 electron
in their outer shell</td><td></td><td>2</td></tr>
<tr><td colspan="3"></td><td>[6]</td></tr>
<tr><td>5a</td><td><table><tr><td></td><td>Colour</td><td>State</td></tr><tr><td>chlorine</td><td>Green</td><td>gas</td></tr><tr><td>bromine</td><td>Brown/orange</td><td>Liquid</td></tr><tr><td>iodine</td><td>Purple/grey</td><td>Solid</td></tr></table></td><td></td><td>4</td></tr>
<tr><td colspan="3"></td><td>[4]</td></tr>
<tr><td>6</td><td>C
Yellow precipitate with silver nitrate shows iodide ions are present
White precipitate with barium chloride shows sulfate ions are present</td><td></td><td>1
1
1</td></tr>
<tr><td colspan="3"></td><td>[3]</td></tr>
<tr><td>7</td><td>Atoms are listed in order of atomic number / number of protons
so that elements with the same number of outer electrons are in the same vertical column / group
Dalton said that each element was made of indivisible atoms
J.J. Thomson discovered electrons
Rutherford discovered that atoms had a small positive nucleus
Bohr, that electrons are in shells</td><td>Any 3
Allow 1 mark for quality of written communication</td><td>1
1
1
1
1
1</td></tr>
<tr><td colspan="3"></td><td>[6]</td></tr>
<tr><td colspan="3"></td><td>[42]</td></tr>
</table>

P3: Introduction

Pages 184–185 in the Student Book provide an introduction to module P3.

When and how to use these pages

These pages summarise what students should already know from KS3 or previous GCSE units and provide an overview of the content that they will learn in this module.

- Use these pages as a revision lesson before you start the first new topic.
- Brainstorm everything that students remember about the different topics using the headings as a starting point. Compare your list with the points in the Student Book.
- Use the questions on the left-hand page as a starting point for class discussions.
- Ask students if they can tell you anything about the topics on the right-hand page.
- Make a note of any unfamiliar / difficult terms and return to these in the relevant lessons.

You can revisit these pages at the following points:

- before the lesson on Forces and motion pages 194–195
- before the lesson on Energy on the move pages 204–205
- before the lesson on Falling safely pages 212–213

Overview of unit

In this section students will learn how to analyse motion, drawing and using distance-time and speed-time graphs. Speed, average speed, velocity, relative velocity and acceleration are discussed.

The need for an unbalanced force to produce acceleration is considered and the equation F = ma introduced. The physics learned so far in this unit is applied to considerations of road safety, including the effect of speed on the stopping distance of a vehicle. The unit goes on to describe work and power, using car brakes and the Eurostar train as applications.

A comparison of petrol and diesel as car fuels is carried out, comparing fuel consumption and emissions. The issue of how we should fuel our cars in the future is discussed, considering electric – both battery and solar-powered – and the advantages of a hybrid vehicle, together with alternatives such as bio-fuels. Some car safety features, both to help to prevent accidents and to minimise injury in the event of a crash, are considered.

Vertical motion is analysed and the effect of the changing forces acting described. The unit ends by considering the energy changes in theme park rides such as roller coasters.

Barriers to learning

Students may need extra guidance with the following terms and concepts:

Speed

Students are confused by the various units used for speed and forget that m/s ***must*** be used in equations.

Distance–time and speed–time graphs

Students often confuse distance–time and speed–time graphs.

Describing motion

Make sure students describe motion unambiguously; for instance, NOT 'the car accelerates at a constant speed' to mean 'the car accelerates uniformly'.

Resultant force

Make sure students realise that the force in the equation 'force = mass x acceleration' refers to the resultant, or net, force acting on the mass.

Mass and weight

Students are often confused about the difference between mass, in kilograms, and weight, in newtons.

Work done

Some students find it difficult to understand that no work is done unless a force moves.

Using data

Encourage students to look for trends or patterns in data and use the information gained to support conclusions.

Considering evidence

Encourage students to express an opinion, backed up by evidence. They often find it difficult to deal with questions to which there is no precise answer.

Calculations

Some students may need extra help with the mathematical content, especially changing the subject of an equation.

Applying knowledge

Some students may need to be encouraged to consider an unfamiliar situation and suggest a solution.

Combining forces

Some students find it difficult to understand that it is the *resultant* force that affects the motion of an object.

Energy transfer

Ensure that students realise that energy cannot be lost, only transferred to other forms. There is a tendency to speak about lost energy in general usage, meaning wasted energy or a particular form of energy.

Practicals in this unit

In this unit students will do the following practical work:

- Investigating speed down a runway
- Obtaining measurements to draw a distance–time graph
- Measuring speed
- Measuring acceleration
- Estimating reaction time
- Investigating work done
- Investigating personal power
- Investigating stopping distance
- Investigating streamlining
- Modelling crumple zones and seat belts
- Designing and making a parachute
- Investigating vertical motion using a ping-pong ball
- Designing and building a roller coaster

Key vocabulary covered in this unit

average speed • instantaneous speed • speed • speed camera

accelerate • best-fit straight line • curved line • decelerate • gradient • straight line

acceleration • area • deceleration • distance • estimate • time

relative velocity • velocity

balanced • force • net • newton (N) • pull • resultant • unbalanced

brake pads • braking distance • reaction time • stopping distance • thinking distance • thinking time • tread • tyres

joule (J) • kinetic energy • mass • weight • work

carbon dioxide • greenhouse gases • kilowatt (kW) • power • watt (W)

bio-fuels • diesel • environment • fossil fuels • non-renewable • oil • petrol • pollution • renewable

air bag • brakes • conservation • crumple zones • escape lane • momentum • seatbelt • velocity •

ABS (anti-lock braking system) • cruise control • electric windows • paddle shift controls • safety cage • air resistance • balanced • drag • free-fall • gravity • molecules • terminal speed

friction • gravitational field strength • gravity • lubricate • streamline

air resistance • efficiency • gravitational potential energy • sound energy • thermal energy

funicular railway • heat • height • roller coaster • sound

P3a: Speed

Resources

Student Book pages 186–187 • Equipment for demonstrations and practical • ICT equipment
Interactive Book News clip: Penalty points!
Files on Teacher Pack CD: p3_a_01_worksheet; p3_a_01_practical; p3_a_01_technician

Learning objectives

- Calculate average speed.
- Describe how average speed is measured.
- Explain how speed cameras work.

Learning outcomes

- Be able to use the equation average speed = total distance / total time, with appropriate units.
- Describe that average speed can be found by measuring the distance covered in a known time.
- Explain how different types of speed camera measure speed and average speed.

Prior knowledge

What is meant by 'speed'.

Key vocabulary

average speed • distance • instantaneous speed • speed • speed camera • time

Barriers to learning

Students are confused by the various units used for speed and forget that m/s ***must*** be used in equations.

Curiosity and starter suggestions

- Match speeds to various objects.

OR

- Show video/photographs of cars over the last 100 years.

Learning activities

Worksheet p3_a_01 + Practical p3_a_01

Low demand

Discuss what is meant by 'speed'. Suggest suitable units depending on its value. Students can do the first starter activity, if not already used, to get an idea of speed values. Show video clips/photographs of things that move at different speeds.

Introduce the idea of average speed = distance / time. Work an example. Ask students to answer worksheet question 1 *Average speed.*

Ask what we need to measure to determine speed and discuss how, for a car passing the school and for an athletics race, we can measure distance and time. Explain why both will be average speeds. This may have been done experimentally at KS3, but it is still a useful 'thought experiment'. If not done previously, it can be used as an alternative class experiment (see standard demand). Measuring speed using a light gate can be demonstrated.

Look at a photograph of a speed camera such as Figure 1 on page 186 of the Student Book and explain how they work using that page. Now show photographs or a video clip of average speed cameras, as used in motorway road works for example. Ask students to suggest how they work. Discuss why speed cameras are used and the advantages of a particular type for a given situation.

Ask students to answer questions 1–3 on page 186 of Student Book.

Teaching and learning notes: *Ensure that students understand why most calculations involve average speed.*

Standard demand

Talk about the effect an increase in speed has on: ***a*** the distance travelled in a certain time and ***b*** the time taken to travel a certain distance.

Students use a light gate and a data logger to measure speed with the support of the practical.

Distinguish between instantaneous and average speed. Introduce standard notation for the average speed equation and show students how to rearrange it to calculate the distance travelled. Ask students to answer questions 4–6 on page 187 of Student Book.

Ask students to answer worksheet question 2 *More about speed.*

High demand

Show students how to change km/h to m/s, and vice versa. Explain that m/s is the standard unit for speed and ***must*** be used in equations, but km/h is used for things that travel fast. Mention mph but emphasise that in Science we use metric units; speeds in mph are given for comparison. Ask them to answer questions 7–9 on page 187 of Student Book.

Students carry out a brief research task using the Internet to find out about speed records in various categories suggested by the teacher, for example cars, animals, aircraft or people.

Ask students to answer worksheet question 3 *Average speed gain.*

Teaching and learning notes: *Make sure that students are familiar with the units of speed and can handle them with ease. Provide a hint for worksheet question 3b Average speed gain if necessary: 'Let the distance be x (or put in a number) and calculate the times there and back.'*

Plenary suggestions

Complete a 'cross-number'. [See technician notes.]

OR

Local authorities have reduced the use of speed cameras. In groups, students discuss their effectiveness.

Assessment opportunities

Answers to Worksheet p3_a_01 and observation of student practical work can give a good indication of how well the lesson has been understood.

Answers

Student Book

Q1 Priya • **Q2** 0.33 (1/3) m/s • **Q3** E.g. road junctions, bends, road conditions • **Q4** Cannot tell; ***average*** speed = 100 km/h • **Q5** E.g. straighter, several lanes, no pedestrians • **Q6** 0.25 hour (15 minutes) • **Q7** 180 cm • **Q8a** 10 m/s **Q8b** 36 km/h • **Q9** 400 m

Fig 1 measures speed of passing car • **Fig 2** driver keeps within speed limit throughout • **Fig 3** e.g. cause accident, hurt pedestrian

Worksheet

Q1 120 km/h, 60 km/h,120 km/h,17 km/h 30 m/s • **Q2ai** Measure distance using tape or trundle wheel; time using stop watch; divide distance by time • **Q2aii** 1500 m • **Q2bi** 900 km/h • **Q2bii** 4800 km • **Q2biii** 845 km/h • **Q3a** 7.5 m/s, 100 s, 1.44×10^8 km, 7.5 s, 2.5 km • **Q3b** 58.3 km/h

P3a: Speed

Resources

Student Book pages 188–189 • Equipment for demonstrations and practical • ICT equipment
Interactive Book Naked Scientist animation: What forces are involved when we are in motion?
Files on Teacher Pack CD: p3_a_02_worksheet; p3_a_02_practical; p3_a_02_technician

Learning objectives

- Interpret simple graphs of distance against time.
- Describe the gradient of a distance–time graph.
- Draw distance–time graphs.

Learning outcomes

- Be able to interpret distance–time graphs qualitatively.
- Interpret the gradient of a distance–time graph as speed.
- Be able to calculate speed from the gradient of a distance–time graph for uniform speed (high demand).

Prior knowledge

Average speed = distance/time.

Basic graph drawing skills.

Key vocabulary

accelerate • best-fit straight line • curved line • decelerate • gradient • straight line

Barriers to learning

Curiosity and starter suggestions

- 'Find the treasure'; a game to introduce the idea of graphs and coordinates.

OR

- Walk or run across the laboratory, varying your speed and stopping for a few seconds at one point. Ask students to describe your motion and decide what measurements could be made to describe the motion in more detail.

Learning activities

Worksheet p3_a_02 + Practical p3_a_02

Low demand

Use a position sensor to draw a distance–time graph of a student walking in front of it. Repeat with different students moving at different speeds. Relate the graphs produced to the motion.

Look at the distance–time graphs shown in Figures 4 and 5 on page 188 of the Student Book. Link:

- a straight line (constant gradient) to a steady speed (same distance travelled each second);
- a straight horizontal line to a stationary object

Ask students to answer questions 10 to 12 on page 188 of the Student Book.

Teaching and learning notes: *Ensure that students realise that a straight line does not have to be horizontal.*

Standard demand

Students use a data-logger and position sensor to obtain a distance–time graph for a toy car or trolley pushed across the floor or bench top. Repeat with a bigger push; watch the motion of the car or trolley and compare the two graphs. Relate the gradient of the graphs to the speed of the car or trolley. Point out that If the distance *increases* as time increases the line has a positive (+) gradient and if the distance *decreases* as time increases the line has a negative (–) gradient.

Alternative class experiment: Working in groups, students obtain distance and time data for a student running 100 m. They then plot a distance–time graph of the motion. The practical supports this activity.

Ask students to answer questions 13–15 on page 189 of Student Book and worksheet question 1 *Distance–time graphs.*

Teaching and learning notes: *The first practical activity can be repeated with a different car or on an inclined plane if time permits. It can be a demonstration, with student participation, if there are insufficient data loggers or the alternative class practical is preferred and time is short.*

High demand

Discuss the shape of some simple distance–time graphs, provided as a white board resource, quantitatively for uniform acceleration and qualitatively for non-uniform acceleration.

Ask students to answer worksheet question 2 *More about distance–time graphs.*

Teaching and learning notes: *Make sure that students can interpret the distance–time graphs confidently, providing as much detail as possible.*

Plenary suggestions

Sketch a distance–time graph for your journey to school.

OR

A luxury car has a top speed of 140 mph. In groups, students discuss whether this is sensible when the speed limit, even on motorways, is 70 mph.

Assessment opportunities

Answers to Worksheet p3_a_02 can give a good indication of how well the lesson has been understood.

Answers

Student Book

Q10 Distance–time graph showing constant gradient from (0,0) to (200,2), horizontal line to (200,2.5) and then a line of constant gradient to (280,3.5) • **Q11** E.g. distance–time graph showing constant gradient • **Q12** Constant speed and then stopped • **Q13** Experimental error • **Q14** Check graph • **Q15** E.g. distance–time graph showing constant gradient from (0,0) to (120,1.5) • **Q16** Speed decreases • **Q17** straight line from (0,0) to (10,200) then horizontal; 20 m/s (72km/h)

Fig 4 Constant • **Fig 5** zero • **Fig 6** E.g. all vehicles travel in same direction; several lanes for safer overtaking; no right turns, no roundabouts • **Fig 7** Distance is zero at start and finish • **Fig 8** Steeper gradient, higher speed • **Fig 9** Constant • **Fig 10** Steeper / larger gradient • **Fig 11** The larger the gradient the greater the speed

Worksheet

Q1a 2; gradient greatest/graph steepest/covers biggest distance in an hour • **Q1bi** After 3 hours • **Q1bii** distance does not change • **Q1biii** 2 hours • **Q1c** 30 km • **Q1d** 10 km/h • **Q1e** 6.5 km/h (6–7 km/h) • **Q1f** Straight line from (1,0) to (6,42) • **Q1g** After approximately 4.5 hours • **Q2ai** 7.5 m/s • **Q2aii** Stopped • **Q2aiii** 5 m/s • **Q2aiv** 4 m/s • **Q2bi** distance–time graph • **Q2bii** 100 km/h • Q2b(iii) Swindon–Bristol • **Q2biv** Bristol–Cardiff • **Q2bv** Value correctly read from graph (12.42 pm)

P3b: Changing speed

Resources

Student Book pages 190–191 • Equipment for demonstrations and practical ▪ Video of Formula 1 race • ICT equipment
Interactive Book Practical investigations: Speedy sums
Files on Teacher Pack CD: p3_b_01_worksheet; p3_b_01_practical; p3_b_01_technician

Learning objectives

- Analyse graphs of speed against time.
- Calculate acceleration from a speed–time graph.
- Find the distance travelled from a speed–time graph.

Learning outcomes

- Be able to interpret speed–time graphs qualitatively.
- Interpret the gradient of a speed–time graph as acceleration.
- Be able to calculate the distance travelled from the area under a speed–time graph for uniform acceleration.

Prior knowledge

Basic graph drawing skills.

Analysis of distance–time graphs.

Key vocabulary

acceleration • area • deceleration • distance • estimate • gradient • speed • time

Barriers to learning

Students often confuse distance–time and speed–time graphs. They should always look at the axes carefully.

Curiosity and starter suggestions

- Two students use a 'Scalextric' set or radio-controlled car. Ask another student to provide a commentary.

OR

- Show a video of parts of a Formula 1 Grand Prix. Talk about the speed changes during a lap.

Learning activities

Worksheet p3_b_01 + Practical p3_b_01

Low demand

Demonstrate the use of a motion sensor and data-logger to plot a speed–time graph for (a) a falling ball, (b) a ball thrown up into the air, (c) a radio-controlled car (or similar). Get students to discuss the changes in speed shown on the graphs. Make sure that they can recognise the graph shapes that represent constant (horizontal line), increasing speed (positive gradient) and decreasing speed (negative gradient).

Ask students to answer worksheet question 1 *Speed–time graphs*.

Teaching and learning notes: *Compare the meaning of graph shapes for distance–time and speed–time graphs.*

Standard demand

Introduce the idea of acceleration as a change in speed. Link the shape of some simple speed–time graphs to uniform / non-uniform and high/low acceleration.

[Mention the unit of acceleration – m/s^2.]

Ask students, working in groups, to use a motion sensor and data-logger to monitor the speed of a ball down a ramp at two different heights. Plot speed–time graphs for each motion. Interpret the graphs qualitatively to decide how the acceleration changed. The practical supports this activity.

Describe the area under a speed–time graph as the distance travelled. Relate this to the speed–time graphs obtained in the class practical. Calculate the distance travelled from a simple speed–time graph for uniform acceleration.

Ask students to answer worksheet question 2 *Drawing speed–time graphs.*

Teaching and learning notes: *The practical activity can be carried out as a demonstration with pupil involvement if there is insufficient data logging equipment.*

High demand

Explain that the numerical value of the acceleration is found from the gradient of a speed–time graph.

Explain how the acceleration and distance travelled can be found from the gradient of and area under a speed–time graph for uniform acceleration.

Interpret speed–time graphs qualitatively for non-uniform acceleration.

Ask students to answer worksheet question 3 *More about speed–time graphs.*

Plenary suggestions

Summarise distance–time and speed–time graphs by asking students to complete a table projected on board.

OR

Play a game of bingo in which the answers to questions about motion are all numerical. Small white boards can be used. The set of questions can be used alone if preferred.

Assessment opportunities

Answers to worksheet p3_b_01 and responses during discussions can give a good indication of how well the lesson has been understood.

Answers

Student Book

Q1 Negative gradient • **Q2** Line of positive gradient from (0,0), followed by horizontal part, then returns to zero with line of negative gradient (motion need not be uniform) • **Q3a** B • **Q3b** Graph – accept anything sensible: e.g. rapid acceleration, greater for B, then constant speed, perhaps to end of race • **Q3c** Area under graph for race (both travel 100 m) • **Q4** 600 m • **Q5** Uniform acceleration of 0.25 m/s^2 for 1 minute, constant speed of 15 m/s for 3.5 minutes; uniform deceleration of 0.5 m/s^2 to stop after 5 minutes; 3825 m or 3.8 km

Fig 1 car would go off road / would not get around bend • **Fig 3** the speeds of cars C and D are decreasing; line D is steeper than line C; it has a larger negative gradient; the speed of car D is decreasing more rapidly than that of car C; Car D has a larger deceleration than car C • **Fig 4** uniform acceleration from rest of 2 m/s^2 for 15 s • **Fig 5** increases at first, then decreases as car approaches maximum speed of 10 m/s

Worksheet

Q1ai OA uniform acceleration, AB constant speed, BC uniform deceleration • **Q1aii** E.g. train between two stations • **Q1bi** after 13 s • **Q1bii** 3 s • **Q1biii** Decelerate uniformly • **Q1biv** Accelerate uniformly but less rapidly than acceleration OA) • **Q1bv** 9 s • **Q2a** and **Q2b** speed–time graph • **Q2c** 24 m/s • **Q2d** 2880 m • **Q2ei** 160-200 s • **Q2eii** Steepest gradient • **Q3ai** OA uniform acceleration = 2 m/s^2, AB constant speed = 10 m/s, BC uniform deceleration = 3.3 m/s^2, CD no motion, DE uniform acceleration = 1 m/s^2, EF constant speed = 5 m/s • **Q3aii** 90m • **Q3aiii** 122.5 m • **Q3bi** Increasing acceleration from rest then constant speed • **Q3bii** Constant speed then decreasing deceleration to stop • **Q3ci** Speed–time graph • **Q3cii** 1.25 m/s^2 • **Q3ciii** 0.5 m/s^2 • **Q3civ** 1760 m

P3b: Changing speed

Resources

Student Book pages 192–193 • Equipment for demonstrations and practical • Video of passing trains • ICT equipment
Interactive Book Matching pairs: Velocity calculations
Files on Teacher Pack CD: p3_b_02_worksheet; p3_b_02_practical; p3_b_02_technician

Learning objectives

- Calculate acceleration.
- Understand about positive and negative acceleration.
- Describe the difference between speed and velocity.
- Explain the meaning of relative velocity.

Learning outcomes

- Be able to use the equation acceleration = change in speed / time taken.
- Associate an increase in speed as a positive acceleration and a decrease in speed as a negative acceleration (deceleration).
- Understand that the velocity of an object is its speed combined with its direction.
- Be able to calculate the relative velocity of objects moving in parallel.

Prior knowledge

Speed and average speed and how to calculate them.

The units of speed and acceleration.

Key vocabulary

acceleration • deceleration • speed • relative velocity • velocity

Barriers to learning

Make sure students describe motion unambiguously; for instance, NOT ‘the car accelerates at a constant speed’ to mean ‘the car accelerates uniformly’.

Curiosity and starter suggestions

- Video clip of two trains on parallel tracks passing (i) in the same direction (ii) in opposite directions.

OR

- Show various things that move, e.g. bouncing ball, pendulum, car moving down a ramp. Ask a student to describe the motion in as much detail as possible.

Learning activities — Worksheet p3_b_02 + Practical p3_b_02

Low demand

Look at the speed–time graphs on page 192 of Student Book. Introduce the equation acceleration = change in speed/time taken. Do questions 6 and 7 on page 192 of Student Book.

Show the class a weight hanging from a spring. Pull weight down and release it. Ask students to watch closely. Then ask a student to describe how the speed changes. Get others to add extra details. Use the terms ‘acceleration’ and ‘deceleration’ to describe ‘speeding up’ and ‘slowing down’. Use this demonstration to introduce velocity as speed in a certain direction.

Ask students to answer worksheet question 1 *Acceleration and velocity*.

Teaching and learning notes: *Ensure that students use the correct terminology when describing motion.*

Standard

Students carry out a class experiment to measure acceleration down a ramp using light gates and a data logger. The practical supports this activity.

Show pupils how to change from km/h to m/s.

Look at some car advertisements that quote the speed change in a certain time.
Use the equation 'acceleration = change in speed / time taken' to calculate their acceleration. Ask students to answer questions 9–11 on page 193 of Student Book.

Reinforce the idea of velocity having magnitude ***and*** direction.

Introduce the idea of relative velocity. Refer back to the Starter video if used, or show it now. Look at Figure 6 and answer question 8 on page 193 of Student Book.

Ask students to answer worksheet question 2 *Relative velocity.*

Teaching and learning notes: *The practical activity can be carried out as a demonstration with pupil involvement.*

Higher

Show how to rearrange the equation 'acceleration = change in speed / time taken' to calculate the change in speed or time taken.

Whirl a weight on the end of a string around in a horizontal circle; try to maintain a constant speed. Repeat rotating it in a vertical circle.

Use this to introduce the idea of a change in direction, and hence an acceleration, even though the speed is constant, which must be towards the centre of the circle. Point out that we should write acceleration = change in velocity/time taken, but in most cases speed can be used.

Ask students to answer worksheet question 3 *More about motion.*

Teaching and learning notes: *Velocity and circular motion are covered in more detail in P5.*

Plenary suggestions

Ask students to solve anagrams connected with how things move and then use each word in a sentence.

OR

"UK TV adverts target 'speeding majority'."/ "In their adverts manufacturers should promote acceleration, not speed."

In groups, pupils discuss these two newspaper comments.

Assessment opportunities

Answers to Worksheet p3_b_02, observation of students during practical work and responses during discussions can give a good indication of how well the lesson has been understood.

Answers

Student Book

Q6 B • **Q7** 0.25 m/s^2 • **Q8** 80 m/s • **Q9** 2.5 m/s^2 • **Q10** 0.8 m/s^2 • **Q11a** 20 m/s • **Q11b** 1.25 m/s^2 • **Q12** 9 s • **Q13** direction changing

Fig 6 constant acceleration • **Fig 7** constant deceleration to stop • **Fig 8** to travel into space and not fall back to Earth • **Fig 9** slowly • **Fig 10** direction changing

Worksheet

Q1ai 0.5 m/s^2 • **Q1aii** 0.75 m/s2 • **Q1b** Direction not known • **Q1ci** 15 m/s • **Q1cii** 15 m/s due W • **Q2a** 2 m/s E • **Q2**b 5 m/s W • **Q2c** 5 m/s S • **Q2d** 35 m/s S • **Q2e** 80 m/s E • **Q2f** 0 m/s • **Q2g** 20 m/s W • **Q2h** 30 m/s N • **Q3ai** 12 m/s • **Q3aii** 120 m • **Q3aiii** 2 m/s^2 • **Q3bi** 100m/s • **Q3bii** Speed–time graph showing speed increase from 70 m/s to 100 m/s in 5 s (see opposite) • **Q3biii** 425 m • **Q3c** Direction changing

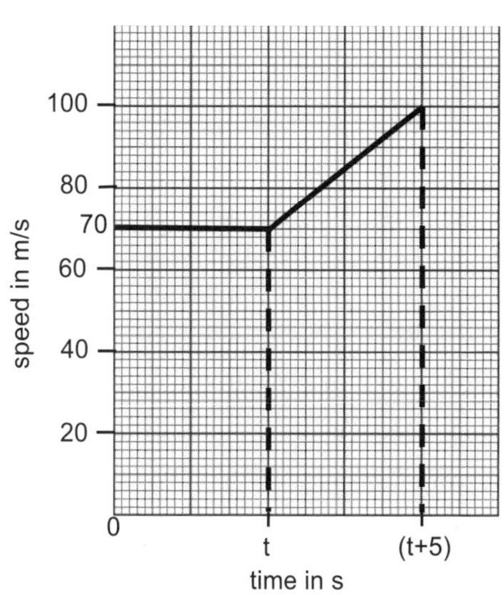

P3c: Forces and motion

Resources

Student Book pages 194–195 • Equipment for demonstrations and practical • Video of athletes or gymnasts landing • ICT equipment

Files on Teacher Pack CD: p3_c_01_worksheet; p3_c_01_practical; p3_c_01_technician

Learning objectives

- Recognise simple situations where forces affect the motion of an object.
- Describe and interpret the relationship between force, mass and acceleration.
- State and use the equation: 'force = mass x acceleration'.

Learning outcomes

- Recognise simple situations where forces cause things to speed up, slow down or stay at the same speed.
- Be able to interpret the relationship between force, mass and acceleration in everyday examples.
- Be able to use the equation 'force = mass x acceleration' including a change of subject, and (high demand only) first calculate the accelerating force.

Prior knowledge

Types of force.

What a force can do.

Key vocabulary

acceleration • balanced • force • net • newton (N) • pull • resultant • speed • unbalanced

Barriers to learning

Make sure students realise that the force in the equation 'force = mass x acceleration' refers to the resultant, or net, force acting on the mass.

Curiosity and starter suggestions

- Ask students to write down five things that a force can do, using small white boards or paper. The teacher then collates ideas and compiles a list of correct suggestions on board.

OR

- Show a video clip of athletes or gymnasts landing. Ask the students what they notice. [Come back to **this at the** end of lesson.]

Learning activities — Worksheet p3_c_01 + Practical p3_c_01

Low demand

Discuss the forces acting on a car when it speeds up, slows down or travels at a constant speed. Refer to balanced and unbalanced forces. Look at worksheet question 1ai *Forces and motion* with the class and decide on the correct answer. Ask students to answer worksheet questions 1aii–v *Forces and motion.*

Use light gates connected to a data-logger as a demonstration, with student involvement, to find the acceleration of a trolley down a friction compensated ramp when:

- the same trolley is pulled by two different forces;
- two trolleys of different masses are pulled by the same force.

Discuss the results qualitatively and lead students, if necessary, to spot the effect of increased force or mass on acceleration.

Introduce the equation $F = ma$ to calculate force.

Ask students to answer worksheet question 1b *Forces and motion*.

Teaching and learning notes: *The demonstration should be set up ready to use. There is no need to mention friction compensation at this stage.*

Standard demand

Ask students, working in groups, to use an air track, light gates and data logger to measure the speed of a vehicle at two different places and compute its acceleration when pulled by a known force. Repeat for (i) different pulling forces and (ii) different vehicle masses. Half the class could vary the pulling force and the other half the mass. The practical supports this activity.

The friction-compensated runway used in low demand can be used with trolley, light gates and data logger. If available, a force sensor and an accelerometer can be used to link force, mass and acceleration using a data logger.

Use the results of the practical work to show that $F = ma$.

Show how the equation $F = ma$ can be rearranged to calculate the acceleration or resultant force on an object.

Ask students to answer worksheet question 2 *Using $F = ma$*.

Teaching and learning notes: *The practical activities can be carried out as demonstrations with pupil involvement if there is insufficient equipment or a circus of practical tasks could be set up to suit the apparatus available.*

High demand

The results of the practical work can be analysed in more detail, plotting graphs of a against F or a against 1/m, for example.

Consider how to calculate the accelerating force acting on a mass. Link this to the unbalanced, resultant or net force. Use this force to calculate mass or acceleration using $F = ma$.

Ask students to answer worksheet question 3 More about $F = ma$.

Plenary suggestions

Working in small groups, students discuss the truth, or otherwise, of the statement: 'If something is moving there must be a force acting on it.' Collate ideas and use $F = ma$ to lead students to conclude that there is no resultant force on an object travelling at a constant speed.

OR

Follow up on second starter activity. Show video clip again. Discuss why a person bends their knees on landing, reducing their deceleration (negative acceleration), and hence the force on them, by taking longer to stop. Make sure all students can write down the correct explanation.

Assessment opportunities

Answers to worksheet p3_c_01 and responses during discussions can give a good indication of how well the theoretical parts of the lesson have been understood. Observation of pupils carrying out the experimental work will inform on their practical skills and organisation.

Answers

Student Book

Q1a Bigger acceleration • **Q1b** Smaller acceleration • **Q2** 5200 N • **Q3** Increases the backwards force, slowing it down more quickly • **Q4** 3.5 m/s^2 • **Q5** Small mass gives large acceleration for given force ($F = ma$) • **Q6ai** 0.5 m/s^2 **Q6aii** 600 N • **Q6bi** 600 N • **Q6bii** 0.2 m/s^2

Fig 1 experience will improve driving skills • **Fig 2** decelerates; constant speed • **Fig 3** car d • **Fig 4** golf ball accelerates; space shuttle decelerates • **Fig 5** accelerates forwards at 4 m/s^2

Worksheet

Q1ai To the left • **Q1aii** To the right • **Q1aiii** Remains at rest • **Q1aiv** To the right • **Q1av** To the left • **Q1b** 72 N • **Q1c** 18 000 N • **Q2ai** Balanced • **Q2aii** Increases forward force/thrust from engine/puts foot on accelerator • **Q2aiii** 2 m/s^2 • **Q2aiv** 2400 N • **Q2b** 1.67 m/s^2 • **Q2c** 800 kg • **Q2di** Accelerates • **Q2dii** Decelerates • **Q2diii** Constant speed • **Q2div** Decelerates • **Q2dv** Accelerates – all to left • **Q3ai** D • **Q3aii** B • **Q3aiii** A and C • **Q3b** 3 m/s^2 • **Q3c** Car has a greater acceleration for the same net forward force • **Q3d** She takes longer to stop, her deceleration is less and so is the force on her ($F = ma$) • **Q3ei** 5 m/s^2 • **Q3eii** 6000 N

P3c: Forces and motion

Resources

Student Book pages 196–197 • Equipment for demonstrations and practical • Video of car crashes • ICT equipment
Interactive Book Quick starter: What factors affect stopping distances?
Files on Teacher Pack CD: p3_c_02_worksheet; p3_c_02_practical; p3_c_02_technician

Learning objectives

- Understand the meaning of thinking, braking and stopping distances.
- Recall the factors that affect thinking, braking and stopping distances.
- Explain why a knowledge of stopping distance is important in road safety.

Learning outcomes

- Describe thinking, braking and stopping distances.
- Explain how certain factors may increase thinking and braking distances.
- Explain the implications of stopping distances in road safety and the effect of increased speed on them.

Prior knowledge

How to calculate speed.

Key vocabulary

brake pads • braking distance • reaction time • stopping distance • thinking distance • thinking time • tread • tyres

Curiosity and starter suggestions

- Show a video clip or photographs of car crashes and / or some road safety material.

OR

- Challenge a student to catch a £10 note when you drop it, without warning, directly above their thumb and first finger, held to catch it.

Learning activities — Worksheet p3_c_02 + Practical p3_c_02

Low demand

Project the typical stopping distances diagram from page 196 of Student Book (or from *The Highway Code*) on board. [This is useful throughout this lesson.] Explain the meaning of '*thinking distance*' and '*braking distance*'. Add them to obtain '*stopping distance*'. Look at the effect of increased speed on the stopping distance. Discuss why thinking, braking and stopping distances are important in road safety.

Working in pairs students carry out an experiment to estimate their thinking (reaction) time by catching a ruler dropped by their partner, using a table to convert the distance fallen before catching it into their thinking time.

Practical p3_c_02 supports this activity. Compare results. Ask students to suggest why their thinking time is (probably) less than that assumed in *The Highway Code*.

Ask students to answer worksheet question 1 *Stopping distances.*

Teaching and learning notes: *Make sure students do not confuse thinking distance and thinking time.*

Standard demand

Discuss the factors that might affect a person's thinking time. List them on board. Link this to thinking distance on the road.

Discuss the factors that affect braking distance. Link these to road safety looking again at the stopping distances diagram used above.

Ask students to list the factors affecting a) thinking distance, b) braking distance.

Talk about the implications of stopping distances in road safety.

Ask students to answer worksheet question 2 *More about stopping distances.*

In groups, ask students to draw up a strategy to improve road safety. [This can be nationally or in the local area.] They can use the internet and other resources to gain information and prepare a presentation to present to the rest of the class. After the presentations the class can vote for the best plan.

Teaching and learning notes: *The research task can be completed for homework.*

High demand

Look again, in more detail, at the typical stopping distances diagram from page 196 of Student Book.

Consider some everyday situations where braking distance is changed. This should include friction (wet/icy road, bald tyres), mass (heavily laden car), speed (dependent on road conditions), braking force (condition of brakes).

Look at the graphs of thinking distance and braking distance against speed shown in Figure 10 on page 197 of Student Book. Consider the effect of increased speed quantitatively on a) thinking distance (straight line through the origin so increases linearly), b) braking distance (curve showing a squared relationship – if speed doubles the braking distance quadruples).

Ask students to answer worksheet question 3 *...and more about stopping distances.*

Teaching and learning notes: *This section covers similar material to the earlier sections but quantitatively and in much more detail.*

Plenary suggestions

Ask students to make 'key facts' cards based on the lesson, and test each other.

OR

Students complete a word search. The words can be given or students told there are eleven hidden words.

Assessment opportunities

Answers to worksheet p3_c_02 will indicate how well the basic material has been understood. Observation of students carrying out the research task and subsequent presentations will inform on their ability to communicate a sensible strategy supported by scientific facts.

Answers

Student Book

Q7 Takes time to react (thinking time) • **Q8** 96 km/h (60 mph), 55 m, 73 m, 23 m • **Q9** Greater speed has much greater stopping distance; impact at higher speed makes serious injury more likely • **Q10** 21 m • **Q11a** 13.5 m, about 32–34 m, 45–48 m • **Q11b** 27 m (double), about 130 m (quadruple), 155–165 m (sum of thinking and braking distances) • **Q12** Tread channels water to avoid aquaplaning

Fig 6 e.g. wet road increases braking distance and hence stopping distance • **Fig 7** car travels further in braking since less friction between brake and wheel • **Fig 8** no tread to channel water when wet; car can aquaplane • **Fig 9** straight line through the origin; braking distance is proportional to $(\text{speed})^2$

Worksheet

Q1a 36 m • **Q1b** 48 km/h (30 mph) • **Q1c** 24 m (goes up by 3 every 10 mph) • **Q1d** 20–22 m (not proportional) **Q2ai** Increases **Q2aii** No change **Q2aiii** Increases • **Q2b** Two from drugs, tiredness, lack of concentration, distractions, etc. • **Q2c** Worn brakes, wet or icy road • **Q2di** Thinking distances – 15 m, 18 m; stopping distances – 29 m, 47m, 71 m, 98 m • **Q2dii** (Just over) 18 m (or thinking distance at 30 m/s from Q2di). The front car driver will travel 18 m before applying the brakes; the following car driver is not aware of the need to brake until this point • **Q3ai** • 7m • **Q3aii** 21 m • **Q3aiii** Thinking distance is proportional to speed • **Q3aiv** Quadruples • **Q3b** Worn brakes increase braking distance as there is less friction between brakes and wheels • **Q3c** Worn tyres increase braking, and hence stopping distance and increase risk of aquaplaning in wet weather

P3d: Work and power

Resources

Student Book pages 198–199 • Equipment for demonstrations and practical • Video of people doing work, astronauts in flight and on the Moon, dropping something on Moon • ICT equipment

Interactive Book Quick starter: Acceleration due to gravity • Naked Scientist animation: How are weight, mass and gravity linked?

Files on Teacher Pack CD: p3_d_01_worksheet; p3_d_01_practical; p3_d_01_technician

Learning objectives

- Recall the connection between mass and weight.
- Understand that energy is needed to do work.
- Calculate work done.

Learning outcomes

- Be able to use the equation 'weight = mass × gravitational field strength', with appropriate units.
- Realise that work is only done when a force moves and that this requires energy.
- Be able to use the equation 'work done = force × distance moved'.

Prior knowledge

Types of force and how to measure the size of a force.

Key vocabulary

force • joule (J) • kinetic energy • mass • weight • work

Barriers to learning

- Students are often confused about the difference between mass, in kilograms, and weight, in newtons.
- Some students find it difficult to understand that no work is done unless a force moves.

Curiosity and starter suggestions

- Show pictures / video of people doing work. Students discuss which person they think is doing the most work.

OR

- Show video of astronauts in situations where they appear to weigh more or less than usual; for instance, at blast off, in orbit (in Space Shuttle), on the Moon.

Learning activities

Worksheet p3_d_01 + Practical p3_d_01

Low demand

Drag a box or suitcase across the floor. Explain that work is done as we are moving it against the force of friction.

Move it further and get the class to tell you that you do more work. Move a heavier object and get class to tell you that you do more work.

Demonstrate other examples of doing work, e.g. pushing a pram / shopping trolley, climbing stairs / steps, lifting weights. Identify the force moved in each case.

Conclude that the amount of work done depends on the size of the force in N and the distance moved in m.

Introduce the equation 'work done = force × distance moved by the force'. State that work done is measured in joules (J) where the force is in N and the distance moved in m. Ask students to answer question 2 on page 198 of Student Book.

Talk about how energy is transferred from one type to another when work is done. Explain that the unit of both work and energy is the joule (J).

Ask students to answer worksheet question 1 *Work done.*

Teaching and learning notes: *Ensure that students use the correct units when substituting in the equation for work done.*

Standard demand

Remind students of the difference between mass and weight. Drop a ball. Ask students the value of its acceleration.

Then use $F = ma$ with $a = g$ to explain that weight, $W = mg$. Ask students to answer question 3 on page 199 of the Student Book.

Try to move a heavy object (e.g. a cupboard) but do not succeed. Explain that no work is done if the object does not move as there is no energy change. **Students should be told to take care when lifting items.**

Show how to rearrange the equation 'work done = force x distance moved' to calculate force or distance.

Point out that 1 joule = 1 newton metre (1 J = 1 Nm). Explain that a joule is the work done when a force of 1 N is moved through 1 m. Reinforce the idea that 1 joule is a small amount of energy by doing 1 J of work, for example by raising an apple through a height of 1 m. Ask students to answer questions 4 and 5 on page 199 of Student Book.

Students carry out a class experiment to calculate the work done in various situations by measuring the size of the force and the distance it is moved. The practical supports this activity.

Ask students to answer worksheet question 2 *Mass, weight and work.*

Teaching and learning notes: *Ensure that students understand the difference between mass and weight and can calculate the weight of a mass if g is known. Some students find it hard to realise that no work is done if an object does not move, no matter how much effort has gone into the attempt. 'Work' has a specialised meaning here.*

High demand

Contrast the value of g on Earth with its value on the Moon. Show a video clip of an astronaut dropping an object on the Moon. Repeat, or show for the first time, the video for the second Starter activity. Explain the meaning of the G-force. Show how to rearrange the equation $W = mg$ to calculate g or m. Ask students to answer question 6 on page 199 of Student Book.

Show pupils a disc brake from a car (or picture of one). Explain how car brakes do work by producing a large friction force. Explain how to calculate the braking distance and how it depends on the speed at which the car was travelling before applying the brakes. Look at the example about car brakes on page 199 of Student Book and ask students to do question 7 on that page.

Ask students to answer worksheet question 3 *More about mass, weight and work.*

Plenary suggestions

- Students identify three objects in the lab or at home that do work and identify the energy source. Compile list.

OR

- Solve the anagrams. Then use each word in a sentence to show its meaning.

Assessment opportunities

Answers to Worksheet p3_d_01 and observation of student practical work can give a good indication of how well the lesson has been understood.

Answers

Answers to the Student Book and Worksheet can be found on the Teachers Pack CD.

P3d: Work and power

Resources

Student Book pages 200–201 • Equipment for demonstrations and practical • Video of old and new methods of transport • ICT equipment

Interactive Book Quick starter: Can you unjumble the sentences to find the scientific definition of power?

Files on Teacher Pack CD: p3_d_02_worksheet; p3_d_02_practical; p3_d_02_technician

Learning objectives

- Recall the meaning of power.
- Calculate power.
- Interpret fuel consumption data.

Learning outcomes

- Describe power as a measurement of how quickly work is being done.
- Be able to use the equation 'power = work done / time' and derive 'power = force × speed' (high demand)
- Be able to interpret fuel consumption figures from data on cars, including environmental issues and cost.

Prior knowledge

How to calculate work done (= force × distance) and speed (= distance / time).

Key vocabulary

carbon dioxide • greenhouse gases • kilowatt (kW) • power • watt (W)

Barriers to learning

Encourage students to look for trends or patterns in data and use the information gained to support conclusions.

Curiosity and starter suggestions

- Show video clip or photographs of old and new methods of transport, e.g. fast car and vintage model, jet aircraft and early plane, steam train and bullet train / TGV; penny farthing bicycle and racing bike.

OR

- Carry out a task (e.g. lifting a weight onto a shelf or walking across the room) first slowly and then quickly. **Care must be taken with heavy objects**.

Learning activities

Worksheet p3_d_02 + Practical p3_d_02

Low demand

Look at the pairs of transport models from the first starter activity. Recognise that all the examples do work but some more quickly than others. Link this with the idea of power as a measurement of how quickly work is being done. This means the more modern methods of transport are the most powerful. Ask students to answer question 9 on page 200 of the Student Book.

Ask students for other examples of machines that develop power. Encourage them to choose examples from a wide range of 'machines' including themselves.

State that power is measured in watts (W).

Look at the data about the cars on page 200 of the Student Book. Ask students to answer question 8.

Students can use the Internet to find similar data about various other cars. They can draw up a table similar to the one on page 200 of Student Book to display their findings.

Students discuss the data obtained and list anything significant.

Ask students to answer worksheet question 1 *Fuel consumption.*

***Teaching and learning notes:** Ensure that students associate power with time – the rate of doing work or the rate of energy transfer.*

Standard demand

Show students how to calculate power using the equation

$$\text{power} = \frac{\text{work done}}{\text{time}}$$

Ask students to answer questions 10 and 11 on page 201 of Student Book.

Students carry out a class experiment to measure their personal power when they carry out various activities.

Practical p3_d_02 supports this activity.

In groups, students discuss the environmental issues associated with fuel consumption and carbon dioxide emissions from cars. They prepare a presentation to summarise their discussions, possibly using the Internet.

Ask students to answer worksheet question 2 *Power and more fuel consumption data.*

***Teaching and learning notes:** Some students may need guidance to extract the key points from the environmental issues discussed before preparing their presentations.*

High demand

Show students how to calculate the amount of work done or time taken using the equation

$$\text{power} = \frac{\text{work done}}{\text{time}}$$

Remind them that they may need to calculate the amount of work done using the equation 'work done = force x distance' introduced in the previous lesson before calculating power or time.

Show students how to derive and use the power equation in the form 'power = force × speed' from work done = force × distance/time.

Ask students to answer questions 13 and 14 on page 201 of Student Book and worksheet question 3 *Power.*

***Teaching and learning notes:** This section is very mathematical in content. Less able mathematicians may need some support in manipulating the equations.*

Plenary suggestions

Definitions – students pair up key words with their definitions. This can be a whiteboard or interactive activity.

OR

In groups, students discuss ways to reduce pollution from cars in our cities. One person from each group reports back to the class.

Assessment opportunities

Opportunities for assessment are provided by students' answers to worksheet p3_d_02 and observation of students carrying out practical work and the research task.

Answers

Student Book

Q8 First car• **Q9a** Same force and same distance moved • **Q9b** B takes less time • **Q10** 20 W • **Q11** 44 W • **Q12** First car – 32.5 litres; second car – 97.5 litres • **Q13** 8 s • **Q14** 24 000 N

Fig 4 first car for a and b • **Fig 5** no – same force (her weight) moved the same vertical distance • **Fig 6** 222 km/h

Worksheet

Answers to Worksheet can be found on the Teacher Pack CD.

P3: Applying your knowledge

Pages 202–203 in the Student Book prepare students for assessment.

When and how to use these pages

This task provides an opportunity for students to apply their science knowledge in a different context.

Ask students to:

- read through the context and tasks, listing any terms that they do not understand
- as a whole class or in small groups, discuss the tasks to ensure all students understand the terminology used and to clarify what is required
- work individually to answer the questions for each task.

If time allows, ask students to mark each other's work using the mark scheme provided.

Notes

The task focuses on the section on road safety in P3c. It is set in the context of a group of young people driving along a country road leading to a beach where they plan to surf. The task tests students' knowledge and understanding of thinking, braking and stopping distances and their ability to apply this knowledge in an unfamiliar context.

Answers

This mark scheme is also available on the Teacher Pack CD.

Task	Answer	Notes
1	there is loud music playing several people in the car there is sand on the road	Stating one or two reasons why Will's brother takes longer to stop than expected is indicative of a student operating at grade F standard
2	Distractions such as loud music mean the driver is not concentrating fully on driving so his thinking (or reaction) time is greater. This means his thinking distance – the distance he travels during his reaction time – is greater.	A good description of how thinking distance is affected by distractions in the car is expected of a student working towards a grade C
3	Kinetic energy increases with increased mass and speed. Kinetic energy = $\frac{1}{2} mv^2$ so if speed doubles the kinetic energy quadruples. When braking the car's kinetic energy is transferred mainly into heat in the brakes. The work done by the brakes in stopping is equal to the braking force x braking distance. Work done also equals the change in kinetic energy so the braking distance is equal to the change in kinetic energy divided by the braking force. When the speed doubles the kinetic energy, and so the braking distance, quadruples.	Stating the factors that affect kinetic energy is a grade C task To raise their answer to a grade A students must be able to explain the relationship between kinetic energy and braking distance
4	When a car driver applies the brakes friction between the brakes and wheel provide a retarding force which slows the car down. Will's brother brakes hard so although he slows down at first the wheels lock and so the car slides, made worse by the sand.	A grade C student should be able to explain the role of friction in stopping a vehicle
5	ABS brakes give a vehicle stability and maintain steering when braking hard or going into a skid. Hard continuous pressure activates anti-lock brakes which then work by automatically pumping on and off to avoid skidding. The driver gets the maximum braking force without skidding and can still steer the car. The driver does not necessarily stop more quickly but he maintains control of the car.	A good explanation of how ABS brakes work is expected of students aiming at an A or A* grade

Notes

P3e: Energy on the move

Resources

Student Book pages 204–205 • Equipment for demonstrations and practical • Video of a traffic jam, video of alternatives to fossil fuels • ICT equipment

Interactive Book Quick starter: Kinetic energy – can you translate this? • News clip: Designing an eco boat • icould career video: The environmental impact of generating electricity

Files on Teacher Pack CD: p3_e_01_worksheet; p3_e_01_practical; p3_e_01_technician

Learning objectives

- Find out about kinetic energy and (high demand) how to calculate it.
- Find out about renewable energy sources for vehicles.
- Understand how braking distance changes with speed.

Learning outcomes

- Understand that kinetic energy depends on the mass and speed of an object.
- Describe how electricity can be used for road transport.
- Apply ideas about kinetic energy to link braking distances and speed.

Prior knowledge

Understand about thinking, braking and stopping distances.

Key vocabulary

bio-fuels • diesel • environment • fossil fuels • kinetic energy • mass • non-renewable • oil • petrol • pollution • renewable • speed

Barriers to learning

Encourage students to express an opinion, backed up by evidence. They often find it difficult to deal with questions to which there is no precise answer.

Curiosity and starter suggestions

- Show video, photo or computer image of a traffic jam. Students suggest why so many people prefer to travel by car, despite the congestion and pollution caused.

OR

- Quick quiz to recap some of the terms already met that come up again in this lesson.

Learning activities

Worksheet p3_e_01 + Practical p3_e_01

Low demand

Show some examples of moving objects, e.g. model car or train, throwing a ball, walking/running, model/paper aeroplane, falling water. Could include pictures/video clips.

Explain that all these objects have kinetic energy. Ask students to suggest which are likely to have the most kinetic energy. Lead them to decide that an increase in mass and/or speed increases the kinetic energy of an object.

Talk about the need for a fuel to provide the energy source. Ask students to answer worksheet question 1a *Fuels*.

Recognise the current reliance on fossil fuels. Get students to suggest alternatives. Show photos/videos of some alternatives, including bio-fuels and solar energy.

Show video clips/photos of electric cars. Point out that these can be battery-driven or have solar panels on the roof. Discuss some of the advantages and disadvantages of both methods.

Ask students to answer worksheet question 1b *Fuels*.

Teaching and learning notes: *Encourage students to express their opinion about the issues raised.*

Standard demand

Discuss factors that increase kinetic energy – greater mass and greater speed. Introduce KE = ½ mv^2.

Students answer question 3 on page 205 of the Student Book.

Link kinetic energy with road transport. Explain why a lorry has more KE than a car when travelling at the same speed. Students should realise this makes it more dangerous if involved in a collision. Show some photos or video clips of road accidents.

Point out that fossil-fuelled cars cause environmental pollution, especially on crowded urban roads. Discuss the benefits of electric cars but make sure students realise that although battery-powered cars do not pollute at point of use the electricity to recharge the battery is probably produced in a fossil-fuelled power station that is a major source of pollution. Ask students to answer questions 4–6 on page 205 of Student Book.

Ask students to work in groups to consider the best method of powering a car. Worksheet question 2 *Fuelling a car* supports this. Leave time for each group to present their choice of car fuel, setting a time limit for each group.

Teaching and learning notes: *The presentations relating to worksheet question 2* Fuelling a car *could be used as the plenary activity. This task will differentiate between standard demand and high demand students.*

Higher

Use the equation KE = ½ mv^2. Students answer question 7 on page 205 of the Student Book.

Students carry out a class practical to relate KE and stopping distance. Practical p3_e_01 supports this activity. Discuss the questions at the end of the practical task.

Show how the kinetic energy equation relates to the work done by the brakes of a car.

Ask students to answer question 8 on page 205 of the Student Book.

Teaching and learning notes: *If teaching this section it may be sensible to do it before the last item in the Standard section if the presentations form the Plenary activity.*

Plenary suggestions

Groups present their conclusions to Worksheet question 2 *Fuelling a car.*

OR

Show class a list of speed limits from the Highway Code. Discuss the reasons for speed limits and why there are many different ones.

Assessment opportunities

The opportunity to assess students' ability to discuss, work with others as part of a team and prepare a presentation is provided by worksheet question 2 *Fuelling a car.*

Answers

Answers to Student Book and Worksheet can be found on the Teacher Pack CD.

P3e Energy on the move

Resources

Student Book pages 206–207 • Equipment for demonstrations and practical • Video of streamlined and non-streamlined objects • ICT equipment

Files on Teacher Pack CD: p3_e_02_worksheet; p3_e_02_practical; p3_e_02_technician

Learning objectives

- Describe how the shape of cars can affect their top speeds and fuel consumption.
- Explain how alternatives to fossil fuels can be used for road transport.
- Interpret data on fuel consumption.

Learning outcomes

- Understand that a streamlined shape increases a car's top speed and improves fuel consumption.
- Explain the advantages of bio-fuelled and solar-powered cars.
- Describe the factors that affect fuel consumption and analyse fuel consumption data.

Prior knowledge

Understand about collecting energy from the Sun.

Some ways in which electricity is used to power road transport.

Key vocabulary

battery • bio-fuels • efficient • environment • fuel consumption • pollution • refined • solar power • streamlining

Barriers to learning

Encourage students to look for trends when analysing data.

Curiosity and starter suggestions

- Look at the introduction to this item on page 204 of Student Book. Ask students to estimate the cost of driving this car from, for example, London to Bristol (about 200 km).

OR

- Show video clips of streamlined objects (e.g. dolphin, sports car, racing cyclist, athlete with tight-fitting clothes) and non-streamlined objects (e.g. frogfish, Jeep, cyclist, athlete from 50 years ago).

Learning activities

Worksheet p3_e_02 + Practical p3_e_02

Low demand

Show some adverts for petrol and diesel cars and discuss them. Explain both use fossil fuels.

Show students petrol and diesel engines if possible. [Large detailed photographs could be used as an alternative.] Outline how each works, highlighting the main differences between them.

Compare fuel consumption figures from page 206 of Student Book. Ask students to answer questions 9–11 on page 206 of Student Book.

Students carry out a class experiment to investigate streamlining. Practical p3_e_02 supports this activity.

Project Figure 4 from page 206 of the Student Book and photographs of a shaped sports car and a car with its windows open on board. Ask students to point out the features that increase or decrease their top speeds. Explain how friction can be reduced by streamlining the shape. Look at a photo showing airflow around a car.

Ask students to answer worksheet question 1 *Streamlining*.

Teaching and learning notes: *Students may have carried out the practical activity in KS3. If so they can be reminded of it with a quick demonstration.*

Standard demand

Remind students of the work on alternative fuels for cars from the previous lesson. Recap the key points about the use of solar and battery powered electric cars.

Look at the table on page 207 of Student Book. Discuss how the data are obtained and why less favourable results are likely to be obtained in practice. Ask students to answer questions 13–16 on page 207 of Student Book.

Talk about the advantages and problems associated with the use of bio-fuels to power cars.

Ask students to answer worksheet question 2 *Alternative fuels*. If you wish students may access the internet to research bio-fuelled and electric cars.

Teaching and learning notes: *If there was not enough time for all the presentations relating to worksheet question 2* Fuelling a car *in the last lesson the remainder could be used here as part of the recap of key points about electric cars.*

High demand

Mention some more factors that affect fuel consumption, including a) the amount of energy required to increase the kinetic energy of the car; b) the amount of energy required to do work against friction; c) the speed of the car; d) the driving style of the driver; e.g. rapid acceleration and deceleration; e) road conditions; e.g. rough road surface, constant braking and speed changes. Ask students to answer worksheet question *3 Factors affecting fuel consumption data.*

Ask students to answer questions 17–19 on page 207 of Student Book. [Question 20 on page 207 of Student Book could be set for homework.]

Plenary suggestions

Show students a data sheet of the ten best fuel consumption figures for petrol and diesel cars. Compare the two lists and answer the questions that follow.

OR

In groups, ask students to reflect on what they have learnt about road transport in the last two lessons and make their suggestions for a sustainable, environmentally friendly strategy.

Assessment opportunities

Students' ability to analyse data can be assessed by considering how they coped with the work on fuel consumption tables.

Answers

Student Book

Q9 Bigger engine uses slightly more fuel; diesel uses less fuel than petrol to go 100 km • **Q10** E.g. load carried; driving style; urban or non-urban travel; speed • **Q11** Diesel produces less CO_2 emissions than petrol engine; engine size makes little difference • **Q12** Greater • **Q13** Less fuel used to travel 100 km; less CO_2 emissions • **Q14** Ford Focus diesel • **Q15** Greater fuel consumption has more CO_2 emissions • **Q16** Lower for petrol engine • **Q17** Steadier speed • **Q18** Produced under ideal conditions; traffic jam; stop/start etc increases fuel consumption • **Q19** E.g. reduced speed / steadier driving; drive less; buy a 'greener' car • **Q20** Sensible comments, presented logically, with evidence quoted from table, including comparison of engine size, petrol and diesel engines, fuel consumption, urban/non-urban driving, emissions

Fig 4 increases top speed and improves fuel consumption • **Fig 5** Sun does not always shine

Worksheet

Q1 Balanced, steady air resistance, drag, shape, speed, streamlined, decreases, faster, thrust, friction • **Q2a** Student's own ideas • **Q2bi** E.g. advantages: fuel cheap, less CO_2 emissions, no toxic emissions; disadvantages: expensive to purchase, low top speed, few refuelling stations • **Q2bii** E.g. good in town but poor choice for longer journeys, M-way driving, etc.; high cost may lead to conclusion that electric car is not a wise purchase • **Q3a** E.g. more speed changes • **Q3bi** Increases • **Q3bii** Increases • **Q3biii** Speed; doubling the mass doubles the kinetic energy but doubling the speed quadruples the kinetic energy

P3f: Crumple zones

Resources

Student Book pages 208–209 • Equipment for demonstrations and practical • Videos of car crashes with and without seat belts; crumple zones, air bags and seatbelts; dummies • ICT equipment

Interactive Book Quick starter: Ask the science teacher.com

Files on Teacher Pack CD: p3_f_01_worksheet; p3_f_01_practical; p3_f_01_technician

Learning objectives

- Find out about momentum.
- Describe how seatbelts, crumple zones and air bags act in a crash.
- Explain how forces can be reduced in a crash.

Learning outcomes

- Use the equations momentum = mass ×velocity and force = change in momentum/time.
- Describe how seatbelts, crumple zones and air bags change the momentum of a person in a car crash more slowly.
- Explain how these reduce or avoid injury.

Prior knowledge

The properties of forces.

Newton's Second Law – $F = ma$.

Key vocabulary

acceleration • air bag • brakes • conservation • crumple zones • escape lane • force • impact • kinetic energy • momentum • seatbelt • velocity

Barriers to learning

Some students may need extra help with the mathematical content, especially changing the subject of an equation.

Curiosity and starter suggestions

- Demonstrate a model rocket, Stomp rocket or water rocket. [Outside activity.]

OR

- Show video clips of two car crashes in one of which people have not been wearing seatbelts.

Learning activities

Worksheet p3_f_01 + Practical p3_f_01

Low demand

Demonstrate the meaning of momentum using toy cars and a wall made from small bricks of polystyrene (or similar). Students note the effect of increasing the speed of a car and compare cars of small and large mass moving at the same speed.

Define momentum with unit (kg m/s). Emphasise that momentum is a vector; it has direction. Work an example to calculate momentum. Ask students to answer question 1 on page 208 of Student Book.

Explain that a sudden change in momentum in a collision results in a large force that can cause injury. Talk about the safety features found in a modern car including crumple zones, seat belts and air bags. Show photographs and/or video clips of these features. Point out that the person is stopped more slowly. This means the momentum change is less sudden and so the force on them is less.

Ask students to answer worksheet question 1 *Momentum*.

Teaching and learning notes: *Ensure that students understand that all the safety features mentioned reduce deceleration and hence the force on a person.*

Standard demand

Consider the equation 'momentum = mass × velocity'. Use it to show that the greater the mass and/or velocity of an object the greater its momentum in its direction of motion. Show how to rearrange the equation to calculate mass or velocity. Ask students to answer question 4 on page 209 of Student Book.

Introduce the equation '$F = (mv - mu) / t$'; i.e. 'force = change in momentum / time'.

Point out that a rapid change in momentum results in a large force. Apply this to the effect of seatbelts, air bags and crumple zones. Show video clips of these safety features if the 'low demand' section has not been covered. Note how they all increase the time a person takes to stop, reducing the force on them. Explain that some injuries in car accidents are due to a very rapid deceleration of parts of the body, for example forcing the brain against the skull, tearing blood vessels. This can happen even at moderate speeds such as 45 mph.

Ask students to answer worksheet question 2 *Force and momentum*.

Working in small groups students *either* design, build and test model crumple zones with trolleys, paper, straws, etc. *or* test seatbelt materials for stretching. Practical p3_f_01 supports this activity.

Care should be taken if using bricks in this activity.

Teaching and learning notes: *Different groups can carry out each class practical activity, depending on their ability.*

High demand

Interpret the principle of conservation of momentum to the collision of two objects moving in the same straight line.

Demonstrate trolleys colliding with different masses and velocities. This is only qualitative as the topic is covered in more detail in p5_d_01 and p5_d_02. Work through an example. Link the principle to the collision of cars, comparing large and small cars. Ask students to answer question 7 on page 209 of the Student Book.

Show how the equation '$F = (mv - mu) / t$' can be obtained by substituting $a = (v - u) / t$ in Newton's Second Law, ($F = ma$). Ensure that students can change the subject of this equation. Use the equation to explain how forces can be reduced when stopping by using features such as crumple zones, seat belts and air bags.

Ask students to answer worksheet question 3 *More force and momentum*.

Teaching and learning notes: *This section provides a more rigorous mathematical analysis of car safety features.*

Plenary suggestions

Word search based on words related to the lesson.

OR

In groups, students think up an idea for a slogan, advert or poster to publicise one of the safety features learnt about in the lesson.

Assessment opportunities

Worksheet p3_f_01 provides an opportunity to assess students' ability to cope with mathematical ideas as well as to explain the physics behind car safety features.

Answers

Answers to Student Book and Worksheet can be found on the Teacher Pack CD.

P3f: Crumple zones

Resources

Student Book pages 210–211 • Equipment for demonstrations • Videos of safety features • ICT equipment
Interactive Book Matching pairs: Falling objects
Files on Teacher Pack CD: p3_f_01_worksheet; p3_f_01_technician

Learning objectives

- Find out about some typical safety features of modern cars.
- Describe how safety features can make driving safer.
- Explain how ABS brakes work.

Learning outcomes

- Recall safety features which are intended to prevent accidents.
- Describe safety features which are intended to protect occupants in the event of a crash.
- Explain how ABS brakes allow greater control over steering and avoid skidding.

Prior knowledge

Recall basic facts about momentum and forces.

Key vocabulary

ABS (anti-lock braking system) • cruise control • electric windows • paddle shift controls • safety cage • seatbelt • traction control

Barriers to learning

Some students may need to be encouraged to consider an unfamiliar situation and suggest a solution.

Curiosity and starter suggestions

- Students solve anagrams of key words and then describe them.

OR

- Show photos of a vintage car and a modern car after an accident. Show Figure 4 on page 210 of Student Book.

Learning activities

Worksheet p3_f_02

Low demand

Recall the safety features of modern cars described in the previous lesson. Point out that these features – crumple zones, air bags, seatbelts and heating in the brakes – all absorb energy when vehicles stop suddenly.

Consider safety features that are designed to prevent accidents – ABS brakes, traction control, electric windows, paddle shift controls. Show photos/video clips of these features. Consider safety features that are designed to protect occupants in the event of an accident – crumple zones, safety cage, air bags, seat belts, collapsible steering column.

Ask students to answer worksheet question 1 *Car safety features* and questions 8–10 on page 210 of Student Book.

Show video clips from the previous lesson of two car crashes, in one of which people have not been wearing seatbelts. Recap the work done in the last lesson on seatbelts. Explain why seatbelts have to be replaced after a crash. In groups students discuss the risks and benefits of wearing seatbelts. Compare their responses.

Teaching and learning notes: *Ensure that students understand the difference between safety features that prevent accidents and those that protect occupants in the event of a crash.*

Standard demand

Recall how seatbelts, crumple zones and air bags are useful in a crash because they change shape, absorb energy and reduce injuries. Recap the work of the last lesson explaining their use in terms of momentum.

Show a computer model of a car that can be used to test how safe the design of the car is in a crash. The virtual car can be crashed over and over again, the effects investigated and the design easily changed until it is as safe as possible. This is much quicker and cheaper than building and crashing real cars.

Show video(s) of tests on safety features (such as cars being driven into a concrete wall at 70 mph on YouTube. Point out how such tests provide useful data to improve the design of existing safety features and suggest new additions to make driving safer. Explain that such tests, though expensive (car wrecked) are still used in addition to computer modelling as they can give a better approximation to a real accident, particularly with the new improved dummies that are available. Ask students to answer questions 11 and 12 on page 211 of Student Book.

Teaching and learning notes: *This section provides an opportunity to show students the techniques used and benefits of scientific research in a field that is familiar to them.*

High demand

Use $F = ma$ or $F = (mv - mu) / t$ to explain why forces can be reduced when stopping by increasing the stopping or collision time or distance, so decreasing acceleration. Show how this applies to secondary safety features. Explain the difference between these and primary safety features.

Ask students to answer questions 13 and 15 on page 211 of the Student Book.

Project Figure 7 from page 211 of Student Book on the board to support an explanation of how ABS brakes work. Show a video clip of cars with and without ABS brakes on a skid pan. Make it clear that ABS brakes *may* reduce braking distances but this is not their prime purpose.

Working in groups, students consider each secondary safety feature mentioned earlier in the lesson and produce a rank order list for their effectiveness in saving lives. [They may wish to refer to some of the information gathered earlier in the lesson, or use the Internet briefly to gain more data.]

Ask students to answer worksheet question 2 *Seatbelts*. Leave time for a general discussion on seatbelts.

Teaching and learning notes: *Ensure that students realise that ABS brakes are designed to avoid skidding, not to reduce braking distance, though this may also occur.*

Plenary suggestions

Project graph of road casualties over the last 40–50 years. Ask students to suggest reasons for the changes.

OR

In groups, students consider the advantages and limitations of computer models of car accidents.

Assessment opportunities

Observation of discussion groups allows assessment of students' ability to express themselves orally.

Answers

Student Book

Q8 Only need to push a button; can keep eyes on road • **Q9** Prevents steering column being forced into driver's chest in accident • **Q10** Risks: trapped in burning car, risk of chest injuries; benefits: prevent person being thrown through windscreen or out of car, reduce injuries because rear passengers could hit those in front in a crash; students' own ideas about why compulsory • **Q11** Can simulate what would happen to people in an accident so that improvements can be made • **Q12** To see the effect on people of different shapes and sizes • **Q13** Primary: help to prevent a crash; secondary: protect occupants in event of a crash • **Q14a** Hard continuous pressure activates anti-lock brakes, which then pump on and off automatically to avoid skidding • **Q14b** 7200 N • **Q15** Student's own ideas

Fig 4 prevents passenger compartment being crushed • **Fig 5** higher centre of mass so topples more easily • **Fig 6** not forward into windscreen if in front or pushing front occupants forward if in rear • **Fig 7** driver has better control over steering; avoids skidding

Worksheet

Answers to Worksheet can be found on the Teacher Pack CD.

P3g: Falling safely

Resources

Student Book pages 212–213 • Equipment for demonstrations and practical • Video of Red Devils • Animation of elephant and feather • ICT equipment

Files on Teacher Pack CD: p3_g_01_worksheet; p3_g_01_practical; p3_g_01_technician

Learning objectives

- Find out about the motion of falling objects.
- Describe how air resistance slows down falling objects.
- Find out about terminal speed.

Learning outcomes

- Realise that objects accelerate as they fall.
- Describe how air resistance, or drag, increases with speed, reducing the acceleration of falling objects.
- Explain how a falling object reaches a constant (terminal) speed when the forces on it are balanced.

Prior knowledge

Balanced and unbalanced forces.

Newton's Second Law – $F = ma$.

Key vocabulary

accelerate • air resistance • balanced • drag • force • free-fall • gravity • molecules • terminal speed

Barriers to learning

Some students find it difficult to understand that it is the *resultant* force that affects the motion of an object.

Curiosity and starter suggestions

- Show a video clip of the Red Devils display team (or similar).

OR

- Measure the bounce height when a ping-pong ball is dropped from 30 cm, 60 cm, 90 cm and 120 cm.

Learning activities

Worksheet p3_g_01 + Practical p3_g_01

Low demand

Drop a ball. Repeat several times. Ask students to describe its motion and explain why it falls. [Make sure you elicit the idea that the ball accelerates because it is pulled by its weight (gravity) towards the centre of Earth.] Repeat with a different ball.

Drop a ball and an A4 sheet of paper. Repeat holding the paper with a different area of cross-section. Ask students to comment on the time each takes to fall.

Demonstrate the 'Guinea and feather' experiment (drop a small ball and a feather in a glass tube, with and without air in it). Draw free body diagrams of the forces acting on the ball and the feather with and without air in the tube to introduce the idea of a frictional force (air resistance or drag) that slows down a falling object. This can be reinforced by an animation showing, for example, a falling elephant and feather. Describe how objects falling through Earth's atmosphere reach a terminal speed.

Consider the effect of cross-sectional area on the motion of the sheet of paper and the feather. Link its motion to the displacement of air molecules providing a drag force that increases with cross-sectional area.

Ask students to answer questions 1 and 2 on page 212 of Student Book.

Ask students to answer worksheet question 1 *Forces on a cyclist*. [The list of missing words can be omitted and used only to support less able students.]

Teaching and learning notes: *Check that students have remembered the work on balanced and unbalanced forces from p3_c_01 and p3_c_02 before starting on the new material.*

Standard demand

Drop ball bearings through tall measuring cylinders of water and cooking oil to show liquid friction / drag. Position light gates connected to a data logger or accurate timers to decide whether terminal velocity is reached. If terminal velocity is reached note its value.

Show a video clip of Red Devils. Repeat and link the motion to the graph on page 213 of Student Book. Project graph on screen or OHT so that both can be viewed together. Pause the video at appropriate points to aid explanation. Analyse each stage of the parachutist's motion, explaining it in terms of the forces acting on a parachutist.

Answer questions 3–5 on page 213 of Student Book.

In small groups ask students to make parachutes and test them. Practical p3_g_01 supports this activity.

Teaching and learning notes: *Ensure students can explain each stage of the parachutist's fall in terms of the forces acting on him/her and how these forces change.*

High demand

Look again at the graph showing the motion of a free fall parachutist on page 213 of the Student Book. Explain the motion in more detail, in terms of the balance of forces at each stage of the motion. The video could be shown again, possibly linked with the graph as above.

Ask students to answer questions 6–8 on page 213 of the Student Book.

Ask students to answer worksheet question 2 *Sky diving*.

Teaching and learning notes: *This section provides a more rigorous mathematical analysis of terminal speed.*

Plenary suggestions

Definitions – students define key words from this item and use each in a sentence to make their meaning clear.

OR

'High flying sky-diver'.

Assessment opportunities

Practical p3_g_01 provides an opportunity to assess students' ability to plan, carry out and evaluate practical work. Students' responses to worksheet p3_g_01 indicate how well the lesson has been understood.

Answers

Student Book

Q1 It decelerates • **Q2** No air resistance/drag force • **Q3** Continue to fall at a high terminal speed • **Q4** To increase cross-sectional area, displacing more air molecules, increasing air resistance • **Q5** Forward force becomes greater than backward force • **Q6** Charlie; terminal speed occurs when air resistance = weight, so need bigger air resistance force to balance Charlie's weight → higher speed • **Q7** see graph • **Q8** E.g. pedal faster; become more streamlined

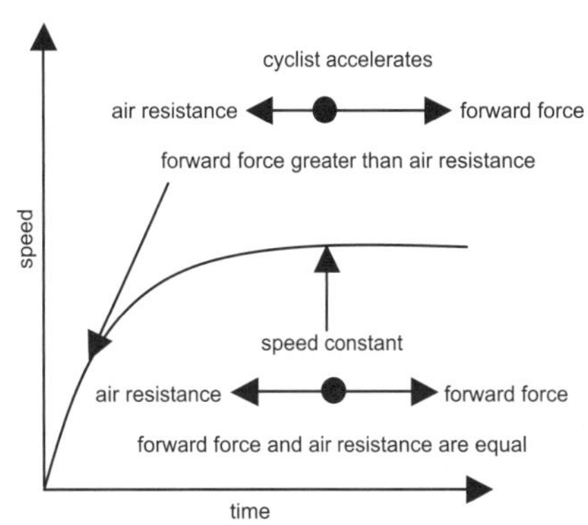

Fig 1 parachute gives bigger upward force • **Fig 2** smaller weight down, larger air resistance force up • **Fig 3** air resistance / drag • **Fig 4** they are balanced • **Fig 5** decreases

Worksheet

Q1 Balanced, constant, air resistance, drag, streamlined, decreases, faster, forward, friction • **Q2a** Zero • **Q2b** 10 m/s^2 • **Q2ci** Decreases • **Q2cii** Upward force of air resistance increases as her speed increases • **Q2d** 700 N • **Q2ei** • Parachute has a large cross-sectional area so she displaces more air molecules each second creating bigger upward force • **Q2eii** 7.14 m/s^2 • **Q2f** 700 N • **Q2gi** Smaller • **Q2gii** Large surface area of parachute means it displaces more air molecules so the air resistance force equals her weight at a lower speed • **Q2h** Increases her cross-sectional area and so the air resistance force is greater, decreasing her terminal speed

P3g: Falling safely

Resources

Student Book pages 214–215 • Equipment for demonstrations • Video of astronaut dropping a spanner on the Moon and walking on the Moon ▪ Video of pursuit cyclists • ICT equipment

Files on Teacher Pack CD: p3_g_02_worksheet; p3_g_02_technician

Learning objectives

- Describe how friction forces affect motion.
- Explain how changes to the shapes of moving objects can influence their terminal speed.
- Find out about the acceleration in free-fall.

Learning outcomes

- Recognise that frictional forces oppose motion, leading to energy loss and inefficiency.
- Explain how streamlined shapes have less resistance to motion so achieve higher terminal speeds.
- Understand that acceleration due to gravity is the same for any object at a given point on Earth's surface.

Prior knowledge

How balanced and unbalanced forces affect the motion of an object.

How the shape of moving objects can affect their speed.

Key vocabulary

acceleration • friction • gravitational field strength • gravity • lubricate • streamline • terminal speed

Barriers to learning

Curiosity and starter suggestions

- Watch the motion of two similar pendulums, one lightly damped and the other heavily damped. Ask students to account for the difference in their motion.

OR

- Show video clip of astronaut dropping a spanner on the Moon.

Learning activities

Worksheet p3_g_02

Low demand

Release two similar toy cars / trolleys at the top of a ramp, one half of which is covered with carpet or sandpaper. Use this to talk about friction as a force that slows things down, leading to energy loss and inefficiency. Explain how friction can be reduced by lubricating (oiling), e.g. moving parts of a car engine.

Show photographs of streamlined objects, e.g. dolphin, sports car, racing cyclist, diver, athlete with tight-fitting clothes. Remind students that cars having a streamlined shape have a higher top speed and use less fuel. Mention the effect of roof racks, open windows, etc. Look at Figure 7 on page 214 of Student Book.

Ask students to answer questions 9 and 10 on page 214 of Student Book.

Ask students to answer worksheet question 1 *Streamlining*.

Teaching and learning notes: *The idea of drag was introduced via falling objects in the last lesson as it affects all falling objects except when there is no atmosphere. It applies equally to other objects moving in a fluid so aim to include a range of situations that are relevant to your students.*

Standard demand

Remind students that objects fall towards Earth due to gravitational attraction.

Students carry out a class experiment to measure the acceleration due to gravity. The method used will depend on the resources available. You may choose to have a circus of different methods and compare the accuracy of each at the end of the activity. For this reason no practical worksheet is provided. Possible methods include:

- ticker tape attached to a falling ball (gives a poor result but good as one of several methods)
- ball with built-in timer
- electromagnet simultaneously releasing steel ball bearing and starting timer, which is stopped when ball opens trap door
- two light gates with card to interrupt light beams and two accurate timers or data logger
- one light gate attached to data logger and computer with 'picket fence' or U-shaped card to interrupt light beam.

Discuss the results.

Ask students to answer questions 11 and 12 on page 215 of Student Book.

Point out that the acceleration due to gravity (*g)* is the same for any object at a given point on Earth's surface.

Compare *g* on Earth with *g* on the Moon. Show second Starter activity if not already used. Show video clip of astronauts walking on the Moon.

Ask students to answer worksheet question 2 *Freefall*.

Teaching and learning notes: *Ensure students can describe one method of measuring 'g'.*

High demand

Talk about the slight variation in *g* at different points on Earth's surface (a) due to the shape of the Earth (b) due to altitude (*g* is slightly smaller at the top of Everest than down a mineshaft).

Discuss some of the problems caused by the slightly lower value of *g* for climbers of Mount Everest.

Ask students to answer questions 13 to 14 on page 215 of the Student Book and worksheet question 3 *About* g.

Teaching and learning notes: *Students could be asked to research the variation in* g *if time permits.*

Plenary suggestions

'Quick quiz' – multiple choice questions.

OR

Show a video clip of pursuit cyclists. Ask students to explain why they change places.

Assessment opportunities

Students' responses to worksheet p3_g_02 indicate how well the lesson has been understood.

Answers

Student Book

Q9 To move faster through the water / to catch prey more easily • **Q10** e.g. by bending over handlebars, helmet style, tight fitting clothes • **Q11** Air molecules present, so gravity is not the only force acting • **Q12a** Increases • **Q12b** Acceleration reduces • **Q12c** B • **Q13** Larger; nearer to centre of Earth • **Q14** Slightly less acceleration when dropped; less KE on reaching ground, less deceleration as it rises after bounce

Fig 6 oppose motion • **Fig 7** airflow is smooth

Worksheet

Q1a Smooth shape that reduces friction / drag / air resistance • **Q1bi** To go faster • **Q1bii** E.g. crouch over handlebars, wear sleek helmet, wear tight fitting clothes • **Q1ci** To increase top speed / fuel consumption • **Q1cii** Remove luggage on roof • **Q2ai** Falling under influence of gravity only • **Q2aii** E.g. object falling above Earth's atmosphere • **Q2cbi** Much further away • **Q2bii** 0.003 m/s^2 • **Q2biii** Earth falls away from Moon due to its curvature • **Q2biv** 0.003 N • **Q3a** Earth has slightly smaller radius at poles than at equator • **Q3bi** Balanced • **Q3bii** Resistive force (e.g. drag), mass of car and load, engine size • **Q3biii** Streamlined design • **Q3ci** Fall more rapidly; much greater acceleration • **Q3cii** 750 N • **Q3ciii** 2250 N • **Q3civ** 6 m/s^2 (6 N/kg) • **Q3cv** Mass of Zog is greater than that of Earth; mass of Hoki is less than that of Earth

P3h: The energy of games and theme rides

Resources

Student Book pages 216–217 • Equipment for demonstrations and practical • Video clips of vertical drop ride at a theme park and space flight lift-off • ICT equipment

Files on Teacher Pack CD: p3_h_01_worksheet; p3_h_01_practical; p3_h_01_technician

Learning objectives

- Find out about gravitational potential energy.
- Calculate gravitational potential energy.
- Explain that there is usually a transfer of gravitational potential energy to kinetic energy as an object falls.

Learning outcomes

- Recognise that objects have gravitational potential energy because of their mass and position in Earth's gravitational field.
- Use the equation GPE = *mgh*.
- Interpret examples of energy transfer between gravitational potential energy and kinetic energy.
- Understand what happens to the gravitational potential energy lost by an object falling at terminal speed (high demand).

Prior knowledge

- The effect of air resistance on falling objects.
- Terminal speed.

Key vocabulary

air resistance • efficiency • gravitational potential energy • kinetic energy • mass • sound energy • terminal speed • thermal energy • work

Barriers to learning

Ensure that students realise that energy cannot be lost, only transferred to other forms. There is a tendency to speak about lost energy in general usage, meaning wasted energy or a particular form of energy.

Curiosity and starter suggestions

- Bounce several different balls. Repeat. Ask students to comment on their motion and suggest reasons for their observations.

OR

- Show video clip of vertical drop ride at a theme park (e.g. Oblivion at Alton Towers)

Learning activities

Worksheet p3_h_01 + Practical p3_h_01

Low demand

Hold (i) two similar balls at different heights; (ii) a heavy ball (e.g. golf ball) and a light ball (e.g. ping-pong ball) at the same height. Ask students which ball has the greater gravitational potential energy in each case. Show other examples using everyday objects if time.

Conclude that gravitational potential energy increases with: (a) more mass, (b) more height.

Ask students to answer questions 1 and 2 on page 216 of Student Book and / or worksheet question 1 *Riding on a roller coaster.*

Teaching and learning notes: *Make sure students realise that gravitational potential energy depends on the mass of an object as well as its position in Earth's gravitational field.*

Standard demand

Introduce the equation GPE = *mgh*. Work an example and talk about the correct units for each quantity. Ask students to answer question 4 on page 217 of Student Book.

Show class some examples of energy transfer between GPE and KE. For example, drop a ball, or look at an oscillating pendulum. Notice that falling objects convert GPE to KE and rising objects convert KE to GPE. Point out that the objects eventually stop moving. Ask what has happened to the apparently lost energy and get students to suggest what other energy forms are involved.

Students carry out an experiment to measure the bounce height when a ping pong ball is dropped from various heights. Bounce a ball to explain what is meant by the efficiency of the bounce. Practical p3_h_01 supports this activity. Ask students to answer question 5 on page 217 of Student Book.

Show a video clip of the lift-off of a space flight. Explain that during lift-off astronauts experience much greater gravitational forces than usual (the so-called G-force). Relate this to the changes in G-force during theme park rides.

Ask students to answer Worksheet question 2 *Gravitational potential energy*.

Teaching and learning notes: *It is difficult to record accurate values for the bounce heights in the practical activity. It provides an opportunity to discuss best practice in this situation.*

High demand

Show how the equation 'GPE = *mgh*' can be rearranged to calculate *m* or *h*. Work an example. Ask students to answer question 6 on page 217 of Student Book.

Ask students to look at the graph they obtained for the class experiment with a ping pong ball. Ask them to sketch the shape of the graph they would expect if they had dropped the ping pong ball from greater heights.

Pick a student who has shown it reaching terminal velocity to sketch his/her graph on board. Relate this to the GPE and KE of the ball. Point out that at terminal speed the KE is constant but the GPE is decreasing. Explain that the GPE lost is used to do work against friction with the air particles, heating the ball and air a little. Ask students to answer questions 5 and 7 on page 217 of the Student Book.

Talk about why squash players 'warm up' by hitting the ball around with their racquets before a game. Demonstrate the bounciness of cold and warm squash balls to illustrate this.

Ask students to answer Worksheet question 3 *More gravitational potential energy*.

Plenary suggestions

Play a 'Loop game' to remind pupils of some of the key points from the lesson

OR

Each pupil writes three questions based on the lesson and, working in pairs, asks his/her partner to answer them.

Assessment opportunities

The practical task provides an opportunity to assess students' ability to plan, carry out and evaluate practical work. Students' responses to worksheet p3_h_01 indicate how well the lesson has been understood.

Answers

Student Book

Q1 GPE • **Q2** Sam's Dad • **Q3a** GPE + KE • **Q3b** Energy changed to other forms – heat, sound – due to friction • **Q4** 42 000J • **Q5** Take up a horizontal position / increase his cross-sectional area • **Q6** 125 km/h (34.6 m/s); some energy is converted to heat and sound due to friction • **Q7** 60 000J

Fig 1 increases • **Fig 2** to gain GPE (to convert to KE as it falls) • **Fig 3** GPE → KE → GPE • **Fig 4** energy transferred to other forms such as sound, thermal energy • **Fig 5** becomes constant

Worksheet

Q1a To gain GPE • **Q1bi** Ali feels four times his normal weight • **Q1bii** 240 N • **Q2a** 30 000 J • **Q2bi** 1 J • **Q2bii** KE at B; elastic potential energy at C • **Q2biii** 0.6 J • **Q2biv** 0.4 J • **Q2bv** Changed to thermal and sound energy • **Q2bvi** 40% • **Q3a** 4 m • **Q3bi** 105 000 J • **Q3bii** Does not change • **Q3biii** Lost GPE transferred to heat in air due to friction

P3h: The energy of games and theme rides

Resources

Student Book pages 218–219 • Equipment for demonstrations and practical • Video clips of roller coaster rides, how a roller coaster works • Video of a water-powered funicular railway • ICT equipment

Files on Teacher Pack CD: p3_h_02_worksheet; p3_h_02_practical; p3_h_02_technician

Learning objectives

- Suggest everyday examples in which objects have gravitational potential energy.
- Describe the physics behind a gravity ride (roller coaster).
- Understand the effect of mass and speed on the kinetic energy of an object.

Learning outcomes

- Recognise examples of everyday objects that have gravitational potential energy.
- Interpret a roller coaster in terms of kinetic energy, gravitational potential energy and energy transfer qualitatively and (high demand only) quantitatively.
- Describe that doubling the mass of an object doubles its kinetic energy but doubling its speed quadruples its kinetic energy.

Prior knowledge

How to calculate gravitational potential energy and kinetic energy.

Key vocabulary

air resistance • funicular railway • friction • gravitational potential energy (GPE) • gravity • heat • height • kinetic energy (KE) • mass • roller coaster • sound • speed • terminal

Barriers to learning

The lesson develops students' ability to calculate energy types and to use equations for energy transfers in the context of roller coasters. Low demand students may find it easier to explain observations in terms of forces first.

Curiosity and starter suggestions

- Show students a model roller coaster, e.g. one made from a child's construction kit.

OR

- Show video of a water-powered cliff railway, e.g. the one connecting Lynton and Lynmouth in Devon.

Learning activities

Worksheet p3_h_02 + Practical p3_h_02

Low demand

Remind students of the factors that affect the gravitational potential energy and kinetic energy of an object, using balls and model cars to illustrate. Ask students to answer questions 8 and 9 on page 218 of Student Book.

Look at a video clip of a roller coaster ride. Repeat and pause if necessary, so that students notice how the speed changes during the ride and where gravitational potential energy and kinetic energy have their greatest and least values.

Show the video clip of a water-powered cliff railway, like the one connecting Lynton and Lynmouth in Devon, shown in Figure 6 on page 218 of Student Book. This may have been used as a Starter activity but is worth showing again. Explain how it works. Ask students to answer worksheet question 1 *The Lynton and Lynmouth Cliff Railway.*

Teaching and learning notes: *The examples fit the theme of the lesson but should be used to reinforce the work on energy forms and energy transfers from earlier in the unit.*

Standard demand

Show a video clip of a roller coaster ride at a theme park if low demand section has not been used to introduce an explanation of how a roller coaster works in terms of energy changes. Discuss the principle of energy conservation in this context. A video clip of how a roller coaster works is also useful to illustrate your explanation.

Ask students to answer questions 10 and 11 on page 219 of Student Book.

Students work in small groups to design their own roller coaster. They could be shown the first Starter activity to aid understanding of what is expected and the type of apparatus from which they will construct their model. This can be done using research from the internet or by studying some pictures of roller coasters and deciding on the necessary parameters for it to work. Students build a model of their design using plastic track and toy cars. They calculate the efficiency of their ride (= drop height/climb height x 100). Practical p3_h_02 supports this activity.

Consider the effect of changing mass and speed on kinetic energy. In particular, consider the effect of doubling the mass and then the speed. Ask students to answer question 12 on page 219 of Student Book.

Consider everyday examples in which objects use gravitational potential energy, such as hydroelectric power, a falling weight operating an old fashioned pendulum clock, roller coaster. Discuss the energy transfers involved.

Ask students to answer worksheet question 2 *Roller coasters*.

Teaching and learning notes: *Students could be asked to prepare a presentation on their roller coaster design.*

High demand

Using a roller coaster as an example, explain that, ignoring friction, as the carriage falls, loss of GPE = gain in KE so $mgh = \frac{1}{2} mv^2$. Show that, for an object falling to Earth, this can be rearranged to give $h = v^2 / 2g$. Point out that this is independent of the mass of the falling object. Explain that this means that all objects dropped through the same vertical height reach the same speed, in the absence of friction. Work an example. Ask students to answer questions 13 and 14 on page 219 of the Student Book. Ask students to answer worksheet question 3 *Falling to Earth.*

Plenary suggestions

Crossword using key words from the unit.

OR

Ask some students to demonstrate the model roller coaster they made and describe the physics principles they used in its design.

Assessment opportunities

The practical task provides an opportunity to assess students' understanding of the physics principles involved in roller coasters and their ability to use their knowledge to design and construct a working model.

Answers

Student Book

Q8 Increase mass; increase height • **Q9** Increase mass; increase speed • **Q10** GPE to KE conversion not perfect as energy is transferred to sound/thermal energy due to friction; less energy available to convert to GPE at each successive climb • **Q11** To give extra GPE to roller coaster so it can continue for longer • **Q12a** Sam has half as much KE (9 000J) as his Dad (18 000 J) • **Q12b** 2250 J • **Q12c** 4500 J • **Q13a** At B: 14.1 m/s • **Q13b** At D: 18.4 m/s • **Q13c** calculation assumed perfect GPE–KE conversion; some energy transferred to sound/thermal energy

Fig 6 down • **Fig 7** no – speeds and masses not known; racehorse has greater speed but less mass • **Fig 8** GPE as it rises, KE as it falls

Worksheet

Q1a E.g. very steep cliff separates villages; in 1888 roads not good/no cars • **Q1b** No pollution as local water used but returned to river; water not pumped • **Q1c** Down • **Q1d** Decrease • **Q1e** Weight of top car pulls bottom car up / loss of GPE by 'down' car equates to gain of GPE by 'up' car (+ sound/thermal energy) • **Q1f** Gravity gives top car weight so that it can pull bottom car up • **Q2a** X marked at A • **Q2b** Y marked at lowest point of track • **Q2c** GPE → KE → GPE etc not perfect; some energy transferred to sound/thermal energy • **Q2d** 50% • **Q2e** New peaks less high than B; second less high than first extra one • **Q3a** 200 000J • **Q3b** 150 000J • **Q3c** 17.3 m/s • **Q3d** Some energy transferred to sound/thermal energy • **Q3e** None • **Q3f** E.g. winch car up a slope part way round course/ winch car up higher at first

P3: Analysis and evaluation

Pages 220–221 in the Student Book prepare students for assessment.

When and how to use these pages

This task provides an opportunity to build and assess the skills that students will use when analysing and evaluating data.

Annotated hints and tips guide students through the tasks. Ask students to:

- read through the context and tasks, listing any terms that they do not understand
- as a whole class or in small groups, discuss the tasks to ensure all students understand the terminology used and to clarify what is required
- work individually to answer the questions for each task.

If time allows, ask students to mark each other's work using the mark scheme provided.

Pages 278–290 provide further guidance on Practical and Enquiry Skills.

Notes

Students are asked to find out if there is a simple relationship between the drop height and the bounce height of a ball and whether all balls bounce in the same way. They can produce their own results or use the data provided on page 221 of the Student Book. If time permits students could obtain their own experimental results in the previous lesson.

Students are asked to calculate mean values for the bounce height of two different balls for a range of drop heights. They then use the same set of axes to plot graphs of mean bounce height (*y*-axis) against drop height (*x*-axis) for each ball. Some students may need some support, in addition to that provided in the Student Book, to decide on the best scales to use. The task leads students through the key points that should be addressed to obtain a good mark for analysing and evaluating data so that on future occasions they can carry out a similar task without prompting.

Answers

This mark scheme is also available on the Teacher Pack CD.

ping-pong ball			
drop height in cm	bounce height in cm 1	bounce height in cm 2	mean bounce height in cm
110	74.4	74.2	74.3
100	70.0	69.0	69.5
90	65.8	66.2	66.0
80	61.0	60.7	60.9
70	54.6	54.4	54.5
60	47.2	47.0	47.1
40	32.1	31.7	31.9

tennis ball			
drop height in cm	bounce height in cm 1	bounce height in cm 2	mean bounce height in cm
110	70.8	71.3	71.1
100	63.8	64.2	64.0
90	58.4	58.8	58.6
80	50.2	50.6	50.4
70	45.5	45.9	45.7
60	39.1	38.8	39.0
50	33.2	32.7	33.0

Values of the mean bounce height should be given to the same degree of accuracy as the experimental values.

The vertical axis could start at 30 cm using a larger scale but most students would not have the mathematical skills required to be able to check for proportionality. Both graph lines must pass through the origin (0,0).

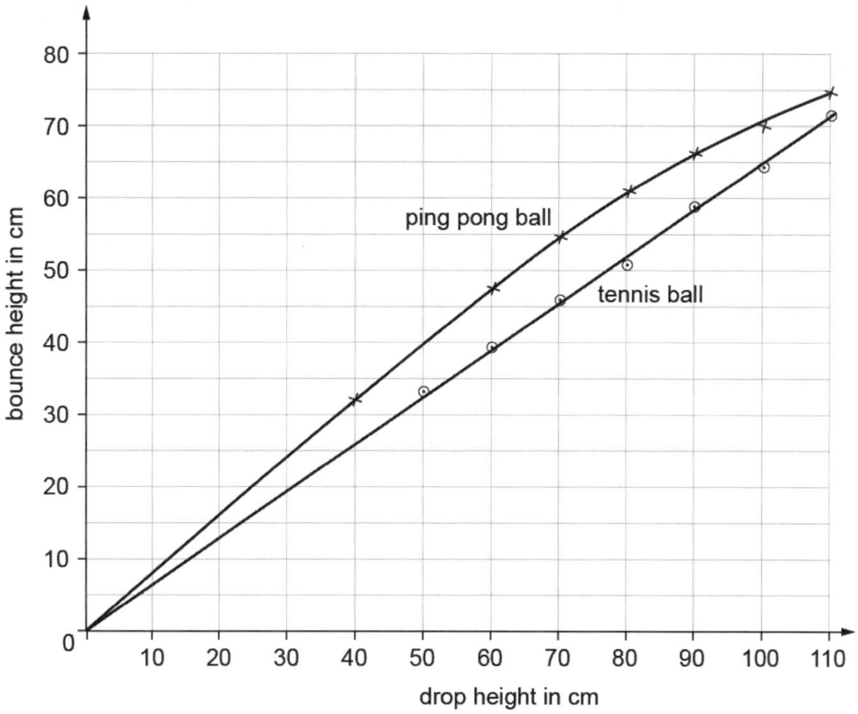

The graph for the tennis ball is a straight line through the origin showing proportionality. The graph for the ping pong ball starts linearly but curves above a drop height of about 80 cm.

The results show that all balls do not bounce in the same way.

The bounce height is hard to measure. Students could ensure that the height is read at eye level to the bottom of the ball and drop the ball first to get an idea of how high it bounces so that they know where to look. It would be sensible to repeat each measurement more than once.

The experiment is quite reliable, considering the difficulty of measuring the bounce height, as the repeat readings are all fairly similar.

The tennis ball weighs more than the ping pong ball and although it displaces more air molecules as it moves the air resistance force, or drag, is always very small compared to its weight so bounce height is proportional to drop height. [Remember drag increases as speed increases.] The ping-pong ball has a smaller air resistance force acting on it but this force is a bigger proportion of its weight (typically only about 0.25 N) so the resultant force on it when dropped from above about 80 cm is significant, reducing the bounce height.

P3: Checklist

Pages 222–223 in the Student Book provide a student-friendly checklist for revision.

When and how to use these pages

This checklist is presented in three columns showing progression, based on the grading criteria.

Remind students that they need to be able to use these ideas in various ways, such as:

- interpreting pictures, diagrams and graphs
- applying ideas to new situations
- explaining ethical implications
- suggesting some benefits and risks to society
- drawing conclusions from evidence they have been given.

These pages can be used for individual or class revision using any combination of the suggestions below.

- Ask students to construct a mind map linking the points on this checklist.
- Work through the checklist as a class and note the points that need further class discussion.
- Ask students to tick the boxes on the checklist worksheet (Teacher Pack CD) if they feel confident that they are well prepared for the topics. Students should refer back to the relevant Student Book pages to revise the points that they feel less confident about.
- Ask students to use the search terms to do further research on the different points in the checklist.
- Students could work in pairs, and ask each other what points they think they can do, and why they think that they can do those, and not others.

Pages 278–299 provide further assessment guidance.

Module summary

In the introduction to this section, students were presented with a number of new ideas. Work through the list below as part of their revision. Ask students to write their own summaries and mind maps, using this list as a starting point:

- speed and average speed
- interpreting distance–time and speed–time graphs
- calculating acceleration
- the relationship between force, mass and acceleration
- relative velocity of objects moving in parallel
- describe thinking, braking and stopping distances
- the factors that may affect thinking, braking and stopping distances
- alternatives to petrol and diesel as fuels for cars
- evaluating data about fuel consumption and emissions
- the importance of thinking, braking and stopping distances in road safety
- the meaning of 'work' in physics and how to calculate work done
- the meaning of power and how to work it out
- the meaning of momentum and its link with force
- safety features in cars designed to prevent accidents, such as ABS brakes and traction control
- safety features in cars to protect occupants in an accident, including crumple zones, airbags and seatbelts
- how the balance of forces affects motion
- how objects falling through Earth's atmosphere reach a terminal speed
- energy transfer between gravitational potential energy and kinetic energy
- the physics of roller coasters and other theme park rides

Notes

P3: Exam-style questions: Foundation

Pages 224–225 in the Student Book are exam-style questions for Foundation students.

When and how to use these pages

These questions are based on module P3 and cover a range of different types of questions that students will encounter in their written exams.

- Questions could be used as a revision test once you've completed the section.
- Work through the questions as a class as part of a revision lesson.
- Ask students to mark each other's work, using the mark scheme provided.
- As a class, make a list of the questions that most students did not get right. Work through these as a class.

Notes on worked example

The worked example concerns some safety features of modern cars.

The student starts well, explaining two advantages of electric windows although there is only one mark available. Part a(ii) asked for a feature that prevents accidents but 'airbags', as quoted by the student, help to reduce injury in the event of a crash; ABS brakes or traction control would have been acceptable responses.

Part b focuses on seatbelts. Two marks are available in part b(i) for explaining how seatbelts protect a car's occupants if there is an accident, suggesting that two good points are required. The student's answer is much too brief. Again in part b(ii) the student's response is too vague; reference to the possible overstretching of the fabric is expected.

Assessment objectives

These exam-style questions cover the Assessment objectives as described below.

Assessment objectives		Questions
AO1	Recall, select and communicate their knowledge and understanding of science	2b, 2c, 2d, 4b
AO2	Apply skills, knowledge and understanding of science in practical and other contexts	1, 2a, 3, 4a, 4c, 5
AO3	Analyse and evaluate evidence, make reasoned judgements and draw conclusions based on evidence	2e, 6

Answers

These answers are also supplied on the Teacher Pack CD so that students can mark their own, or their peer's work.

Question number	Answer	Additional notes	Mark
1a	7.03 km/h	Accept 7030 m/h / 1.95 m/s for 3 marks. 7.03 / 6, 7030 / 6, 7030 / (6 × 3600) scores 1 with consistent unit scores 2	3
b	speed not constant / Darren goes faster and slower than this at times		1
			[4]
2a	15 m, 14 m, 46 m, 72 m		4

b	braking distance increases so stopping distance increases		1
c	braking distance increases so stopping distance increases		1
d	thinking distance increases so stopping distance increases		1
e	Any two from Thinking distance and / or braking distance increase with speed; Braking distance increases more than thinking distance; Stopping distance increases very rapidly as speed increases making a collision more likely		2
			[9]
3a	0.5 m/s^2	10 / 20 scores 1 mark	2 1
b	400 or '800 × answer to part a' N	800 × 0.5 or '800 × answer to part a' scores 1	2 1
c	bigger		1
			[7]
4a	600 J	400 × 1.5 scores 1 mark	2 1
b	gravitational potential energy / GPE		1
c	Transferred to kinetic energy		1
			[5]
5a	3000 J	500 × 6 scores one mark	2 1
b	400 or 'answer to part a /7.5' W	3000 / 7.5 or 'answer to part a / 7.5'scores 1 mark	2 1
			[6]
6	**Level 3** **Level 2** **Level 1** Additional guidance for each 6 mark question is provided on the CD-rom..	(5–6 marks) (3–4 marks) (1–2 marks)	
			[6]
			[27]

P3: Exam-style questions: Higher

Pages 226–227 in the Student Book are exam-style questions for Higher students.

When and how to use these pages

These questions are based on module P3 and cover a range of different types of questions that students will encounter in their written exams.

- Questions could be used as a revision test once you've completed the section.
- Work through the questions as a class as part of a revision lesson.
- Ask students to mark each other's work, using the mark scheme provided.
- As a class, make a list of the questions that most students did not get right. Work through these as a class.

Notes on worked example

The worked example takes students through a question about a car journey.

In part a the student demonstrates good ability to select the correct equations and to substitute the appropriate values, but loses one mark as the whole expression in a(ii) has been squared, rather than just the velocity, when calculating kinetic energy using the equation $KE = ½ mv^2$. The writing of 202 for 20^2 does not incur a further penalty but is indicative of the student's failure to understand the meaning of the equation, as also shown in the answer to part c.

Part b asks for an *explanation* for the decrease in acceleration using ideas about forces. The student should have linked the additional backward force to the component of the weight of the car down the hill. This extra resistive force reduces the resultant force, F (= forward force – backward force) and hence the acceleration since, by rearranging the equation *F* = *ma*, the acceleration, a = resultant force / mass.

In part c the student has failed to appreciate the significance of squaring the velocity when calculating kinetic energy (KE = ½ mv^2). While correctly spotting that the speed is halved, the student fails to realise that the kinetic energy will be quartered.

Assessment objectives

These exam-style questions cover the Assessment objectives as described below.

Assessment objectives		Questions
AO1	Recall, select and communicate their knowledge and understanding of science	2a(i), 2b, 2c
AO2	Apply skills, knowledge and understanding of science in practical and other contexts	1, 2a(ii), 2a(iii), 3, 4
AO3	Analyse and evaluate evidence, make reasoned judgements and draw conclusions based on evidence	5

Answers

These answers are also supplied on the Teacher Pack CD so that students can mark their own, or their peer's work.

Question number	Answer	Additional notes	Mark
1a	0.2 m/s^2	3 / 15 scores 1 mark.	2 1
b	112.5 m	Attempt to calculate the area under the graph scores 1 mark.	3
c	45 s		1

d	No Area under graph (= distance travelled) would be less so does not travel as far.		2
			[9]
2a(i)	10 m/s^2		1
a(ii)	Air resistance / drag increases as speed increases. Resultant force is less so acceleration (= F/m) is less.		2
a(iii)	Make body horizontal / spread arms and legs (to maximise cross-sectional area and so drag).		1
b	Any two from: > As speed increases, drag increases so resultant force decreases. > When forward force / weight equals drag there is no resultant force, > so no acceleration – terminal velocity reached.	Forces acting must be named. These forces become balanced is acceptable for 'no resultant force'	2
c	Energy dissipated into surroundings / heats up air a little.		1
			[7]
3a(i)	600 N	Both number and unit must be correct.	1
a(ii)	12 000 J	600 × 0.25 × 80 scores 1 mark 25 cm not changed to m, giving answer 1 200 000 J scores 1 mark.	2 1
a(iii)	100 W	12 000 / (2 x 60) scores 1 mark.	2 1
b	Andy weighs more than Beckie.		1
			[7]
4a	24 000 kg m/s	1200 x 20 scores 1 mark.	2 1
b	Crumple zones increase the time taken by car to stop. Force = rate of change of momentum / $F = (mv - mu) / t$. If time, *t*, increases, force, *F*, decreases.		3
			[6]
5	**Level 3** **Level 2** **Level 1** Additional guidance for each 6 mark question is provided on the CD-ROM.	(5–6 marks) (3–4 marks) (1–2 marks)	
			[6]
			[35]

P4: Introduction

Pages 228–229 in the Student Book provide an introduction to module P4.

When and how to use these pages

These pages summarise what students should already know from previous GCSE units and provide an overview of the content that they will learn in this module.

- Use these pages as a revision lesson before you start the first new topic.
- Brainstorm everything that students remember about the different topics using the headings as a starting point. Compare your list with the points in the Student Book.
- Use the questions on the left-hand page as a starting point for class discussions.
- Ask students if they can tell you anything about the topics on the right-hand page.
- Make a note of any unfamiliar / difficult terms and return to these in the relevant lessons.

You can revisit these pages at the following points:

- before the lessons on Ultrasound pages 242–245
- before the lessons on What is radioactivity? pages 248–251
- before the lessons on Uses of radioisotopes pages 252–255.

Overview of module

In this section students will learn what causes static electricity and how it is used in some everyday applications. They will study how static electricity can be a nuisance and, in some situations, even dangerous. Methods that can be used to overcome the problems caused by static electricity will also be studied.

Students will learn about current electricity in the home and how it can be used safely. They will study earth wires, fuses and circuit breakers as safety devices.

Students will learn about ultrasound and how it can be used in medicine for both diagnosis and for treatment.

They will look at the nature and properties of alpha, beta and gamma radiation and their respective uses. How to calculate radioactive half-life and what happens to a nucleus when it emits alpha or beta radiation.

Students then move on to learning how objects are dated using radioactive carbon and how power is produced by fission of uranium. Finally the potential of fusion power is explored as a new and exciting alternative to current methods of power production.

Barriers to learning

Students may need extra guidance with the following terms and concepts:

Terminology

Students may become confused between magnetic attraction and repulsion and static electrical attraction and repulsion. Encourage them to say like *charges* repel and not like *poles*.

Charges and conducting

Students may not realise that anything can be made to conduct electricity if a high enough voltage is used.

Make sure that higher students understand that electrons carry a negative charge and that an absence of electrons leaves an object positively charged.

Make sure students realise that liquids can be charged and if all drops have the same charge they will repel equally from each other and produce an even spray.

Current, voltage and resistance

Students always have difficulty with the difference between current and voltage in a circuit.

More able students will be required to rearrange the equation for resistance.

Mains electricity

Students may be confused by the plug having 3 wires when they are used to two connections in a circuit – positive and negative. The Earth wire is only used when there is a problem.

Make sure students appreciate that mains current is alternating which is different to cells and batteries which provide direct current.

Ultrasound

Students will have studied sound in KS3 and it is important to emphasise that the only difference with ultrasound is the high frequency.

Students may have seen ultrasound scan pictures but may be less familiar with ultrasound being used as a method of treatment.

Radioactivity

Emphasise that background radiation is all around us and that we have evolved in a radioactive environment.

Students may find it difficult to understand how atoms of one element can change into another totally spontaneously.

Students will be unfamiliar with the idea that neutrons and protons are not fundamental particles and that they can be broken down (or changed).

Uses of radioactivity

Students may have ideas about radioactivity being dangerous especially gamma radiation. Misconceptions on radioactivity are common due to films and television.

Students may believe that half-life is literally as it sounds half of the whole life of the sample and it is important to emphasise that the activity halves and halves again and that this can go on indefinitely.

Imaging

Students will be familiar with the use of X-rays for imaging the inside of the body but will be less familiar with gamma rays being used in this way.

Treatment

Students may have relatives who have been diagnosed with cancer. This should be handled sensitively.

Nuclear power

Students may view nuclear power stations as dangerous as any accidents are always reported widely and usually sensationalised.

It is vital to emphasise the difference between fission and fusion as these terms are so similar.

Practicals in this unit

In this unit students will do the following practical work:

- Investigating static electrical charge
- Investigating the resistance of a wire
- Investigating the threshold of hearing
- Investigating radioactive half-life
- Measuring resistance
- Wiring a three pin plug

Key vocabulary covered in this unit

electron • positive • negative • attract • repel • insulator • conductor

atom • electron • charge • friction • induction • attract • repel • electrostatic

negative • defibrillator • electrostatic • paddle • conductor • charge • dust precipitator

atom • charged • attract • repel • electrostatics

resistor • current • resistance • ohms • potential difference • volt • conductor • circuit • voltmeter • ammeter

live • neutral • earth • power • fuse • circuit breaker • double insulated

ultrasound • frequency • longitudinal • transverse • rarefaction • compression • wavelength • hertz • vibrate

scan • ultrasound • X-ray • vibrations • image • reflect • pulse • longitudinal • frequency

alpha • beta • gamma • ionising • decay • half-life • activity • becquerels • GM tube

atom • alpha • beta • gamma • decay • nuclear • isotope

background radiation • cosmic rays • radioisotope • alpha • decay • tracer • gamma

radiocarbon dating • isotope • ratio • half-life • Uranium

X-rays • gamma • absorption • wavelength • electromagnetic wave • exposure • half-life • diagnosis • therapy

diagnosis • sterilisation • tracer • radiotherapy • radiographer • emitter • X-rays• gamma • beta

fission • fusion • nuclear • chain reaction • graphite moderator • control rods • uranium • reactor

fission • fusion • energy • Joules

P4a: Sparks

Resources

Student Book pages 230–231 • Equipment for practical
Interactive Book Quick starter: Here's the question – what's the answer? • Quick starter: Insulators Dragon's Den
Files on Teacher Pack CD: p4_a_01_worksheet; p4_a_01_practical; p4_a_01_technician

Learning objectives

- Understand how insulating materials can become charged.
- Recognise that there are two types of charge and describe how these interact.
- Realise that charged objects contain ions.

Learning outcomes

- Describe how insulators are charged by friction.
- State that charges are either positive or negative.
- Recognise that like charges repel and unlike charges attract.
- Explain how the transfer of electrons is responsible for static charge and describe the formation of ions.

Prior Knowledge

KS3 – Basic structure of the atom.

Existence of positive and negative charges.

Key vocabulary

electron • positive • negative • attract • repel • insulator • conductor

Curiosity and starter suggestions

- Rub balloons and stick to the wall.

OR

- Charge a Van de Graaff generator and bring an uncharged metal dome towards it.
  (Or if you are lucky enough to have a Fun Fly Stick, available from Amazon and other supplier; it is a hand-held generator that students will be amazed to see.)

Learning activities — Worksheet p4_a_01 + Practical p4_a_01

Low demand

Ask the students to give examples of where they have come across consequences of static electrical charge such as how clothes will cling or hair can stick to a comb – also include sparks when removing synthetic clothes or touching a car after travelling in it. Encourage them to think of what is common to all these examples, e.g. attraction or small sparks.

Students carry out a circus of experiments to investigate the effect of static charge. Include rubbing a metal rod, which will not become charged, so that they realise it is insulators and not conductors that hold static charge. Use Practical p4_a_01.

Summarise the results of the circus by asking groups to feedback their answers. Main points to emphasise are that there are two types of charge – positive and negative and that some materials when rubbed will become charged and attract other (uncharged) objects. Give some examples of where this could be useful, e.g. in dusting cloths or brushes. Students complete Worksheet question 1 *Investigating static electrical charge.*

Teaching and learning notes: *There are many different short experiments that can be carried out in the circus depending on the equipment available.*

Students may become easily confused as to the type of object that will hold a static charge as they are used to the idea that electricity has so far always been linked to conductors.

Standard demand

Students carry out a class practical where they charge polythene and acetate rods and bring them close to each other to illustrate the fact that opposite charges attract and like charges repel using Practical p4_a_01. Students complete Worksheet question 2 *Behaviour of charges*.

Explain to the students that electrostatic phenomena are caused by the transfer of electrons, which have a negative charge. It may help if they have a clear idea of atomic structure so that they can link this with the idea that electrons are small and light and on the outer part of the atom. Use the illustration on page 230 of the Student Book to explain this.

Teaching and learning notes: *How this is tackled depends on time available – students find it difficult to charge the rods and then balance them without discharging them. Therefore, they may get incorrect attraction when rods are of same type because one is uncharged.*

High demand

Explain how an object becomes positively charged due to a lack of electrons or negatively charged due to an excess of electrons. Explain that an atom or molecule that has become charged is an ion. Students complete Worksheet question 3 *Transfer of electrons*.

Teaching and learning notes*: Students often become confused by the idea that* ***excess*** *electrons makes an object* ***negatively*** *charged and* ***lack of*** *electrons leaves it* ***positively*** *charged.*

Plenary suggestions

Demonstrate the Van de Graaff generator again with a small pot of rice crispies on it. Ask students to predict what will happen to the crispies before showing them. (Alternatively a stack of upside down small aluminium pie dishes.)

OR

Students return to their original descriptions of electrostatic phenomena and write an explanation based on what they have learned from the lesson.

Assessment opportunities

Worksheet p4_a_01, along with questioning during class practical, may be used to draw out blocks to learning.

Worksheet question 2 *Behaviour of charges* and question 3 *Transfer of electrons* might provide good checkpoints for students' progress.

Answers

Student Book

Q1 Iron • **Q2** Charges can move through a conductor so will not build up • **Q3** Repel, repel, attract • **Q4** 6 electrons • **Q5** The duster will become positive • **Q6** The insulator will have lost electrons to the cloth • **Q7** It has lost electrons

Fig1 previously separated charges jump causing a spark • **Fig 2** yes • **Fig 3** four • **Fig 4** they repel • **Fig 5** all hairs gain the same charge so repel • **Fig 6** electrons are transferred from the cloth onto the rod

Worksheet

Q1a Acetate, polythene, rubber, ebonite, etc. (not metals) • **Q1b** All insulators • **Q1c** Attract or stick to them • **Q1d** Dusting cloths could be designed to pick up dirt by attracting it • **Q1e** Positive and negative • **Q2** Charged, insulators, move, attract, opposite, same • **Q3a** C, A, D, B, E • **Q3b** Same except for electrons transferred **from cloth to rod** now rod has **more** electrons and cloth has **fewer** so rod is **negative** and cloth **positive** • **Q3c** An ion

P4a: Sparks

Resources

Student Book pages 232–233
Interactive Book Naked Scientist animation: What is static electricity?
Files on Teacher Pack CD: p4_a_02_worksheet; p4_a_02_technician

Learning objectives

- Describe how electrostatic charge can be a nuisance and sometimes even dangerous.
- Explain how problems caused by electrostatic charge can be minimised.

Learning outcomes

- Describe how an electrostatic shock can be caused by charge being earthed.
- Describe how static charge can be a nuisance and how anti-static sprays and cloths can help.
- Explain how static electricity can be dangerous when flammable substances are present and how the risks can be reduced.

Prior knowledge

Content from p4_a_01.

Key vocabulary

atom • electron • charge • friction • induction • attract • repel • electrostatic

Curiosity and starter suggestions

- Show a video of a spark causing an explosion with no sound.

OR

- Show pictures of lightning and ask students for the link with the previous lesson.

Learning activities

Worksheet p4_a_02

Low demand

Use the starter activity to lead into a discussion about what will happen when lots of charge builds up in one place.

Most students will have experienced a 'crackle' when removing a sweater made from a synthetic material (insulator). Some may have seen sparks if they removed it in the dark. Ask students to use words such as 'friction' and 'charged' to explain why this happens. Explain that it can be likened to 'mini-lightning'.

Make sparks using a Van de Graaff generator and metal sphere. Ask students how they could become charged by walking on a synthetic carpet or vinyl floor and how this could cause a shock when they touch something connected to the Earth like a tap or metal hand rail.

Students complete Worksheet question 1 *Shocking*.

Teaching and learning notes: *Remind students of the way they charged up rods in lesson p4_a_01 by rubbing them with a cloth and ask them to think about how this is similar to their jumper rubbing on their shirt during the school day.*

Standard demand

Explain that static charge can be a nuisance, e.g. when clothes cling together while we are wearing them or when they have been in a tumble dryer. Manufacturers of anti-static sprays and dusters claim that these will stop the build-up of static charge, e.g. tumble dryer sheets. Show some examples of these and discuss how they work.

Use a spark lighter to ignite inflammable gas using a Bunsen burner. Link this to the risk of explosion posed by static electricity when inflammable materials are present. Mention some examples, with photographs if possible, such as cleaning oil tankers, refuelling aircraft, etc.

Show a film clip of static charge setting off an explosion, e.g. the 'Brainiac' episode where they blow up a caravan using static electricity from a man in nylon clothes.

Demonstrate that an electric current is a flow of electric charge by using the Van de Graaff generator connected to a sensitive milliammeter. Explain that even small currents can be fatal – project the table of current and effect on the body in page 233 of Student Book.

Students complete Worksheet question 2 *Problems of electrostatic charge*.

Teaching and learning notes: *The Van de Graaff demonstration is a good way of linking the idea of static charge with that of moving charge, i.e. electric current. It may be worth re-emphasising that static occurs when the charge cannot move (in insulators) and current when it can (in conductors).*

High demand

Explain how the chance of receiving an electric shock can be reduced by correctly connecting to earth via insulating mats or shoes with insulating soles. Sometimes aviation fuel has anti-static additives added to it to prevent build-up of static charge.

Give examples of each solution, e.g. project onto the board photographs of aircraft being refuelled, rubber mats around machines in a factory and operatives wearing rubber shoes or boots. Explain why it is necessary to earth trucks or tankers containing inflammable materials before unloading. Students complete Worksheet question 3 *Safety precautions.*

Teaching and learning Notes: *Students may have some difficulty understanding why connecting to the earth reduces the chance of a shock. It may help to think how much charge is there likely to be in the entire Earth and how insignificant a few extra (or a few fewer) electrons would be to the Earth.*

Plenary suggestions

Play word pairs – Give pairs of students two words and ask them to discuss what they have in common and what is different about them. Examples of words: conductor/insulator, positive/negative, current/voltage, charged/earthed, static electricity/current electricity, attract/repel.

Show students a video clip showing static charge causing a problem at petrol stations (e.g. Mythbusters – can static electricity cause a gas station fire?)

Assessment opportunities

Worksheet p4_a_02 provides staged opportunities to assess students' learning, particularly question 2 *Problems of electrostatic charge*.

Answers

Student Book

Q8 The car tyres were rubbing on the road so become charged • **Q9** The water pipes are metal and connected to the ground • **Q10** Build-up of charge will lead to sparks, which could lead to a fire if there is a lot of oxygen • **Q11** These clothes can become charged and are attracted to uncharged objects • **Q12** So that any charge cannot build up on the plane • **Q13** Machinery may have lots of parts that are rubbing together • **Q14a** All of the coffee grains were charged the same and repelled missing the jar • **Q14b** The inside of the jar could be given the opposite charge to the grains and they would then be attracted to it

Fig 7 the hair is charged and is attracted to the hat • **Fig 8** the charge has nowhere to go to • **Fig 9** first fill tank with nitrogen • **Fig 10** because the electronic parts could be ruined by charge • **Fig 11** to prevent the build-up of a separation of charge

Worksheet

Q1 B, F, D, E, G, A, C • **Q2a** Use anti-static spray or cloth • **Q2b** Use hair conditioner or gel • **Q2c** Use a tumble dryer sheet • **Q2d** Wear a thimble or carry a coin • **Q2e** Refuelling, charge, friction, spark, explosion, charges, difference, ignite, earth • **Q3a** Connect the tanker to the earth first • **Q3b** Wear conducting shoes and conducting tiles on floor • **Q3c** Wear natural fibres and conducting shoes • **Q3d** Earth the lorry before unloading

P4b: Uses of electrostatics

Resources

Student Book pages 234–235 • Equipment for demonstration
Interactive Book Drag and drop: Electrostatics and electromagnets
Files on Teacher Pack CD: p4_b_01_worksheet; p4_b_01_ technician

Learning objectives

- Understand the use of electrostatics in:
  - dust precipitators
  - defibrillators.

Learning outcomes

- Describe how smoke particles, etc. are removed from chimneys using charged plates.
- Explain how the use of high voltages ensures the dust is attracted to plates inside the chimney.
- Explain how electrical charge can be used to restart the heart.

Prior knowledge

Content from p4_a _01.

Key vocabulary

negative • defibrillator • electrostatic • paddle • conductor • charge • dust precipitator

Barriers to learning

Students may not realise that anything can be made to conduct electricity if a high enough voltage is used.

Make sure that high demand students understand that electrons carry a negative charge and that an absence of electrons leaves an object positively charged.

Curiosity and starter suggestions

- Show a patient having treatment with a defibrillator.

OR

- Some anagrams of key words on electrostatics.

Learning activities

Worksheet p4_b_01

Low demand

Show some pictures or video clips on uses of electrostatics.

Explain how each one works and why it is important. Include how dust particles are collected from chimneys using charged metal plates. Photocopiers and laser printers use charged particles to produce an image on paper. A patient's heart can be restarted using a controlled electric shock. Paints and crop sprays use static to ensure an even coverage.

Students complete Worksheet question 1 *Uses of static electricity*.

Teaching and learning notes: *Details of the actual method by which the static charges are used in these is not required at this level.*

Standard demand

Remind students how charged rods will attract small pieces of paper or polystyrene – demonstrate the fact that a rubbed polythene or acetate rod can attract lots of uncharged objects, e.g. Pringles tin, empty drink can, empty plastic bottle. Remind them that oppositely charged objects will have an even greater force of attraction between them (the greater the charge the greater the force in fact).

Putting this attraction to use – explain in more detail how the electrostatic dust precipitator works including the grid or rods. These are placed in the chimney connected to a high voltage negative supply and the plates earthed so that they will gain the opposite charge to the grid. Any particles in the smoke will then pick up a negative charge from the grid as they pass through it and so will be attracted to the positively charged plates. The clean smoke then leaves the chimney and the plates can be vibrated or knocked periodically to make the dust fall down into collectors underneath. Work through questions 4 and 5 of Student Book.

Students complete Worksheet question 2 *Electrostatic dust precipitators*.

Move on to explain how defibrillators use electric charge to restart the heart. First, the paddles must be charged to around 300 V. They are then placed on the patient's chest. A special gel is usually applied to make sure the charge can pass through and the operator has to make sure everyone is clear of the patient before the shock is administered.

Use Figure 1 on page 234 of Student Book to help with the explanation and perhaps a short video clip. Students answer questions 9–13 on page 237 of Student Book.

Teaching and learning notes: *Students at this level will be required to explain the uses of electrostatics in some detail but inclusion of transfer of electrons is not required.*

High demand

Explain how the transfer of electrons is important in the dust precipitator. First, the positive metal grid will induce a negative charge on the earthed plates. When the smoke passes through the negative grid the solid particles will gain more electrons and become negatively charged. The positive plates then attract the negatively charged particles and they stick to it until they are later removed.

Students complete Worksheet question 3 *It's all about electrons*.

Teaching and learning notes: *There is a lot of potential for confusion here and it may help to have a physical model of this to help students understand the transfer of the electrons and the principle of induction.*

Plenary suggestions

Play true or false where students hold up true or false cards (or just mini white boards) in response to statements read out by the teacher.

OR

Students write out the definitions of the keywords from the starter activity and share them.

Assessment opportunities

Worksheet question 3 *It's all about electrons* might provide good checkpoints for students' progress.

Answers

Student Book

Q1 So that they spread out and give an even coverage • **Q2** Crop sprayer, photocopier, dust precipitator, defibrillator, etc. (any 2) • **Q3** To restart the heart using a controlled electric shock • **Q4** There could be a lot of harmful particles in the environment and people could be harmed by breathing in the particles • **Q5** The smoke particles would become positively charged and be attracted to the negative plates • **Q6** The powder becomes charged as it passes the wire and is attracted to the paper, fingerprints show up where the powder sticks • **Q7** As the dust particles pass close to the wires they gain or lose electrons, becoming charged. The dust particles induce the opposite charge on the earthed metal plate. Opposite charges attract so the dust particles are attracted to the plate

Fig 1 to restart a patient's heart • **Fig 2** they used charged ink particles to form an image • **Fig 3** it removes harmful smoke and soot particles from chimneys • **Fig 4** dust particles are charged by passing through a charged grid, then attracted to oppositely charged plates

Worksheet

Q1 1C, 2E, 3A, 4B, 5D • **Q2** F, C, E, B, D, A • **Q3a** No charge • **Q3b** Negative • **Q3c** It is attracted • **Q3d** So that the electrons can flow away • **Q3e** The negative charge on the grid repels electrons from the plates to the earth leaving the plates positive

P4b: Uses of electrostatics

Resources

Student Book pages 236–237
Files on Teacher Pack CD: p4_b_02_worksheet; p4_b_02_ technician

Learning objectives

- Understand the use of electrostatics in:
  - Crop spraying
  - Paint spraying.

Learning outcomes

- Explain how the sprayed particles produce a fine mist due to being of the same charge.
- Explain how an object will be given an even coat when it is charged oppositely to the paint.

How Science Works

Content from p4_a_01 and p4_b_01.

Key vocabulary

atom • charged • attract • repel • electrostatics

Barriers to learning

Make sure students realise that liquids can be charged and if all drops have the same charge they will repel equally from each other and produce an even spray.

Curiosity and starter suggestions

- Show pictures of spray painting or crop spraying.

OR

- Word puzzle.

Learning activities

Worksheet p4_b_02

Low demand

Review the uses of electrostatics studied in lesson p4_b_01 particularly emphasising the similarities and linking it to what they have learned about static charge. Students could research another use of electrostatics not previously studied and produce a short information leaflet to share (e.g. the photocopier or finger printing)

Students complete Worksheet question 1 activity 1 *Using electrostatics.*

Teaching and learning notes: *Students at this level simply need to recall the uses of electrostatics.*

Standard demand

Use a water spray and Figure 9 on page 237 of Student Book to explain how paint spraying makes use of electrostatics. The fine spray is achieved by charging all of the particles with the same charge as they come out of the nozzle so that they repel each other and spread out. The object being sprayed can then be charged opposite to this and will attract the paint, making sure it covers the whole object even at the back. This results in an even coat of paint and a lot less paint being wasted in the process.

Students complete Worksheet question 2 *Paint spraying.*

Teaching and learning notes: *Make sure both the point about the droplets repelling to give an even spread and the paint and object attracting to reach awkward places is covered.*

High demand

Explain that when an uncharged object is being sprayed with charged paint it will become more and more charged by the paint collecting on its surface. This would eventually lead to a limit where it has become so charged that more paint will be repelled from it. This problem can be overcome by earthing the object so that the charge can move away to earth and prevent any build up. This works well for small objects.

On a larger scale it is better to give the object to be painted an opposite charge to the paint. This way you can ensure the paint will be attracted to the object and will spread evenly across the whole object even getting into awkward places giving a good coverage. Advantages of this method are the reduction in wasted paint and the even coating given to the object, even in 'hard to reach' places. Remind students that if the paint has lost electrons it will be positively charged and so the object must gain electrons giving it an overall negative charge.

Students complete worksheet question 3 *More on uses of electrostatics*.

Teaching and learning notes: *It is very important to emphasise the transfer of electrons at this level.*

Plenary suggestions

Students are given a discussion card and work together to give reasons why the situation described occurs. Each group then selects a spokesperson to give feedback to the group.

OR

Students showcase their leaflets on uses of electrostatics.

Assessment opportunities

Worksheet p4_b_02 provides staged opportunities to assess students' learning (afl). In addition, thoughtful questioning during class discussions may be used to draw out blocks to learning.

Activity 1 and the students' own leaflets might provide good checkpoints for their progress.

Answers

Student Book

Q8 All the paint droplets have the same charge and repel each other • **Q9** By increasing the charging voltage • **Q10** 48A • **Q11** In case they accidently receive a shock too • **Q12** It is applied directly across a heart only for a very short time • **Q13** If it needs maintenance the patient will have to be operated on again • **Q14** To make the droplets spread out evenly and cover a wide area • **Q15** The paint will give an even coverage and reach even awkward places so there will be less paint wasted • **Q16** The paint loses electrons leaving it positively charged and the object being sprayed gains electrons making it negatively charged. This means the paint is attracted onto the object

Fig 5 to attract the paint droplets • **Fig 6** to place on the patient's chest and deliver the charge • **Fig 7** it can be used very quickly and this makes chances of survival higher • **Fig 8** it can monitor and sense changes and then respond immediately • **Fig 9** less wasted paint; even coat of paint; paint reaches awkward places • **Fig 10** by charging the drops of pesticide so they repel and spread out evenly.

Worksheet

Q1 Charged; same; charge; like; charges; repel; charge; paint; charges; attract; attracted; sticks; laser; static; dust; smoke; chimneys; chimney; voltage; smoke; attracted • **Q2** To the negative; frame attracts paint; paint reaches shadow areas; even coverage; less wasted paint • **Q3** Students' own leaflets on the uses of electrostatics

P4c: Safe electricals

Resource

Student Book pages 238–239 • Equipment for practical

Interactive Book Naked Scientist animation: How is household wiring kept safe? • Practical investigations: Currents in circuits • Drag and drop: Voltage (V), current (I) and resistance (R) • Naked Scientist animation: How are resistance and current linked?

Files on Teacher Pack CD: p4_c_01_worksheet; p4_c_01_practical; p4_c_01_technician

Learning objectives

- Understand how resistors can be used to change the current in a circuit.
- Calculate resistance and understand the effect of length and thickness on the resistance of a wire.

Learning outcomes

- Describe circuits in terms of flow of electrical charge.
- Use the formula resistance = voltage/current.
- Recall that resistance is measured in ohms.
- Explain that
  - longer wires have more resistance
  - thinner wires have more resistance.

Prior knowledge

KS3 Series and parallel circuits.

Key vocabulary

resistor • current • resistance • ohms • potential difference • volt • conductor • circuit • voltmeter • ammeter

Barriers to learning

Students always have difficulty with the difference between current and voltage in a circuit.

More able students will be required to rearrange the equation for resistance.

Curiosity and starter suggestions

- Circuit components treasure hunt (students are given a card with component on and they must find it). First group with one of each laid out on table wins. (Could add challenge that they must also make a circuit and draw circuit diagram.)

OR

- Quick revision questions on electric circuits to check existing knowledge.

Learning activities

Worksheet p4_c_01 + Practical p4_c_01

Low demand

Remind students of (or show again) the demonstration with the Van de Graaff generator connected to a sensitive milliammeter. Explain that electrical current is a flow of charge. Electrons move through the wires in an electrical circuit in the opposite direction to conventional current (which was defined before the discovery of electrons!)

Students construct circuits using cells, resistors and ammeters to investigate the effect of resistance in a circuit. Summarise the results and highlight how adding cells to the circuit increases the current and adding resistance decreases the current. Current is the rate of flow of electrical charge, adding a resistor to the circuit reduces the rate of flow of charge and so reduces the current on the ammeter. The greater the value of resistor the more effect it has. Resistance is measured in ohms.

Students add a rheostat to a circuit with the cells, an ammeter and a bulb and test what happens to the current when the length of resistance wire in the circuit is increased or decreased. Compare this to a dimmer switch in a lighting circuit. Students complete Worksheet question 1 *Current and resistance*.

Teaching and learning notes: *If a Van de Graaff generator is unavailable use two charged metal plates with a conducting ball on a thread between. Use an EHT supply (5 kV), do NOT use an HT supply (120 V). More able students may be able to explain what is happening in detail; others will appreciate the idea of charge transfer completing a circuit.*

Students may not have set up electrical circuits for some time and may need help especially with the ammeters and rheostats.

Standard demand

Class experiment – relating current, voltage and resistance in a circuit. Students complete the experiment to show that for a given resistor, current increases as voltage increases and vice versa and that for a fixed voltage, current decreases as resistance increases and vice versa.

Class experiment – resistance of a wire. Students complete the experiment investigating the effect of length and diameter on resistance.

Explain how to use the equation: *resistance = voltage ÷ current*. Students complete Worksheet question 2 *Calculating resistance*.

Teaching and learning notes: *How this is tackled depends on time available. It is worth demonstrating how each circuit is set up and training students how to troubleshoot for themselves.*

High demand

Explain resistance in microscopic terms. Use Figure 7 from page 239 of Student Book, or an animation from commercial software, projected onto the board to help with the explanation. Explain why the wire gets hot and give the example of a filament lamp where the wire gets so hot that it glows and gives off light.

Show how to rearrange the equation: *resistance = potential difference (or voltage) ÷ current*. Students complete Worksheet question 3 *More calculations on resistance*.

Teaching and learning notes: *students may have difficulty relating microscopic and macroscopic models of current and resistance.*

Plenary suggestions

Play 'What am I?' where a student describes a component and the others guess what it is.

OR

Quick quiz on resistance calculations using mini white boards.

Assessment opportunities

Worksheet p4_c_01 provides staged opportunities to assess students' learning (afl).

Activities 2 and 3 might provide good checkpoints for students' progress.

Answers

Answers to the Student Book and Worksheet can be found on the Teacher Pack CD.

P4c: Safe electricals

Resources

Student Book pages 240–241 • Equipment for demonstration
Interactive Book Matching pairs: Mains electricity • Matching pairs: Wiring a plug
Files on Teacher Pack CD: p4_c_02_worksheet; p4_c_02_ technician

Learning objectives

- Recognise the colour coding in a three-pin plug and describe the functions of the live neutral and earth wires.
- Explain how fuses, earth wires and circuit breakers work and understand the term 'double insulated'.
- Use the equation for electrical power to choose the correct fuse for an appliance.

Learning outcomes

- Recall the colours of the live, neutral and earth wires and describe their functions.
- Explain how the fuse and earth wire protect a user and describe a circuit breaker as a 'resettable fuse'.
- Explain the term 'double insulated'.
- Use the equation power = voltage x current to select an appropriate fuse.

Prior knowledge

KS3 Electric circuit; content from p2_d_01 and p4_c_01

Key vocabulary

live • neutral • earth • power • fuse • circuit breaker • double insulated

Barriers to learning

Students may be confused by the plug having three wires when they are used to two connections in a circuit – positive and negative. The Earth wire is only used when there is a problem.

Make sure students appreciate that mains current is alternating, whereas cells and batteries provide direct current.

Curiosity and starter suggestions

- Display a picture showing overloaded sockets or other electrical safety hazard. Discuss some dos and don'ts.

OR

- Ask students to list all the things they have used today with a plug.

Learning activities

Worksheet p4_c_02

Low demand

Show a correctly wired three-pin plug and project Figure 8 from page 240 of the Student Book. Point out that an earthed conductor cannot become live because it is connected to the ground and any charge will flow away to earth.

Class activity – wiring a plug. Students wire a plug themselves. Check that it has been done correctly. (If the class works slowly, give each group a correctly wired plug to examine.) Ensure the plug is disabled, e.g. by putting a rivet through the earth pin. In addition, ensure mains sockets in the lab are turned off.

Class demonstration – fuses and circuit breakers. Show the class a fuse and circuit breaker, or photographs, and describe why they are used.

Class demonstration – double insulation. Show some examples of double insulated appliances. Explain that they do not need to be earthed. Point out the double insulated symbol and the earth symbol on some appliances.

Students complete Worksheet question 1 *Three-pin plug*.

Teaching and learning notes: *Students are very tempted to try out the plugs they have wired so it is vital that these are disabled and that the sockets in the room are turned off to avoid accidents. Also watch out for any students using the screwdrivers to look inside the sockets if there are some on the bench!*

Standard demand

Point out the differences between mains electricity and the cells used in the previous lesson. Show AC and DC waveforms on a cathode ray oscilloscope. Emphasise that mains voltage is high (230 V) and so is dangerous.

Give groups of students a correctly wired plug to examine. Explain the functions of the live, neutral and earth wires.

Class demonstrations – fuses, double insulation and RCDs. Show the action of a wire fuse using two different thicknesses of wire. Link this to the current passing through different appliances when working normally. Use a mains ammeter to measure the current in various appliances. Link to the fuse rating required. Use power = voltage x current to work out the electrical power of some appliances.

Show some examples of double insulated appliances. Explain why they do not need to be earthed. Point out the double insulated symbol on the appliances.

Show students a residual current device (RCD). Describe a situation in which an electric lawnmower, or similar, is being used and the cable is cut. Explain why this is a serious hazard and the current must be switched off quickly.

Class activity – residual current device advert. Students use the Internet to find out more about residual current devices. They produce a public safety advertisement telling the public why they should buy one.

Students complete Worksheet question 2 *Fuses and circuit breakers*.

Teaching and learning notes: *Steel wool can be used to demonstrate to students that very thin metal will glow and melt when a current is passed through it. This must be tried out first.*

High demand

Give a detailed explanation of how a wire fuse protects an appliance.

Show students a circuit breaker, or a picture. Explain its use as a re-settable fuse. Explain how the combination of wire fuses and earth connections protect you.

Explain how the equation for electrical power = current x voltage can be used to find the normal operating current for a device and therefore to select an appropriate fuse.

Students complete Worksheet question 3 *Choosing the correct fuse*.

Teaching and learning notes: *The detailed workings of a circuit breaker are not required at this level. Ensure students can rearrange the formula.*

Plenary suggestions

Students show their public safety advertisements.

OR

Students write down three questions based on what they found out in the lesson and ask other students to answer them.

Assessment opportunities

Worksheet p4_c_02 provides staged opportunities to assess students' learning (afl). In addition, thoughtful questioning during class discussions may be used to draw out blocks to learning

Worksheet question 2 *Fuses and circuit breakers* and question 3 *Choosing the correct fuse* might provide good checkpoints for their progress.

Answers

Answers to the Student Book and Worksheet are available on the Teacher Pack CD

P4d: Ultrasound

Resources

Student Book pages 242–243 • Equipment for demonstrations and class practical
Interactive Book Drag and drop: Wave types
Files on Teacher Pack CD: p4_d_01_worksheet; p4_d_01_practical; p4_d_01_ technician

Learning objectives

- Understand that ultrasound is a longitudinal wave with a very high frequency.

Learning outcomes

- Describe ultrasound as a longitudinal wave with a frequency above 20 000 Hz.
- Describe features of longitudinal waves including – wavelength, frequency, compression and rarefaction.
- Describe and compare features of longitudinal and transverse waves.

Prior knowledge

KS3 Nature of sound waves.

Key vocabulary

ultrasound • frequency • longitudinal • transverse • rarefaction • compression • wavelength • hertz • vibrate

Barriers to learning

Students will have studied sound in KS3 and it is important to emphasise that the only difference with ultrasound is the high frequency.

Curiosity and starter suggestions

- Recap ideas about sound from KS3.

OR

- Play some musical notes of different loudness and pitch and ask students to identify the differences.

Learning activities — Worksheet p4_d_01 + Practical p4_d_01

Low demand

Class demonstration – sound and vibration. Show the class that sound is caused when objects vibrate, by using a tuning fork dipped in water and a loudspeaker with ping pong balls in its cone connected to a signal generator.

Introduce ultrasound by gradually increasing the frequency of the sound produced by the signal generator until the class can no longer hear it. Explain how we hear sound – refer to compressions and rarefactions.

Class demonstration – longitudinal waves. Use a Slinky spring to model a longitudinal wave. 'Label' one coil with string. Ask one student to hold this coil. Ask another to hold several coils and suddenly release all but the end coil.

Introduce the idea of amplitude, wavelength and frequency. Point out the compressions and rarefactions on the Slinky.

Students complete Worksheet question 1 *Sound waves.*

Teaching and learning notes: *Students may have heard of high frequency sound being used to move teenagers away from a shopping area. They will be interested in how your range of hearing may be different to theirs.*

Standard demand

Use the above activity with a slinky spring. Describe features such as wavelength, frequency, compression (a region of higher pressure) and rarefaction (a region of lower pressure) in more detail. Link this to the way sound travels.

Use a signal generator, loudspeaker and cathode ray oscilloscope to see the effect of changing the amplitude and frequency on the sound heard.

Class activity – thresholds of hearing. Working in small groups, students use a signal generator and loudspeaker to find their upper and lower thresholds of hearing. Their results can be compared with yours. Ask, 'What is ultrasound?' Point out that the frequency of ultrasound is higher than the upper threshold of human hearing (20 000 Hz). Note: the volume will need to be carefully monitored to avoid ear damage.

Explain how ultrasound is used to measure distances such as ocean depth (sonar) or room size (ultrasonic tape measure). Remind students how to calculate distances using speed = distance/time and link this to how the depth of structures in the body is computed using ultrasound echoes.

Look at the table on page 243 of Student Book comparing the speed of sound in different materials and ask students to explain why sound travels faster in steel than water and faster in water than in air.

Students complete Worksheet question 2 *Ultrasound.*

Class activity – bats. If time allows, ask students to use books or the internet to find out how bats use ultrasound to navigate.

Teaching and learning notes: *How this is tackled depends on equipment available. If there is only one signal generator and loudspeaker the whole class will have to be tested at once. If no equipment is available there are sound frequency tests available on the internet you could use.*

High demand

Look at water waves in a ripple tank. Set up a Mexican wave with students around the room. Discuss the motion of the 'particles' relative to the wave direction. Compare with a longitudinal wave along a slinky spring.

Describe how we hear sound in terms of the motion of the particles.

Show students a wave machine that models both types of wave, if available.

Describe and compare the wavelength, frequency and amplitude of both types of wave. Link the amplitude of the wave to the loudness of the sound.

Students complete Worksheet question 3 *Transverse and longitudinal waves.*

Teaching and learning notes: *It is important to ensure that students understand that vibrations in a transverse wave are at right angles to the wave direction. In a longitudinal wave the particles vibrate back and forth around a mean position; in both cases it is the energy, and not the particles, which travels forward.*

Plenary suggestions

Play Taboo with keywords from the lesson.

OR

Test the students with a sound quiz.

Assessment opportunities

Worksheet p4_d_01 question 1 *Sound waves* and question 3 *Transverse and longitudinal waves* might provide good checkpoints for students' progress.

Answers

Answers to the Student Book and Worksheet are available on the Teacher Pack CD.

P4d: Ultrasound

Resources

Student Book pages 244–245 • Computer with internet and printer access • Equipment for demonstration
Interactive Book Matching pairs: Ultrasound
Files on Teacher Pack CD: p4_d_02_worksheet; p4_d_02_ technician

Learning objectives

- Recognise the use of ultrasound in medicine for diagnosis.
- Explain how ultrasound can be used to break down, e.g. kidney stones.
- Understand why ultrasound is preferable to X-rays for certain scans.

Learning outcomes

- Describe how ultrasound is used for scanning the body and to measure the speed of blood.
- Explain how ultrasound is used to break down kidney stones and other accumulations.
- Explain the reasons for using ultrasound rather than X-rays for certain scans.

Prior knowledge

KS 3 sound waves content from p4_d_01.

Key vocabulary

scan • ultrasound • X-ray • vibrations • image • reflect • pulse • longitudinal • frequency • diagnosis • therapy

Barriers to learning

Students may have seen ultrasound scan pictures but may be less familiar with ultrasound being used as a method of treatment.

Curiosity and starter suggestions

- Show a video clip of an ultrasound scan of a pregnant woman.

OR

- Students write down 3 things they learned about ultrasound in previous lesson and ask students to read out one each. Compile a list on the board.

Learning activities

Worksheet p4_d_02

Low demand

Lead a discussion about using ultrasound to scan a foetus in the womb. Ask students what the scan might show. Students may have seen scan pictures – show some if available.

Ask the students what other parts of the body could be scanned using ultrasound. Show ultrasound pictures of the heart, liver, etc. and discuss why these parts of the body are scanned with ultrasound.

Explain why ultrasound is a good technique for diagnosis of a problem – no need to cut a patient open, safe to use, can show highly detailed and real time images.

Describe how ultrasound is used to measure the speed of blood in vessels and this could help to find any blockages. Students answer Worksheet question 1 *Ultrasound for diagnosis.*

Teaching and learning notes: *Students do not need to describe the Doppler Effect at this level.*

Standard demand

Remind students that ultrasound is high frequency vibrations. Show an image of stones in the kidney or gall bladder. Explain that high-powered ultrasound can break them up without surgery.

Class activity – ultrasound leaflet. Students use the internet to find out more about body scans or breaking up stones within the body and produce a leaflet to:

inform a pregnant woman and her partner about the purpose of a foetal ultrasound scan, what will happen and the safety of the procedure.

OR

inform a person about to be treated with ultrasound for kidney stones about the procedure.

Students complete Worksheet question 2 *Using ultrasound for therapy.*

Teaching and learning notes: *The use of ultrasound vibrations to break something may be difficult for students to grasp. You could use a clip of an opera singer breaking a glass as an example (Mythbusters did a programme on this).*

High demand

Class demonstration – transmission of ultrasound at various surfaces. Explain that when a beam of ultrasound enters the body, some is transmitted and some reflected at each interface. The returning echoes are used to build up a picture. Use Figure 14 on page 245 of Student Book to help.

Explain how the depth of the reflecting layer can be obtained by using speed = distance/ time and knowing the speed of the ultrasound in each type of body tissue.

Explain why a gel is placed on the body between the probe and the skin and how different layers will reflect different amounts of the ultrasound.

Outline the advantages of using ultrasound over X-rays – show some X-ray pictures and point out that ultrasound shows soft tissue better where X-rays are better for bones and ultrasound does not damage living cells whereas X-rays can cause cancer.

Class activity – ultrasound leaflet. Students can carry out the standard demand activity but including more detail about the techniques. A third option could be offered in which the uses of X-rays and ultrasound are compared.

Students carry out Worksheet question 3 *Ultrasound and X-rays.*

Teaching and learning notes: *The ionising effect of X-rays is dealt with later on in this unit.*

Plenary suggestions

Students showcase their leaflets and give each other positive feedback.

OR

Read out some possible uses of ultrasound and students guess true or false

Assessment opportunities

Worksheet p4_d_02 provides staged opportunities to assess students' learning (afl). In addition, thoughtful questioning during class discussions may be used to draw out blocks to learning.

The students' leaflets should provide a useful check of their understanding.

Answers

Student Book

Q7 To check the development of the foetus; to investigate heart or liver problems; to look for tumours in the body; to measure speed of blood if blockage is suspected • **Q8** The jewellery is put into a cleaning solution then the ultrasound vibrates it and dislodges dirt • **Q9** The stones need a lot of energy from the vibrations to break them up • **Q10** To break up cataract patient's opaque lens • **Q11** X-rays are ionising radiation, which is dangerous for developing cells • **Q12** 15 cm • **Q13** 10.5 cm

Fig 8 the sex of the baby • **Fig 9** no surgery is needed • **Fig 10** densities of the tissues and speed of sound in the tissues • **Fig 11** can show more detail • **Fig 12** narrowing of arteries, etc.

Worksheet

Q1 Longitudinal, frequency, reflects, picture, foetus, tumours, heart, liver, see, surgery, soft, speed, blood • **Q2a** Break them up • **Q2b** It is high powered vibrations • **Q2c** Passed out in urine • **Q2d** No need for surgery • **Q2e** E.g. cleaning teeth; breaking up cataracts • **Q3a** C, A, D, B, H, F, E, G • **Q3b** Ultrasound shows soft tissues and is non-ionising • **Q3c** X-rays can cause cells to mutate and lead to cancer • **Q3d** If an image of bones was needed

P4: Applying your knowledge

Pages 246–247 in the Student Book prepare students for assessment.

When and how to use these pages

This task provides an opportunity for students to apply their science knowledge in a different context.

Ask students to:

- read through the context and tasks, listing any terms that they do not understand
- as a whole class or in small groups, discuss the tasks to ensure all students understand the terminology used and to clarify what is required
- work individually to answer the questions for each task.

If time allows, ask students to mark each other's work using the mark scheme provided.

Notes

This task will test the student's ability to apply their knowledge of ultrasound to a real life situation. They should know that ultrasound is high frequency sound waves and be able to explain how it travels through different layers of a pregnant woman's body to build up a picture of the baby in the womb.

They will need to explain the term density and appreciate that it is the difference in density of the various layers that cause the ultrasound to reflect back to the detector and that the time taken for these echoes is an indication of the depth of each layer.

Students should also appreciate why ultrasound is preferable to X-ray imaging for looking at developing babies.

Answers

This mark scheme is also available on the Teacher Pack CD.

Task	Answer	Notes
1	Ultrasound is above the range of human hearing / 20 000 Hz	This is a simple recall question
2	A 3-dimensional image is built up using information from the time delay between sending the pulses and receiving the echoes back	A good description of how the image is built up is expected of a student working towards a grade C
3	X-rays are ionising radiation which can cause cancer and developing babies are particularly vulnerable to this	This is a simple recall question
4	Density is the mass per unit volume and that bone is most dense followed by fat / muscle then amniotic fluid	
5	A foetus' head should be a certain size at 16 weeks and so the circumference of the head is a good indication of the age	This explanation is indicative of a higher level student
6	A trained operator could use the information from the ultrasound to identify any abnormalities in the development of the foetus	

Notes

P4e: What is radioactivity?

Resources

Student Book pages 248–249 • Equipment for measuring half-life demonstration • Equipment for radioactive decay simulation with dice

Interactive Book Naked Scientist animation: Where does radiation come from? • Naked Scientist animation: What happens when radioactive elements decay? • Drag and drop: Half-lives

Files on Teacher Pack CD: p4_e_01_worksheet; p4_e_01_practical; p4_e_01_ technician

Learning objectives

- Recognise that nuclear decay occurs naturally.
- Describe how the activity of a sample is measured.
- Understand the term 'half-life'.

Learning outcomes

- Recall that alpha, beta and gamma radiation comes naturally from the nucleus of atoms.
- Describe how activity is measured in nuclear decays per second.
- Interpret graphical or numerical data and calculate half-life.

Prior knowledge

P2e.

Key vocabulary

alpha • beta • gamma • ionising • decay • half-life • activity • becquerels • GM tube

Barriers to learning

Emphasise that background radiation is all around us and that we have evolved in a radioactive environment.

Curiosity and starter suggestions

- Have a GM Tube and counter set up in the lab and counting background (attach to a speaker if possible to give an audible sound when it counts)

OR

- Ask students to work in small groups (perhaps using mini-white boards) to write down what they remember about radioactivity from Module P2 (perhaps have a few pictures on a slide show or sheet to remind them).

Learning activities

Worksheet p4_e_01 + Practical p4_e_01

Low demand

Use the starter activity to lead into a discussion about how alpha, beta and gamma radiation come naturally from the nucleus of some elements. The alpha, beta and gamma are called nuclear radiation and the substances these come from are known as radioactive isotopes.

Draw students' attention to the Geiger–Muller tube and rate meter, which are being used to count the number of nuclei that decay. Activity is measured in **counts per second** or becquerels. Use the rate meter to measure the background count for 30 seconds or so and repeat to get an average background count (work out the activity by dividing the count by 30).

Hold one of the radioactive sources in front of the GM tube and note the new average count rate. Point out to the students that the count rate is not regular and will gradually reduce over time. (School sources have a very long half-life and a low activity so they would not notice this happening in the course of a lesson.) Students complete Worksheet question 1 *Measuring radioactive decay*.

Teaching and learning notes: *Students have a lot of preconceived ideas about the dangers of radioactivity and it is worth pointing out that it is all around us and that we evolved in a radioactive world so our bodies are used to a certain amount of exposure. This is a good chance to remind pupils about careful management of risk.*

Standard demand

Demonstrate to the students how to measure the count rate for the alpha, beta and gamma sources following the usual safety precautions for correct handling. Point out to the students that the decay is completely **random** and **spontaneous.** Increasing the temperature, pressure or any other physical conditions will not increase the count rate. (Compare this to chemical reactions.)

Explain to the students that even though the decay is random, since there are millions and millions and millions of atoms in even a small amount of any radioactive sample we can still see an overall pattern in the rate of decay and we can measure this. Use a protactinium generator to demonstrate measuring the half-life of a radioactive source. Students should record the count every 10 seconds and draw a graph to see the pattern of decay and read off the half-life. It is good practice to check the half-life from the graph in more than one place to get an average.

Introduce the radioactivity simulation as a way of explaining how this can be modelled. Students carry out Practical p4_e_01.

Students complete Worksheet question 2 *Half-life.*

Teaching and learning notes: *There is a free simulation called Radiation Lab on the internet which allows students to measure half-life using a simulation of a protactinium generator (if your school does not have a real one available to use).*

High demand

Explain how the rate of radioactive decay is different for different radioisotopes and give some examples. Students complete Worksheet question 3 *Half-life of commonly used radioactive isotopes.*

Students could investigate how scientists identified the radioisotope that was responsible for the death of Alexander Litvenenko using the Sci Upd8 materials. http://www.upd8.org.uk/activity/195/Isotope-kills-ex-spy.html

The BBC news article is at http://news.bbc.co.uk/1/hi/health/6181688.stm

Teaching and learning notes: *Emphasise that a radioactive element can be identified by its half-life and that an appropriate isotope for a particular job can be chosen depending on its half-life.*

Plenary suggestions

Give out alpha, beta and gamma cards and students hold them up in response to properties read out as a revision.

OR

Ask the students to make some suggestions as to the uses of radioactive isotopes and how they could be chosen for a particular job. (Summarise that the important things to consider would be the half-life and the type of radiation emitted.)

Assessment opportunities

Worksheet p4_e_01 question 1 *Measuring radioactive decay* and question 2 *Half-life* provide good opportunities to assess the pupils' understanding.

Answers

Student Book

Q1 2 000 • **Q2** 160Bq • **Q3** They are unstable • **Q4** Because radioactive decay is random and not regular • **Q5** 2 hours • **Q6** 1/8th of the original sample

Fig1 for work on the 3 types of radiation and then for discovering 2 new elements • **Fig 2** the rate of decay of a radioactive sample • **Fig3** 6 days • **Fig 4** they are unstable

Worksheet

Answers to the Worksheet are available on the Teacher Pack CD.

P4e: What is radioactivity?

Resources

Student Book pages 250–251 • 'What am I?' cards
Interactive Book Quick starter: Alpha particles – how many sentences can you make? • Matching pairs: Alpha particles
Files on Teacher Pack CD: p4_e_02_worksheet; p4_e_02_technician

Learning objectives

- Recognise the ionising nature of alpha, beta and gamma.
- Describe how an atom changes when alpha or beta decay happens.
- Construct balanced nuclear decay equations.

Learning outcomes

- Recall that nuclear radiation ionises materials and explain why alpha is such a good ioniser.
- Describe alpha and beta particles and what happens to a nucleus when an alpha or a beta particle is emitted.
- Construct balanced nuclear equations for alpha and beta decay.

Prior knowledge

P2e Nuclear radiation.

Key vocabulary

atom • electron • negative • attract • electrostatic • positive • conductor • insulator • repel

Barriers to learning

Students may find it difficult to understand how atoms of one element can change into another totally spontaneously.

Students will be unfamiliar with the idea that neutrons and protons are not fundamental particles and that they can be broken down (or changed).

Curiosity and starter suggestions

- Put sticky notes on students' heads (or attach to their backs) as they come in to the room and then play 'What am I?' where other students describe what they are without using the word and the student has to guess what word they have been given.

OR

- Ask students to list all the things they have ever heard about radioactivity and compile a true/false board on the wall where these can be organised.

Learning activities

Worksheet p4_e_02

Low demand

Use the true/false idea from the starter activity to lead into a discussion of some of the misconceptions people have about radioactivity and ask students how they feel about soft fruits being irradiated to kill bacteria so they will last longer.

Remind students that alpha, beta and gamma are all ionising radiations. Show cloud chamber tracks of alpha and beta (there are lots of videos on the internet available) and point out the differences between them (alpha – short and fat; beta – long and thin).

Demonstrate a spark counter with an alpha source. Draw attention to the random nature of the sparks and hence of the ionising radiation. By counting sparks you are counting the number of alpha particles emitted. You should find that the range of the alpha particles is about 5 cm.

The sparks are similar to those produced by a Van de Graaff generator. The alpha particles ionise the air forming positive and negative ions. When these ions recombine to form neutral atoms then blue light is emitted. The noise of the spark is due to warming the air in the narrow region of the avalanche current, which produces a sound wave just like in a lightning strike.

A thin sheet of tissue paper or gold foil held between the spark counter and the source will show a reduced range for the alpha particles or even prevent them getting to the counter.

Next show how an electroscope previously charged will discharge when an alpha source is brought near to the top disc.

Remind students that ionising radiations can damage living cells which may result in cancer. Nuclear waste contains isotopes that can remain radioactive for a long time. Highlight the problems this could cause when trying to safely dispose of nuclear waste. Students complete Worksheet question 1 *Ionising radiation*.

Teaching and learning notes: *There are many common misconceptions about radioactivity, e.g. that an object that has been exposed to radiation is itself radioactive OR that radioactive isotopes are somehow different from the stable isotope of the same element. It is worth exploring these ideas.*

Standard demand

Students in groups play the 'nuclear radiation detective game' where they are given pieces of evidence from scientists listing some properties of radioactivity on cards and they have to sort out the evidence to build up a picture of what an alpha particle is. They can then do the same with beta and gamma. Use Worksheet question 2 *Nuclear detective*.

Students could then use the internet to write a short biography of one scientist per group on one sheet of A4 including a picture.

Teaching and learning notes: *How this is tackled depends on time available. If time is short students could be provided with information and asked to summarise the main points.*

High demand

Using small pieces of Lego or counters ask students in groups to make a model of an atom of carbon-12, for example. Discuss how many protons neutrons and electrons their model has and where these are situated. Emphasise that this is a model to help us understand how it behaves. Now change the model to represent carbon-14. In chemistry we are interested in how the electrons take part in chemical reaction: is there any difference in the number of electrons in each of your atoms of carbon? No – so carbon will behave exactly the same way chemically whatever the isotope is.

Now explain that the carbon-14 nucleus is unstable due to the extra neutrons in it and so spontaneously and randomly it will decay. Describe how a neutron will change into a proton and an electron and this will be ejected at high speed from the nucleus, i.e. a beta particle will be formed.

Alpha decay only happens from considerably heavier isotopes that would be difficult to model using the Lego or counter idea but students could still think about the numbers involved. For example, Americium-241, which is used in smoke detectors, has an atomic number of 95 and a mass number of 241. Students could work out what it will turn into after emitting an alpha particle. Students complete Worksheet question 3 *Nuclear decay equations*.

Teaching and learning notes: *Alpha decay may actually be easier to understand than beta decay so you could deal with this first.*

Plenary suggestions

Groups show their biographies and explain the contribution of their scientist to the development of ideas about radioactivity.

OR

Students discuss how they could persuade people that ionising radiations are not always bad e.g. 'Why is eating irradiated fruit a good thing'.

Assessment opportunities

Worksheet p4_e_02 question 2 *Nuclear detective* and question 3 *Nuclear decay equations* might provide good checkpoints for students' progress.

Answers

Answers to the Student Book and Worksheet are available on the Teacher Pack CD.

P4f: Uses of radioisotopes

Resources

Student Book pages 252–253

Interactive Book Quick starter: Gamma rays – can you translate this? • Quick starter: Background radiation doses

Files on Teacher Pack CD: p4_f_01_worksheet; p4_f_01_technician

Learning objectives

- Identify sources of background radiation.
- Understand the use of alpha sources in smoke detectors.
- Understand how radioisotopes are used as industrial tracers.

Learning outcomes

- Recall that background radiation comes from rocks and cosmic rays and some from man-made sources.
- Explain how a smoke detector with an alpha source works.
- Describe how tracers are used in industry and explain why gamma sources are used.

Prior knowledge

Content from P2 Radioactivity.

Key vocabulary

background radiation • cosmic rays • radioisotope • alpha • decay • tracer • gamma

Barriers to learning

Students may have ideas about radioactivity being dangerous especially gamma radiation. Misconceptions on radioactivity are common due to films and television.

Curiosity and starter suggestions

- Have the GM tube and rate meter counting background radiation and also use it to measure some naturally occurring radioactivity depending on what is available.

OR

- Ask students to list any uses of radioactivity they know of.

Learning activities

Worksheet p4_f_01

Low demand

Use the starter activity to lead into a discussion about how radioactivity comes naturally from some materials – remind students that we call this naturally occurring radiation in the environment ‘background radiation’. Background radiation varies from place to place and from day to day. Show the students a map of background radiation and point out the higher levels in areas where granite rock is common.

The granite contains small amounts of naturally radioactive materials such as uranium and thorium. Uranium and thorium decay to other radioactive atoms, including radium, which then decays to radon gas. Since radon is an inert (that is, chemically stable) gas, it moves from the soil, where it is produced, and into the air. Radon is a natural part of the earth's atmosphere. The amount of uranium and radium in soil varies greatly with geographic location and soil type.

Explain that the two main sources of background radiation are rocks/soil and cosmic rays from the Sun. Students complete Worksheet question 1 *Background radiation.*

Demonstrate to students how a radioactive tracer could be used to detect a leak by using a hidden radioactive source and the GM tube and counter to find it. Explain that this can also be done in plants to trace fertiliser uptake or in humans to check for blockages in blood vessels etc.

Show students a smoke detector if available and explain that this contains an alpha particle source to detect smoke and sound the alarm in the event of a fire. Students complete questions1–to 3 from page 252 of Student Book.

Teaching and learning notes: *It may be possible to demonstrate some natural radioactive sources. Low sodium salt may contain enough potassium-40 for example.*

Standard demand

Explain in more detail how the smoke alarm works (could demonstrate it working)

Without smoke: The alpha particles hit air particles and ionise them. The positive **ions** and negative **electrons** move towards the negative and positive plates, respectively. This creates a tiny **current** that is detected.

With smoke: Some alpha particles hit the smoke particles so there is less ionisation of air particles. The smoke detector senses the drop in current and sets off the alarm.

Ask students to identify the reasons why Americium-241 is chosen as the source used in the smoke detector. It emits alpha particles and has a long half-life so that it does not have to be replaced often and so that there is no reduction in ionisation current due to decay of the source. Students complete Worksheet question 2 *Smoke alarms*.

Teaching and learning notes: *Show an old smoke detector if you have access to one but make sure the ionisation chamber is kept intact.*

High demand

Explain that although most of the background radiation is from rocks and cosmic rays there is a small percentage (less than 1%) from human activities such as the nuclear power industry and medical uses.

Students research one of the human activities that contribute by researching industrial tracers, medical tracers, etc. Students complete Worksheet question 3 *Industrial and medical tracers.*

Teaching and learning notes: *It may be surprising to students that only a very small percentage of background radiation is caused by human activity.*

Plenary suggestions

Students share their findings from the research with the rest of the class and everyone notes down key points.

OR

Show an unlabelled diagram of a leak in an underground pipe and ask students to summarise how a tracer works.

Assessment opportunities

Worksheet p4_f_01 provides staged opportunities for assessing students' understanding: question 1 *Background radiation,* question 2 *Smoke alarms* and the students' research findings could provide good checkpoints.

Answers

Student Book

Q1 A radioactive isotope could be added to the fertiliser and it could be traced using a detector • **Q2** Smoke alarms can save lives by warning when there is a fire • **Q3** Radiation, which is always present in the environment • **Q4** Rocks and cosmic rays, etc. • **Q5** A gamma emitting radioactive isotope is introduced into the pipe and a detector on the surface notes a drop in the level detected after the blockage • **Q6** Beta particles would not be stopped by the smoke particles • **Q7a** Different rock types common in different areas • **Q7b** More or less cosmic rays could be reaching us from the Sun at different times • **Q8** Gamma is the only type of radiation capable of passing through the pipe and soil to reach the detector • **Q9** Put a radioactive isotope in one site and if it reaches the silt deposit you can work out where it came from

Fig 1 houses made from granite, which may contain some uranium; uranium emits radon when it decays • **Fig 2** radioactive tracers • **Fig 3** alpha • **Fig 4** because the radioisotope has leaked out and there is less in the pipe • **Fig 5** alpha ionises air causing a current; when alpha is stopped by smoke there is less current; this drop in current can be detected • **Fig 6** radioactivity in the air

Worksheet

Answers to the Worksheet are available on the Teacher Pack CD.

P4f: Uses of radioisotopes

Resources

Student Book pages 254–255
Files on Teacher Pack CD: p4_f_02_worksheet

Learning objectives

- Understand how radioactivity is used to date materials.

Learning outcomes

- Explain how rocks are dated using the ratio of uranium to lead.
- Explain how organic materials can be dated using measurements from radioactive carbon.

Prior knowledge

Content from p2 Radioactivity and p4_e_01 Half-life.

Key vocabulary

radiocarbon dating • isotope • ratio • half-life • uranium

Barriers to learning

Students may believe that half-life is literally as it sounds half of the whole life of the sample and it is important to emphasise that the activity halves and halves again and that this can go on indefinitely.

Curiosity and starter suggestions

- Display a graph showing nuclear decay and ask students to find the half-life from the graph (e.g. Figure 8 from page 254 of the Student Book).

OR

- Have a slide show of archaeological finds and ask students for ideas on how scientists can judge how old they are.

Learning activities

Worksheet p4_f_02

Low demand

Explain which types of rocks may contain radioactive materials. Remind students of the map of background radiation distribution and that areas with a lot of granite rock tend to have higher than average background radioactivity due to some of the isotopes of uranium found in the rocks. Explain to students that over a long period of time the uranium in some rocks will have decayed into lead and scientists can use the ratio of uranium to lead to work out an approximate age of the rock. Students complete Worksheet question 1 *Dating rocks.*

Teaching and learning notes: *Students may have some problems with the idea of atoms of uranium turning into lead.*

Standard demand

Use a simulation to show decay of a radioisotope for example and remind students that half-life is the time when half of the nuclei in the sample have decayed:
http://www.colorado.edu/physics/2000/isotopes/radioactive_decay3.html

Explain how uranium-238 is used to date older rocks and uranium-235 for younger rocks. Students complete Worksheet question 2 *Using uranium to date rocks.*

Describe how carbon-14 is used to date any archaeological find that was once living and is between about 3,000 and 58,000 years old. Give examples of famous artefacts that have been dated using this technique. Students answer questions 12–14 from page 255 of the Student Book.

Teaching and learning notes: *How this is tackled depends on time available. If there is enough time students could work with the simulation in pairs.*

High demand

Explain how carbon-14 is formed when cosmic rays from the Sun collide with atoms and release neutrons. These neutrons are absorbed by the nitrogen atoms in the air and form carbon-14. There is a very small but constant ratio of carbon-14 to carbon-12 in the atmosphere (due to the rate of decay of carbon-14 being approximately equal to its rate of formation). Plants absorb carbon-14 in the form of carbon dioxide during photosynthesis and then animals eat the plants also absorbing the carbon-14. By comparing the amount of carbon-14 in a sample with the amount in a living organism, scientists can work out the age of the sample. Students complete Worksheet question 3 *Radiocarbon dating.*

Teaching and learning notes: *Students may need some reminding of the carbon cycle.*

Plenary suggestions

Show a short video clip of radiocarbon dating without the sound and ask students to write a script.

OR

Students play a game where they have to decide if an object could be carbon dated or not. Teacher describes the object and they use a simple thumbs up or down all at the same time.

Assessment opportunities

The worksheet questions should provide opportunities for assessing the students' level of understanding.

Answers

Student Book

Q10 It contains small amounts of uranium • **Q11** by comparing how much uranium is in it compared to lead • **Q12** iron nail and nylon shirt • **Q13** radioactive elements often end up as lead because it is the heaviest stable element • **Q14a** 9 000 million years • **Q14b** The rock is older than the Earth • **Q15** because it has to be something which was living • **Q16** By comparing the ratio of Carbon-12 to Carbon-14 in the animal to that of living organisms.

Figure 7 by comparing the amount of uranium and lead • **Figure 8** lead-206 • **Figure 9** has shorter half-life so can date younger rocks • **Figure 10** it is too recent to have been worn by Jesus • **Figure 11** the Scroll was radiocarbon dated to the correct historical date • **Figure 12** she was found in ice which would have slowed any decay

Worksheet

Q1a Atoms with the same number of protons but different number of neutrons• **Q1b** The half-life has to be appropriate to the sample they are trying to date • **Q1c** Fossils would not contain any uranium • **Q1d** By decay of uranium • **Q1e** By comparing the relative proportions of uranium and lead • **Q1f** Two • **Q2a** **W** – after 2 half-lives; **X** – 12.5%; **Y** – 50% **Z** – 1:3 • **Q2b** 8.8 billion years • **Q3a** 7 and 8 • **Q3b** Neutron capture • **Q3c** Beta decay • **Q3di** C-12 • **Q3ii** C-14 • **Q3e** 1 000 000 000 000 • **Q3f** True

P4g: Treatment

Resources

Student Book pages 256–257 • X-ray pictures and gamma camera pictures • Equipment for Penetration of radioactivity demonstration

Files on Teacher Pack CD: p4_g_01_worksheet; p4_g_01_ technician

Learning objectives

- Compare the production and properties of X-rays and gamma rays.
- Understand how radioactive materials are produced for medical uses.

Learning outcomes

- Describe some similarities and differences between X-rays and gamma rays.
- Explain how the image is produced by the different amounts of absorption of X-rays by different materials.
- Outline how X-rays and gamma rays are produced.

Prior knowledge

P2e, P4e and P4f.

Key vocabulary

X-rays • gamma • absorption • wavelength • electromagnetic wave • exposure • half-life • diagnosis • therapy

Barriers to learning

Students will be familiar with the use of X-rays for imaging the inside of the body but will be less familiar with gamma rays being used in this way.

Curiosity and starter suggestions

- Display some X-ray pictures and some gamma camera pictures and ask students to compare them.

OR

- Project the electromagnetic spectrum on the board and ask students to point out X-rays and gamma rays and give some information about each type of wave.

Learning activities

Worksheet p4_g_01

Low demand

Use the starter activity to lead into a discussion of the differences and similarities between X-rays and gamma rays. Emphasise that both are electromagnetic waves and so will have similar properties. Both X-rays and gamma rays are used in medicine for **diagnosis** and **treatment**. Emphasise the difference between these two.

Students complete Worksheet question 1 *Using X-rays and gamma rays.*

Explain how X-rays can be produced at any time using the X-ray machine but gamma rays are given off from radioactive nuclei which must have a suitable half-life. The half-life of the isotope should be long enough for the procedure to be completed but not too long so that there is unnecessary damage to the patient. Radioisotopes can be made artificially by placing materials into a nuclear reactor.

Students answer questions 1–3 on page 256 of Student Book.

Teaching and learning notes: *Students may have misconceptions around the similarities of X-rays and gamma rays because they will have much more experience of X-rays and will view them as routine and not at all dangerous and gamma rays as radioactive and very dangerous.*

Standard demand

Use a GM tube and counter to carry out demonstrations to show how penetrating the different nuclear radiations are. Interpret observations made during the demonstrations.

Explain why alpha sources are not useful for diagnosis or for therapy as they will not pass through the skin. Beta will pass through the skin but is absorbed by bone so its medical applications are limited. Gamma sources such as Cobalt-60 are used in radiotherapy because of gamma radiation's ability to pass through the body and because when it is absorbed by living cells it can kill them. There are obvious risk associated with this as healthy cells can also be affected. Students complete Worksheet question 2 *Penetration of nuclear radiation*.

Show the X-ray picture again (and others if you have them) ask the students to identify what each one shows. Describe how X-rays pictures are formed because of the different amounts of X-rays absorbed by different materials. X-rays are hardly absorbed by the soft tissues of the body but are strongly absorbed by bones. If a photographic plate is placed on the other side of the body an image of the bones will show white as that part of the plate was not exposed to the X-rays, all the rest of the plate was exposed to the X-rays and so blackened as a result.

Teaching and learning notes: *Students are not allowed to handle the radioactive sources but they can participate in demonstrations by timing the periods for the count rate and by counting the clicks if using an audible counter. Computer simulations are also useful for emphasising the key ideas.*

High demand

Explain how X-rays are produced by firing a fast moving beam of electrons at a metal target. Some of the electrons kinetic energy is released as X-rays. Use Figure 4 on page 257 of the Student Book projected on the board to aid the explanation. Explain that most of the advantages of using X-rays instead of gamma rays stem from the fact that their production can be controlled.

Students complete Worksheet question 3 *Comparing X-rays and gamma rays*.

Teaching and learning notes: *There is a good article in the Catalyst magazine on medical imaging which may be useful for this lesson. Find it at http://www.sep.org.uk/catalyst/articles/catalyst_16_2_261.pdf*

Plenary suggestions

Ask students to produce a summary comparing X-rays with gamma rays in a table.

OR

Play 'true or false' where the teacher reads out a scenario and the students have to decide which it is. (They could hold up white boards or cards to ensure everyone takes part.)

Assessment opportunities

Worksheet p4_g_01 question 2 *Penetration of nuclear radiation* and the summaries produced in the plenary will provide good checkpoints for students' understanding.

Answers

Student Book

Q1 Diagnosis is finding out what is wrong and therapy is treating the problem • **Q2** Both short wavelength electromagnetic waves; both very penetrating; both can pass into the body ; both can damage living cells • **Q3** They are specially made in nuclear reactors • **Q4** It cannot pass through the skin • **Q5** It is ionising and can damage cells increasing the risk of cancer • **Q6** Gamma • **Q7**So that the electrons can travel across the tube • **Q8** X-rays are produced only when necessary gamma are produced continuously; X-rays can be controlled and the energy adjusted gamma cannot be made with different energies

Fig 1 the radiation must be carefully targeted • **Fig 2** the wavelengths overlap/ are similar • **Fig 3** X-rays are absorbed by the bones they pass through soft tissue • **Fig 4** the anode gets very hot

Worksheet

Answers for the Worksheet are available on the Teacher Pack CD.

P4g: Treatment

Resources

Student Book pages 258–259

Interactive Book icould career video: Applications of radioactivity: how useful is radioactivity? • icould career video: Diagnostic radiography

Files on Teacher Pack CD: p4_ g _02_worksheet; p4_ g _02_ technician

Learning objectives

- Describe the use of nuclear radiation in medicine.
- Understand the role of the radiographer and the safety precautions they must take.

Learning outcomes

- Describe the use of nuclear radiations for:
  - diagnosis and treatment of cancer
  - sterilisation of equipment.
- Explain that nuclear radiation can damage cells.
- Explain how gamma (and sometimes beta) emitters can be used as tracers.
- Describe safety precautions which are necessary when using X-rays or tracers.

Prior knowledge

p4_e_01, p4_e_02, p4_f_01 and p4_f_02.

Key vocabulary

diagnosis • sterilisation • tracer • radiotherapy • radiographer • emitter • X-rays• gamma • beta

Curiosity and starter suggestions

- Show a picture of a patient being prepared for an X-ray and ask students who have been X-rayed to say what they remember (especially the safety precautions used)

OR

- Quick Quiz on Properties of radiations and their uses.

Learning activities

Worksheet p4_g_02

Low demand

Use the picture of a patient and the students' own experience to draw out their ideas about some of the safety precautions for X-rays, e.g. lead apron or bib; radiographer and others out of the room; patient asked if they could be pregnant.

Explain that a radiographer may also be involved in setting up and using a radiotherapy treatment for a patient where large doses of gamma radiation are used to kill cancer cells after surgery to remove a tumour (or sometimes in place of surgery). Explain that this is necessary in case there are any cancerous cells left in the body which could multiply and cause secondary cancers. Students complete Worksheet question 1 *Radiotherapy*.

Explain that gamma radiation can also be used to sterilise medical equipment because of its ability to kill bacteria. Use Figure 5 on page 258 of the Student Book to help describe the stages in sterilisation. Students answer questions 10 and 11 on page 258 of the Student Book.

Teaching and learning notes: *Students may have a relative who has or is having radiotherapy treatment and this needs to be sensitively handled.*

Standard demand

Describe the use of radioactive tracers in the body to investigate any problems without the need to operate on the patient. Explain that different radioisotopes are used to target different parts of the body, e.g. iodine-123 is used to investigate the thyroid for example. Explain that the sources must usually be gamma emitters since the radiation is emitted inside the body and has to be detected outside. Sometimes beta emitters can be used if the area being investigated is not too deep in the body.

Explain that radioactive tracers must have short half-lives so that they do not harm the patient by remaining active in the body for long periods.

Show students how a tracer can be tracked in the body using a gamma emitter hidden in a soft toy or skeleton.

Technitium-99m is a commonly used tracer – it is ideal as it has a half-life of 6 hours, just long enough for a procedure to be completed but not so long that it is around in the body for long after the measurements are taken. Students complete Worksheet question 2 *Using radioactive tracers in the body.*

Teaching and learning notes: *When patients have a radioactive tracer inside they may be asked to avoid children and pregnant women for a while but the half-life is short so the activity should drop quickly.*

High demand

Describe how the patient either takes the radioactive material with food or drink or it may be injected into the body. Explain how a gamma camera connected to a computer is used to monitor the progress of the radioisotope through the body. Show images obtained using radioactive tracers.

For the treatment of cancer high power gamma radiation is used and two methods of reducing the damage to the healthy tissues that the gamma passed through can be used. One is to rotate the source and the other is to use three sources, each providing one third of the dose. Use Figure 8 on page 259 of Student Book to help explain this. Students complete Worksheet question 3 *Treating Cancer.*

Teaching and learning notes: *It may be worth pointing out that patients who have undergone radiotherapy are not radioactive.*

Plenary suggestions

Students share their leaflets on radiotherapy with others in the group and receive constructive feedback from them.

OR

Word puzzle on ideas from the lesson.

Assessment opportunities

Worksheet p4_g_02 provides staged opportunities to assess students' learning (afl). In addition, thoughtful questioning during class discussions may be used to draw out blocks to learning

Answers

Student Book

Q9 Any remaining cancer cells can multiply and cause secondary cancers • **Q10** They leave the room while the radiation source is on • **Q11** gamma emitter with a short half-life • **Q12** Its half-life is about 6 hours and it gives out **only** gamma radiation • **Q13**To prevent unnecessary exposure to the radiation • **Q14** Cobalt-60 has a longer half-life • **Q15a** So that measurements can be made but the sources does not remain active inside the patient for very long • **Q15b** So that it is detected outside the body

Fig 5 to avoid infection • **Fig 6** to protect the rest of the face from the radiation • **Fig 7** the blood with the tracer has not reached that area • **Fig 8** the three beams can all reach the tumour but only 1/3 passes through the healthy tissue on the way

Worksheet

Q1 Students produce their own leaflet • **Q2** Students produce their own poster • **Q3a** It is the only type of radiation that will penetrate the skull • **Q3b** So that the tumour gets the full dose of radiation but healthy tissue only receives one-third of that amount • **Q3c** Rotating source means that all tissue receives a small dose of radiation; three-source method means some tissue does not receive any radiation but other healthy tissue gets more radiation than it would with a rotating source • **Q3d** Healthy tissue only receives a very small dose of radiation

P4h: Fission and fusion

Resources

Student Book pages 260–261

Interactive Book Naked Scientist animation: What's the difference between a nuclear reactor and an atomic bomb? • News clip: Nuclear power

Files on Teacher Pack CD: p4_h_01_worksheet

Learning objectives

- Understand the main stages in the production of electricity in nuclear power stations.
- Describe nuclear fission and how it is controlled.

Learning outcomes

- Describe the main stages in the production of electricity in nuclear power stations.
- Describe nuclear fission as the process that releases energy in a nuclear power station and recall that it produces radioactive waste.
- Describe a chain reaction and how they are controlled.
- Explain that a nuclear bomb is a chain reaction out of control.

Prior knowledge

Content from p4_e_01 and p4_e_02.

Key vocabulary

fission • fusion • nuclear • chain reaction • graphite moderator • control rods • uranium • reactor

Barriers to learning

Students may view nuclear power stations as dangerous as any accidents are always reported widely and sensationally.

Curiosity and starter suggestions

- Display a picture of a nuclear power station without labels.

OR

- Show a short clip of a nuclear explosion and ask how much energy would be released.

(A 1 megaton nuclear weapon is one which produces the same amount of energy in an explosion as does 1 million tons of TNT. One megaton is equivalent to 4.18 × 10^{15} joules.)

Learning activities

Worksheet p4_h_01

Low demand

Use a simulation or video to help describe the stages in the nuclear power station.

Remind the students that one of the disadvantages of nuclear power is the amount of radioactive waste. Students prepare an argument in groups either for or against nuclear power as a solution to future energy needs for the UK. Hold a debate where each side is asked to put its point across and hold a class vote on the issue.

Students complete Worksheet question1 *Power stations*.

Teaching and learning notes: *Instead of the debate students could prepare a report that they then share with the group. If choosing to debate it is important to set ground rules before you begin.*

Standard demand

Use Figure 3 on page 260 of Student Book to help illustrate the size of the fuel rods used in a nuclear reactor. This is called enriched uranium because it has a greater proportion of uranium-235 than would occur naturally.

Explain that a chain reaction occurs in the reactor where the neutrons released go on to react with more uranium and this continually releases energy until all of the uranium has been used up. 1 kg of uranium-235 can release as much energy as 2 million kg of coal.

The chain reaction must be controlled or it could be very dangerous. A nuclear bomb is a chain reaction which is not being controlled.

Students answer questions 4–6 on page 261 of the Student Book.

Teaching and learning notes: *A physical model of a chain reaction would make it easier for students to visualise. An edible one can be made using cakes as the nuclei that can split and Smarties™ as the neutrons.*

High demand

Explain how uranium is bombarded with neutrons to cause a chain reaction and how Boron control rods are used to absorb some of the neutrons and control the rate of fission. Students make their own model of a nuclear reactor with junk – challenge them to make question 2 *How nuclear power stations work.*

Teaching and learning notes: *Add to the model a control rod to 'absorb the neutrons'.*

Plenary suggestions

Students display their model reactors and judge each other's based on mutually agreed criteria.

OR

Word search of key words from the lesson.

Assessment opportunities

Worksheet p4_h_01 question 1 *Power stations* and question 2 *How nuclear power stations work* might provide good checkpoints for students' progress.

Answers

Student Book

Q1 The uranium is used as a fuel in the reactor; it gives off heat to heat the water • **Q2** Coal burns but uranium undergoes fission • **Q3** Radioactive waste is dangerous to humans • **Q4** It has more Uranium-235 than occurs naturally • **Q5** A fission reaction occurs and releases heat • **Q6** The reaction must be carefully controlled and they produce dangerous waste • **Q7** The rate of fission increases, which means more energy is produced. • **Q8** The graphite moderator slows down the neutrons making them more likely to react with the fuel

Fig 1 the effects of the radiation lasted for generations • **Fig 2** fossil fuels, nuclear, etc. • **Fig 3** enriched uranium • **Fig 4** the neutrons which are released • **Fig 5** it could go out of control and explode

Worksheet

Q1a ii, iv, vi, i, v, iii • **Q1b** 1 g • **Q1c** Radioactive waste • **Q2ai** 92 • **Q2aii** 143 • **Q2aiii** 92 • **Q2aiv** 144 on each side • **Q2av** Uranium-235 has a very long half-life, so it decays very slowly; neutron fired at nucleus makes it split • **Q2avi** Chain reaction – three neutrons emitted, which can go on to split three more uranium nuclei, etc. • **Q2bi** 2.5×10^{16} J • **Q2bii** 8.42×10^{16} J • **Q2biii** 4.2 kg • **Q2biv** Very small compared to amount of coal used in 1 year by coal-fired power station • **Q2ci** Boron control rods are placed between the fuel rods. Boron absorbs neutrons so fewer neutrons are available to split more uranium nuclei. The boron rods can be raised or lowered in the reactor, which controls the fission rate. Enough neutrons are always left to keep the process operating • **Q2cii** Graphite rods placed between the fuel rods slow down fast-moving neutrons emitted during fission. The graphite acts as a moderator. Slow-moving neutrons are more likely to be captured by other uranium nuclei, which maintains the chain reaction

P4h: Fission and fusion

Resources

Student Book pages 262–263
Interactive Book Drag and drop: Fusion
Files on Teacher Pack CD: p4_h_02_worksheet; p4_h_02_technician

Learning objectives

- Understand the difference between fission and fusion.
- Recognise that 'cold fusion' is a disputed claim made by some scientists.
- Understand why fusion research is an international joint venture.

Learning outcomes

- Describe how nuclear fusion releases energy.
- Describe the conditions needed for fusion to take place.
- Explain why fusion for power generation is difficult.
- Explain why data on fusion research is shared between scientists.

Prior knowledge

Content from p4_h_01 Fission.

Key vocabulary

fission • fusion • energy • Joules

Barriers to learning

It is vital to emphasise the difference between fission and fusion as these terms are so similar.

Curiosity and starter suggestions

- Show the detonation of the first hydrogen bomb in the Pacific and give figures for how much energy was released compared to Hiroshima.

OR

- Show pictures of cities at night and ask students how much energy they think that the UK consumes in a year.

Learning activities

Worksheet p4_h_02

Low demand

Explain the difference between fission and fusion and point out that stars use fusion of hydrogen as their main power source. The sun gives out 3.8 x 10^{26} joules every second.

Students research the claims made by Pons and Fleischmann that they had achieved fusion at room temperature and write report on it. Ask them why it is so important that other scientists are able to repeat the findings.

Students complete Worksheet question 1 *Fusion*.

Teaching and learning notes: *Students may confuse the two terms fission and fusion.*

Standard demand

Explain that fusion requires extremely high temperatures (10 million degrees Celsius). These high temperatures are very difficult to achieve and to manage safely on Earth and so fusion as a method of large-scale power generation is not yet a reality. Fusion in the Sun is at a much higher pressure so the temperatures are less than this.

Projects such as the JET project have tried for many years to achieve fusion to produce energy safely and economically. For a long time the input energy was greater than the output energy. Now scientists have achieved equality, but a much greater output is needed for commercial use. Such research is very expensive so it is carried out as an international joint venture to share costs, expertise and ultimately the benefits.

Explain to the students that one litre of ordinary water contains enough deuterium to provide the energy content (when fused with tritium) of more than 500 litres of petrol.

Students complete Worksheet question 2 *Energy for the future.*

Teaching and learning notes: *There is lots of information on the JET website that could be useful here.*

High demand

Explain that extremely high temperatures and pressures are present in stars where fusion is happening. A hydrogen bomb is started with a fission reaction to produce these very high temperatures needed to start the reaction. 'Cold fusion' is not really accepted as a realistic possibility but lots of scientists continue to work together and share information because if it were to prove possible it would revolutionise energy production.

Students complete Worksheet question 3 *More about fusion.*

Teaching and learning notes: *There have been a few Hollywood movies recently where fusion is mentioned, e.g.* Spiderman 2 *or* Iron Man. *It may be interesting to discuss the physics (or lack of) in these.*

Plenary suggestions

Show students pictures/video from the Jet project.

OR

Play a loop game to summarise the topic.

Assessment opportunities

Worksheet p4_h_02 question 2 *Energy for the future* and question 3 *More about fusion* might provide good checkpoints for students' understanding of fission and their newspaper articles should allow a check on their appreciation of scientists working together to develop ideas.

Answers

Student Book

Q9 In fission a large nucleus breaks down to form smaller nuclei; in fusion smaller nuclei join together to make a larger nucleus • **Q10** Other scientists have not been able to repeat their findings • **Q11** It would be an energy source with plenty of fuel and less harmful waste products than fission • **Q12** Sharing information can lead to a better understanding and allow lots of new ideas to be suggested • **Q13** So far no one has been able to verify any of the results or replicate the data • **Q14** Fusion would be a much safer way of supplying energy; the fuel would be easily available; the waste would be less dangerous; energy would probably be much cheaper, etc

Fig 6 successfully achieved fusion at room temperature • **Fig 7** hydrogen bombs use fusion atomic bombs use fission • **Fig 8** scientists have to provide the right conditions and this needs sophisticated equipment • **Fig 9**
$^{3}_{1}H + ^{1}_{2}H \rightarrow ^{2}_{3}He + ^{1}_{0}n$

Worksheet

Answers for the Worksheet are available on the Teacher Pack CD.

P4: Planning and collecting primary data

Pages 264–265 in the Student Book prepare students for assessment.

When and how to use these pages

This task provides an opportunity to build and assess the skills that students will use when planning an investigation.

Annotated hints and tips guide students through the tasks.

Ask students to:

- read through the context and tasks, listing any terms that they do not understand
- as a whole class or in small groups, discuss the tasks to ensure all students understand the terminology used and to clarify what is required
- work individually to answer the questions for each task.

If time allows, ask students to mark each other's work using the mark scheme provided.

Pages 278–290 provide further guidance on Practical and Enquiry Skills.

Notes

To set the task in context, students are reminded of how a dimmer switch in a lighting circuit works by altering the resistance in the circuit. They are reminded that changing the resistance is achieved by altering the length of the resistance wire in the variable resistor inside the dimmer switch.

Students plan an investigation into how the length of a resistance wire affects the current through a lamp. It may be useful to remind students how current is measured and where to place the ammeter. Some students may need help with drawing the circuit. Guide students towards planning for at least five different lengths in order to identify a trend. Also encourage them to plan for repeated readings and an average to be calculated. Students may also require help ensuring an accurate length is used as the wire may not be completely straight. They may not appreciate how hot resistance wires can become especially the shorter lengths and how this could affect their results.

Once the students have written a draft of their plan it could be a useful peer evaluation exercise if they were to give their plan to another group in the class for a critique. Each student, or group of students, could be asked to highlight good points in another student's plan and then suggest an improvement.

Once the plan has been approved, the experiment is carried out and the raw results recorded. Points 1 and 2 on page 265 are helpful in guiding the students towards an appropriate table of results and then 3 points out that the next step would be drawing a graph. It may be appropriate to ask the students to draw the graph suggested and write out a conclusion by using points 5 and 6 to help them.

To evaluate the experiment fully, it would be useful to discuss improvements to the experimental technique with the students and then discuss the data itself and identify how precise and how repeatable their results are. It is important to ensure that students know the difference between these terms.

The final two questions on page 265 ask students to consider how they could extend their investigation and modify it to investigate thickness of the wire.

Answers

This mark scheme is also available on the Teacher Pack CD.

1. *The current will be measured using an ammeter connected in series with the resistance wire.*
2. *The length of wire in the circuit could be measured using a metre rule. Remembering to measure between the two connectors so that it is only the length of wire in the circuit that is measured.*
3. *The thickness of the wire, the material of the wire, the temperature (as much as possible). Students should try out the experiment as very short or very thin wires will become very hot affecting the results as well as causing a hazard.*
4. *Use five or more different lengths.*

5. *It is good practice to repeat the readings although the number of repeats should really be determined by how close the repeated values are to each other.*

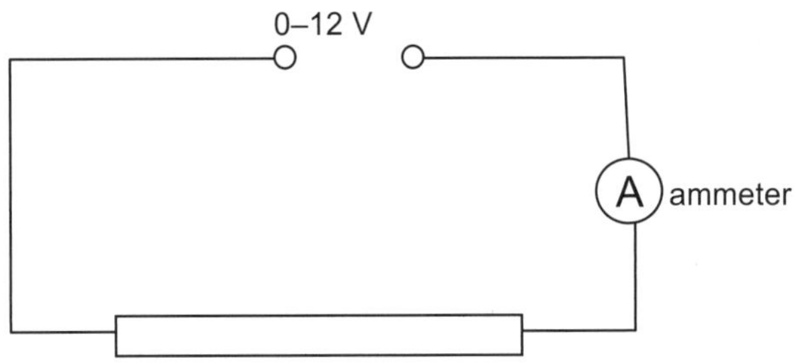

6. *Do not use too short a length or too high a current as it will become very hot; also switch off between readings to avoid the wire heating up. Avoid touching the wire when it is switched on and shortly afterwards in case it is hot.*

7. *Student plans will have to be checked to ensure they have considered all of the above points and that their plan gives a clear step by step outline of how the experiment will be conducted as well as a clear table ready for the results to be entered.*

P4: Checklist

Pages 266–267 in the Student Book provide a student-friendly checklist for revision.

When and how to use these pages

This checklist is presented in three columns showing progression, based on the grading criteria.

Remind students that they need to be able to use these ideas in various ways, such as:

- interpreting pictures, diagrams and graphs
- applying ideas to new situations
- explaining ethical implications
- suggesting some benefits and risks to society
- drawing conclusions from evidence they have been given.

These pages can be used for individual or class revision using any combination of the suggestions below.

- Ask students to construct a mind map linking the points on this checklist.
- Work through the checklist as a class and note the points that need further class discussion.
- Ask students to tick the boxes on the checklist worksheet (Teacher Pack CD) if they feel confident that they are well prepared for the topics. Students should refer back to the relevant Student Book pages to revise the points that they feel less confident about.
- Ask students to use the search terms to do further research on the different points in the checklist.
- Students could work in pairs, and ask each other what points they think they can do, and why they think that they can do those, and not others.

Pages 278–299 provide further assessment guidance.

Module summary

In the introduction to this section, students were presented with a number of new ideas. Work through the list below as part of their revision. Ask students to write their own summaries and mind maps, using this list as a starting point:

- how static electricity is due to the transfer of electrons
- how static electricity can be a nuisance and sometimes dangerous
- some uses of static electricity
- electric circuits and resistance
- the safe use of electricity in the home
- the properties of longitudinal and transverse waves
- how ultrasound is used for diagnosis in medicine, for example, in body scans
- how ultrasound is used for treatment in medicine, for example, to break down kidney stones
- why ultrasound is preferred to X-rays for certain scans
- the properties of alpha, beta and gamma radiation
- the ionising effect of nuclear radiation
- the meaning of half-life and how to calculate it
- X-rays and gamma rays, which are part of the electromagnetic spectrum and have a very short wavelength
- what happens to a nucleus when an alpha particle or a beta particle is emitted
- how alpha sources are used in some smoke alarms
- how radioactive tracers are used to locate blockages in industry and in medicine
- the use of gamma rays to treat cancer
- how measuring the activity of radioactive carbon can lead to an approximate age for certain objects
- how radioactivity is used to date rocks
- fission and fusion.

Notes

P4: Exam-style questions: Foundation

Pages 268–269 in the Student Book are exam-style questions for Foundation students.

When and how to use these pages

These questions are based on module P4 and cover a range of different types of questions that students will encounter in their written exams.

- Questions could be used as a revision test once you've completed the section.
- Work through the questions as a class as part of a revision lesson.
- Ask students to mark each other's work, using the mark scheme provided.
- As a class, make a list of the questions that most students did not get right. Work through these as a class.

Notes on worked example

The worked example takes students through how nuclear radiation is used in hospitals.

The student realises that alpha particles cannot be detected outside the body so are not useful as a tracer. They fail to mention that alpha radiation is very strongly ionising and could cause a serious risk to health if inside the body.

In part (ii) the student fails to explain that the tracer will be emitting harmful radiation whilst in the body and so a tracer with a short half-life is more desirable.

In part b the students answer to (i) is correct but in part (ii) the student fails to explain that the radiation beam can be focussed on the tumour. Some healthy tissue will receive gamma radiation but this will be limited as much as is possible with lead shielding and careful targeting.

Assessment objectives

These exam-style questions cover the Assessment objectives as described below.

Assessment objectives		Questions
AO1	Recall, select and communicate their knowledge and understanding of science	1, 2a, 2b(i), 3, 4, 6
AO2	Apply skills, knowledge and understanding of science in practical and other contexts	2b(ii)
AO3	Analyse and evaluate evidence, make reasoned judgements and draw conclusions based on evidence	5

Answers

These answers are also supplied on the Teacher Pack CD so that students can mark their own, or their peer's work.

Question number	Answer	Additional notes	Mark
1a	Paint drops have same charge; They repel.		1 1
b	To attract the paint.		1
c	Less wasted paint; Covers 'hard to reach' areas.		1 1
			[5]
2a	L on brown wire.		1
b (i)	F on fuse.		1

(ii)	(When fault occurs) high current through fuse; Fuse melts; Breaking the circuit/stopping the current flow.		1 1 1
			[5]
3a	Ultrasound has a higher frequency (above 20 000Hz)		1
b	A; B; B.	1 mark each	1
c	Prenatal scanning /breaking down kidney stones / cleaning teeth	accept other uses	1
			[5]
4a	Removes or adds electrons to an atom		1
b (i)	beta		1
(ii)	gamma		1
(iii)	alpha		1
(iv)	alpha		1
			[5]
5	There is a clear description of the reasons for choosing suitable radioisotopes for each application, referring specifically to the penetrating abilities of the emitted radiation and the half-life of the isotope chosen. All information in answer is relevant, clear, organised and presented in a structured and coherent format. Specialist terms are used appropriately. Few, if any, errors in grammar, punctuation and spelling.		(5-6 marks)
	There is description of which isotope is suitable for which application, which refers at some points specifically to the half-life or penetrating ability of the emitted radiations. There are, however, some details or some steps missing or the answer is not always entirely clear. For the most part the information is relevant and presented in a structured and coherent format. Specialist terms are used for the most part appropriately. There are occasional errors in grammar, punctuation and spelling.		(3-4 marks)
	There is a brief description of some reasons for choosing particular isotopes, but this is incomplete. Answer may be simplistic. There may be limited use of specialist terms. Errors of grammar, punctuation and spelling prevent communication of the science.		(1-2 marks)
	examples of points made in response ▪ alpha particles cannot penetrate skin. ▪ gamma rays can pass through layers of earth or rocks. ▪ alpha particles are very strongly ionising. ▪ living materials contain carbon. ▪ alpha particles can be stopped by smoke. ▪ isotopes with a long half-life would last a long time. ▪ over time, the activity of a source reduces.		
			[6]
6 a)	Fission is when large atoms split and fusion is when small atoms join		1
b)	The results claimed have so far not been able to be reproduced by other scientists		2
			[3]
			[29]

P4: Exam-style questions: Higher

Pages 270–271 in the Student Book are exam-style questions for Higher students.

When and how to use these pages

These questions are based on module P4 and cover a range of different types of questions that students will encounter in their written exams.

- Questions could be used as a revision test once you've completed the section.
- Work through the questions as a class as part of a revision lesson.
- Ask students to mark each other's work, using the mark scheme provided.
- As a class, make a list of the questions that most students did not get right. Work through these as a class.

Notes on worked example

The worked example takes students through a six mark question on how electricity is produced in nuclear power stations.

The student begins with a paragraph where a chain reaction is explained well but the explanation would be improved by a diagram and an explanation of how a graphite moderator is used to slow down the neutrons so that they are more easily captured by another uranium nucleus.

The second paragraph mentions the Boron control rods but would be improved with a more detailed description of how these can be raised or lowered to increase or decrease the neutrons absorbed and hence alter the number of fission reactions that can take place.

The student finishes the explanation with the remaining stages of the power station process but misses out the important final step where the turbine turns a generator to produce electricity.

For the most part the information in this answer is relevant and presented in a structured and coherent format. Specialist terms are used for the most part appropriately. There are occasional errors in grammar, punctuation and spelling.

Assessment objectives

These exam-style questions cover the Assessment objectives as described below.

Assessment objectives		Questions
AO1	Recall, select and communicate their knowledge and understanding of science	1a, 2a, 4a
AO2	Apply skills, knowledge and understanding of science in practical and other contexts	1b, 1c, 2b, 3, 4b
AO3	Analyse and evaluate evidence, make reasoned judgements and draw conclusions based on evidence	5, 6

Answers

These answers are also supplied on the Teacher Pack CD so that students can mark their own, or their peer's work.

Question number	Answer	Additional notes	Mark
1a(i)	Electrons move from the duster onto the rod.		1
(ii)	The duster is left positively charged.		1
b	The balls will both become negatively charged; and repel each other.	1 mark each	2

c	Electrons move onto ball from rod; The electrons on the rod repel those in the wall pushing them further away from the surface; The wall surface is now more positive and the ball is attracted to it.		1 1 1
			[7]
2a	Power = voltage × current 900 = 230 × I I = 900/230 = 3.9 Amps		1 1 1
b	5 A		1
			[4]
3	Non-ionising radiation; Can be used to view soft tissue.		1 1
			[2]
4a	The time taken for the activity of a radioactive sample/ number of radioactive nuclei to reduce to half.		1
b (i)	5 years; lines shown on graph	1 mark each	2
(ii)	$^{60}_{27}Co \rightarrow ^{60}_{28}Ni + ^{0}_{-1}e\ (+\gamma)$	1 for each of the prefixes to Ni	2
			[5]
5	In favour: Produces more energy / kg of fuel than a fossil fuel power station; Does not produce greenhouse gases; Against: waste products are radioactive; An accident could release radiation into the environment.		1 1 1 1
			[4]
6	There is a clear description of the process of ultrasound scanning, including how the density of the layer and the speed of ultrasound in the material affect the amount of reflection. All information in answer is relevant, clear, organised and presented in a structured and coherent format. Specialist terms are used appropriately. Few, if any, errors in grammar, punctuation and spelling.		(5-6 marks)
	There is description of ultrasound scanning, which refers at some points to the effects of density of the layer and speed of ultrasound in the material. There are, however, some details or some steps missing and the answer is not always entirely clear. For the most part the information is relevant and presented in a structured and coherent format. Specialist terms are used for the most part appropriately. There are occasional errors in grammar, punctuation and spelling.		(4-3 marks)
	There is a brief description of some aspects of ultrasound scanning, but this is incomplete. Answer may be simplistic. There may be limited use of specialist terms. Errors of grammar, punctuation and spelling prevent communication of the science.		(2-1 marks)
	examples of relevant points made in response ▪ gel is needed between the transducer and the body ▪ ultrasound would reflect off the body without the gel ▪ ultrasound is partly reflected at the boundaries between different layers ▪ the proportion of ultrasound reflected depends on the density of each layer and the speed of ultrasound in the layer ▪ the time taken for reflections from different layers to arrive is measured ▪ a picture is built up by a computer.		
			[6]
			[28]

Carrying out Controlled Assessments in GCSE Additional Science

Pages 278–290 in the Student Book prepare students for Controlled Assessments.

When and how to use these pages

Carrying out a wide range of practical and investigative work, including fieldwork, with your students will help you to prepare them for their Controlled Assessment.

Pages 278–290 focus on the skills that students need in order to successfully carry out this work and complete their Controlled Assessment.

- Before starting practical work, you may wish to work through a specific part of this section, such as *Variables*, to ensure that students are familiar with the terminology.
- Encourage students to refer to these pages when they are carrying out class practicals to build confidence in their scientific vocabulary and understanding of the different skills they need to develop.
- Use these pages when revising and preparing students for examinations. Knowledge and understanding of scientific terminology is essential for both Written Papers and Controlled Assessment.

Further guidance and skills building resources

Worked Example and Key Technique videos in the Collins Interactive Book support this section.

Overview of this section

The different skills and key components of the practicals are covered in separate sections so that you can focus on one section at a time.

- Research and collecting secondary data (page 278)
- Planning and collecting primary data (page 279–286)
  - Choosing method and apparatus (page 280–281)
  - Working with variables (page 281–284)
  - Assessing and managing risk (page 284–285)
  - Collecting and processing data (pages 285–286)
- Analysis and evaluation (page 286–290)
  - Drawing conclusions and evaluating investigations (page 287–289)
  - Using secondary data (page 289–290)
  - Referencing (page 290)

In addition to the content mentioned above, in this section you will find

- *Examples* which put the skills in context
- *Assessment tips* providing further guidance
- *Definition* boxes highlighting key scientific vocabulary.

Notes on Controlled Assessment

Students will use a range of practical skills and knowledge in one task chosen from those supplied by OCR. The tasks are based on topics in the specification. Teacher guidance will be given with each task. The following guidance is reproduced from The OCR Additional Science B Gateway specification.

Each year, three new controlled assessment tasks will be made available on Interchange from 1st June, two years ahead of the examination series for which the tasks are to be submitted. Tasks will be removed upon expiry. Guidance on how to access controlled assessment tasks from Interchange is available on the OCR website: www.ocr.org.uk.

The same OCR controlled assessment task must NOT be used as practice material and then as the actual live assessment material.

Students require the same set of skills to successfully complete all Controlled Assessments, with the exception that:

- for Science, students will be given a hypothesis to investigate;
- for Additional Science and Separate Sciences, students will be asked to formulate a hypothesis.

Structure of the Controlled Assessment

Controlled assessment tasks have been designed to be an integral part of the teaching of the course. The practical activities will be based on the specification content. It is expected that candidates will complete the task at the appropriate point in the teaching of the specification content.

Opportunities to develop the practical skills required for this task are highlighted in the content of the specification. It is essential that candidates have some advance practice in these skills so that they can maximise their attainment. Candidates will need to take part in a planned learning programme that covers the underpinning knowledge and skills of the unit prior to undertaking the task.

The controlled assessment unit requires the completion of one assessment task. Each task is divided into three parts which are linked into an overall theme. The three parts should be taken in the order of Part 1, Part 2 and Part 3. Stimulus material will be provided which will introduce candidates to the task and direct the work they produce.

Part 1 – Research and collecting secondary data

Part 1 requires candidates to plan and carry out research. The Part 1 stimulus material introduces the task and provides guidance for the research. The research may be conducted either in class or as a homework exercise. The information collected is required for Parts 2 and 3.

Part 2 – Planning and collecting primary data

Part 2 requires candidates to develop a hypothesis in response to the Part 2 stimulus material and to plan and carry out an investigation to collect primary data to test their hypothesis. Collecting the data, as well as an assessed skill, will help candidates in Part 3 of the task by:

- enhancing their awareness of the practical techniques involved
- focusing on the quality of the data collected
- making them aware of the risks and necessary safety precautions.

Part 3 – Analysis and evaluation

Part 3 requires candidates to process and analyse the results from their research (Part 1) and their primary data (Part 2). They will also be required to evaluate their data and the methods used to collect it, and draw and justify a conclusion. Candidates will be guided by questions in an answer booklet.

Planning and managing Controlled Assessment

Controlled assessment tasks are available at an early stage to allow planning time prior to delivery. It is anticipated that candidates will spend a total of about 6 hours in producing the work for this unit. Candidates should be allowed sufficient time to complete the tasks.

While the wording of the stimulus material and questions must remain unchanged, practical aspects of these tasks can be adapted so that they allow the use of resources available to the centre, including the availability of equipment and materials for practical work.

Where controlled assessment tasks are adapted by centres this must be in ways that will not put at risk the opportunity for candidates to meet the marking criteria, including the chance to gain marks at the highest level.

Suggested steps and timings are included below, with guidance on regulatory controls at each step of the process. Teachers must ensure that control requirements indicated below are met throughout the process.

The parts of the task should be taken in the order of Part 1, Part 2 and Part 3. Candidates' work for Parts 1 and 2 should be collected on completion and returned to the candidates for Part 3.

How to be successful in your GCSE Additional Science written examination

Pages 291–299 in the Student Book prepare students for their written examinations.

When and how to use these pages

This section can be used as reference when students are revising for exams and practicing exam-style questions.

- Ask students to read page 297–298 and encourage class discussion of best-practice when revising for exams.
- Remind students of the mathematical skills that they've learnt in their mathematics classes and need to apply in their science assessments (page 299).
- Choose one or two of the types of questions to discuss and encourage students to look for examples of these questions in their student books or past papers.
- Encourage students to refer to these pages on a regular basis to develop confident exam techniques.

Further guidance and skills building resources

Worked Example videos in the Collins Interactive Book support this section.

Overview of the section

The different types of questions and wording that students will encounter are covered in separate sections so that you can focus on one section at a time.

- Language of the assessment paper – verbs used in questions (page 291–292)
- Answering different types of questions (page 293–296)
- Quality of Written Communication in science (page 296)

In addition to the main content, you will find *Assessment tips* providing extra guidance.

Notes and answers to examples

Example 7

A reaction that gives out heat energy.

Example 8

Multiply the load in newtons by the distance moved by the load in metres.

Example 9

The package where the parachute failed to open will hit the ground first.

Sometimes examiners do not award a mark for a statement such as this, but are looking to give credit for the explanation.

Example 10

a) 70 cm^3

b) There are more collisions because there are more acid particles.

c) Less acid is added and the reaction stops before all of the calcium carbonate has reacted.

Example 11

Aluminium is lightest, much cheaper than copper and a relatively good conductor. Copper cables would mean pylons being much closer together to support the weight.

Bad Science for Schools

What is Bad Science?

Bad Science is a book, a newspaper column in the Guardian and a website by Ben Goldacre, an award-winning writer and broadcaster who specialises in unpicking dodgy scientific claims made by scaremongering journalists, dodgy government reports, evil pharmaceutical corporations, PR companies and quacks. It promotes a healthy scepticism as a way of detecting powerful and effective uses of science and misuses and abuses.

How Collins is using 'Bad Science' in our New GCSE Science course

Ed Walsh, Science Advisor for Cornwall Learning, has taken eight of the case studies from the book and turned them into lessons aimed at GCSE level students. The lessons are designed to engage and excite students and encourage them to think for themselves. Pupils in secondary schools are in many cases very capable of understanding the 'Bad Science' approach and making good use of it themselves. Their grasp of scientific concepts and their enquiring minds mean that Bad Science is good for school science.

'Bad Science' lesson plans

Three of the lessons have been included in the Student Book (pages 272–277). You will find the lesson plans on the next few pages, with accompanying worksheets on the Teacher Pack CD.

- bs_goo: Brown goo
- bs_news: Bad news
- bs_mmr: MMR – don't die of ignorance

You can find these and other lesson plans on our website at:

www.collinsnewgcsescience.co.uk/badscience

Partnership

The "Bad Science is good for school science" project is a partnership between:

- Ben Goldacre – author of 'Bad Science'
- Harper Collins – publishers of 'Bad Science and the Collins GCSE Science series
- Cornwall Learning – developers of the teaching materials

Brown goo

Commentary

The key idea for the teacher to get students to engage with is how we can use science, both the procedure and the concepts, to investigate and evaluate claims made by product manufacturers. This provides students with an opportunity to apply their understanding and also to reflect on the implications for society of products being sold in this way. The particular context used here is that of detoxification, which some students may initially find convincing – the body produces waste materials that have to be disposed of. But the students go on to use concepts and processes from their school science to examine further and evaluate the claims.

Students are likely to find the marketing techniques derisory, but nothing more than rather expensive and ultimately harmless. However, there is a more serious point here. These approaches are dangerous, not because they're harmful but because they're a distraction. People who want to live longer, healthier lives could focus on some basic (and well known) advice on not smoking, limiting alcohol intake, eating fresh fruit and vegetables, and getting regular exercise and sleep, but over the course of a whole lifetime. An unnecessary and ineffective focus on 'detoxing' implies an alternative (and easier) way to a healthier life.

Before this lesson student should have knowledge of the process of excretion but this could be used as a starting point for a more detailed treatment. This lesson could also provide an introduction to electrolysis.

Resources

Student Book pages 272–273

ear candling video clip (search for 'ear candling' on YouTube) • ear candles • foot spa advertisement video clip (search for 'detox foot spa' on YouTube) • bs_goo_worksheet_01 'Ear Candling' • bs_goo_worksheet_02 'Collins Detox Foot Bath' • access to reference materials on excretion and electrolysis (not supplied) • model foot bath: see bs_goo_technician

Learning objectives

- To use primary and secondary evidence to investigate scientific claims
- To apply scientific concepts to evaluate 'health products'
- To explore the implications of evaluations of claims

Learning outcomes

By the end of the lesson students will have:

- examined evidence and drawn valid conclusions
- applied concepts such as excretion and electrolysis to evaluate applications of ideas and claims being made
- considered their responses to the ways in which science is used or abused to sell products.

Key vocabulary

electrolysis • excretion

Barriers to learning

Students may hold misconceptions relating to:

- the purpose of 'waste products' such as ear wax
- the nature of excretion

Lesson 1

Starter

Start by asking if anyone has heard of, or tried, ear candling. If possible show a short video clip from YouTube or use the photo shown on bs_goo_worksheet_01.

Explain that this is a technique that is claimed by some people to remove toxins by drawing them out through the ear in ear wax. The candle is actually a cone of waxed cloth. After use the cone can be cut open and the wax displayed.

Ask students to work in small groups to consider and give feedback on these questions:

- Why might such a technique be thought to draw out ear wax?
- Where might the wax in the used candle have come from?
- How could a simple experiment be set up to see if ear candling does remove ear wax?

The technique doesn't work; there is no force acting on the ear wax, and any wax in the used candle has come from the candle itself.

Furthermore, the technique may be dangerous due to the proximity of hot wax to the ear and the side of the head. It should not be demonstrated and it should be made clear that it may be hazardous as well as being ineffective.

Main activity

Draw out from students how they propose to investigate the claim. This is likely to centre upon two distinct approaches:

- Seeing if the candle can produce any drop in pressure to force the wax out.
- Seeing if the wax in the candle is produced even when not used in an ear.

It should be possible to demonstrate the first approach by burning an ear candle in the proximity of some suitable medium, such as chalk powder or smoke from a splint. The force is minimal and certainly not enough to lift wax out of an ear canal.

The second approach can also be demonstrated by burning an ear candle (but not in an ear), cutting open the candle afterwards and displaying the contents. Some students may object, saying that even if the candle produces wax on the inside, that there could be more wax or a different type, if used in the ear. Refer back to the first demonstration. Some students may propose analysing the wax in a used candle and comparing it with ear wax but it is unlikely that this will be feasible.

There are two research tasks that need to be undertaken at this point. Depending upon the facilities available and the students involved, students could all undertake both tasks or some groups do one and some the other.

- Some suppliers of ear candles claim that this is a traditional cleansing technique that originated with the Hopi Indians. Find out if this is true.
- Wax production is a natural process in the body. Find out what its purpose is.

Gather students' findings. Point out that ear candling has nothing to do with the Hopi tribe of America, who have requested to be dissociated from it, and emphasise that wax is produced by the ears for a good reason – it helps to clean the ear and provides some protection against bacteria. General hygiene including the washing of the outer ear is all that most people require. Impacted wax can reduce hearing efficiency but can't be treated by candling (or anything poked in the ear canal).

Plenary

Ask students to discuss what they now think about ear candling; explore with them their feelings about such treatments being marketed. Ask them to consider these points of view:

- 'Some people are convinced it works for them and swear that they feel better afterwards. Just because science can't explain it doesn't mean it doesn't work.'
- 'Ear candling is dangerous and should be discouraged. Every year hospital A&E departments have to deal with wax burns from ear candles.'
- 'In a free society people should be able to do what they want as long as it doesn't affect others.'
- Strange detox rituals like ear candling may do harm, because they can distract people from the real determinants of health, such as diet, lifestyle and income.

Lesson 2

Starter

Start the lesson by inviting students to recall and recount the activities and outcomes from the previous lesson. Briefly revisit the ways that they explored ear candling and their attitudes towards the technique.

Main activity

Introduce the main part of the lesson by explaining that another detox technique is going to be explored. Say that this is the foot spa, in which the patient puts their feet. Salt (or some other electrolyte) is added and a current made to flow using electrodes and a power supply. A good way of showing how this is promoted is by showing a video clip from YouTube.

Ask students to look at sample promotional materials for the detox foot spa (bs_goo_worksheet_01) and to consider:

- What claims are being made?
- What makes these claims seem plausible?
- Why might you be suspicious of these claims?
- How could you test them out?

Explain that promoters using bad science often use scientific terms to sound more convincing. Superficially the device may seem convincing, because:

- the body has to be able to dispose of toxins
- people's feet sweat and sweating is a form of excretion
- the water gradually changes colour

The next part of the lesson involves students working in groups, each of which has a particular job:

- Groups A need to research excretion and produce a summary of how the body disposes of waste materials.
- Groups B need to research electrolysis and produce a summary of what happens when current flows through an electrolyte.
- Groups C need to model the detox process using a model foot bath with electrodes and a low voltage power supply (see bs_goo_technician). If desired, a doll can represent the person. The changes in the water should be observed.

In the discussion following, these points should be drawn out:

- Human metabolism is complex, with the building blocks of molecules constantly being shaped into new arrangements. Sometimes there are waste products, but at different times the same molecule can be a valued ingredient or a waste product. There is no such thing as a 'detox system' in any medical textbook.
- Electrolysis occurs when current flows through water with an electrolyte; the electrolyte separates out and may (depending on the chemicals involved) result in a precipitate in the water and often bubbles and froth on top.
- The water changes colour even if no human feet are present.

Plenary

- Reflect on the way that claims are presented using theatrical techniques, and why the claims may be superficially plausible.
- Discuss why some people believe that these 'cures' work for them.
- Debate whether and how such products should be marketed.

Bad news

Commentary

The main idea to get across to students here is that data can be used and presented selectively to support different, or even opposing arguments – and this is often used in advertising and news stories. Someone looking to support or oppose a particular point of view can often trawl through data to find something to support their case.

The point of this isn't to encourage students to be cynical about data but to develop a more rigorous approach. In relation to health, people should be able to find an answer to 'If I do this rather than that, what, in real numbers, is the likely impact going to be?'

Before this lesson students should know that:

- Our bodies need energy in order to function
- Energy comes from the food that we eat
- Sugar is a common ingredient of food and contains energy
- This lesson can lead to understanding that sugars are carbohydrates, and that unused carbohydrates are turned into fat and stored in the body.

Resources

Student Book pages 274–275

bs_news_worksheet_01 'Brief sheet' • bs_news_worksheet_02 'Student data'

Learning objectives

- To develop an understanding of what makes a 'good' news story
- To consider examples of how science reports can be distorted to make 'good' news stories
- To consider why science reports may be represented in various different ways

Learning outcomes

By the end of the lesson students will have:

- used data and other evidence in particular ways to either support or disprove ideas
- seen that different interpretations can be made of the same evidence, and that often people have a vested interest in supporting or opposing particular points of view

Key vocabulary

energy • data • trend • pattern • correlation

Barriers to learning

Students may have the misconceptions that:

- sugar is always bad for you
- the body always releases energy from food at the same rate

Starter

First take a straw poll using questions such as:

- Who thinks that your body can get energy from a high glucose drink?
- Who thinks that your body can get energy from a jam sandwich?
- Which can you get energy from more quickly?

Then ask students to work in small groups and discuss these questions:

- Who had something sweet for breakfast?
- Sugar is very soluble – what does this suggest about how quickly your body can get energy from it?
- In what way is this a good thing?
- In what way is it a bad thing?

Take feedback and draw out the fact that sugar dissolves quickly in the bloodstream, providing the body with a sudden supply of energy. This is useful if you need to transfer a lot of energy quickly, but less useful if you need a steady supply over a long period of time.

Main activity

Students work in small groups, each with a particular brief, but each (though without knowing it) with the same set of data. The brief will be to make a case for a certain course of action based on the evidence.

Each group needs one of the following briefs, taken from bs_news_worksheet_01:

1. You are marketing managers from 'Gluco-glug' drinks, with a target of increasing sales figures.
2. You are sales executives from the Jam Marketing Board, keen to avoid your products having an image as an unhealthy food.
3. You are project managers from the 'Healthy Foods Project', with the task of encouraging people to follow better diets.
4. You are advertising managers for 'Porridge People', a new outlet selling takeaway porridge pots. You are keen to encourage people to eat porridge for breakfast and are using the slogan 'slow release of energy to keep you going all day long'.

Each group has a set of the figures (bs_news_worksheet_02). Tell them that they have to produce text for a press release, with a title of no more than ten words and text of no more than 50 words, making such use of the data as they can. Emphasise that they have to remember what their job is and be persuasive. Say that the press release won't be used unless it is engaging.

Plenary

Each group will present their case. This might be done by displaying the press releases, getting students to read them out or making key points. Consider asking students to explain how they used the data.

Ask the class why they think that such different outcomes came from the same set of evidence.

Discuss why scientists may sometimes disagree about the meaning of data.

MMR – don't die of ignorance

Commentary

This lesson has two really important ideas. One is that correlation is not the same as causation; agreement between two sets of data doesn't prove that one has caused the other. The other is that small scale studies can be misleading. It uses the well-known example of the MMR vaccination scare and refers to two studies, the case study of the 12 autistic children and a large scale observational study in Denmark.

Students should already have some understanding of how vaccination is used to develop people's resistance to a range of illnesses. This lesson could be used as an introduction to more work on ethical issues in Biology, the treatment of diseases, and lessons in which correlation and cause & effect have a significant role.

Resources

Student Book pages 276–277

bs_mmr_worksheet_01 'Is there a correlation?' • bs_mmr_worksheet_02 'Measles and Immunisation graph'

Learning objectives

- Understand the difference between correlation and cause & effect.
- To apply this understanding to a variety of contexts.
- To explore the professional responsibility of scientists when their research could have serious consequences.

Learning outcomes

By the end of the lesson students will have:

- applied an understanding of data and relationships to a situation
- engaged with the ethical dilemma facing doctors reporting on evidence and decisions.

Key vocabulary

correlation • cause • effect • vaccination

Barriers to learning

Students may hold misconceptions relating to the presence or absence of causal links

Starter

Ask students to look at the two graphs on the resource sheet (bs_mmr_worksheet_01) and answer these questions:

- When does graph A reach a maximum? When is it at its lowest? What is the general trend?
- When does graph B reach a maximum? When is it at its lowest? What is the general trend?

Establish that the overall trend is similar. Now tell the students that one of the graphs shows ice cream sales over a year and the other shows pollen count. Ask them if they can work out which is which. (The difference is that one is based on daily figures and the other is based on monthly figures. That doesn't help answer the question. In fact, A is the ice cream one.) Explain that the idea of correlation is an important one in science. It means agreement between sets of data.

How good is the correlation between these graphs – do they show the same pattern in the data? Explore these questions with the class:

- Did the pollen count cause the ice cream sales to rise?
- Did the sale of ice cream cause the pollen count to rise?
- Is there any link?

There is, of course, a correlation, but it's not a causal link between these two variables. Ice cream sales rise in hot weather and the release of pollen is triggered by long days and warm breezy weather. Emphasise that just because the correlation is strong, it doesn't mean that there is a causal link between these variables. It may mean that there is some other factor (such as long sunny days in this case) that is causing both.

In medical research, scientists are often trying to determine if one thing causes another, but this can be difficult if the proposed cause only creates the outcome in some cases, or if the outcome has lots of possible causes, or if there is a long delay between proposed cause and effect. Looking for a connection between cause and effect (between a treatment and a cure, or a health risk and a disease) can be thought of as a switch and light. It's easy to discover, in a room with a light switch, whether the switch makes the light come on. But in medicine we often encounter more difficult problems: often health risks are like a light switch that makes the light come on, but only sometimes, and sometimes the light comes on even when the switch isn't pressed, and in any case, even when the light does come on, it's several years after the switch is pressed. In situations like these we often need studies with large numbers to detect small, subtle effects.

Main activity

Formally introduced objectives and outcomes, relating back to the starter.

Explain to students that autism is a condition which affects between one and two people in every thousand, affecting neural development and causing restricted and repetitive behaviour. It affects social behaviour and language; its causes are unknown. It is usually diagnosed from the age of three onwards.

In Britain, as in many countries, the majority of children are vaccinated against measles, mumps and rubella using a combined vaccine (MMR). A British doctor wrote a report on 12 children who had been vaccinated with the MMR vaccine and were subsequently diagnosed as autistic. The result of this report was that media interest was raised; many anti-MMR stories appeared and there was a significant fall in the number of children given the MMR vaccine.

Ask students to work in groups to consider these questions:

- Does the fact that the children in the report were diagnosed with autism after being given the MMR vaccine prove that the vaccine caused the autism?
- At the time of the report being written well over 90% of children had the MMR vaccine. Why should it not be a surprise if some of those children are diagnosed with autism?
- What kind of survey would have helped to identify whether the MMR vaccine caused autism?

Ask students to look at the graph on bs_mmr_worksheet_02. This may need some careful introduction as there are two sets of data being displayed. The timing is significant: the story first started to appear in newspapers in 1998 and reached a height of interest in 2002. It then started to wane.

Ask students to look at the graph and consider these questions:

- What happened to the MMR vaccination rates of children?
- What happened to the incidence of measles?
- Is there a causal link?

It was subsequently established beyond reasonable doubt that there is no causal link between MMR vaccination and autism. The doctor had a commercial interest in the alleged link and was subsequently struck off. The scare affected no other countries; MMR vaccination rates are rising again.

Explain to students that one of the things this story illustrates is the importance of working with large-scale surveys wherever possible. Say that such a study was carried out in Denmark: the Madsen study. Because Denmark tracks patients and the care they receive they have been able to study the correlation between vaccination and illness; the data clearly shows that there is no correlation between MMR vaccination and the incidence of autism.

Explain that the study was based on data from over half a million children (nearly 100% of the children born): over 440,000 had been vaccinated and there was no greater incidence of autism amongst children vaccinated as amongst those not vaccinated. Say that the author of the study, Dr Madsen, pointed out that even in developed countries measles kills one in every 3000 people and causes pneumonia in one in 20.

Ask students to identify the features of this study that make its findings reliable and suggest what they might say to someone who still wasn't convinced and decided to 'play it safe' by not having their child vaccinated for MMR?

Plenary

Ask students to consider these points of view, decide what their responses are, and be ready to share their ideas:

- "The doctor who wrote the original report was right to alert people to his concerns and suggest that more research should be carried out."
- "The media got hold of the story and turned it into a huge scare. It's their fault."
- "There was never any evidence to prove a link. Thousands of children have caught diseases that could otherwise have been avoided."

Schemes of Work

Plan your teaching with these Schemes of Work for Modules B3, B4, C3, C4, P3 and P4.

Structure of Science

The Gateway Science Suite comprises eighteen modules of work, six from Biology, six from Chemistry and six from Physics. Each module contains eight items.

Modules 1 and 2 from each subject are the content for Science.

Modules 3 and 4 from each subject are the content for Additional Science.

All six modules from each subject are the content for that subject.

Schemes of Work are provided for each module and can be arranged in many different teaching orders depending on the resources available and the policies within a school's Science department.

Student text books follow the specification from the Awarding Body and each item is covered by two double page spreads – each spread representing the equivalent of one teaching lesson of approximately 1 hour.

subject - examined	year 10						year 11					
science – year 10 additional science – year 11[1]	B1	C1	P1	B2	C2	P2	B3	C3	P3	B4	C4	P4
science – year 10 additional science – year 11	B1			B2			B3			P4		
	C1			C2			C3			C4		
	P1			P2			P3			P4		

subject - examined	year 10						year 11					
science – year 11 additional science – year 11[1]	B1	C1	P1	B3	C3	P3	B2	C2	P2	B4	C4	P4
science – year 11 additional science – year 11	B1			B3			B2			P4		
	C1			C3			C2			C4		
	P1			P3			P2			P4		

subject - examined	year 9		year 10		year 11	
separate sciences – year 11	B1	B2	B3	B4	B5	B6
	C1	C2	C3	C4	C5	C6
	P1	P2	P3	P4	P5	P6

[1] If several classes are taught simultaneously, the order in which each block of three modules is taught can be changed to allow resources to be more available.

Lesson number	Lesson name	Learning Objectives	Assessable Learning Outcomes	Specification reference	Student Book pages	Teacher Pack materials	Personal resources e.g. videos / websites
B3a1	Molecules of Life	Explain that DNA is found in the nucleus of the cell. Describe how Watson and Crick built a model of DNA. Explain the function of mitochondria and ribosomes.	Recall that mitochondria are needed for respiration. Recall that Watson and Crick used data from other scientists to develop their ideas about the structure of DNA. Explain why new discoveries are not always accepted and that ribosomes are the site of protein synthesis.	B3a.1 B3a.3	10-11	Lesson plan. Worksheet. Technicians' notes.	
B3a2	Molecules of Life	Describe the structure of DNA. Explain how DNA is used to make proteins.	Recall that genes are made from DNA and that DNA controls the production of proteins. Recall that DNA is a double helix and that each gene contains a different sequence of bases. Explain the base sequence is used to determine the order of amino acids in a protein.	B3a.2	11-12	Lesson plan. Worksheet. Model DNA practical. Technicians' notes.	
B3b1	Proteins and mutations	Describe the function of some proteins. Explain how DNA mutations can affect the function of the protein.	Recall example of proteins and describe a mutation as changes to genes. Describe the function of different proteins and understand that mutations can be harmful or beneficial. Explain that genes can be switched on or off and that mutations can alter the sequence of amino acids in a protein.	B3b.1 B3b.3	14-15	Lesson plan. Worksheet. Technicians' notes.	
B3b2	Proteins and mutations	Describe the role of enzymes in the body. Explain why enzymes are specific. Explain how enzyme activity is affected by temperature and pH.	Recall that enzymes are proteins that speed up chemical reactions. Describe the effect of temperature and pH on enzyme activity and use the lock and key mechanism to explain why enzymes are	B3b.2	16-17	Lesson plan. Worksheet. Temperature and enzymes practical. Technicians' notes.	

			specific. Explain effect of temperature and pH on enzyme activity and calculate Q10 values.				
B3c1	Respiration	Describe the process of aerobic respiration. Describe how to measure the rate of respiration. Explain why respiration rate is affected by temperature and pH.	Recall the word equation for aerobic respiration and be able to name some processes that require energy from respiration. Recall the balanced symbol equation for aerobic respiration, use data to compare respiration rates and be able to calculate RQ values Explain that respiration is controlled by enzymes which are affected by pH and temperature. Recall that ATP molecules are produced during the process of respiration.	B3c.1	18-19	Lesson plan. Worksheet. Respiration rate practical. Technicians' notes.	
B3c2	Respiration	Describe an experiment to measure resting pulse rate and recovery time after exercise. Explain why anaerobic respiration takes place during hard exercise in addition to aerobic respiration. Explain fatigue in terms of lactic acid build up (oxygen debt) and how this is removed during recovery	Describe how to measure recovery time and explain that breathing rate and pulse rate increases during exercise because the muscles need more oxygen and need to remove more carbon dioxide. Recall the word equation for anaerobic respiration and explain that anaerobic respiration occurs when the muscles do not get enough oxygen. Explain that lactic acid builds up because of the incomplete breakdown of glucose due to a lack of oxygen in the cells.	B3c.2	20-21	Lesson plan. Worksheet. Recovery time practical. Technicians' notes.	
B3d1	Cell division	Describe the difference between unicellular and multicellular organisms. Explain why cell division takes place. Explain the advantages of being multicellular Describe DNA replication and mitosis	Describe difference between unicellular and multicellular organisms and recall that cell division is needed for growth repair and asexual reproduction. Explain the advantages of being multicellular and explain that mitosis produces genetically identical cells	B3d.1 B3d.2	22-2	Lesson plan. Worksheet. Mitosis practical. Technicians' notes.	

			needed for an organism to grow. Describe the process of DNA replication to include 'unzipping and complimentary base pairing. Describe how chromosomes line up and divide during mitosis.				
B3d2	Cell division	Describe the role of gametes in sexual reproduction. Explain why fertilisation results in genetic variation and how the structure of a sperm cell is adapted to its function. Explain why, in meiosis, the chromosome number is halved and each cell is genetically different.	Recall that in sexual reproduction gametes join in fertilisation and that a unique individual forms with half their genes coming from each parent. Describe gametes produced by meiosis are haploid and that the joining of gametes to form a diploid zygote results in genetic variation. Explain that sperm cells require mitochondria to provide energy and an acrosome that releases enzymes to digest the egg membrane. Explain that in meiosis the chromosome number is halved when pairs of chromosomes move to opposite poles and that each new cell is genetically different.	B3d.3	24-25	Lesson plan. Worksheet Technicians' notes.	
B3e1	The circulatory system	Describe the functions of components of the blood and name the different blood vessels. Explain how red blood cells are adapted to their function and describe the role of arteries veins and capillaries in the transport of blood. Describe how haemoglobin is used to transport oxygen.	Recall that blood moves through arteries, veins and capillaries, they should also describe the function of red blood cells, white blood cells and platelets. Explain how haemoglobin in red blood cells, their size, shape and lack of nucleus help them carry oxygen. Describe the function of plasma in the transport of substances and the role of arteries veins and capillaries in the transport of blood. Describe the how haemoglobin reacts with oxygen to form	B3e.1 B3e.2	28-29	Lesson plan. Worksheet. Technicians' notes.	

			oxyhaemoglobin. Explain how arteries veins and capillaries are adapted to their function.				
B3e2	The circulatory system	Describe the functions of the heart and explain why blood flows round the body. Identify the different parts of the heart and explain why the left ventricle has a thicker wall than the right ventricle. Explain the advantage of the double circulatory system in mammals.	Recall that the heart pumps blood to the lungs and the rest of the body and that the blood flows because of pressure differences. Label a diagram of the heart and explain that the left ventricle has a thicker muscle wall to pump the blood at higher pressure so that it reaches all parts of the body. Explain advantages of the double circulatory system in mammals in that it can produce a higher pressure and increase the rate of flow to the tissues.	B3e.3	30-31	Lesson plan. Worksheet. Heart dissection practical. Technicians' notes.	
B3f1	Growth and development	Describe how to make a stained slide of an onion cell and the functions of the parts of a plant cell. Identify simple differences between bacterial cells and plant and animal cells and discuss the use of stem cells. Describe the difference between the arrangement of DNA in a bacterial cell and a plant/animal cell.	Describe how to prepare a stained slide using iodine solution. Recall that bacteria cells are smaller than plant and animal cells and that cell division is followed by specialisation. Recall that bacteria lack a 'true' nucleus mitochondria and chloroplasts. Describe uses of stem cells to treat medical conditions and discuss the issues involved. Describe bacterial DNA as a single circular strand and explain that embryonic stem cells have the ability to differentiate into many different types of cells.	B3f.1 B3f.3	32-33	Lesson plan. Worksheet. Plant cells practical. Technicians' notes.	
B3f2	Growth and development	Describe how growth can be measured and interpret data on increases in mass. Describe and explain why plant growth is different to animal growth. Explain the advantages and disadvantages of the different	Describe how to use height, wet mass and dry mass to measure growth and explain that plants grow continually at specific points but all parts of an animal grow during their early stages. Recall that dry mass is a	B3f.2 B3f.4	34-35	Lesson plan. Worksheet. Technicians' notes.	

		methods of measuring growth.	better measure of growth and that plan.t growth is restricted to meristems but unlike animal cells plan.t cells retain the ability to differentiate. Explain that to measure dry mass the organism cannot be living and that different parts of an organism may grow at different rates.				
B3g1	New genes for old	Describe the process selective breeding. Discuss the issues involved in selective breeding.	Recall that selective breeding involves selection of characteristics, cross breeding and selection of offspring over many generations. Recall that selective breeding can lead to inbreeding and health problems. Explain that selective breeding reduces the gene pool which reduces variation and cause the accumulation of harmful recessive characteristics.	B3g.1	36-37	Lesson plan. Worksheet. Technicians' notes.	
B3g2	New genes for old	Describe the process of genetic engineering. Discuss the issues involved in genetic engineering and gene therapy.	Recall that genetic engineering involves the transfer of genes from one organism to another and that it may be possible to use genetic engineering to cure certain genetic disorders. Describe how genetic engineering is used to make golden rice, insulin and disease resistant plants. Use the terms selection, isolation, insertion and replication to describe the principles of genetic engineering and explain why gene therapy using gametes is controversial.	B3g.2 B3g.3	38-39	Lesson plan. Worksheet. Technicians' notes.	
B3h1	Cloning.	Describe the process cloning that produced Dolly the sheep. Discuss the issues involved in cloning.	Recall that cloning produces genetically identical copies and that twins are natural clones. Recall cloning dolly involved the process of nuclear transfer and be able to describe some uses of cloning and discuss	B3h.1	40-41	Lesson plan. Worksheet. Technicians' notes.	

Lesson number	Lesson name	Learning Objectives	Assessable Learning Outcomes	Specification reference	Student Book pages	Teacher Pack materials	Personal resources e.g. videos / websites
			the dilemmas concerning human cloning. Describe in detail how nuclear transfer involves removing the nucleus from a body cell and placing it in an egg cell; they should also be able to implications of using cloning to supply organs for humans.				
B3h2	Cloning	Describe how to clone different plants. Discuss the advantages and disadvantages of cloning plants. Describe how to clone plants using tissue culture.	Recall how to take cuttings and how spider plants, strawberries and potatoes reproduce asexually. Describe the advantages of cloning to include mass production and a guarantee of the required characteristics. Describe the process of tissue culture to include, selection of characteristics the use of small pieces of tissue, aseptic techniques and a suitable growth medium. Explain that cloning of animals is difficult because animal cells lose the ability to differentiate.	B3h.2	42-43	Lesson plan. Worksheet. Cloning practical. Technicians' notes.	
B4a1	Ecology in the local environment	Use the terms ecosystem, habitat, community and population in the correct context. Explain data that shows zonation of organisms. Explain differences between biodiversity in different ecosystems.	Explain the differences between ecosystem, habitat, community and population. Explain how the distribution of organisms within a habitat is affected by various factors. Define biodiversity and compare the biodiversity of natural ecosystems and artificial ecosystems.	B4a.3	54-55	Lesson plan. Worksheet.	
B4a2	Ecology in the local environment	Make decisions on the best methods of counting and collecting data. Develop practical skills to collect data and use it to estimate population size.	Describe how to use different collecting and counting methods. Use keys to identify plants and animals. Use data from collecting and	B4a.1 B4a.2	56-57	Lesson plan. Worksheet. Using quadrats practical. Technicians' notes.	

		Understand why estimates and real population sizes may differ.	counting methods to calculate an estimate of the population size. Explain the effect of sample size on the accuracy of an estimate of population size. Explain the need to make certain assumptions when using capture-recapture data.				
B4b1	Photosynthesis	Understand that the products of photosynthesis can be used by the plant to produce all the substances that it needs.	Recall and use the word and balanced symbol equation for photosynthesis. Recall that glucose can be converted to other substances in plants to be used for different functions. Explain why insoluble substances are used for storage. Explain how experiments using isotopes have shown that photosynthesis as a two stage process.	B4b.1 B4b.2	58-59	Lesson plan. Worksheet. Testing leaves for starch practical. Technicians' notes.	
B4b2	Photosynthesis	Appreciate that understanding of the process of photosynthesis has developed over time. Use data from photosynthesis experiments to determine limiting factors. Explain the relative rates of photosynthesis and respiration in plants.	Describe the development of the understanding of the process of photosynthesis. Describe how the rate of photosynthesis can be increased. Explain the effects of limiting factors on the rate of photosynthesis.	B4b.1 B4b.4 B4b.5	60-61	Lesson plan. Worksheet. Gas production by pondweed practical. Technicians' notes.	
B4c1	Leaves and photosynthesis	Explain how light is trapped by plants for photosynthesis.	Name and locate the parts of a leaf. Explain how the cellular structure of a leaf is adapted for efficient photosynthesis. Recall that chlorophyll pigments in chloroplasts absorb light energy for photosynthesis.	B4c.1	62-63	Lesson plan. Worksheet. Stomata practical. Technicians' notes.	
B4c2	Leaves and photosynthesis	Explain the structure of a leaf in terms of the needs of photosynthesis. Explain the effect of different	Explain how leaves are adapted for efficient photosynthesis. Interpret data on the	B4c.1	64-65	Lesson plan. Worksheet. Technicians' notes.	

		colours of light on photosynthesis.	absorption of light by photosynthetic pigments.				
B4d1	Diffusion and osmosis	Use concentration gradients to explain the direction of diffusion. Apply the principles of diffusion to movement of different substances in plants and animals.	Recall that substances move in and out of cells by diffusion through the cell membrane. Describe how molecules enter and leave cells by diffusion. Explain how the rate of diffusion is increased by various factors. Explain how leaves are adapted to increase the rate of diffusion of gases.	B4d.1 B4d.4	66-67	Lesson plan. Worksheet. Moving molecules practical Technicians' notes.	
B4d2	Diffusion and osmosis	Predict the direction of water movement in osmosis. Explain why plants wilt. Use the effect of osmosis on animal cells to appreciate the need to keep the concentration of the blood constant.	Recognise that water moves in and out of plan.t cells by osmosis through the cell membrane. Explain the term partially-permeable. Explain how plants are supported by the turgor pressure within cells. Describe the effects of the uptake and loss of water on animal cells.	B4d.2 B4d.3 B4d.5	68-68	Lesson plan. Worksheet. Osmosis in living potato cells / Change in length of potato cores / osmosis in onion cells practicals. Technicians' notes.	
B4e1	Transport in plants	Explain the results of experiments with dyes in terms of transport in xylem.	Describe how water travels through a plant. Describe transpiration as the evaporation and diffusion of water from inside leaves. Describe the arrangement of xylem and phloem in a dicotyledonous root, stem and leaf. Describe the structure of xylem and phloem.	B4e.1 B4e.4	72-73	Lesson plan. Worksheet. Stalks and dye practical Technicians' notes.	
B4e2	Transport in plants	Interpret the results of transpiration experiments. Explain how plants can cope with hot conditions by having certain adaptations to their leaves.	Describe the effect of environmental factors on transpiration rate. Explain how the structure of a leaf is adapted to reduce excessive water loss.	B4e.2 B4e.3 B4e.4	74-75	Lesson plan. Worksheet. Measuring transpiration practical. Technicians' notes.	
B4f1	Plants need minerals	Understand that converting sugars to other substances requires elements other than	Recall that fertilisers contain minerals.	B4f.1 B4f.2	76-77	Lesson plan. Worksheet.	

		carbon, hydrogen and oxygen.	Describe how elements obtained from soil minerals are used in the production of compounds in plants.				
B4f2	Plants need minerals	Interpret data on NPK values. Explain why gardeners need to provide suitable conditions in the soil for active transport.	Relate mineral deficiencies to the resulting poor plan.t growth. Explain how minerals are taken up into root hair cells by active transport.	B4f.1 B4f.2 B4f.3	78-79	Lesson plan. Worksheet.	
B4g1	Decay	Explain that bacteria and fungi are the main decomposers and need certain conditions to work. Understand the importance of surface area on the rate of decay.	Recall the key factors in the process of decay. Explain why changing temperature and the amounts of oxygen and water affect the rate of decay. Explain how saprophytic fungi digest dead material. Explain how detritivores increase the rate of decay.	B4g.1 B4g.2 B4g.3	80-81	Lesson plan. Worksheet. Decomposers practical. Technicians' notes.	
B4g2	Decay	Appreciate that removing one of the factors needed for decay can preserve food.	Recognise the various food preservation techniques that reduce the rate of decay. Explain how food preservation methods reduce the rate of decay.	B4g.4	82-83	Lesson plan. Worksheet. Measuring bacterial activity practical. Technicians' notes.	
B4h1	Farming	Appreciate that although intensive farming maximises yields it can cause environmental problems.	Recall that intensive farming means trying to produce as much food as possible from the land available. Describe how intensive farming methods can increase productivity. Explain how intensive food production improves the efficiency of energy transfer. Explain the disadvantages of using pesticides.	B4h.1 B4h.2	84-85	Lesson plan. Worksheet.	
B4h2	Farming	Understand that organic farming may produce lower yields than intensive farming. Discuss some of the arguments for and against organic farming.	Describe organic farming techniques. Explain the advantages and disadvantages of organic farming. Explain the advantages and	B4h.3 B4h.4	86-87	Lesson plan. Worksheet.	

			disadvantages of biological control.				

Lesson number	Lesson name	Learning Objectives	Assessable Learning Outcomes	Specification reference	Student Book pages	Teacher Pack materials	Personal resources e.g. videos / websites
C3a1	Rates of reaction	Recognise that reactions occur at very different rates. Understand that the fastest reaction has the shortest reaction time. Interpret data in tabular, graphical or written form.	Recognise that some reactions can be fast and others very slow. Describe what is meant by the rate of reaction. Recognise that reaction times are shorter for faster reactions. Interpret data about the rate of reaction or reaction time. Calculate the rate of reaction from the slope of a graph (HT). Extrapolate and interpolate graphs (HT).	C3a.1 C3a.2	98-99	Lesson plan. Worksheet. Measuring a reaction rate practical. Technicians' notes.	
C3a2	Rates of reaction	Explain that reactions stop when one reactant is used up. Recall that the limiting reactant is the one that is not in excess. Explain how the amount of product depends on the amount of the limiting reactant (HT).	Explain why reactions eventually stop. Recognise and use the idea that the amount of product formed is directly proportional to the amount of the limiting reactant because it is all used up at the end of the reaction. Explain why the amount of product formed is directly proportional to the amount of limiting reactant used (HT).	C3a.3 C3a.4	100-101	Lesson plan. Worksheet. Comparing reactions practical. Technicians' notes.	
C3b1	Rates of reaction	Describe how temperature, concentration and pressure affect reaction rates. Use the collision theory to explain the way temperature, concentration and pressure effect reaction rates.	Recognise that a chemical reaction takes place when reactant particles collide. Understand that the rate of reaction depends on the frequency of successful collisions. Describe the effect of changing the temperature, concentration or pressure on the rates of chemical reactions. Explain, in terms of collisions between reacting particles,	C3b.1 C3b.2	102-103	Lesson plan. Worksheet. Technicians' notes.	

			why changes in temperature, concentration or pressure, change the rate of reaction.				
C3b2	Rates of reaction	Interpret data about the effects of temperature, concentration and pressure on the rates of reactions.	Read values from a graph and (HT) extrapolate or interpolate graphs. Compare rates of reaction by comparing reaction times or the gradients of graphs and decide when a reaction has finished. Draw sketch graphs to show the effect of changing temperature, concentration or pressure on the rate of reaction or the amount of product formed in a reaction. Calculate the rate of reaction from the slope of an appropriate graph (HT).	C3b.3	104-105	Lesson plan. Worksheet. Measuring the effect of concentration on a reaction rate practical. Technicians' notes.	
C3c1	Rates of reaction	Describe how surface area affects reaction rates and why powders can explode. Use the collision theory to explain how the surface area affects reaction rates.	Recall that the rate of a reaction can be increased by using powdered reactant rather than a lump. Describe an explosion as a very fast reaction which releases a large volume of gaseous products. Explain, in terms of collisions between reacting particles, the difference in rate of reaction between a lump and powdered reactant. Explain the dangers of combustible powders in factories.	C3c. 2 C3c. 3	106-107	Lesson plan. Worksheet. Measuring the effect of surface area on a reaction rate practical. Technicians' notes.	
C3c2	Rates of reaction	Describe how catalysts affect reaction rates and why only small amounts are needed. Interpret data about the effects of catalysts.	Recall that the rate of a reaction can be increased by the addition of a catalyst, which is a substance that changes the rate of reaction and is unchanged at the end of the reaction. Understand why only a small amount of a catalyst is needed to catalyse large amounts of reactants and that a catalyst is specific to a particular	C3c.1 C3c.4	108-109	Lesson plan. Worksheet. Measuring the effect of catalysts on a reaction rate practical. Technicians' notes.	

			reaction. Read values from graphs and (HT) interpret the data about the effects of catalysts. Compare rates of reaction by comparing gradients of graphs and calculate the rate of reaction from the slope of an appropriate graph (HT). Decide when a reaction has finished. Draw sketch graphs to show the effects of a catalyst on the rate of reaction and the amount of product formed.				
C3d1	Reacting masses	Calculate relative formula masses.	Calculate the relative formula mass of a substance from its formula (with and without brackets) given the appropriate relative atomic masses.	C3d.1	110-111	Lesson plan. Worksheet. Technicians' notes.	
C3d2	Reacting masses	Use equations to determine the masses of reactants and products.	Understand that the total mass of reactants at the start of a reaction is equal to the total mass of products made and that this is called the principle of conservation of mass Use the principle of conservation of mass to calculate the mass of reactant or product, including the mass of gaseous product formed during decomposition And the mass of oxygen that reacts with a known mass of magnesium to make magnesium oxide. Use simple ratios to calculate reacting masses and product masses given the mass of a reactant and a product. Use relative formula masses and a provided symbol equation (1:1 molar ratio) to show that mass is conserved during a reaction, and (HT) when not in a 1:1 molar ratio. Recognise and use the idea that the mass of product	C3d.2 C3d.3	112-113	Lesson plan. Worksheet. Mass conservation practicals. Technicians' notes.	

			formed is directly proportional to the mass of limiting reactant used. Interpret chemical equations quantitatively, and calculate masses of products or reactants from balanced symbol equations using relative formula masses (HT).				
C3e1	Percentage yield and atom economy	Use percentage yields to determine how much product has formed. Recognise factors which lower yields.	Understand percentage yield as a way of comparing amount of product made (actual yield) to amount expected (predicted yield). 100% yield means that no product has been lost, 0% yield means that no product has been made. Recognise possible reasons for why the percentage yield of a product is less than 100%, such as loss in filtration, loss in evaporation, loss in transferring liquids, not all reactants react to make product. Recall and use the formula: percentage yield = actual yield x100 predicted yield Explain why an industrial process wants as high a percentage yield as possible, including reducing the reactants wasted and reducing cost (HT).	C3e.1 C3e.2	116-117	Lesson plan. Worksheet. Preparation of ammonium sulfate practical. Technicians' notes.	
C3e2	Percentage yield and atom economy	Use atom economy to determine the percentage of reactant atoms converted to useful products. Recognise why chemists aim to maximise atom economy.	Understand atom economy as a way of measuring the amount of atoms that are wasted when manufacturing a chemical, appreciating that 100% atom economy means that all atoms in the reactant have been converted to the desired product. Understand that the higher the atom economy, the 'greener' the process. Recall and use the formula: atom economy =	C3e.3	118-119	Lesson plan. Worksheet. Preparation of magnesium sulfate practical. Technicians' notes.	

			Mr of desired products × 100 sum of Mr of all products Calculate atom economy when given balanced symbol equation and appropriate relative formula masses. Explain why an industrial process wants as high an atom economy as possible, including to reduce the production of unwanted products and to make the process more sustainable (HT). Be able to interpret complex atom economy and percentage yield data.				
C3f1	Energy	Distinguish between exothermic and endothermic reactions. Explain why reactions involve energy changes.	Recall that an exothermic reaction is one in which energy is transferred into the surroundings (releases energy). Recall that an endothermic reaction is one in which energy is taken from the surroundings (absorbs energy). Recognise exothermic and endothermic reactions using temperature changes. Recall bond making as an exothermic process and bond breaking as an endothermic process. Explain why a reaction is exothermic or endothermic using the energy changes that occur during bond breaking and bond making (HT).	C3f.1	120-121	Lesson plan. Worksheet. Comparing reactions practical. Technicians' notes.	
C3f2	Energy Using fuels	Compare the amounts of energy transferred when different fuels burn.	Describe a simple calorimetric method for comparing the energy transferred in combustion reactions, including using a spirit burner or a bottled gas burner, heating water in a copper calorimeter, measuring mass of fuel burnt and measuring the temperature change.	C3f.2	122-123	Lesson plan. Worksheet. Comparing fuels practical. Technicians' notes.	

			Describe fast and reliable calorimetric methods Interpret and use data from simple calorimetric experiments related to the combustion of fuels to compare which fuel releases the most energy. Use the formula energy transferred (in J) = m × c × ΔT to calculate the amount of energy transferred and (HT), the mass of water heated (m) and temperature change (ΔT). Calculate the energy output of a fuel in J/g by recalling and using the formula: energy per gram = energy released in J mass of fuel burnt in g (HT).				
C3g1	Batch or continuous?	Compare batch and continuous industrial processes.	Describe the differences between a batch and continuous process. Explain why batch processes are often used for the production of pharmaceutical drugs but continuous processes are used to produce chemicals such as ammonia. Evaluate the advantages and disadvantages of batch and continuous manufacturing processes given relevant data and information (HT).	C3g.1	124-125	Lesson plan. Worksheet. Technicians' notes.	
C3g2	Batch or continuous?	Explain why pharmaceutical drugs are often expensive.	List the factors that affect the cost of making and developing a pharmaceutical drug, including research and testing, labour costs, energy costs, raw materials, time taken for development and marketing. Explain why pharmaceutical drugs need to be thoroughly tested before they can be licensed for use. Explain why it is difficult to test and develop new pharmaceutical drugs that are	C3g.2 C3g.3 C3g.4	126-127	Lesson plan. Worksheet. Oil extraction practical. Technicians' notes.	

			safe to use (HT). Recall that the raw materials for speciality chemicals such as pharmaceuticals can be either made synthetically or extracted from plants, and describe how chemicals can be extracted from plan.t sources, including crushing, boiling and dissolving in a suitable solvent, and chromatography. Explain why it is important to manufacture pharmaceutical drugs to be as pure as possible. Explain why it is often expensive to make and develop new pharmaceutical drugs Interpret melting point, boiling point and chromatographic data relating to the purity of a substance.				
C3h1	Allotropes of carbon and nanochemistry	Recall the properties of diamond and graphite and explain why they are so different.	Explain why diamond and graphite are allotropes of carbon. Recognise the structures of diamond and graphite and explain why they have a giant molecular structure. List the following physical properties of diamond: lustrous, colourless and clear (transparent), hard and has a high melting point, insoluble in water, does not conduct electricity. Explain, in terms of properties, why diamond is used in cutting tools and jewellery. Explain, in terms of structure and bonding, why diamond does not conduct electricity, is hard and has a high melting point (HT). Explain, in terms of properties, why graphite is used in pencil leads, in lubricants. Explain, in terms of structure and bonding, why graphite	C3h.1 C3h.2 C3h.3	128-129	Lesson plan. Worksheet. Technicians' notes.	

			conducts electricity, is slippery, and has a high melting point (HT). List the following physical properties of graphite, black, lustrous and opaque, slippery, insoluble in water, conducts electricity. Predict and explain the properties of substances that have a giant molecular structure (HT).				
C3h2	Allotropes of carbon and nanochemistry	Explain why fullerenes are allotropes of carbon and explain why they are useful.	Explain why fullerenes are allotropes of carbon. Recognise the structure of Buckminster fullerene. Recall that nanotubes are used to reinforce graphite in tennis rackets because nanotubes are very strong. Recall that nanotubes are used as semiconductors in electrical circuits. Explain why fullerenes can be used in new drug delivery systems. Explain how the structure of nanotubes enables them to be used as catalysts (HT).	C3h.4	130-131	Lesson plan. Worksheet.	

Lesson number	**Lesson name**	**Learning Objectives**	**Assessable Learning Outcomes**	**Specification reference**	**Student Book pages**	**Teacher Pack materials**	**Personal resources e.g. videos / websites**
C4a1	Atomic structure	Describe the structure of atoms. Use ideas about atoms to compare elements and their isotopes.	Recall that an atom has a nucleus made of protons and neutrons, surrounded by electrons. Recall the relative charge of electrons are –1 and have a mass of 0.0005 , protons have a charge of +1 and mass 1, neutrons have a charge of 0 and mass 1 and (HT) explain why that makes atoms neutral. Understand that atoms have a very small mass - 10-23g - and a very small size -10-10m	C4a.1 C4a.3 C4a.4	142-143	Lesson plan. Worksheet. Technicians' notes.	

			(HT). Identify the atomic number of an element or vice versa by using a periodic table. Recall that atomic number is the number of protons in an atom. Recall that mass number is the total number of protons and neutrons in an atom Describe isotopes as varieties of an element that have the same atomic number but different mass numbers. Deduce the number of protons, electrons and neutrons in a charged particle given its atomic number, mass number and the charge on the particle using data in a table and using the conventional symbolism – e.g. carbon-12. Identify isotopes from data about the number of electrons, protons and neutrons in particles.				
C4a2	Atomic structure	Distinguish formulas of elements and compounds. Use electronic structures to identify elements. Explain how ideas about atomic structure developed.	Explain why a substance is an element or a compound given its formula. Deduce the number of occupied shells or the number of electrons from the electronic structure of an element. Describe and explain the significance of Dalton's atomic theory and how the work of J.J. Thomson, Rutherford and Bohr contributed to the development of the theory of atomic structure, noting how the atomic theory changed as new evidence was found and that science explanations are more convincing when predictions are later confirmed, and (HT) how unexpected results led to the theory of a nuclear atom. Describe the arrangement of elements in the periodic table. Explain how the identity of an	C4a.2 C4a.5	144-145	Lesson plan. Worksheet. Technicians' notes.	

			element can be deduced from its electronic structure and (HT) deduce the electronic structure of the first 20 elements in the periodic table.				
C4b1	Ionic bonding	Explain how and why ions form. Deduce the formulas of ionic compounds.	Recall that an ion is a charged atom or group of atoms. Recognise an ion, an atom and a molecule from given formulae. Understand that atoms with an outer shell of 8 electrons have a stable electronic structure. Explain how and why metal atoms form positive ions. Explain how and why non-metal atoms form negative ions. Understand that, in ionic bonding, a metal and non-metal combine by transferring electrons to form positive ions and negative ions which then attract one another. Deduce the formula of an ionic compound from the formula of the positive and negative ions. Explain, using the "dot and cross" model, the ionic bonding in simple binary compounds (HT).	C4b.1	146-147	Lesson plan. Worksheet. Technicians' notes.	
C4b2	Ionic bonding	Compare the properties of ionic compounds. Relate the structures of ionic compounds to their properties.	Compare the electrical conductivity of sodium chloride in solid, molten liquid and solution. Compare the melting points of sodium chloride and magnesium oxide Recall that sodium chloride solution conducts electricity. Recall that magnesium oxide and sodium chloride conduct electricity when molten. Describe the structure of sodium chloride or magnesium oxide as a giant ionic lattice in which positive ions are strongly attracted to negative ions.	C4b.2	148-149	Lesson plan. Worksheet. Comparing properties practical. Technicians' notes.	

			Explain, in terms of structure and bonding, some of the physical properties of sodium chloride, including its high melting point, its electrical conductivity as a solid, a molten liquid and in solution (HT). Explain, in terms of structure and bonding, why the melting point of sodium chloride is lower than that of magnesium oxide (HT). Predict and explain the properties of substances that have a giant ionic structure (HT).				
C4c1	The periodic table and covalent bonding	Describe how non-metals combine by sharing electron pairs.	Recall that there are two types of bonding – ionic bonding between metals and non-metals, and covalent bonding between non-metals. Recall that non-metals combine together by sharing electron pairs and this is called covalent bonding. Describe carbon dioxide and water as simple molecules with weak intermolecular forces between molecules. Explain, using the "dot and cross" model, the covalent bonding in simple binary compounds or molecules containing single and double covalent bonds (HT).	C4c.1	150-151	Lesson plan. Worksheet. Technicians' notes.	
C4c2	The periodic table and covalent bonding	Relate an elements position in the periodic table to its atomic structure. Describe how the periodic table came to be developed.	Recall that carbon dioxide and water do not conduct electricity. Deduce, using a periodic table, elements that are in the same group. Describe a group of elements as all the elements in a vertical column of the periodic table and that the elements have similar chemical properties Deduce, using a periodic	C4c.2 C4c.3 C4c.4 C4c.5	152-153	Lesson plan. Worksheet. Technicians' notes.	

			table, elements that are in the same period. Describe a period of elements as all the elements in a horizontal row of the periodic table. Describe the main stages in the development of the classification of elements, including Dobereiner, Newlands and Mendeleev, and understand that classification of elements was provisional, based on evidence gathered at the time. Recognise that the group number is the same as the number of electrons in the outer shell. Deduce the group to which an element belongs from its electronic structure (limited to the s and p blocks). Recognise that the period to which the element belongs corresponds to the number of occupied shells in the electronic structure. Deduce the period to which the element belongs from its electronic structure. Explain, in terms of structure and bonding, some of the physical properties of carbon dioxide and water, such as low melting points and inability to conduct electricity (HT). Predict and explain the properties of substances that have a simple molecular structure (HT). Describe the evidence or observations that caused Newlands and Mendeleev to develop new models of periodic classification of elements, and (HT only) explain how further evidence confirmed Mendeleev's ideas about the periodic table, including confirmation of his predictions about unknown elements, and how				

			investigations on atomic structure (mass number and electronic structure) agreed with his ideas.				
C4d1	The group 1 elements	Describe the physical and chemical properties of group 1 elements. Write equations for their reactions with water.	Recognise sodium, lithium and potassium as Group 1 elements. Explain why the Group 1 elements are known as the alkali metals. Explain why Group 1 elements are stored under oil. Describe the reaction of lithium, sodium and potassium with water, noting that hydrogen is formed, and an alkali is formed which is the hydroxide of the reacting metal. Construct the word equation for the reaction of a Group 1 element with water. Predict the physical properties of rubidium and caesium and how they react with water. Construct a balanced symbol equation for the reaction of a Group 1 element with water (HT).	C4d.1 C4d.2	154-155	Lesson plan. Worksheet. Technicians' notes.	
C4d2	The group 1 elements	Use flame test results to identify Group 1 metal ions. Use ideas about ion formation to explain the similarities and differences between Group 1 metals. Use ionic equations to deduce when oxidation is taking place.	Note that the reactivity of Group 1 metals with water increases down Group 1, and that potassium gives a lilac flame. Recall the flame test colours for lithium, sodium and potassium compounds. Interpret information about flame tests e.g. deduce the alkali metal present from flame colours. Describe how to use a flame test to identify the presence of lithium, sodium and potassium compounds, describing the use of moistened flame test wire, dipped into a solid sample, and then put into blue Bunsen flame.	C4d.2 (HT) C4d.3	156-157	Lesson plan. Worksheet. Technicians' notes.	

			Explain why Group 1 elements have similar properties, in terms of forming positive ions with stable electronic structures (HT). Construct a balanced symbol equation to show the formation of an ion of a Group 1 element from its atom (HT). Explain, in terms of electron loss, the trend in reactivity of the Group 1 elements with water. (HT) Recall the loss of electrons as oxidation, and explain why a process is oxidation from its ionic equation (HT).				
C4e1	The group 7 elements	Describe the physical and chemical properties of group 7 elements. Write equations for their reactions with Group 1 elements.	Recall that the Group 7 elements are known as the halogens. Recognise fluorine, chlorine, bromine and iodine as Group 7 elements. Describe the physical appearance of the Group 7 elements at room temperature – chlorine is a green gas, bromine is an orange liquid, iodine is a grey solid. Describe the uses of some Group 7 elements, including that chlorine is used to sterilise water, chlorine is used to make pesticides and plastics, and iodine is used to sterilise wounds. Recognise that Group 7 elements react vigorously with Group 1 elements. Identify the metal halide formed when a Group 1 element reacts with a Group 7 element. Construct the word and symbol equations for the reaction between a Group 1 element and a Group 7 element.	C4e.1 C4e.2	160-161	Lesson plan. Worksheet. Technicians' notes.	
C4e2	The group 7 elements	Use ideas about ion formation	Recall that the reactivity of the	C4e.3	162-163	Lesson plan.	

		to explain the similarities and differences between Group 1 metals. Use ionic equations to deduce when reduction is taking place.	Group 7 elements decreases down the group. Construct the word and symbol equations for the reaction between a Group 7 element and a metal halide. Predict the properties of fluorine or astatine given the properties of the other Group 7 element, e.g. physical properties, melting point, boiling point and displacement reactions. Describe the displacement reactions of Group 7 elements with solutions of metal halides – chlorine displaces bromides and iodides, and bromine displaces iodides. Predict the feasibility of displacement reactions e.g. will bromine react with sodium astitide solution (HT). Explain why Group 7 elements have similar properties, (HT) in terms of forming negative ions with stable electronic structures. Construct an equation to show the formation of a halide ion from a halogen molecule (HT). Explain, in terms of electron gain, the trend in reactivity of the Group 7 elements (HT). Recall the gain of electrons as reduction, and explain why a process is reduction from its ionic equation (HT).			Worksheet. Technicians' notes.	
C4f1	Transition elements	Describe the properties and uses of elements and their compounds.	Identify whether an element is a transition element from its position in the periodic table. Recognise that all transition elements are metals and have typical metallic properties. Deduce the name or symbol of a transition element using the periodic table. Recall that copper and iron are transition elements. Recall that compounds of	C4f.1	164-165	Lesson plan. Worksheet. Technicians' notes.	

			transition elements are often coloured, such as copper compounds are often blue, iron (II) compounds are often light green, iron (III) compounds are often orange/brown. Recall that transition elements and their compounds are often used as catalysts – iron in the Haber process, and nickel in the manufacture of margarine.				
C4f2	Transition elements	Describe the thermal decomposition of transition metal carbonates and write equations for the reaction. Describe the precipitation of transition metal hydroxides and write equations for the reactions.	Describe thermal decomposition as a reaction in which a substance is broken down into at least two other substances by heat. Describe the thermal decomposition of carbonates of transition elements including $FeCO_3$, $CuCO_3$, $MnCO_3$ and $ZnCO_3$; noting that a metal oxide and carbon dioxide is formed and that a colour change occurs. Construct word equations for thermal decomposition reactions. Construct the balanced symbol equations for the thermal decomposition of $FeCO_3$, $CuCO_3$, $MnCO_3$ and $ZnCO_3$ (HT). Recall that the test for carbon dioxide is that it turns limewater milky. Describe precipitation as a reaction between solutions that makes an insoluble solid. Describe the use of sodium hydroxide solution to identify the presence of transition metal ions in solution, where Cu^{2+} gives a blue solid, Fe^{2+} gives a grey/green solid, Fe^{3+} gives an orange/brown solid, and note that the solids are called precipitates. Construct balanced symbol equations for the reactions between Cu^{2+}, Fe^{2+} and	C4f.2 C4f.3	166-167	Lesson plan. Worksheet. Decomposition and precipitation practicals. Technicians' notes.	

			Fe3+ with OH– (without state symbols) given the formulae of the ions (HT).				
C4g1	Metal structure and properties	Relate the properties of metals to their most important uses.	Explain why iron is used to make cars and bridges. Explain why copper is used to make electrical wiring List the physical properties of metals, including: lustrous, hard, high density, high tensile strength, high melting and boiling points, good conductors of heat and electricity. Interpret data about the properties of metals e.g. hardness, density and electrical conductivity. Suggest properties needed by a metal for a particular given use. Explain why metals are suited to a given use (data will be provided). Recognise that the particles in a metal are held together by metallic bonds. Explain, in terms of structure, why metals have high melting points and boiling points and conduct electricity. Describe metallic bonding as the strong attraction between a sea of delocalised electrons and close packed positive metal ions (HT).	C4g.1 C4g.2 C4g.3	168-169	Lesson plan. Worksheet. Technicians' notes.	
C4g2	Metal structure and properties	Relate the properties of metals to their structures.	Describe what is meant by the term superconductor. Recall that at low temperatures some metals can be superconductors. Describe the potential benefits of superconductors, including loss free power transmission, super-fast electronic circuits and powerful electromagnets. Explain some of the drawbacks of superconductors (HT).	C4g.4	170-171	Lesson plan. Worksheet. Technicians' notes.	

C4h1	Purifying and testing water	Explain why clean water is essential. Explain how and why water is purified. Explain why purification leaves soluble salts in water.	Interpret simple data about water resources in the United Kingdom (no recall is expected). Recall different types of water resources found in the United Kingdom, including lakes, rivers aquifers, and reservoirs. Explain why water is an important resource for many important industrial chemical processes, and why it must be conserved. List some of the pollutants that may be found in domestic water supplies, including nitrate residues, lead compounds, and pesticide residues, and explain why water may contain some of these. List the types of substances present in water before it is purified, e.g. dissolved salts and minerals, microbes, pollutants, insoluble materials. Recall that chlorination kills microbes in water. Describe the water purification process to include filtration, sedimentation and chlorination. Explain why some soluble substances are not removed from water during purification (HT). Explain the disadvantages of using distillation of sea water to make large quantities of fresh water (HT).	C4h.1 C4h.2 C4h.3	172-173	Lesson plan. Worksheet. Technicians' notes.	
C4h2	Purifying and testing water	Describe how the soluble salts in water can be identified.	Understand that the reactions of barium chloride with sulfates and silver nitrate with halides are examples of precipitation reactions. Recall that barium chloride solution is used to test for sulfate ions and gives a white precipitate. Recall that silver nitrate solution is used to test for	C4h.4	174-175	Lesson plan. Worksheet. Insoluble salts practical. Technicians' notes.	

			halide ions, and chloride ions give a white precipitate, bromide ions give a cream precipitate, and iodide ions give a pale yellow precipitate. Interpret data about the testing of water with aqueous silver nitrate and barium chloride solutions. Construct word and symbol equations for the reactions of barium chloride with sulfates and silver nitrate with halides.				

Lesson number	Lesson name	Learning Objectives	Assessable Learning Outcomes	Specification reference	Student Book pages	Teacher Pack materials	Personal resources e.g. videos / websites
P3a1	Speed	How to calculate average speed. Describe how average speed is measured. Explain how speed cameras work.	Be able to use the equation average speed = total distance / total time, with appropriate units. Describe that average speed can be found by measuring the distance covered in a known time. Explain how different types of speed camera measure speed and average speed.	P3a.1 P3a.2	186-187	Lesson plan. Worksheet. Measuring speed practical. Technicians' notes.	
P3a2	Speed	How to interpret simple graphs of distance against time. Describe the gradient of a distance –time graph. How to draw distance-time graphs.	Be able to interpret distance-time graphs qualitatively. Interpret the gradient of a distance-time graph as speed. Be able to calculate speed from the gradient of a distance-time graph for uniform speed (HT).	P3a.3	188-189	Lesson plan. Worksheet. Obtaining data to plot a distance-time graph practical. Technicians' notes.	
P3b1	Changing speed	How to analyse graphs of speed against time. How to calculate acceleration from a speed–time graph. How to find the distance travelled from a speed-time graph.	Be able to interpret speed-time graphs qualitatively. Interpret the gradient of a speed-time graph as acceleration. Be able to calculate the distance travelled from the area under a speed-time graph for uniform acceleration.	P3b.1	190-191	Lesson plan. Worksheet. Using a data logger to monitor motion practical. Technicians' notes.	

P3b2	Changing speed Acceleration and velocity	How to calculate acceleration. Understand about positive and negative acceleration. The difference between speed and velocity. Relative velocity.	Be able to use the equation acceleration = change in speed / time taken. Associate an increase in speed as a positive acceleration and a decrease in speed as a negative acceleration (deceleration). Understand that the velocity of an object is its speed combined with its direction. Be able to calculate the relative velocity of objects moving on parallel paths.	P3b.2 P3b.3	192-193	Lesson plan. Worksheet. Measuring acceleration practical. Technicians' notes.	
P3c1	Forces and motion	How to recognise simple situations where forces affect the motion of an object. How to describe and interpret the relationship between force, mass and acceleration. How to state and use the equation: 'force = mass x acceleration'.	Recognise simple situations where forces cause things to speed up, slow down or stay at the same speed. Be able to interpret the relationship between force, mass and acceleration in everyday examples. Be able to use the equation 'force = mass x acceleration' including a change of subject, and (HT) first calculate the accelerating force.	P3c.1	194-195	Lesson plan. Worksheet. Force, mass and acceleration practical. Technicians' notes.	
P3c2	Forces and motion	The meaning of thinking, braking and stopping distances. The factors that affect thinking, braking and stopping distances. Explain why knowledge of stopping distance is important in road safety.	Describe thinking, braking and stopping distances. Explain how certain factors may increase thinking and braking distances. Explain the implications of stopping distances in road safety and the effect of increased speed on them.	P3c.2	196-197	Lesson plan. Worksheet. Reaction time practical. Technicians' notes.	
P3d1	Work and power	The connection between mass and weight. Energy is needed to do work. How to calculate work done.	Be able to use the equation 'weight = mass x gravitational field strength', with appropriate units. Realise that work is only done when a force moves and that this requires energy. Be able to use the equation 'work done = force x distance moved'.	P3d.1 P3d.2	198-199	Lesson plan. Worksheet. Work done practical. Technicians' notes.	

P3d2	Work and power	The meaning of power. How to calculate power. How to interpret fuel consumption data.	Describe power as a measurement of how quickly work is being done. Be able to use the equation 'power = work done / time' and derive 'power = force x speed' (HT). Be able to interpret fuel consumption figures from data on cars, including environmental issues and cost.	P3d.3	200-201	Lesson plan. Worksheet. Personal power practical. Technicians' notes.	
P3e1	Energy on the move	Find out about kinetic energy and how to calculate it (HT). Find out about renewable energy sources for vehicles. How braking distance changes with speed.	Use and apply the equation KE = ½ mv2, including (HT) a change of subject.. Describe how electricity can be used for road transport. Apply ideas about kinetic energy to link braking distances and speed.	P3e.1 P3e.2	204-205	Lesson plan. Worksheet. Kinetic energy and stopping distance practical. Technicians' notes.	
P3e2	Energy on the move	Describe how the shape of cars can affect their top speeds and fuel consumption. How alternatives to fossil fuels can be used for road transport. More on how to interpret data on fuel consumption.	Understand that a streamlined shape increases a car's top speed and improves fuel consumption. Explain the advantages of bio-fuelled and solar-powered cars. Describe the factors that affect fuel consumption and analyse fuel consumption data, including emissions. Evaluate and compare data about fuel consumption and emissions.	P3e.2 P3e.3	206-207	Lesson plan. Worksheet. Streamlining practical. Technicians' notes.	
P3f1	Crumple zones	Find out about momentum. How seatbelts, crumple zones and air bags act in a crash. How forces can be reduced in a crash.	Use the equations momentum = mass x velocity and force = change in momentum/time. Describe how seatbelts crumple zones and air bags change the momentum of a person in a car crash more slowly. Explain how this reduces or avoids injury.	P3f.1 P3f.2	208-209	Lesson plan. Worksheet. Testing crumple zones or seatbelt material practical. Technicians' notes.	
P3f2	Crumple zones	Find out about some typical	Recall safety features which	P3f.3	210-211	Lesson plan.	

		safety features of modern cars. How safety features can make driving safer. How ABS brakes work.	are intended to prevent accidents. Describe safety features which are intended to protect occupants in the event of a crash. Explain how ABS brakes allow greater control over steering and avoid skidding.			Worksheet. Technicians' notes.	
P3g1	Falling safely	Find out about the motion of falling objects. How air resistance slows down falling objects. Find out about terminal speed.	Realise that objects accelerate as they fall. Describe how air resistance, or drag, increases with speed, reducing the acceleration of falling objects. Explain how a falling object reaches a constant (terminal) speed when the forces on it are balanced.	P3g.1	212-213	Lesson plan. Worksheet. Making parachutes pracical. Technicians' notes.	
P3g2	Falling safely	How friction forces affect motion. How changes to the shapes of moving objects can influence their terminal speed. Find out about the acceleration in free-fall.	Recognise that frictional forces oppose motion, leading to energy loss and inefficiency. Explain how streamlined shapes have less resistance to motion so achieve higher terminal speeds. Understand that acceleration due to gravity is the same for any object at a given point on Earth's surface.	P3g.2	214-215	Lesson plan. Worksheet. Technicians' notes.	
P3h1	The energy of games and theme rides	Find out about gravitational potential energy. How to calculate gravitational potential energy. How there is usually a transfer of gravitational potential energy to kinetic energy as an object falls.	Recognise that objects have gravitational potential energy because of their mass and position in Earth's gravitational field. Use the equation GPE = mgh. Interpret examples of energy transfer between gravitational potential energy and kinetic energy. Understand what happens to the gravitational potential energy lost by an object falling at terminal speed (HT).	P3h.1	216-217	Lesson plan. Worksheet. Bouncing ball practical. Technicians' notes.	
P3h2	The energy of games	Everyday examples in which	Recognise examples of	P3h.2	218-219	Lesson plan.	

	and theme rides	objects have gravitational potential energy. The physics behind a gravity ride (roller coaster). The effect of mass and speed on the kinetic energy of an object.	everyday objects that have gravitational potential energy. Interpret a roller coaster in terms of kinetic energy, gravitational potential energy and energy transfer qualitatively and (H only) quantitatively. Describe that doubling the mass of an object doubles its kinetic energy but doubling its speed quadruples its kinetic energy.			Worksheet. Design and build a model roller coaster practical. Technicians' notes.	

Lesson number	Lesson name	Learning Objectives	Assessable Learning Outcomes	Specification reference	Student Book pages	Teacher Pack materials	Personal resources e.g. videos / websites
P4a1	Sparks	Understand how insulating materials can become charged. Recognise that there are two types of charge and describe how these interact. Realise that charged objects contain ions.	Describe how insulators are charged by friction. State that charges are either positive or negative. Recognise that like charges repel and unlike charges attract. Explain how the transfer of electrons is responsible for static charge and describe the formation of ions.	P4a.1	230-231	Lesson plan. Worksheet. Static charges practical. Technicians' notes.	
P4a2	Sparks	Describe electrostatic charge can be a nuisance and sometimes even dangerous. Explain how problems caused by electrostatic charge can be minimised.	Describe how an electrostatic shock can be caused by charge being earthed. Describe how static charge can be a nuisance and how anti-static sprays and cloths can help. Explain how static electricity can be dangerous when flammable substances are present and how the risks can be reduced.	P4a.2	232-233	Lesson plan. Worksheet. Technicians' notes.	
P4b1	Uses of Electrostatics	Understand the use of electrostatics in dust precipitators and defibrillators.	Describe how smoke particles etc. are removed from chimneys using charged plates. Explain how the use of high voltages ensures the dust is	P4b.1	234-235	Lesson plan. Worksheet. Technicians' notes.	

			attracted to plates inside the chimney. Explain how electrical charge can be used to restart the heart.				
P4b2	Uses of Electrostatics	Understand the use of electrostatics in crop spraying paint spraying	Explain how the sprayed particles produce a fine mist due to being of the same charge. Explain how an object will be given an even coat when it is charged oppositely to the paint.	P4b.2	236-237	Lesson plan. Worksheet. Technicians' notes.	
P4c1	Safe Electricals	Understand how resistors can be used to change the current in a circuit. Calculate resistance and understand the effect of length and thickness on the resistance of a wire.	Use the formula resistance = voltage/current. Recall that resistance is measured in Ohms. Explain that longer wires have more resistance thinner wires have more resistance.	P4c.1	238-239	Lesson plan. Worksheet. Resistance practical. Technicians' notes.	
P4c2	Safe Electricals	Recognise the colour coding in a three pin plug. Describe the functions of the live neutral and earth wires in the plug. Explain how fuses, earth wires and circuit breakers work. Calculate electrical power. Understand the term 'double insulated'.	Recall the colours of the live, neutral and earth wires. Describe the functions of live, neutral and earth wires. Explain how the fuse and earth wire protect a user and describe a circuit breaker as a 're-settable fuse.' Use the equation power = voltage x current. Explain the term 'double insulated'.	P4c.2	240-241	Lesson plan. Worksheet. Technicians' notes.	
P4d1	Ultrasound	Understand that ultrasound is a longitudinal wave with a very high frequency. Describe how the cost of domestic electricity is worked out.	Describe ultrasound as a longitudinal wave with a frequency above 20 000Hz. Describe features of longitudinal waves including – wavelength, frequency, compression and rarefaction. Describe and compare features of longitudinal and transverse waves.	P4d.1	242-243	Lesson plan. Worksheet. Threshold of hearing practical. Technicians' notes.	

P4d2	Ultrasound	Recognise the use of ultrasound in medicine for diagnosis. Explain how ultrasound can be used to break down e.g. kidney stones. Understand why ultrasound is preferable to X-rays for certain scans.	Describe how ultrasound is used for scanning the body and to measure the speed of blood. Explain how ultrasound is used to break down kidney stones and other accumulations. Explain the reasons for using ultrasound rather than X-rays for certain scans.	P4d.2	244-245	Lesson plan. Worksheet. Technicians' notes.	
P4e1	What is Radioactivity?	Recognise that nuclear decay occurs naturally. Describe how the activity of a sample is measured. Understand the term 'half-life'.	Recall that alpha, beta and gamma radiation comes naturally from the nucleus of atoms. Describe how activity is measured in nuclear decays per second Interpret graphical or numerical data and calculate half-life.	P4e.1	248-249	Lesson plan. Worksheet. Decay practical. Technicians' notes.	
P4e2	What is Radioactivity?	Recognise the ionising nature of alpha, beta and gamma. Describe how an atom changes when alpha or beta decay happens. Construct balanced nuclear decay equations.	Recall that nuclear radiation ionises materials and explain why alpha is such a good ioniser Describe alpha and beta particles and what happens to a nucleus when an alpha or a beta particle is emitted. Construct balanced nuclear equations for alpha and beta decay.	P4e.2	250-251	Lesson plan. Worksheet. Technicians' notes.	
P4f1	Uses of Radioisotopes	Identify sources of background radiation. Understand how radioisotopes are used as industrial tracers.	Recall that background radiation comes mainly from rocks and cosmic rays and that some also comes from man-made sources. Describe how tracers are used in industry and explain why gamma sources are used.	P4f.1	252-253	Lesson plan. Worksheet. Technicians' notes.	
P4f2	Uses of Radioisotopes	Understand the use of alpha sources in smoke detectors. Understand how radioactivity is used to date materials.	Explain how a smoke detector with an alpha source works. Explain how rocks are dated using the ratio of uranium to lead. Explain how organic materials	P4f.2	254-255	Lesson plan. Worksheet.	

			can be dated using measurements from radioactive Carbon.				
P4g1	Treatment	Compare the production and properties of X-rays and gamma rays. Understand how radioactive materials are produced for medical uses.	Describe some similarities and differences between X-rays and gamma rays. Explain how the image is produced by the different amounts of absorption of X-rays by different materials. Outline how X-rays and gamma rays are produced.	P4g.1	256-257	Lesson plan. Worksheet. Technicians' notes.	
P4g2	Treatment	Describe the use of nuclear radiation in medicine. Understand the role of the radiographer and the safety precautions they must take.	Describe the use of nuclear radiations for diagnosis treatment of cancer sterilisation of equipment. Explain that nuclear radiation can damage cells. Explain how gamma (and sometimes beta) emitters can be used as tracers. Describe safety precautions which are necessary when using X-rays or tracers.	P4g.2	258-259	Lesson plan. Worksheet. Technicians' notes.	
P4h1	Fission and Fusion	Understand the main stages in the production of electricity in nuclear power stations. Describe nuclear fission and how it is controlled.	Describe the main stages in the production of electricity in nuclear power stations. Describe nuclear fission as the process that releases energy in a nuclear power station and recall that it produces radioactive waste. Describe a chain reaction and how they are controlled. Explain that a nuclear bomb is a chain reaction out of control.	P4h.1	260-261	Lesson plan. Worksheet.	
P4h2	Fission and Fusion	Understand the difference between fission and fusion. Recognise that 'cold fusion' is a disputed claim made by some scientists. Understand why fusion research is an international joint venture.	Describe how nuclear fusion releases energy. Describe the conditions needed for fusion to take place Explain why fusion for power generation is difficult. Explain why data on fusion research is shared between scientists.	P4h.2	262-263	Lesson plan. Worksheet. Technicians' notes.	

